PALESTINE DIARIES

Award-winning historian Dr Jonathan King has been producing books and films about World War I since 1994. He leads battlefield tours to Gallipoli and the Western Front, and is a regular television and radio commentator, as well as a writer for newspapers. After lecturing at The University of Melbourne for many years, he has written more than 30 books and produced 20 documentaries. He is based in Sydney with his fellow adventurer and wife, Jane. They have four daughters and seven grandchildren.

Other books (selected) by Jonathan King

The Other Side of the Coin:
a political cartoon history of Australia (1976)

Stop Laughing, This is Serious!:
a social cartoon history of Australia (1978)

Waltzing Materialism: attitudes that shaped Australia (1978)

A Cartoon History of Australia (1980)

Governor Phillip Gidley King (with R. John King, 1982)

The First Fleet: convict voyage that founded a nation (1982)

The First Settlement: convict village that founded a nation (1985)

In the Beginning:
the founding of Australia from the original documents (1986)

Voyage into History (1987)

Australia's First Fleet: the original voyage and the re-enactment (1988)

Battle for the Bicentenary (1989)

The Man from Snowy River (1995)

Australia's First Century: a pictorial history of Australia (2000)

Gallipoli Diaries: the Anzacs' own story, day by day (2003)

Gallipoli: our last man standing (2004)

Mary Bryant: her life and escape from Botany Bay (2004)

Gallipoli Untold Stories:
from Charles Bean and frontline Anzacs (2005)

Historica: 1000 years of our lives and times (2006)

Western Front Diaries: the Anzacs' own story, battle by battle (2008)

Great Moments in Australian History (2009)

Great Battles in Australian History (2011)

Great Disasters in Australian History (2013)

Tall Ships and Tall Tales: a life of dancing with history (2014)

Gallipoli Diaries:
the Anzacs' own story, day by day (revised ed.) (2015)

Western Front Diaries:
the Anzacs' own story, battle by battle (revised ed.) (2016)

PALESTINE DIARIES

JONATHAN KING

THE LIGHT HORSEMEN'S OWN STORY, BATTLE BY BATTLE

SCRIBE
Melbourne · London

Scribe Publications
18–20 Edward St, Brunswick, Victoria 3056, Australia
2 John St, Clerkenwell, London, WC1N 2ES, United Kingdom

First published by Scribe 2017

Printed and bound in Australia by Griffin Press

 The paper this book is printed on is certified against the
Forest Stewardship Council® Standards. Griffin Press holds
FSC chain of custody certification SGS-COC-005088.
FSC promotes environmentally responsible, socially beneficial
and economically viable management of the world's forests.

ISBN 9781925322668 (Australian edition)
ISBN 9781947534216 (UK edition)
ISBN 9781925548556 (e-book)

A CiP entry for this title is available from the National Library of Australia

scribepublications.com.au
scribepublications.co.uk

This book is dedicated to Trooper Ion L. Idriess, (1889–1979) from the Australian Light Horse, 2nd Brigade's 5th Regiment, who wrote such wonderful diaries during the Light Horse campaign in Palestine. An adventurous gold prospector from outback Australia who had learnt how to survive from Aboriginal tribes, he was at home in the desert. During the war, he was the most dedicated of all scribes and kept updating those little books in his saddlebag day after day, year after year, despite enemy bullets, shrapnel, shells, bombs, desert sand storms, scorching heat, hunger, thirst, and malaria — right up until he was wounded in action and repatriated back to Australia, where he became one of our nation's leading authors of adventure books.

Trooper Ion 'Jack' Idriess, the greatest scribe of all, kept a colourful diary throughout the Light Horse campaigns at Gallipoli and in Palestine.

CONTENTS

PART 4: JORDAN 1918

PART 5: SYRIA 1918

FOREWORD

Two costly assaults in March and April 1917 had failed to capture Gaza. As a part of the fresh offensive in October, Lieutenant-General Sir Harry Chauvel was instructed to 'take Beersheeba'. At 4.30pm on 31 October, the relatively untested 4th (Victoria) and 12th (New South Wales) Light Horse Regiments charged into Beersheeba, history, and folklore.

Gaza fell to the British a week later, the Turks retreated to Palestine, and the gateway to victory in 1918 was opened — by the Australians.

The official historian, 'Harry' Gullett wrote: 'The enemy was beaten by the sheer recklessness of the charge, rather than the very limited fighting powers of this handful of Australians'.

One Light Horseman simply said, 'It was the horses that did it — those marvellous bloody horses'.

But it was also something about these men. They served with courage dismounted at Gallipoli, and ran unflinchingly to their certain deaths at the Nek.

Standing silent sentinel above the Tomb of the Unknown Australian Soldier at the Australian War Memorial are fifteen stained-glass windows. Each depicts a serviceman and nurse from the First World War. At the base of each is a single word — a value, a virtue-informing character observed in those depicted above.

Beneath the image of the Light horseman is *Audacity* — nothing of value in life is achieved without taking a risk. And risk these remarkable men certainly took.

Official War Correspondent, Charles Bean.

The Australian War Memorial was the vision of Charles Bean, Australia's First World War official historian.

At Pozières, a dying Australian had asked Bean, 'Will they remember me in Australia?' From there, he subsequently conceived and resolved that at the war's end he would build the finest memorial and museum to these men of the Australian Imperial Force and the nurses.

Bean determined to collect not only the official records of war, but to preserve and protect the private records of those who had fought it. Bean acquired personal letters, diaries, and sketches to complement the battlefield reports, personnel records, and unit war diaries held by the AIF. These records, the words of the men and women who were actually there, enable us to learn more about the first-hand experience of war.

It was the first time that Australia's 'working class' had put pencil to paper on a major scale.

More than a century after Charles Bean started collecting the personal experiences of Australians at war, they have become more valuable and popular than ever. The dedicated staff in the Memorial's Research Centre

Official War Artist James McBey rode with this Australian camel patrol in Palestine for five days to sketch 'Strange Signals' as the hardened bushmen peered through the shimmering mirage searching for enemy Turks or troublesome Bedouins.

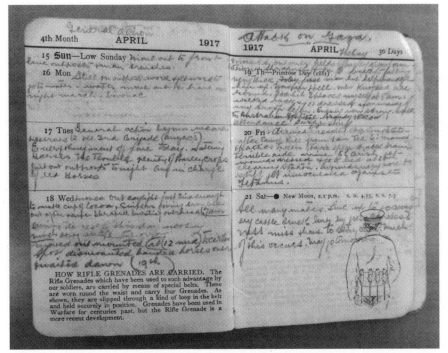

To keep a detailed record of his service in Palestine, Trooper Arthur Adams used a military issue diary full of useful instructions with explanatory pictures for things like carrying 'Rifle Grenades'.

facilitate thousands of these incredible private records being available each year to not only scholars and authors like Dr King, but to families and descendants.

The final book in his First World War centennial trilogy, *Palestine Diaries: the Light Horsemen's story battle by battle* is informed by hundreds of diaries and letters held at the Memorial, and completes his exploration of the Australian soldiers' experience of that terrible conflict. Skilfully weaving the words of the Light Horsemen themselves into a thoroughly researched historical narrative, he illustrates the experience of the Light Horse at Gallipoli and in Palestine, exploring the very different war they fought in the desert compared to the slime and blood-soaked mud of the Western Front.

Jonathan King gives us the gift of understanding. Through the writing of Light Horsemen like Ion Idriess, one of the most prolific and talented

Australian diarists of the war, and Sergeant Colin Bull, who would be killed in the Charge at Beersheba, we learn their war may have been different, but it was no less dangerous. Further to this, despite popular perception, it was a war no more glamorous than the trench warfare in France and Belgium. Men served, fought, suffered, and died. So too did their beloved horses.

Dr King's work is an eloquent validation of the vision of Charles Bean of the Australian War Memorial as a place of learning and understanding, and a fitting tribute to the men of the Light Horse.

They are 'remembered' — all of them. Within the pages of this book is revealed much about a remarkable generation, its courage, horsemanship, mateship, and what it means to be an Australian.

The Hon Dr Brendan Nelson AO
Director
Australian War Memorial
August 2017

PREFACE

At a mile distant their thousand hooves were stuttering thunder, coming at a rate that frightened a man — they were an awe inspiring sight, galloping through the red haze — knee to knee and horse to horse — the dying sun glinting on bayonet points …

TROOPER ION IDRIESS,
5TH LIGHT HORSE REGIMENT, PERSONAL DIARY 1916–18

———————————

This book is the third in a World War I centennial trilogy covering all three major theatres of war in which Australians fought between 1914 and 1918. It follows on from *Gallipoli Diaries: the Anzacs' own story day by day* (Scribe, 2014) and *Western Front Diaries: the Anzacs' own story battle by battle* (Scribe, 2015), which told the story of the battles through the words of those frontline soldiers who were there, on the spot.

Now, *Palestine Diaries: the Light Horsemen's own story battle by battle* tells the story through the diaries and letters of eyewitnesses who served in this third important theatre, Palestine. In fact, this book has been published to commemorate the centenary of the most important battle of all — the glorious cavalry charge at Beersheba, history's last successful cavalry charge, which took place on 31 October 1917.

The 100th anniversary of that great charge provides Australians with an opportunity to replace the tired old cornerstone of our national identity — Gallipoli — with a new foundation stone for our identity — Beersheba, the peak moment of the breathtaking achievements of the Australian Light Horse in World War I. Instead of basing our identity on a failed campaign in which the British sent 8,709 Australians to their unnecessary deaths, we should use the 100th anniversary to replace that tragic base with the stunningly successful series of Australian-led victories in the Middle East, culminating with Beersheba.

Nothing could be more Australian than young country bushmen riding Australian-bred stock horses (Walers) to defeat an enemy; it should appeal much more to Australians than honouring the deaths of our foot soldiers trapped in the trenches of Gallipoli. When World War One Prime Minister Billy Hughes claimed, 'Australia was born on the shores of Gallipoli', he was praising the bravery and sacrifice of that disastrous 1915 campaign. When he told Parliament, in 1919, 'In the history of the world, there never was a greater victory than that which was achieved in Palestine, and in it (also as in France) the soldiers of Australia played a great part', he was talking about horsemanship, intelligent and skilled military tactics, and fierce fighting. It is time, 100 years later, to hold our national head up proudly, knowing our identity can be based on success instead of failure. From 2018 onwards, to mark the anniversary of the end of the war these Light Horsemen helped win, the Australian government should organise a new annual commemoration day, like Anzac Day, but on 31st October, to be called Beersheba Day, to build up the importance of this new foundation stone for our national identity.

As many of the troopers had worked on their horses together back in Australia, they shared a camaraderie that helped them become a formidable fighting force.

The words those brave troopers wrote after charging Beersheba — and after all the other battles threaded through the narrative — collectively tell the story of all the main battles fought by the Australian Light Horse serving with Britain's Egyptian Expeditionary Force as it drove the Turks out of Palestine and dismantled the centuries-old Ottoman Empire. These diaries and letters were kindly provided by generous descendants of those gallant Light Horsemen, who fought so hard to help win those battles. Many diaries also came from the Australian War Memorial.

Other writers have produced many books on the Australian Light Horse. I particularly like *Light Horse: the story of Australia's mounted troops* by my late friend and great horsewoman Elyne Mitchell of Towong Station, Victoria — the daughter of Lieutenant-General Sir Harry Chauvel, who commanded the Australian Light Horse and the charge at Beersheba. Other Australians have also produced films on the Light Horse, starting with the 1940 classic *Forty Thousand Horsemen*, which was directed by Charles Chauvel, the nephew of Sir Harry Chauvel.

This book attempts to tell the story mainly through the words of the ordinary Light Horsemen who were there — those troopers who found time to write up their diaries or pen letters home. Their writing is littered with mistakes — of fact, grammar, and spelling — and may seem politically incorrect and also racist to the modern reader, but they were writing more than 100 years ago, when people had different attitudes. The book tries to give as many of them as possible a platform — a testament to life in and around the battlefields. I often quote from the greatest Light Horse scribe of all, the late Ion 'Jack' Idriess from the 5th Light Horse Regiment, who wrote thousands of words in his diaries, brimming with colour, enthusiasm, excitement, and love for his fellow troopers — and it is to him that this book is gratefully dedicated.

Fortunately, over my life I have gained enough useful experience to help me to write this book. I was lucky enough to interview one of the last surviving Light Horsemen just before he died: the heroic trooper Len Hall, from Western Australia, who served mainly as a Gunner with the 10th

Light Horse Regiment and who featured in my Foxtel History Channel documentaries: *Gallipoli: untold stories* (2005); *Winning World War I* (2008); *Gallipoli: last Anzacs tell all* (2015), which was also shown at the Centennial Anzac Day Service at Gallipoli as part of the pre-dawn Reflective Program, and *Palestine: last Lighthorsemen tell all* (2017). Hall had landed at Gallipoli, been involved in the bloody Battle of The Nek, served throughout the Palestine campaign where he met Lawrence of Arabia, and then ridden with the Light Horse into battles like Beersheba; he died in February 1999, but is remembered each year in the Len Hall Tribute Game, an Anzac Day AFL football match played by the Fremantle Dockers against various other clubs.

I also interviewed the last Light Horseman to die, Albert Whitmore, who passed away in Barmera, South Australia, on 29 July 2002 at the age of 102. I wrote his obituary for *The Australian* newspaper. He was Australia's last living link with the Light Horsemen, that legendary mounted force that had captured Beersheba in 1917. He was lucky to survive, let alone live to 102, as he caught malaria during a record-breaking heat wave in Jordan: 'When one of my fellow troopers saw me lying on the ground sick as a dog he said, "We'll never see old Whit again"; but they carted me off to hospital and I pulled through', he said. Such was the resilience of the Light Horsemen.

Gunner John King Lethbridge of Tregeare, St Marys, a descendant of NSW Governor Philip Gidley King, was one of the author's ancestors who served in Palestine.

I also grew up riding horses: first, on family sheep properties in Victoria, and then as a mounted jackaroo and stockman in the early 1960s, for the New Zealand and Australian Land Company in New South Wales on 'Bundure' Station, 'New Camp' near Jerilderie, and 'Wingadee' between Walgett and Coonamble. I also have family roots in Tamworth, where many of the troopers' horses came from — the home of the famous Walers — because my ancestor, the Hon. Philip Gidley King II, helped found the town in the 1850s as the head of the Australian Agricultural Company (AA Co), managing nearby 'Gunoo Gunoo' sheep station. My parents, R. John Essington King and Zelma King, (nee Sprague), were also born and bred in Tamworth; and I, with my wife, Jane, also live in the former AA Co homestead in Stroud, New South Wales, where in the 1840s, my ancestor Admiral Phillip Parker King (AA Co director) lived, as did his son, the above mentioned Hon. Philip Gidley King II (who was Superintendent of Flocks).

But my interest in the Australian Light Horse was really aroused by Lieutenant-General Harry Chauvel's daughter, Elyne Mitchell, who had me to stay at her homestead in 1995 at Towong Hill, near Corryong, while I was directing the centennial celebrations for an event I conceived to celebrate great Australian horsemen — Banjo Paterson's 'Man From Snowy River'. The popularity of this fabulous ballad (which is printed on the $10 note with Paterson's portrait and a picture of the Man From Snowy River) confirms the importance of horse riding in our culture. Elyne proudly showed me her father's memorabilia from World War I and gave me a copy of the book she wrote based on her father's letters to her mother about his campaigns, *Light Horse: the story of Australia's mounted troops*. After I appointed her Patron of the 1995 Man From Snowy River Centennial Celebrations, she wrote an introduction to our brochure that recalled the days of Banjo Paterson and also the Light Horse: 'Those were the days of great horses and great horsemen. Everyone rode a horse: the cantering rhythm of a horse was the rhythm to which Australia moved. This was the rhythm which Banjo caught'.

Major Paterson, Commander of the Remount Squadron, a great horseman himself, also took that rhythm with him as the officer in charge of the horses in Palestine; where for some years I also led historical tours through the Middle East, guiding tourists through many of the towns mentioned in this book, towns that the brave troopers of the Light Horse captured — as we will now see.

*The author, who travelled through Palestine to research this book, saw the same monasteries —
like Beit Sahour, north of Jerusalem — that the Light Horse troopers visited.*

INTRODUCTION

EQUAL TO THE WORLD'S BEST

The Australian Light Horseman was generally very quick in summing up a situation for himself. No doubt his early training in the wide spaces of the Australian bush had developed to an extraordinary degree his individuality, self reliance and power of observation; and the particularly mobile style of fighting he was called upon to take part in suited him and brought out his special qualities far more than any trench warfare would have done.

GENERAL SIR HARRY CHAUVEL,
COMMANDER DESERT MOUNTED CORPS INTRODUCTION TO
'THE DESERT COLUMN', 1932, BY ION IDRIESS.

Using the words of the troopers wherever possible, this book tells the story of one of Australia's finest hours — the victorious desert campaign of the Australian Light Horse during World War I, serving with Britain's Egyptian Expeditionary Force (EEF) in Palestine. These were the Australian horsemen who, against great odds, between 1916 and 1918 helped British and Allied forces defeat the Turks and liberate Palestine from the centuries-old Ottoman Empire — peaking with the great Light Horse cavalry charge which captured Beersheba on 31 October 1917. And it is these achievements that should, 100 years later, become the new cornerstone of the Australian identity (in place of the failed campaign at Gallipoli), as I argued in the preface.

In this book, Palestine refers to what is now known as the Middle East. In World War I, well before the creation of the state of Israel, most people called that part of the world Palestine, so I have used that name,

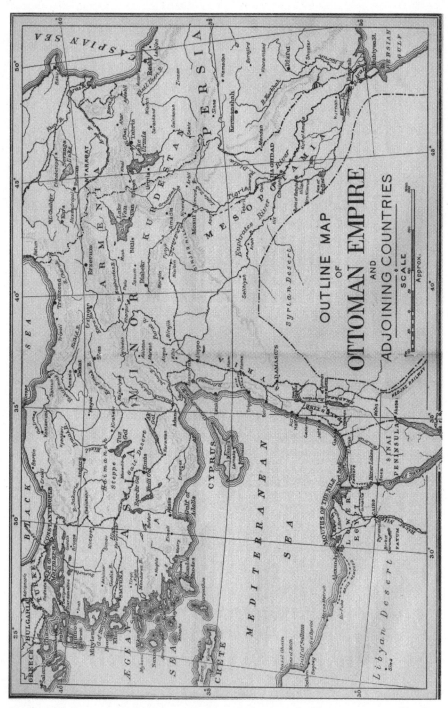

To dismantle the centuries-old Ottoman Empire, which occupied such a vast expanse of land, Britain's Egyptian Expeditionary Force planned to start driving the Turks back from the Suez Canal in the south-west corner, east through the Sinai desert into Palestine, then north through Jordan and Syria until they captured the last stronghold of Damascus, forcing the enemy to flee north to Aleppo and back into Asia Minor towards their capital, Constantinople.

even though today the term refers only to the state of Palestine, a much smaller area. I also use the term Ottoman Empire to describe the overall geographic spread of that Empire. Although the Empire had its Ottoman Army (composed of many nationalities and led by German generals), I have referred to their soldiers as Turks because most of them were Turkish.

As Australian Light Horse contingents had served in the 1899–1902 Boer War, there was no shortage of experienced veterans willing to train officers and men in the art of war in preparation for future conflicts.

The desert campaign I describe in this book drove the Turks 640 kilometres east from the edge of the Suez Canal in Sinai, then north through today's Israel and Palestine, then through Jordan and Syria and right through to Damascus. At that point, the Turks — and their German leaders — surrendered, and the Ottoman Empire was on its last legs. The EEF mounted a massive military campaign with large units of heavily armed British infantry, mobile artillery batteries, aircraft, and thousands of mounted men from Britain's colonial empire, including Australians on horses and also camels. All these units helped win battles at a series of Turkish strongholds standing in the way of the EEF's path to Damascus.

Although conditions could be harsh in the Australian deserts, none of the Light Horsemen were prepared for the terrible thunderstorms that hit them in the deserts of the Sinai, during which even the local Arabs took fright.

The book starts with a prelude at Gallipoli, where the Light Horsemen made a false start. The British had sent them there to fight without horses. It tells the story chronologically in five parts — Gallipoli, Sinai, Palestine, Jordan, and Syria — where they fought. There are chapters on each of the major battles within those regions, as well as the smaller battles within that framework, from start to finish. The main fortified towns they conquered include, in geographical order: Romani and Magdhaba in the Sinai; Rafa on the Sinai/Palestine border; Beersheba, Jerusalem, Bethlehem, and Gaza in Palestine; Amman and Es Salt in Jordan; then Megiddo (Armageddon) before capturing their final objective, Damascus in Syria, where they forced the Turks to surrender.

Because these were the places where the stories of the Old Testament and New Testament happened, they had great religious significance for many of the Light Horsemen. For the Christian soldiers marching onwards through some of the towns, it must have seemed like travelling through the pages of the Bible, especially towns such as Bethlehem, where Jesus Christ was born, then Jerusalem the Holy City, where he was crucified (and which was, of course, holy to Christian, Jews, and Muslims). These religious associations were celebrated by some of the Light Horsemen in their journals and letters, especially by the most colourful Light Horse scribe, Ion (Jack) Idriess, the outback bushman and gold prospector who'd enlisted in Queensland in the 5th Regiment.

Another significant religious association was that of the Crusades — the medieval Christian Holy Wars against the Muslims for control of the Holy Land, including Jerusalem. The Light Horsemen were among the first Christian forces to liberate Jerusalem, which had come under Muslim rule more than 650 years earlier. Some religious scholars even claimed liberation was predicted by prophecies. Andrew Adams, in his book with the title taken from the biblical text of Isaiah 31:5, *As Birds Flying*, claimed that Beersheba was always destined to be the site where good triumphed over evil as it opened the way for the liberation of the most holy city, Jerusalem.

As this book went to press, Christians and Muslims were again fighting over many of the same towns that the Light Horse fought for and captured. For me, it was distressing to turn on the television after a day's writing and watch the news reports of bloody battles over places like

Gaza, Aleppo, Homs, and Damascus, where the Light Horse sacrificed so many lives. What the Australian Light Horsemen would have thought of this historical re-run is any reader's guess; but for the author it was an uncanny experience — writing about the Light Horse capturing Damascus in 1918, and then watching the modern battle for Damascus on the TV news that night.

Today's conflicts in the Middle East are extremely complex and resolution is incredibly difficult. Back then, the conflict between the British and Turks was more straightforward and, for the British, relatively easily won. In fact, on their way northwards the British forces, with their Australian and New Zealand mounted troops, captured 40,000 Turkish (and German) prisoners, with less than 100 Light Horsemen captured by the enemy.

The Light Horsemen were the greatest mounted warriors Australia has ever produced, and we shall never see their like again. That mould has been thrown out, and in any case, warfare has become too mechanised for wonderful riders and marvellous horses. At the end of the Palestine campaign, the commander-in-chief of the Egyptian Expeditionary Force, General Sir Edmund Allenby, said: 'The Australian combines a splendid physique and restless activity of mind, rendering him somewhat impatient of rigid and formal discipline, but giving him the gift of adaptability mounted or on foot. Eager in advance and staunch in defence, the Australian light horseman has proved himself equal to the world's best, earning the gratitude of the Empire and admiration of the world'.

Allenby was talking about the handsome young horsemen from outback Australia who most famously captured the Turkish stronghold village of Beersheba in history's last great successful mounted cavalry charge, brandishing nothing but .303 Lee–Enfield rifles and bayonets — rather than the traditional lance and sabre. For this battle of all battles, many had to ride nearly 300 kilometres in four days to get there, in temperatures above 37°C, and with very little water. They fought 36 battles over those three bloody years and won most of them.

These brave horsemen were also stoic, accepting death and making light of wounds. Writing to his father from Lemnos Hospital, Trooper Bert Merrell, 7th Regiment, from Wellington, New South Wales — one of four brothers who enlisted from the family that founded Ashton's Circus — said: 'Just a few lines to let you know I am out of the trenches after six months and I am glad to be out I can tell you. It is quite a treat to be able to walk about free and easy and have a good night's sleep'. Merrell was lucky not to be killed in those trenches, as he then wrote: 'It's not much of a snap to be in the trenches because the cold weather has set in and there is plenty of rain and snow on the peninsular [sic]. I was blown up in a trench with a few more mates. The Turks mined it early on Sunday morning and blew it up and I was one who went up with it. I was blown about six feet in the air and one of my mates was killed — so I was lucky'. Fortunately, all four Merrell brothers returned from the war, some with decorations. When their local newspaper saluted them with a prominent

Mrs Merrell (pictured centre), from the family that founded Ashton's Circus, considered it such a miracle that all of her four sons returned from World War I that she contacted her local newspaper in Wellington, New South Wales, which published this montage as a tribute.

article as the 'Fighting Merrells', Bert's brother John corrected the newspaper, admitting honestly: 'Never mind about the Fighting Merrells, we were the Bloody Frightened Merrells'.

The fact that these Australians were so independently minded and were such great characters gave them an edge over their conservative British comrades, but it also got them into trouble. Ed de Rose, C Squadron Machine Gun Section, who was a mate of Philip Tod of 9th Light Horse, confirmed that men slipped away from their training camp in front of the Pyramids (Mena Camp) to visit nearby Cairo. They got up to all sorts of tricks in Cairo, living up to the notion that these Australians were certainly 'impatient of rigid and formal discipline', as when in town they did what they liked — eating all kinds of food, drinking, and having sex with prostitutes, despite the serious health risks. 'The deaths in camp here average from two to three a day', de Rose wrote in his diary, 'so I reckon it's a shame to keep our troops in a place like this. We also heard the natives are dying of Cholera which seems to be true. Half the regiment had leave today and I believe they were involved in a great riot in Cairo with two of our men killed last night — one of these lads being stabbed by a girl — and six wounded. So no leave is granted now to any of the lads just because a few have played up'.

Food was a big source of complaint. Some troopers were tempted to sneak away from their Mena camp near the pyramids and into town because of the poor food and rations. Tom Crase, 3rd Light Horse Regiment, reported: 'Our rations are of very poor quality and vegetables and fresh meat are unheard of. When we open a tin of bully beef, as soon as the tin is pierced, the hot liquid fat inside spurts out likes a small geyser. As often as not our bread does not turn up and we have to use Army Biscuits instead — special Army quality biscuits — no taste and hard as granite. To make matters worse some Back Room Boffin got the idea that kerosene was good for the troop's blood etc. So a special brew of marmalade was made and it was well seasoned with kerosene. It was enough to put a chap off marmalade for life. Our time in the Sinai was also beset by scorpions, flies, mosquitoes and malaria fever. Join all that with a lack of sleep, strenuous rides (mostly at night) and battle fatigue — it is a wonder that we achieve what we do'.

Throughout the whole desert campaign, the Light Horsemen had also competed with Bedouins, Arabs, Turks, and Germans for water — which they all mainly got from sought-after wells. In the dry, arid moonscape of the desert, water was everything. Campaigns were planned around the availability of water, with one big exception: Beersheba. For the big decisive charge on 31 October 1917, both men and horses had to survive many hours without water.

Yet despite these challenging circumstances, Crase reported, they achieved great things: 'While British Generals conducted warfare from increasingly tenuous distances in Cairo, the Light Horse and the Camel Corps moved against the Turkish troops and their German advisers from the Sinai onwards through Palestine and beyond. The Anzac Mounted Divisions were the Spearhead of the Campaign. This formation achieved results unequalled by any other of Horse, Allied or Enemy engaged in any front in the War. We carried the can and did all the dirty work and the hard fighting on the Sinai right through to El Arish'.

Their horses — the wonderful Walers — were, of course, first class, mostly bred in New South Wales. They had their origins in English thoroughbred stallions and Australian breeding mares, which were sometimes part brumby (wild horses); their progeny were called Walers. These strong, hardy stock horses had great endurance and were ideal for riding into battle. The famous poet, bushman, champion horseman, and lawyer, Major Andrew 'Banjo' Paterson, who was in charge of the unit responsible for caring for their horses, wrote: 'The war was a good test of horses, and our troop horses under Palestine conditions were better than any others. They stood more work and they recovered quicker when they came back to us to be patched up after

Already famous for his 1895 ballad about the legendary horse ride 'The Man From Snowy River', and for his newspaper reports from the Boer War, Major A.B. 'Banjo' Paterson became a real favourite with the troopers when he was put in charge of caring for their horses in Egypt.

being knocked around. Our horses had more thoroughbred blood than any others and I think that accounted for their toughness'.

Tom Crase described the toughness of these horses in the worst of conditions in the Sinai: 'A desert dust storm hit our camp at about 9 p.m. the wind was searing hot even at night time and must have been at least 100 mph. The desert gravel was lit up with electricity. And when the airborne gravel hit the ground there were sparks flying everywhere. There were electrical flares about 4 inches long on the end of the horses' ears. Our horses were tethered to the horse lines with metal chains and all these chains were ablaze with electricity. If we held up our hand each fingertip has a two-inch electrical flare on its end. In the storm the entire place was lit up like a large city. Our horses were very frightened indeed and they broke the horse lines and just bunched up in a mob and stood with their tails turned into the blast. Just as well for us that they did; if they had stampeded they could have galloped over the top of us, as we had no getaway at all. Of course all our tents were flattened, most of our felt hats were blown miles away (and we had to be issued with new hats). All our gear and personal belongings, food and tents were buried under about six feet of sand and gravel. The storm must have lasted about two hours'.

Yet despite their great achievements and winning the war in Palestine, the Light Horsemen have never achieved the recognition the infantry achieved after their defeat at Gallipoli. In Australia, both during the war and for many years after, there was little respect for the Light Horse: they were not considered to be as important as the brave boys who had landed and paid such a high price on the beach at Gallipoli. Nor were the Light Horsemen considered as valuable as the Australian Imperial Force (AIF), who fought in the more important theatres like the Western Front. Major Wilfred Kent Hughes, 3rd Light Horse Brigade, wrote in his book *Modern Crusaders* shortly after the war: 'A short-sighted Red Cross enthusiast enclosed a note in the toe of a sock that she had knitted to the effect that she hoped the socks would be sent to one of the brave boys in France, and not to a cold footed light-horseman in Egypt'. This 'caused much indignation throughout the Light Horse units' and combined with the casual remarks in odd letters which were received from Australia made the men feel rather slighted'.

Yet, as the Australian Light Horse Studies Centre confirms, the Light Horse could trace its origins back to early colonial times. The first horses were brought to New South Wales on the First Fleet by my ancestor, Lieutenant Philip Gidley King, and other officers, who'd bought them in Cape Town en route. For the first hundred years of European settlement, horses were the only means of transport. The ability to ride a horse was almost as basic as the ability to walk. Mounted soldiers had served since 1804, when redcoats of the New South Wales Corps set out in pursuit of a large force of rebel convicts who had broken out of the Castle Hill Prison Farm near Sydney. King, by then Governor of New South Wales, rode through the night to successfully suppress this Irish rebellion. Governor King's mounted bodyguard, soon described as 'Lighthorsemen', became forerunners of a semi-military mounted police force, and British infantry regiments stationed in Australia then created special mounted units. One of these units took part in the attack on the Eureka Stockade at Ballarat in 1854.

Three of the colonial governments created their own small cavalry forces, motivated by fear of Russian invasion following the Crimean War of 1853 to 1856. Australia's mounted citizen soldiers then sprang up everywhere — men who rode their own horses and trained in their spare time.

In 1899, as soon as the Boer War started, the Australian colonies sent some of these self-trained mounted troops to fight in the imperial cause. Although the British senior officers were nervous about using untried, unprofessional, and undisciplined colonial cavalrymen, the slouch-hatted, mounted Australian 'bushmen' out-rode and out-fought the fast-moving and unconventionally mounted commandos of the Boers, and so helped win the war.

On a world stage for the first time, they showed they were both skilled, rough-riding horsemen and good shots. Used to going for long periods with little food and water, they also had an uncanny knack of finding their way in strange country and working out where to shelter behind protective cover, and when and where to launch an attack.

Some of the Australian Light Horse officers and troopers had learned valuable skills while fighting on horseback in the South African bush against the Boers, who were tough, cutthroat guerrilla fighters who fought to the death.

After a few hundred Australians and a small group of Rhodesians held out successfully against several thousand encircling Boers at the Battle of Elands River, the Australians helped create a new tradition of winning against the odds. This contrasted with the massacre of England's famous 17th Lancers, wiped out by Boers, which was seen by the English as part of a noble 'death or glory' tradition, with its origins in the disastrous defeat of the British Light Brigade in the Crimean War immortalised by Alfred, Lord Tennyson in his poem 'The Charge of the Light Brigade'. But Australian horsemen showed how they could win, time and time again. Lord Kitchener, who commanded the relieving troops at Elands River and would become Secretary of State for War in 1914, commented: 'Only colonials could have held out and survived in such impossible circumstances!'

When Australia became a Commonwealth in 1901, the different colonial mounted contingents that had served in the Boer War united to form the Commonwealth military forces, which included the Light Horse brigades and regiments that would serve in World War I. By the outbreak of war in August 1914, there were already 23 Light Horse regiments within Australia's part-time military force, consisting of 9,000 people.

When the war started, Australia offered a volunteer expeditionary force of 20,000 personnel — the AIF — that initially included an infantry division and a Light Horse brigade. But as Australia's commitment increased, the size of the Light Horse contingent expanded, with second and third Light Horse brigades being raised in late 1914 and early 1915. By the end of the war, Australia had contributed five brigades, all of them voluntary; in fact, Australian forces were the only all-volunteer forces serving in World War I.

There was no problem getting recruits — adventurous young horsemen from the country flocked to join — and there was no problem getting horses either, as many men brought their own. If the horse met army standards, it was bought by the Commonwealth for about £30. Each horse was branded with the Government broad arrow and the initials of the purchasing officer, and an army number on one hoof. Other men were given 'remounts' — army horses bought by Commonwealth purchasing officers from graziers and breeders.

The recruits took a riding test in which they had to ride an army horse bareback over a water jump and/or a low wall, or jump a log fence. Once they passed a strict medical test, they were sworn in and issued with their uniforms — a standard AIF jacket, smart cord riding breeches, leather 'puttee' leggings bound by a spiral strap, a leather bandolier that carried 90 rounds of ammunition, and, most importantly, an Australian slouch hat, to which was later added an emu plume under the hat-band.

Everything was well organised. At night, the horses were tethered by head and heel ropes between long ropes called picket lines, and a saddle was placed in front of each horse. The riders slept close by in bell tents — eight men to a tent, feet to the centre like the spokes of a wheel.

The Light Horse troopers' secret weapon was their Waler, which was not only exceptionally big and strong but could also go for long periods without food and water and still gallop into battle. Artist, George Lambert.

The Light Horsemen watered, fed, and groomed their horses and cleaned the horse lines before breakfast. After breakfast, they trained in mounted-infantry fighting techniques.

The men got to know each other well. Each regiment lived and fought as a series of four-man sections. In a typical battle, three men would dismount to fight as infantry while the fourth man led the four horses to cover until they were needed for further action.

Everything the Light Horse trooper needed for living and fighting had to be carried by him and his horse. He carried clothing, food, and personal possessions in a canvas haversack slung over one shoulder, and a vital life-saving one-litre water bottle over the other. He was armed with his .303 rifle — also slung over his shoulder — containing ten rounds of ammunition; another 90 rounds of ammunition were in his bandolier, plus 50 rounds in pouches on his belt, which also supported the bayonet and scabbard. Later, some men were also issued swords.

A Light Horsemen was issued with a special military saddle, built on a pair of felt-padded wooden 'bars' that sat on either side of the horse's spine, joined by steel arches with a shaped leather seat laced between them. His rolled greatcoat and waterproof ground sheet were strapped across the front. He carried his personal blanket either in a roll, or spread under the saddle on top of the saddle blanket. At the back of the saddle he attached a mess tin, a billy and a tin or enamel plate, a canvas water bucket, and a nosebag with a day's grain ration. He also carried a heel rope, removable length of picket line, and a leather case with two horseshoes and nails. It was a good thing the Walers were big and strong, with all this weight to carry. Fully loaded, Walers often carried up to 150 kilograms in scorching heat, sometimes for long distances, walking, trotting, cantering or galloping, sometimes without water, for 70 hours at a stretch. No wonder the men grew to love the horses they depended on to survive as the war years went on, and no wonder they were so distraught after the war when the British War Cabinet ordered them to leave their horses behind. Rather then leave them to the mercy of hard-hearted Arabs, many Light Horsemen shot their mounts, which would have been traumatic.

Many animals got sick or died during the war, up to 640 a week in 1916 (both horses and mules). Horses that died or were destroyed while on active service were buried two miles (3.2 kilometres) from the nearest camp, their carcasses transported to a suitable site away from troops, where they were disembowelled and left to disintegrate in the dry desert air and high temperatures. After four days' drying in the sun, the carcases were stuffed with straw and burnt; the skins were sold to local contractors.

These Australian Light Horse units fought like mounted infantry, using their horses as transport to the battlefield then usually fighting dismounted, and then remounting as a means of swift disengagement when retreating. However, the charge of the 4th and 12th Light Horse Regiments at Beersheba on 31 October 1917 became a famous exception to this tradition. The advance on Damascus in 1918 was another exception, as some Light Horse regiments were equipped with sabres so they could charge on horseback and fight in a conventional cavalry role. The Australian Light Horse also performed certain cavalry roles, such as scouting and screening, while mounted.

Organised along cavalry rather than infantry lines, a Light Horse regiment, although technically equivalent to an infantry battalion in terms of command level, contained only 25 officers and 400 men, as opposed to an infantry battalion that consisted of around 1,000 men. A regiment was divided into three squadrons, designated A, B and C (similar to an infantry company), and a squadron divided into four troops (similar to an infantry platoon). Each troop was divided into about ten four-man sections.

Each regiment initially had a troop of two Maxim guns, and in 1916, these were consolidated into Light Horse machine-gun squadrons, each with 12 Vickers machine guns. Later, the troops were issued the Lewis Gun, and then later again the Hotchkiss M1909 Benét–Mercié machine gun, in April 1917. Before the end of the war each troop had a Hotchkiss gun, which increased the mobile firepower of each regiment.

The troopers in the Light Horse served in a complicated structure commanded by the British. The Australian Mounted Division originally formed as the Imperial Mounted Division in January 1917, as a mounted infantry, Light Horse, and yeomanry division. The division was formed in Egypt, and, along with the Anzac Mounted Division, formed part of Desert Column, Egyptian Expeditionary Force (EEF) in World War I.

It could have been difficult for the ordinary trooper to keep up with the name changes of the overall units, as they changed so often, as well as with who was who. The mounted troops were restructured in February 1917 into the Anzac Mounted Division consisting of the 1st and 2nd Light Horse Brigades, the New Zealand Mounted Rifles Brigade, and the British

22nd Mounted Brigade. Meanwhile, the Imperial Mounted Division was formed from the 3rd and 4th Light Horse Brigades and the British Yeomanry 5th and 6th Mounted Brigades. The Imperial Mounted Division's name was then changed to the Australian Mounted Division at the request of the Australian government.

Then, when more British yeomanry arrived in June 1917, the authorities created the Yeomanry Mounted Division (6th, 8th, and 22nd Yeomanry Brigades). The three mounted divisions and the Imperial Camel Brigade together formed the Desert Mounted Corps under the command of Australia's Lieutenant-General Sir Harry Chauvel.

Later, the Imperial Camel Corps was broken up when Britain demanded its Yeomanry forces transfer to their main Western Front theatre, and Australia's newly formed 5th Light Horse Brigade joined the Australian Mounted Division. Two Indian cavalry divisions recruited to take the place of the Yeomanry forces joined the Desert Mounted Corps.

By the time the war got underway, Australia organised its Light Horse into five brigades with regiments as follows:

1st Light Horse Brigade consisted of the 1st, 2nd, and 3rd Light Horse Regiments.

2nd Light Horse Brigade consisted of the 5th, 6th, and 7th Light Horse Regiments.

Major Chauvel — decorated for leadership in the Boer War and, through successful command in Palestine, becoming the commander of the whole of the Desert Column, Australian Mounted Division, Anzac Mounted Division, and Imperial Camel Brigade — was the first Australian to reach the rank of Lieutenant-General and command a Corps.

3rd Light Horse Brigade consisted of the 8th, 9th, and 10th Light Horse Regiments.

4th Light Horse Brigade consisted of the 4th, 11th, and 12th Light Horse Regiments.

5th Light Horse Brigade consisted of the 14th and 15th Light Horse Regiments, as well as the French 1er Regiment Mixte de Cavalerie du Levant and the New Zealand 2nd Machine Gun Squadron.

Finally, after months of anticipation, on 1 November 1914, the first four Light Horse regiments sailed for England in a fleet of transport ships (with Australia's First Infantry Divisions). Special stalls were built for the horses below decks, where the Light Horsemen cared for their mounts, even exercising them in the limited space available. Sadly, some horses died on the voyage, and all of them suffered terribly in the tropics.

This diary of Charles Poynton was typical of the troopers' diaries: full of cryptic entries scribbled in between battles, often while they were grabbing a meal on the run before collapsing into their tent (or onto the ground) to get some badly needed sleep.

Then, suddenly, mid-voyage plans were changed, and the Light Horse landed in Egypt instead of England to complete their training there with another two brigades that joined them later, increasing the number to six regiments of Light Horse. But instead of then sailing with the horses to serve on the Western Front in France, they were unexpectedly ordered to sail for the steep cliffs of Gallipoli in Turkey as infantrymen, leaving their horses behind.

This is where we take up the story to see just what the Light Horse did and did not do — where possible, in their own words — from Gallipoli right through to Damascus, letting their actions speak for themselves.

NOTHING is to be written on this side except the date and signature of the sender. Sentences not required may be erased. If anything else is added the post card will be destroyed.

[Postage must be prepaid on any letter or post card addressed to the sender of this card.]

I am quite well.

I have been admitted into hospital

{ sick } *and am going on well.*
{ wounded } *and hope to be discharged soon.*

I am being sent down to the base.

I have received your { letter dated _____
{ telegram „ _____
{ parcel „ _____

Letter follows at first opportunity.

I have received no letter from you
{ lately
{ for a long time.

Signature only }

Date_____

Wt. W65—P.P.948. 8000m. 5-18. C. & Co., Grange Mills, S.W.

The Egyptian Expeditionary Force issued standard correspondence cards to troopers like James Williamson, hoping to control what the troopers told their folks back home and trying to keep information coming from the frontline to a minimum.

PART I
GALLIPOLI 1915

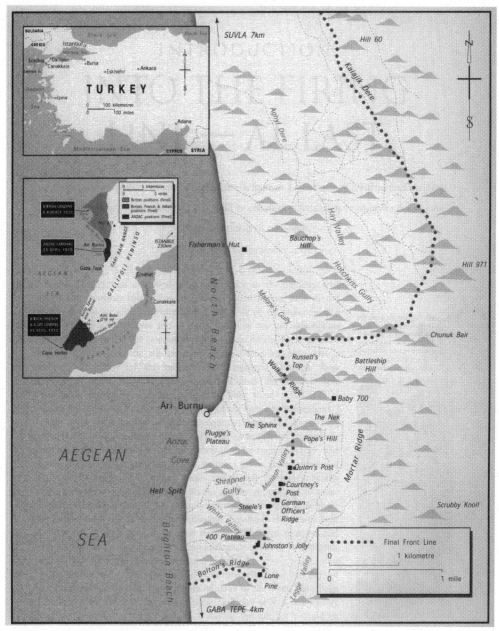

Top Insert: *Turkey, with the Gallipoli peninsula just west of the town of Canakkale.*
Bottom Insert: *Gallipoli peninsula, showing the 25 April 1915 British landing spot, Cape Helles, to the south; the Anzacs landing spot at Ari Burnu to the north; and Suvla Bay, where British reinforcements landed in August 1915, at the top.*
Main Map: *The extent of territory occupied by the Anzacs is shown by the dotted line, including Anzac Cove and positions like Lone Pine on the frontline, which they occupied, and battlefields like The Nek, where Light Horse troopers were slaughtered when they tried to capture this position on 7 August 1915.*

PRELUDE: GALLIPOLI 1915

MASSACRE OF THE UNMOUNTED AT THE NEK, 7 AUGUST 1915

Unfortunately, the Anzacs landed at the wrong spot at Gallipoli: the beach was too narrow to accommodate the thousands of soldiers who came ashore, and the cliffs were so steep they could hardly climb up them to dig themselves in, especially with Turkish defenders shooting at them.

During the long hours of the day the summit of the Nek could be seen crowded with the bodies of Light Horsemen. At first here and there a man raised his hand to the sky, or tried to drink from his water bottle. But as the sun of that burning day climbed higher, such movement ceased. Over the whole summit the figures lay still in the quivering heat.

CHARLES BEAN, OFFICIAL WAR CORRESPONDENT,
The Story of Anzac: the first phase, 1921

BACKGROUND TO THE BATTLE

Apart from their risky landing on the beach in May 1915, the Light Horse also fought in a number of costly battles at Gallipoli including Quinn's Post, The Nek, Russell's Top, and Hill 60 — all without the horses they had enlisted to ride as mounted troopers. The Nek on 7 August alone would claim the lives of 234 of these horsemen turned foot soldiers.

By far the most terrible of the battles they fought during their seven months at Gallipoli was The Nek, which would scar the 8th and 10th Regiments for the rest of the war, and continue to send a shudder of fear through the rest of the Light Horse until they disbanded in 1919. World War I Correspondent Charles Bean wrote later that this was when 'the flower of Australian youth, the sons of the old pioneering families rushed to their death'.

These gallant horsemen were only at Gallipoli because of a last-minute change of plans when British commanding officers sent them to fight on the steep cliffs of Gallipoli instead of the flat fields of the Western Front. After declaring war on Germany, Australia had sent its first contingent of troops to Egypt for training to fight against Germany in Europe, which included the Light Horse regiments recruited specifically to fight on horseback. Many had taken their prized horses with them, housed in stables on the transport ships. Both horses and men, mainly from the outback, were trained for mounted cavalry operations.

But despite their expectations, the Light Horse, along with other troops, were suddenly assigned to attack the Ottoman Empire, which had unexpectedly joined the war on the side of Germany. And to make matters worse, these experienced horsemen, whose *raison d'être* was riding horses, were ordered to leave their mounts behind in Egypt.

That was the worst thing about Gallipoli for the troopers, who had never dreamed they would have to fight on foot. Yet they had no alternative, because mounted troops were not suited to the steep terrain of Gallipoli.

'It is practically decided we go in a few days,' wrote the commander of the 1st Light Horse Brigade, Harry Chauvel, on 4 May 1915, and 'I have offered to go dismounted'. On 11 May, he confirmed: 'The men — although very disappointed would rather come dismounted than not at all'.

After their ships arrived in Egypt, the Australian military forces set up camp near the pyramids at Giza, where the Light Horsemen pitched their tents, tethered the horses they had brought with them, and gave them a feed of chaff.

Meanwhile, not knowing when they could sail for Gallipoli, commanding officers banned the Light Horsemen from going back into Cairo, where they had been playing up and causing trouble. According to Ed de Rose, C Squadron Machine Gun Section, this ban did not stop two larrikins from continuing the fun in camp. Trooper Albert Edward Merrell and his best mate decided to create their own entertainment, putting on a show entitled 'Dancing Ducks', with an affordable entry price, inside a crudely erected viewing tent. Bert, as he was known, captured a couple of ducks from an unsuspecting Egyptian farmer, clipped their wings, placed them on a tin surface mounted on a metal stand that the patrons could see, then lit a secret fire behind this stand, which of course made the poor ducks dance so the patrons got their money's worth. This caper lasted until the officers found out about the illicit circus act, confiscated the ducks and equipment, and arrested Bert and his accomplice for misbehaviour. Unfortunately, the humourless officers did not take into account the important fact that Bert was the grandson of the founder of Ashton's Circus. Ed de Rose was right when he concluded that the sooner the troopers sailed for Gallipoli, the better.

When they did eventually sail to Gallipoli, some of the men would still dream of getting their horses back, as one anonymous trooper wrote in his diary later: 'We were hoping that in a couple of weeks at the latest, once more mounted, we would canter gaily along the Gallipoli road to Constantinople [capital of Turkey]. We were mostly young and optimistic! We were soon to find what a long, long road it was'.

Sadly, it was their very flexibility that would prove to be their undoing. There would be no cantering on horseback into Constantinople, and hundreds of slaughtered Light Horsemen would lie buried on that fatal shore within months, far from the horses they had expected would serve them well as they rode into battle. And there was no shortage of battles — despite their lack of training in trench warfare, once these unmounted horsemen landed at Gallipoli they were assigned to some of the toughest trenches, which they had to defend against murderous enemy fire.

The action at The Nek was part of an ill-conceived final Allied offensive mounted in early August by the British War Council, which still believed the Allies could occupy the Gallipoli peninsula successfully, if not from the south at Cape Helles (where the British had landed on the first day, 25 April 1915) then from the north-west part of the peninsula from Suvla Bay, where more British were to be landed and ordered to march up the long, narrow peninsula to Constantinople, which they would capture. Despite all the earlier failed offensives, the Allied commander-in-chief, General Sir Ian Hamilton, and his staff officer, Lieutenant Andrew Skeen, masterminded the boldest but most complicated strategy yet.

The British decided to have an all-out assault on the Turkish defences at the top of the Sari Bair range, from which the Turks overlooked the Anzacs and fired down upon them. The generals created a complicated plan to fight a number of battles to achieve their objective; and they ordered the Light Horse to help. The overall big-picture objective was to capture the Sari Bair ridge, including the towering Hill 971, which at

971 feet (295 metres) was the commanding peak above Anzac Cove — the Mount Everest of the maze of surrounding hills on the Sari Bair range. If the British captured those heights, they could look down on the Turks on the inland side. The British plan was to land 20,000 reinforcements, north of Anzac Cove at Suvla Bay, to secure the bay and foothills just inland. Although these inexperienced troops would be commanded by the ageing Sir Frederick Stopford (who had never served in a war), they were meant to help capture the Sari Bair range from the north-west, which the Turks would not expect. At the same time, Anzacs of the 4th Brigade under General John Monash would capture Hill 971; and New Zealand troops would capture Chunuk Bair (which scouts claimed was poorly defended), with the strategically important 700-foot high hilltop known as Baby 700 as a supplementary objective if all went well.

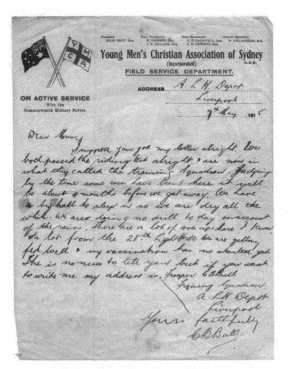

Trooper Colin Bull's mother would treasure letters like this one from her son saying he had passed the riding test on his horse, because he was shot dead on that very horse as he charged Beersheba on 31 October 1917.

But to achieve these ultimate goals they had to distract Turks with diversionary battles. This would force the Turks to send troops to these sideshows, which is where the Light Horse came into the picture — and as it turned out, these horsemen would be asked to fight at the worst sideshow of all.

The first of these diversionary actions would be at that hopeless old southern battlefield of Cape Helles, which was littered with thousands of unburied British corpses. Here, the British would pretend to attack the impenetrable Turkish trenches yet again. The second sideshow would be at Lone Pine, inland from Anzac Cove, where the Anzacs would put on a big show and create the impression they were mounting an all-out attack. The final sideshow would be The Nek.

Unfortunately, the brilliant Turkish leader Mustafa Kemal had predicted Britain's big-picture strategy and had been getting ready for months with reinforcements and stronger defences — especially at The Nek. So the Allies did not have a chance of succeeding.

ARRIVAL AND PREPARATIONS FOR BATTLE

12 May

The first of the Light Horse arrived at Gallipoli on 12 May — Chauvel's 1st Regiment (New South Wales) and 2nd Regiment (Queensland). Anzac Cove, scene of the first infantry landing, was already a bustling little port. Hundreds of men swam in the cove, ignoring the Turkish shells that burst over them.

As the Light Horsemen clambered to their camping areas up the steep, winding ravine of Shrapnel Gully, Turkish bullets cracked high over their heads. Infantrymen, who were old hands by now, laughed when the newcomers ducked. Very soon, the newcomers, too, were old hands. They quickly proved themselves to be excellent soldiers and readily adapted to the dreadful living conditions at the Anzac front.

The 3rd Regiment (South Australia and Tasmania) arrived the next day and was soon followed by other Regiments.

19 May

Brigadier-General Granville Ryrie's 2nd Light Horse Brigade landed at Gallipoli on 19 May, delivering more skilled horsemen, some of whom would soon become canon fodder. This brigade included the 5th Light Horse Regiment from Queensland, the 6th from New South Wales, and the 7th, also from New South Wales. One of the Queensland troopers in the 5th was the diligent diary-keeper Ion Idriess, who reported that 'the gullies were swarming with Turks and machine guns' when they landed. Apart from recording the Light Horse's experience at Gallipoli, Idriess, who went on to fight in the Middle East, kept the best records of that campaign, and after the war published them in a book called *The Desert Column* (1932).

Although the Light Horse troopers were disappointed they could not take their horses to Gallipoli, at least they did not have to land against heavy enemy fire with the Anzacs — as reinforcements, they landed later (and against less opposition) in May.

A concerned Lieutenant Reg Garnock of 6th Regiment, who had just attended a church service from which 'very few were absent', reported in his diary: 'We will probably get it hot if we land in daylight' then added, 'In case this diary is never finished for obvious reasons I will bid a fond farewell here'. But he survived, adding: 'Landed today after getting orders earlier in the day that that we would not land till dark, as anticipated we were shelled with shrapnel, a couple of shells hitting the boat but fortunately no damage was done. Had a long walk up the hill to our bivouac where we had to dig in at once, most of us with bayonets the only implements available, even so we were shelled pretty severely and one chap had his eye knocked out with a piece of shrapnel'. Things got worse, as the next day, 'One of our chaps was shot through the head while walking along the road'.

As carrying dispatches between the different headquarters on the beachfront was the only horse work available, this dangerous job proved the most popular with the Light Horsemen, who competed for the honour.

But the only thing the Light Horse was really suited for at Gallipoli was using the few horses that had landed for riding with dispatches. Eventually, these skilled horsemen would ride from the northern British beachhead of Suvla Bay about 10 kilometres down south to the Anzac beachhead at Ari Burnu in the morning, and then back with dispatches in the afternoon. Riding with these daily messages was extremely dangerous, as the Turks shot at the riders from the hilltops, but the Light Horsemen galloped at great speed and got away with it most of the time. As Chauvel wrote: 'The rider was fired at the moment he left the shelter of Lala Baba until he reached the wide communication trench near Anzac' yet all the brave young Light Horsemen were 'tumbling over each other to get the job'; such was their desire to do what they had enlisted to do — to ride horses.

May: Quinn's Post and Pope's Hill

The Light Horsemen were quickly assigned to one of the hottest spots — the extreme frontline trench of Quinn's Post, right up the top end of the deadly Monash Valley and only 20 metres from the nearest opposing Turkish trench. According to Chauvel, whose dugout headquarters were also in Monash Valley, this was 'the most poisonous part of the whole front line'; yet his inexperienced 1st Regiment was meant to defend this vulnerable outpost. The 2nd Regiment was sent to the less deadly Pope's Hill.

It was a lot to ask the unsuspecting horsemen from country New South Wales, and as Charles Bean wrote in *The Story of Anzac*, 'The mere strain of holding the post was the equivalent of a battle'. Anzacs back down in Monash Valley would hear the bombs bursting at Quinn's, Bean said, and look up 'as a man looks at a haunted house'.

At Gallipoli, the Light Horsemen were stuck in crowded trenches, just like the infantry, where they lived for safety's sake and from where they climbed up to attack positions like The Nek.

Many of these young horsemen were killed within days by Turkish shrapnel, snipers, or 'bombs' (grenades) thrown, into Quinn's especially. The Australians tried to throw back the bombs before they exploded in their hands, which was possible until the Turks shortened the fuses, giving the troopers very little time before the bombs exploded.

This kind of trench warfare was difficult for anybody, as Major T.A. Kidd explained: 'Being the fittest I remained on duty last night. Men were very tired and some in a state of stupor. 2nd Lieut. Howard who rested during the day remained during night to help. We have a bomb fight practically from dusk to dawn but more than hold our own. Turks managed to hurl several bombs in our trench, but my bags on trench floor successfully stopped them and very little damage was done. I allowed three men only (2 Throwers 1 Observer) to remain in bomb throwing trench. Before daylight this morning a bomb prematurely exploded resulting in fatal injuries to Trooper Fletcher. Through faulty fuse, bomb exploded in Fletcher's hand. His two hands and one leg were blown off, both eyes blown out and stomach pierced. He was conscious for an hour and calmly gave instruction re personal effects'. Even senior officers were not immune: General Sir William Bridges was mortally wounded while visiting Chauvel's dugout, becoming the highest-ranking officer killed at Gallipoli.

THE OFFENSIVE BEGINS

The Light Horse's main jobs — defending Quinn's Post and assaulting the Turkish trenches whenever they got a chance — were difficult enough, but why the British then decided to use these specialist horsemen, rather than trained infantry foot soldiers, to charge enemy trenches at The Nek in the most suicidal battle of all is hard to understand.

One Light Horse officer was certainly aware of the dangers. South Australian wine grower Lieutenant Colonel Carew Reynell, acting commander of the 9th Regiment (which would be in reserve), wrote in his diary in early August that he had heard 'through the secret service that the Turks have been reinforced by upwards of 100,000 and intend to make a grand attack on us'. Against these great odds, he was now worried about the planned attack on The Nek. 'We are going to make a big attack — our casualties are bound to be very heavy indeed as we shall have to cross a confined space under fire from a half circle of Turkish trenches. However I have every confidence in our fellows and even if 75% of us are knocked out I believe the other 25% will get there. I am going to talk to them and prepare their minds for heavy losses and impress on them the necessity of getting there or dying in the attempt. However I believe they will behave well and do or die anyway. I see a big stack of new stretchers being made just near our bivouac'. Fearing for his own life, having calculated that 19 per cent of his men had by now become casualties in earlier battles, he now confided in his diary: 'All my pals wounded now and my turn next I suppose — damned nuisance if I have to provide the 20% of the said casualties'.

Although Lieutenant Colonel Carew Reynell, a South Australian wine producer, predicted he would become a casualty, he could not have known he would actually be killed as he bravely led his men into battle.

That battle was sheer bloody murder and a terrible waste of talented horsemen. More Light Horsemen were killed at The Nek than in any other battle they fought in World War I.

The results alone proved the stupidity — 372 valuable horsemen killed or wounded for no territorial gain at all. 'No doubt today has been the fiercest battle in the history of the war,' wrote 3rd Light Horse Sergeant A.S. Hutton in his diary after the 6 August battle. 'The first Light Horse were absolutely cut up.'

4 August

On 4 August, Reg Garnock asked in his diary, 'Today is the anniversary of the declaration of war, I wonder if it will be celebrated?'. Lieutenant Colonel Carew Reynell reported optimistically: 'Our first definite orders about the attack last night. The attack is to be general and a big left flanking attack to be made in co-operation. Apparently the artillery support for the frontal attack will be good. Our 3rd L H. Brigade is to take the trenches on the neck [sic.] with good covering fire by rifle machine and artillery fire after a very heavy and prolonged bombardment and so it should present no difficulties'. Sadly for the Light Horse, it would be this bombardment that would let them down, along with the covering fire, which never eventuated. 'From what I can guess of the plan of attack', the trusting Reynell continued, 'and the numbers we are to have I anticipate a great and glorious victory during the next few days with such a stunning blow to the Turks that it may end the Turkish hash in one hit. I have been busy all day with preliminary arrangements for the attack, which is to start on the day after tomorrow either just before or after daylight.' Perhaps sensing his own death soon after, he added, ' I feel I ought to be writing home sort of good bye letters in case of a wash out … I am looking forward to the attack very much as I am very hopeful that it may result in a glorious stroke'.

6 August

At last, the long-awaited day of the offensive arrived. Some Anzacs believed it would be as successful as their landing on 25 April — which they had achieved against such great odds, securing a beachhead on the narrow strip of sand at Anzac Cove, with the Turks shooting down at them from the steep cliffs above. That had been 104 days ago, and this was the biggest 'stunt' since then, and long overdue. Lieutenant Reg Garnock wrote, 'This is an extremely important day in the operations here'.

The first sideshow battle launched by British soldiers on 6 August at Cape Helles failed, at the cost of many lives. This battle was shockingly mismanaged. In this first diversionary battle, 26,000 British and 13,000 French troops charged towards 40,000 well-entrenched Turks with machine guns, who were defending their homeland yet again from a long-expected attack. Sadly, many were slaughtered, as they ran out of ammunition. Corporal Alec Riley reported: 'Once more the long procession of wounded, dirty, ragged, torn and bloody men came down to the dressing station' as 'others lay just 25 yards in front of the trench in the hot sun not daring to move till night when some of them might be able to crawl slowly back to the lines'. The battle did not even succeed as a diversion, because the Turks expected the main attack to come from the north-west.

But much to everyone's amazement, the second diversionary action, which took place at Lone Pine and was also launched on 6 August, succeeded. Even though the Turkish trenches were covered with heavy logs for protection, Australian infantry tore the logs apart, jumped into the trenches, and shot or bayoneted the Turks in hand-to-hand fighting in the dark caverns below. The Anzacs actually succeeded at Lone Pine, capturing the new frontline trenches from the Turks in a bloody but victorious battle in which they won seven Victoria Crosses, although there were more than 2,000 killed or wounded securing these trenches. As Private J.K. Gammage reported: 'We felt like wild beasts but were calm and never fired reckless but were deliberate', and 'we rushed them out of their 2nd and 3rd line of trenches in half an hour'. But it was a bloody battle, he said, as 'bombs simply poured in and as fast as our men went down another would take his place', and soon 'the wounded were piled up three or four deep', but 'the moans of our own poor fellows and also the Turks we tramped on was awful'. Charles Bean concurred: 'The dead lay so thick that the only respect which could be paid to them was to avoid treading on their faces'; that went for both friend and foe as 'you could not tell the difference between our dead and Turkish dead because their faces went so black'.

It was one of the bloodiest battles of Gallipoli, as an anonymous soldier confirmed after the battle: 'The conditions are unspeakable. The dead, Turkish and Australians, are lying buried and half buried in the trench bottom, in the sides of the trench and even built into the parapet — of all the bastards of places this is the greatest bastard in the world'.

THE NEK: 7 AUGUST

But the third sideshow battle at The Nek was a very different story. This battlefield was just a flat piece of open ground on a plateau, just below the top of the cliffs rising up from the beach; and it was tiny — only about the size of a tennis court, as Charles Bean noted in his official history. 'This narrow bridge of land stretched between Russell's Top and Baby 700 across the top of Monash Valley. The Turkish trenches on the slopes of Baby 700 allowed them to dominate the Australian positions below'.

The Light Horsemen's trenches were at the beach end of this tennis court and the Turkish trenches were on the inland end. Worst of all, deeply entrenched at the enemy's end were rows of riflemen and machine gunners, ready to shoot right across the open ground. Mustafa Kemal had done his homework.

Despite this murderous set-up, the Light Horsemen would be asked to crawl up out of their trenches and run across this open space towards the enemy's backline, against a hail of machine-gun fire from that end. Having been trained to ride into battle safely in the saddle, these horsemen must have wished they had not left their trusty steeds back in Egypt.

The generals ordered the 3rd Brigade Light Horse — consisting of the 8th Regiment (Victorians), 9th Regiment (South Australians and Victorians) and 10th Regiment (West Australians) — to do the hardest fighting. These men and their actions were immortalised in Peter Weir's 1981 film, *Gallipoli*, which made this senseless tragedy the best known to Australians of all the hopeless battles fought at Gallipoli.

The Nek is one of history's greatest examples of shocking military leadership. The generals' plans went horribly wrong from the start: the senior officers failed to synchronise their watches, which led to the pre-battle bombardment against the Turkish trenches from the ships offshore stopping several minutes *before* the charge was due to start. In that gap, the Turks were able to get back into their trenches and line up their guns for the Light Horsemen's charge. This incompetence at the top level presented a gift to the enemy.

Officers in charge included the antiquated British Boer War veteran Major-General Sir Alexander Godley (whose father had fought in the Crimean War), 48, who knew nothing about machine guns but who had overall command; his ageing and sickly Australian subordinate, Colonel Frederic Hughes, 57, a civilian soldier who had direct command despite never commanding men before (and who was invalided back to Australia several weeks later); and Lieutenant-Colonel Jack Macquarie 'Bull' Antill, 49, a noted Boer War veteran of cavalry charges and a controversial short-tempered professional soldier who was the hands-on leader in the trenches.

Although these men knew that the essential preparations for the battle had failed, they went ahead and ordered the Light Horse to attack — simply because it was already planned. They knew the heavy artillery bombardment from the ships had stopped too early, and they knew infantry troops could not provide covering fire because they had failed to capture objectives higher up the cliffs, at, for example, Chunuk Bair. But they still gave the orders to charge.

Predictably, this decision had disastrous consequences. For rather than running across a small area of open ground that had been deserted by supposedly bombarded Turks, who would also be fired upon by their Australian infantry comrades from higher positions, these horseless horsemen faced a wall of Turks with rifles and machine guns who were by then entrenched in their defending position and were waiting for them as daylight lit the scene!

4am

As planned, the ships off Anzac Cove began the half-hour bombardment of the Turkish trenches at 4am, aiming for the inland end of The Nek. The intention was to force the Turks to flee and leave their trenches empty.

4.23am

The ships stopped shelling the Turkish trenches seven minutes before the planned Light Horse attack, allowing the Turks to return to their trenches and aim their machine guns and rifles towards the sea side of The Nek, where they knew the Australians would mount their attack.

4.30am

Despite this gift to the Turks, at the appointed time of 4.30am, the officer in charge of the first line of the 8th Light Horse, Lieutenant-Colonel Alexander White (who was soon shot dead), called out, 'Go!', and 150 fine young men from Victoria climbed over the top of their trench and charged across no-man's-land into the hail of machine gun and rifle fire only 40 metres away. Some men were shot the moment they jumped up out of the trench and into view. Most were shot to pieces within seconds of starting their charge, dropping to the ground dead or wounded. 'We got over and cheered but they were waiting and ready for us and simply gave us a solid wall of lead,' noted one survivor, Sergeant Cliff Pinnock, in his diary. 'We did not get ten yards. Everyone fell like lumps of meat'. An observer on Pope's Hill added: 'They only ran a few yards before they seemed to go limp like rag dolls, sinking to the ground as though their limbs suddenly became strings'.

4.32am

Despite this carnage, and the dead and wounded already lying groaning in the trench or just over the parapet in no-man's-land, the officers ordered the second line of the 8th Regiment to jump up over the top a few minutes later. Major Arthur Deeble, who commanded this second wave, gave the fatal order, leading his men to certain death. At 4.32am, the 150 men of this second wave — also from the 8th Light Horse — jumped over the top and were mostly mown down. One of the few survivors, Captain George Hore, recalled: 'We bent low and ran as hard as we could. Ahead we could see the trench aflame with rifle fire. I ran past our first wave of men who were all dead or dying it seemed. All around were smoke and dust kicked up by the bullets. I felt a sting on my shoulder. Most of my men were also hit. So I lay down behind a very little fold in the ground with a dead Turk above me who had been dead about six weeks!'

Sergeant Cameron, watching from the 9th Light Horse reserve positions, wrote: 'They were cut down like corn before a scythe. The enemy trench was less than 50 yards yet not one of the first two waves got anywhere near it'. Trooper Vernon Boynton said: 'Well the first wave were all mown down except one or two who staggered back wounded. Then our turn came and we made a dash for it. We had to trample over dead bodies of our first line'. Then he wrote: 'I was hit everywhere, in my right leg, right forearm, my right hand, the first finger of which was hanging off and blood pouring everywhere'.

One very fast runner — a lean and lanky 19-year-old champion amateur athlete called Geoffrey Grant — may have reached the Turkish trench with a red-and-yellow flag he carried to claim possession of the enemy trench, before he was slaughtered at close quarters. Lieutenant William Oliver claimed he saw the flag hoisted briefly before the Turks tore it down. Whatever the case, Grant's superior, Sergeant Albert Pearce, certainly wrote a sympathy letter to the parents of this only son: 'he carried the signaling flag, although wounded, right to the Turkish trench'.

4.45am

Then, despite these suicidal charges, at 4.45am the commanding officer, Lieutenant-Colonel Noel Brazier, ordered the third wave of 150 men to charge; this time, the men came from the 10th Regiment (West Australians). Being on the spot, Brazier had had second thoughts before ordering the third wave and had even reported the carnage to his superior officer, Jack Antill, who was directing the battle from his remote headquarters. But Antill claimed that because somebody had seen a red-and-yellow flag flying above the Turkish trench, it meant that some of the Light Horse had already occupied part of the Turkish trench and so had to be supported by reinforcements. Despite passionate pleas to Antill from Brazier, who did not believe any Light Horsemen had reached the enemy, let alone survived, Antill just shouted at him, 'Push on!'

So Brazier returned to the trench and told his men: 'I am sorry, lads, but the order is to go'. So these poor souls, who had hoped the charge would be called off, shook hands, blessed each other, said goodbye, and were also sent over the top, led by Major Tom Todd, who gave the order to charge. They were mostly mown down, too. And now the Turks had

added a 75mm field gun, in addition to the machine guns, rifles, and hand-thrown bombs. Survivor Lieutenant Andy Crawford recalled: 'I could see the Turks standing up two deep in their trench. I could see one soldier firing over another chap's shoulder. We had no chance against that fire storm'. Major Todd, who had taken cover, scribbled a note on a pink sheet of paper and sent a runner back with it to Brazier saying that this wave was pinned down, unable to move forward, and he wanted fresh orders.

Brazier had said, 'this whole thing is sheer bloody murder'. He now decided to ignore Antill and ran off to get another opinion.

Although a frontline officer told Lieutenant Colonel Jack 'Bull' Antill that the daylight attack at The Nek was 'sheer bloody murder', Antill ordered wave after wave of brave Light Horsemen to keep charging.

5.15am

Then came the worst mistake of all. At 5.15am, despite bodies choking the trench and the parapet, while the officer in charge of the fourth wave, Lieutenant Colonel J.B. Scott, was anxiously waiting for Brazier to come back, some of his nervous troopers jumped over the top of the trench and started charging anyway. 'By God', Scott called out in horror, 'I believe the right flank of my men has gone in without orders', Brazier reported later in his official despatch.

So the fourth wave went to their deaths by mistake. These West Australian troopers knew they were running to their deaths. Many of them shook hands beforehand, said goodbye, asked God to bless them and their mates, prayed they would go to heaven, wrote hasty notes to loved ones, pinned their watches or special photos of their wives or sweethearts to the side of the trench, and choked back tears.

Meanwhile, Lieutenant-Colonel Antill refused to stop this senseless slaughter — even though Brazier begged for this fourth wave to be cancelled. Orders are orders, Antill said.

One of the survivors of this fourth wave, Sergeant Sanderson, claimed a signal had come, passing along the waiting troopers in their trench and reaching the men on the right, who acted on it. Sanderson did not know in what part of the line of 150 men the signal had started. But Scott knew it did not come from him. It was a false order, probably started by an extremely jumpy and frightened trooper saying to the agitated man on his right something like: 'We may have to go soon, so its better to get it over with'. And as the man next to him asked, 'What did he say?', this message could have rippled along the line, getting distorted as verbal messages do, so that it ended up as an order: 'We have to go'. They certainly went before Brazier returned to the trench.

Luckily, Scott was able to scream out an order over the noise of the fresh firing to 'Stand down', so some of the men in this fourth wave were spared.

Lieutenant Kidd wrote that the troopers were 'practically annihilated before they could advance 5 yards'. He wrote that soon a new order was passed down the line, to 'Halt and dig in'.

It was fortunate that one of the leading officers of this fourth wave, Hugo Throssell, responded quickly to this order. He survived and went on to win the Light Horse's only Victoria Cross at a later battle, before they left Gallipoli.

AFTERMATH

In three-quarters of an hour, of 600 officers and men who charged, 234 Light Horsemen were killed. Of those killed, 154 were from the 8th Light Horse (Victoria) and 80 were from the 10th Regiment (Western Australia). The bodies of those killed were left on that bloody tennis court, and the only survivors among the wounded were those with enough strength to crawl back into the trench. There were 138 wounded altogether. Some were so badly shot-up that their lives were ruined. Sadly, many of those young men killed were the cream of the Australian crop, hailing from the finest cattle and sheep properties, and they left a gap, not only in these well-known families, but also in these important pastoral industries. Some brothers who had enlisted together were killed at The Nek, and some only sons.

Sergeant Pinnock wrote how 'all your pals whom you had been with for months [were] blown and shot out of all recognition', and when the roll was called afterwards, 'I cried like a child'. Charles Bean, who heard a 'tremendous fusillade break out', said, 'God help anyone that was out in that tornado'. The men had shown remarkable courage and discipline. Never again would these qualities be wasted so tragically. Bean later wrote: 'For sheer bravery, devoted loyalty and that self-discipline which seldom failed in Australian soldiers, they stand alone in the annals of their country'.

Writing about the mass slaughter of these unsuspecting horsemen at The Nek, Lieutenant-Colonel Brazier confirmed he had at least tried to stop it, towards the end: 'The Regiment took up position in trenches at 4 a.m. when bombardment commenced. Bombardment continued to 4.30 when a murderous machine gun and rifle fire upon our parapets commenced. At 4.40 Major Todd in charge of 3rd line, reported he could not advance as 8th Regt. Was held up. Referred matter to Brigade H.Q. and informed them the task was impossible under such a fire. Was ordered to advance at once. Major Scott almost immediately reported he was held up; again referred matter to H.Q. and was told to advance. As the fire was murderous again referred matter personally to Brigadier who said to get what men I could and go round by BULLY BEEF Sap and MONASH GULLY. Meanwhile Majors Love and Todd had discussed matters in some dead ground in front of trenches, where to advance was impossible, and on returning received orders to go by BULLY BEEF Sap as above. The fire here was also deadly and as the casualties were then very heavy, were ordered to retire. Meanwhile I remained observing in No. 8 Sap, and at

5.35 Lieut. Lyall and 8 men of 10th and some men of 8th, returned to No. 8 Sap and reported that no one had reached the Turk's trenches. Reported at 5.40 after observing again, and held on here till relieved. The attack seemed premature and in view of the heavy machine gun fire, should have been held up — and many valuable lives saved'.

When wave after wave of troopers from the 8th and 10th Light Horse Regiments charged against entrenched Turkish machine guns at The Nek, 234 of them were killed for no territorial gain. Painting by George Lambert in Elyne Mitchell's Light Horse, *also Australian War Memorial.*

As it was too dangerous to retrieve dead bodies killed in 'No Man's Land' during battles like The Nek, they became a breeding ground for flies, which in turn spread disease through the trenches, creating even more casualties through cholera and dysentery.

The surviving Light Horsemen grieved for their dead comrades. Sergeant Pinnock tried to put these senseless events into logical order: 'The General "Ian Hamilton", ordered that the whole line would advance on yesterday week. We all knew what that would mean to the poor 8th. They took all our kit, including our tunics, four days before the advance and simply left us with a shirt, pants, puttees and boots. Well, we simply perished those four nights … Had very little sleep … on the Friday we were told that the advance would take place on the following morning early at half past four … but they were waiting ready for us … we did not get ten yards … The second line came on and got the same reception, and so on until the whole of the 8th and 10th were practically wiped out. Really too awful to write about … There was no chance whatever of us gaining our point, but the roll call after was the saddest, just fancy only 47 answered their names out of close to 550 men … It is really too awful. I got mine shortly after I got over the bank, and it felt like a million ton hammer falling on my shoulder. However, I managed to crawl back and got temporarily fixed up till they carried me to the Base Hospital'.

Although difficult to write the truth as the days passed, Light Horsemen like Second Lieutenant W.M. Cameron did their best to record that nightmare: 'It is twelve days since I saw this book; we had some severe fighting and it turns out that we have gained little in territory or position, yet sacrificed thousands of lives. On that eventful Friday when the advance was ordered, I was placed in charge of the Regtl. Sharp Shooters and took up position on the left at three o'clock in the morning and waited the rush forward of our comrades. The eighth Regt. was the first out. We saw them climb out and move forward about ten yards and lie flat. The second line did likewise; meantime the Turkish fire increased in intensity.' Then, in perhaps the most graphic image of all used to describe the horrible massacre, Cameron confirmed that, 'as they rose to charge the Turkish Machine Guns just poured out lead and our fellows went down like corn before a scythe'.

Sergeant A.S. Hutton wrote: 'No doubt today has been the fiercest battle in the history of the war. The first Light Horse were absolutely cut up' as 'the Turks evidently expected us to make a supreme attempt to drive them back from here, which resulted in them concentrating most of their troops to oppose us ... our first brigade paid the price heavily ... the sights of mangled bodies has been sickening and the stench also. I have had quite a notable birthday'.

Lieutenant-Colonel Carew Reynell tried to make sense of the senseless massacres: 'After 4 days continuous scrapping there has been a lull today and both sides seem fairly tired. Our Brigade made an attack on the trenches in front of us at 4.30a.m. on the morning of the 7th. It failed and the 8th Regt. which found the first line was wiped out — all the officers on the spot with the exception of the 2nd in Command and a couple of subalterns being killed or wounded (mostly the former). The Regt. Lost 240 out of 400 and most of them were killed. The 10th Regt. were to follow but when the first line were cut down they remained on the edge of the trenches and although their casualties were heavy they were light in comparison'. Reynell concluded: 'The main cause of failure of our brigades attack was machine gun fire — some men's legs were completely severed by this fire'.

The deaths were all in vain. The Light Horse lost their battle and the British lost the overall August Offensive. That offensive was too complicated, with too many assumptions. The plan assumed New Zealanders would have captured the high adjacent hill of Chunuk Bair and would be attacking Turks from the rear, driving the Turks away from The Nek, so the coast would be clear for the Light Horse to mount their action there. It was not the New Zealanders' fault either, because although they had briefly reached the summit of Chunuk Bair, the ships off the beach (which had stopped firing too early for The Nek charge) thought the New Zealanders on the hilltop must be Turks, so they bombarded them with heavy artillery. This friendly fire drove the New Zealanders back down the slopes, allowing the Turks to regain the summit.

Even worse, the 20,000 British troops landing at Suvla Bay also failed to advance because their inexperienced commander, Lieutenant-General

Stopford, gave them a day's holiday on arrival for swimming, picnicking, playing football, and so on — and this gave the Turks time to move in reinforcements that soon stopped the British. Anzac signaller Corporal Ted Matthews remembered: 'Those damn fool British just sat down, had a picnic, drank cups of tea and played soccer for so long that the Turks were able to muster reinforcements — which means they lost any advantage of surprise'. With no support from the British, Australian troops in an associated offensive also failed to capture Hill 971.

So it was all pointless.

'Things are pretty deadly at the Lone Pine these days,' 6th Regiment diarist Lieutenant Reg Garnock then revealed. 'There are hundreds of dead bodies of both sides lying about everywhere and the stench is appalling and of course it is impossible to remove them, any attempt is greeted with a hail of bullets. The only thing to do is put up with it and breathe through special respirators. Of course it affects the Turks the same as it does our men and we get it down here too at night chiefly. It's almost unbearable at times.' Garnock was also becoming critical of his superior officers telling him what to do, writing in his diary, 'Orders have been issued for two officers to be in the firing line every night (one awake the other asleep) which is of course quite ridiculous, one of many pin pricks of this military life!'

After The Nek, a frustrated Lieutenant-Colonel Reynell (whose 9th Regiment was in reserve at The Nek) complained: 'We are still in these dirty damned dusty lousy trenches and no more prospect of getting out of them than flying to the moon. Our offensive has come to a stop everywhere and there is no sign of a revival'. He blamed the British, who he claimed were 'the absolute bally limit. A more miserable useless lot of Devils I can't imagine. They seem to have no spirit or pride of any sort', and 'one could do more with one battalion of Australians or New Zealanders than 5 battalions of these men whose officers are a wretchedly incompetent lot'. But 'if we have a fair sample of Australians here then Australians are a damned sight better tribe than I ever thought'. Reynell reckoned they had 'dash, pluck, initiative, resource, dogged determination, patience and cheerful fortitude'.

In his last diary entry before being killed in action a few hours later, when he bravely volunteered to lead his men into another attack against Turkish trenches at Hill 60, Reynell wrote: 'I hear we are to be withdrawn in a day or two ... to be sent to Imbros or Lemnos for a few days' rest. We can all do with a rest I think. Personally I am pretty run down and have had a cold for a long time and am lousy'. Reynell, who had already predicted his own death, noted in his diary: 'Well some of us will be making room for others before long and it's all in the game'.

The surviving troopers of the Light Horse did take part in other smaller battles at Gallipoli, in which they fought bravely. For example, in that futile battle for Hill 60, where, although wounded many times, Lieutenant Hugo Throssell fought so hard that he won the Victoria Cross (the only Australian Light Horseman to win a VC in the Great War.) But none of these battles was anything like as bloody or tragic as The Nek. In 1933, the Australian War Memorial produced a publication that likened the tragedy at The Nek to the 1854 Charge of the Light Brigade against Russian guns at the Battle of Balaclava. The AWM felt that the following lines from Tennyson's well-known poem about the charge (in which, coincidentally, 600 soldiers took part) also suited the 600 Light Horsemen who charged at The Nek:

They that had fought so well
Came thro' the jaws of Death,
Back from the mouth of Hell,
All that was left of them,
Left of six hundred

The news of the disastrous mismanagement of the August Offensive and the deaths of thousands of soldiers soon reached the British War Cabinet. Hamilton sacked Stopford, and then the British War Cabinet sacked Hamilton.

When Hamilton's replacement as commander-in-chief, Lieutenant-General Charles Monro, arrived, he said the 'rabbit warrens' at Gallipoli reminded him of the burrow Alice went down in *Alice's Adventures in Wonderland*. He soon understood it was impossible to defeat the Turks, and passed on this view to Lord Kitchener, the Minister for War, who then visited the site himself and quickly recommended evacuation.

All troops were evacuated in December 1915. The surviving Light Horse troopers were transported to Egypt, to be reunited with their horses and train for the mounted warfare for which they had enlisted.

Bloody though it had been at Gallipoli, the Light Horse had certainly learnt some valuable lessons for their next theatre of operations, Palestine. So far, they had lost every battle. From 1916 onwards, however, these Light Horsemen — now mounted — would win almost every battle, starting with Romani.

After the slaughter at The Nek, a survivor, Sergeant C. Pinnock wrote, 'All your pals whom you had been with for months [were] blown and shot out of all recognition', and when the roll was called afterwards, 'I cried like a child'.

PART II
SINAI 1916

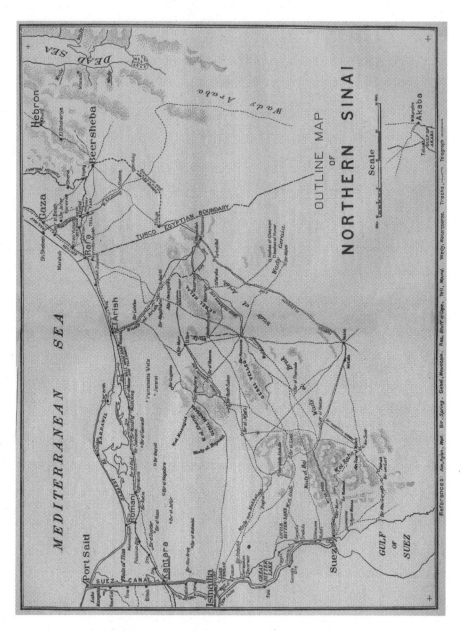

Britain's Egyptian Expeditionary Force, which was based in Romani at the start of the war, had to defend the vital Suez Canal, just west of their position. The Turks — who controlled the territory to the east in their Ottoman Empire, from Constantinople down south as far as the 'Turco-Egyptian boundry' — occupied El Arish and other villages in the Sinai, and began marching towards the Canal. They got as far as Romani, where they fought a make-or-break battle with the EEF.

1.
ROMANI,
3–5 AUGUST 1916

SAND-DUNE STRUGGLES
IN SINAI

The terrain for the Battle of Romani was so difficult for the Light Horsemen to negotiate, because it was surrounded by soft sand dunes and sandy mountains, that some of the troopers were shot after their horses got bogged in the sand.

The troops have been fighting day and night in fierce charges — attack and counter attack — galloping their horses to within point blank range of the Turks — scrambling on their horse when the Turks came raging around them only to gallop back to turn around and fight again. Men and horses are desperately in need of sleep.

TROOPER ION IDRIESS, 2ND BRIGADE, 5TH REGIMENT

AUGUST 1916

BACKGROUND TO THE BATTLE

The strategic British-held village of Romani stood near the Mediterranean coast in the north-western corner of the Sinai Peninsula, just east of where the Suez Canal flows into the Mediterranean. The Turks attacked Romani to threaten the vital canal — which the Allies increasingly needed to transport troops and supplies from the Indian Ocean — and to try and capture a string of life-giving wells in that region. In the successful defence of Romani, the Light Horsemen proved themselves highly effective warriors in the saddle in a way they never could at Gallipoli, where they had fought on foot.

Romani would turn out to be just the first successful battle for Britain's Egyptian Expeditionary Force (EEF), which would be charged with the task of tackling a series of Turkish towns between Suez and Damascus to dismantle the Turks' Ottoman Empire that had ruled Palestine for centuries. These towns would include Magdhaba, Rafa, Gaza, Beersheba, Jerusalem, Es Salt, Amman, and, finally, the Turkish heartland headquarters of Damascus.

The fighting at Romani started overnight on 3 August 1916, when the Turks attacked. Britain's EEF, commanded by General Sir Archibald Murray, included many different units from Britain and her colonies, with a major force known as the Desert Column that, in addition to British forces, included the Anzac Mounted Division of Australian and New Zealand Light Horsemen who in this battle were outnumbered by more than ten to one. Fortunately, Major-General Harry Chauvel, commanding the Anzac Mounted Division, had anticipated the attack and made careful preparations.

Not surprisingly, the Turks initially pushed the outlying Light Horse units of the Anzac Mounted Division back towards their Romani base. But when reinforcements arrived, the Light Horsemen held their ground — although initially with a fighting withdrawal — demonstrating the best mounted-infantry tactics. By the night of 4 August, reinforcements including New Zealanders, British cavalry, and infantry helped the Light Horse make a stand, and together they turned the tide, driving the Turks back. The Turks had to give up their dream of capturing the canal, and retreat.

This first big battle the Light Horse fought in the Middle East was a pivotal one, because it stopped the Turks advancing further through Sinai and getting control of the Suez Canal. Yet the Allies could well have lost this turning-point battle. In fact, they would certainly have lost if that strong-minded British General Sir Archibald Murray, commander of all Allied forces in Egypt, had not had the vision to keep the all-volunteer Australian Light Horse in this less important theatre rather than send them to France. He had refused to obey orders when Britain's War Cabinet told him that the Australian Light Horse units still under his command were to be transferred to France to make up the numbers after heavy AIF battle casualties. He understood that the only way to stop the predicted Turkish advance was with the battle-hardened veterans of Gallipoli — the Anzac Mounted Division. He also feared they could be slaughtered, especially after the 19–20 July 1916 Battle of Fromelles on the Western Front, in which nearly 2,000 Australians were killed in action on the one day. Murray thought it would be sheer bloody murder to send the Light Horse to France where they would be massacred as foot soldiers, as they had been at The Nek a year earlier at Gallipoli. In the end, not only did Murray save their lives, but he also enabled the Light Horse to win glorious victories from the saddle.

He knew he would need the Anzac Mounted Division to counter the German-led Turkish forces already slowly advancing through Palestine, intent on capturing the Canal. Under the German General Friedrich Kress von Kressenstein, the Turks had so far defeated all British cavalry and infantry formations that tried to stop their advance. By coincidence, their path though Palestine followed the same well-tried route that Napoleon had used in 1798 when his army invaded Egypt, and Murray knew these

Turks could get through to the Suez Canal the way Napoleon's forces had reached Cairo. But if the British could not stop them, he hoped the Australians would.

This would be the first of a long series of battles in Palestine, as Lieutenant Reginald Garnock of the 6th Regiment says: 'On 23rd April 1916 we started on the long ride, which began at Salhia and ended two and a half years later on the Tablelands of Moab'. It may have been a long ride for Reg, a lawyer from Bombala, but he was twice 'Mentioned in Dispatches', promoted to Staff Captain in the Second Cavalry Brigade HQ, and had the rare distinction of being awarded the Order of the Nile by the Sultan of Egypt. On his return, he married his patient fiancée, Alice Wynne Lovegrove, and settled in Linfield, Sydney.

Major Thomas Bird, from Gresford, New South Wales, sent this photo of British mounted troops home saying, 'This unit of Yeomanry were cut up by the Turks in 1916' and his 'Light Horse went out to help, but the Turks had completed the job and gone back' which he said 'started the desert campaign for us'.

THE BATTLE OF ROMANI

June: First Australian moves

Well before the Romani battle, Murray ordered Chauvel and his Anzac Mounted Division to prepare to halt the gradual enemy advance. Chauvel spent days surveying large areas of desert before finally deciding where to take a stand to halt the Turks — the Romani tableland. To be sure, while the enemy was still miles away, Chauvel also deployed his Light Horse units around Romani itself, acclimatising them to the extreme heat and teaching them to survive on the limited water supplies of that desert region.

July: Setbacks

Chauvel's first action, in late July, failed. He had ordered small patrols to stage a series of independent hit-and-run raids on enemy camps to test the enemy's resistance. The Turks either hit back or just advanced regardless, getting closer to Romani.

In his diary, Trooper Ion Idriess, 5th Regiment, gave an eyewitness account of some of the dangers of these patrols: 'We manoeuvred ever closer towards a great hill, for we had to find out if whether [that] portion of the Turkish army behind it were marching out to cut in behind Romani'. Soon after, he noted, 'we saw two figures silhouetted on the skyline gazing in our direction. As we had approached under perfect cover, they had almost certainly not seen us however as we rode on further they just vanished'. Riding further up the sand hill he said 'a camel sauntered across the skyline. We grinned, expecting a shot every second none came', and then reaching the top he spied a line of Turks 'lying on their bellies. How we laughed. It looked absurd; almost a whole regiment had been turned out to one tiny patrol. But, by Jove, how alert we felt!'

Idriess's patrol leader, Lieutenant Stanfield, had orders to observe and report on troop movements. After seeing the Turks, Stanfield said, 'The game is up, boys, but I'd still just like one glance down the hill, as there may be a movement of troops'. Hoping the Turks would not fire, they dismounted and climbed the hill on foot. At the top, they saw even more Turks, 'their rifles at the ready'. Then Idriess had a narrow escape: 'The sight of all those waiting Turks took our breath away. Three big chaps crouched up trying to level their rifles through the bushes to get a clear shot at our heads. I jerked up my rifle and at that very moment only twenty feet away appeared the black cloth elbow, then the rifle muzzle, then very slowly the head of a Bedouin. I bit my lip in taking aim, to keep steady, then crack, crack three bullets in a second and the Bedouin threw out his arms and bit with his mouth in the sand'.

"On your horses, boys, quick!' shouted Stanfield and in one jump, Idriess said, 'each man was in his saddle, digging in his spurs and laughing as our horse leapt away with Stanfield shouting, "Come on boys, and we'll give these Turks a go for it. Ride like the hammers of hell".' But on the way down the hill, Idriess's horse stumbled and fell on top of Idriess, who had to get out from under his mount and get back on as his comrades dashed ahead. As the last man riding, he was lucky to escape: 'I swung into the saddle as the first bullets hissed by and in seconds I was galloping through what sounded like a shower of red hot hail'. As game as the bushranger Ned Kelly, the exhilarated trooper got away on that occasion, reporting, 'That ride was simply grand!'

1 August

Despite these unsuccessful and dangerous patrols (in which some troopers were killed), before long the Turks were again threatening Light Horse outposts closer to Romani. Always on the lookout (for good food and Turks) Idriess noted, 'Poor tucker again. The Turks are nearly at Katia. They are swarming towards Romani'.

The battle looming for Romani was not just on land. As Trooper Hubert Billings noted: 'A hostile plane reported and he flew all around the joint but didn't drop bombs evidently just had a squiz at us. But our planes went up and gave Jacko a doing dropping 72 bombs on his lines and camps in general'. Things were improving back down on the ground

too: 'in a raid yesterday our casualties were 32 but only a few killed —
much less than the June 1st raid'.

2 August

After dark on 2 August, the Turks approached as close as the tiny Katia
settlement, only 8 kilometres south-east of Romani, convincing Chauvel
that the enemy could attack Romani the next night. Idriess wrote of,
'Heavy gun-fire with rifles rattling in waves of sound, sighing across the
desert' and patrols reporting the appearance of 'two thousand Jackos'.

Stuart Robertson Macfarlane, riding with the 1st Brigade, confirmed
both how fast the Anzac Mounted Division responded and the unexpected
dangers: 'We had to gallop for about half a mile then dismount and
advance on foot'. Then, 'We were trying to take up a position behind a
"skyline" when the Turks appeared out of a gully 100 yards away. When
three men were wounded we had to retire about 300 yards and then took
up a position which we held all day'.

Having noted, 'Air activity very noticeable', Hubert Billings wrote:
'Two shells fell in the palm trees we were in and we had to prepare to belt
but no more bombs fell so we stopped. We had five casualties and one
man got acute appendicitis and had to be brought in!' Then, 'two men
went out to bring in a wounded man and they were wounded by machine
gun fire as was the original wounded man a second time'. Billings and his
comrades were getting very jumpy as he admits, in his diary under the
heading 'MYSTERY???'. He wrote: 'A white kite, shaped like a German
Zeppelin plane was seen directly above, not visible to the naked eye but
through the glasses. All hands saw it and much speculation as to what it
was. We reported it to HQ and suggested a plane be sent up to investigate
— but they refused explaining it was just a NEW MOON'.

3 August

Under the cover of darkness on 3 August, the Turks attacked the Allied
forces in earnest. The Battle of Romani had begun. Murray was determined

to turn the Turks back east, into the largely waterless desert from whence they had come.

Unfortunately, the Turks had captured Katia en route to use as a base for attacking the Allies at Romani. The Turks were also becoming a nuisance in the aerial battle, as Macfarlane reported: 'A Taube [enemy plane] came over this morning and dropped one bomb. The Turks have a battery of anti-aircraft guns at Oghratina and they shell our planes heavily … Our guns bombard their position every day sending heavy shells back to Oghratina'. Not that things were much better on the ground: 'One man in our patrol last night is reported missing'.

Despite Chauvel's warnings just before the battle about how sneaky the Turks could be, the Allied forces were caught by surprise. In fact, none of the Australian listening posts east of Romani (which had been trying to get news of the enemy's rapid advance towards Romani for some time) — or patrols like those mounted by Idriess — heard the sounds of Turkish troop movements. So it was not until the last minute that the Australians spotted the first Turks creeping out of the dark night at about 11.30pm on 3 August.

Not that all advancing Turks reached their objective, because, cleverly, Chauvel had set up even more heavily armed and isolated military outposts spread around the Romani tableland which sometimes diverted advancing Turks. At other times, however, the silent, desert-savvy Turks destroyed these outposts and the troopers manning them. Idriess, who was still serving in these outposts, reported: 'There has been some desperate night fighting out in front — some of our night outposts have been bayoneted'. The British also had well-armed outposts dotted along a series of towering sand dunes, which sometimes stopped Turkish advances.

Just after midnight, the Australian Light Horse could clearly see the shadowy figures of Turkish soldiers stealthily advancing out of the Sinai Desert towards the Romani tableland. Much to their horror, it looked as though the attackers greatly outnumbered the Allied forces. Idriess reported, 'The Turks seem to arise out of the very sand in overwhelming numbers' and 'appear like transparent shadow men, the harder to realise as our men are dazed for want of sleep'. They realised then that thousands of Turks must have crept close to Australian outposts without being spotted. Only the 1st Light Horse Brigade was in the right position to stop the attack, and they were badly outnumbered.

The challenges in the air continued. Hubert Billings recorded: 'Two hostile planes flew over during the day and were chased by our Bristol Scout until his rudder seized and he had to come down'. Then later, 'Our plane dropped bombs on Hill 11 held by us whom the pilot thought the Turks held but luckily the bombs went wide and missed'. On the ground, getting ready for the showdown, he confided, 'Our troops are now moving out in all directions'.

One of the challenges during the Battle of Romani was negotiating the steep sand dunes, as even those troopers who had worked as stockmen in the outback and had brought their own horses found it difficult.

Even though most of the fighting was inland in the desert, the Egyptian Expeditionary Force was able to use the ancient towns and villages with port facilities along the Mediterranean coast for transporting men, equipment, and supplies by boat.

4 August, 1am

Nervous night patrols spying on enemy movements were predicting imminent attack as Billings reported, in the early hours of 4 August, 'a body of about 500 Turks seen moving towards us,' then just before 1am: 'Enemy are reported in great strength opposite our right flank' then 'firing is now general on that flank'.

Suddenly, just after 1am, the first wave of Turks burst right upon them, screaming, 'Allah, Allah. Finish Australia.' The desert night exploded into action as the defending Light Horse began shooting at these dark shapes charging at them, the flashes of gunfire from both sides lighting up the darkness. But no sooner had the Light Horse killed or wounded the first wave of attackers then another wave arrived, followed by more and more seemingly suicidal Turks. 'Both sides blazed away point-blank at one another's rifle flashes, which when the quarter moon had set made the intense blackness seem aflame,' Idriess wrote. Pitch black though it was, these inexperienced Australians now had to stand and fight or die in bloody hand-to-hand fighting, as the Turks exploited their advantage of surprise.

After charging forward in great numbers, the attacking Turks broke through the outnumbered defences, killing or wounding many of the Light Horse troopers. At the same time, because the enemy were charging in a line close together (with just bayonets outstretched before them), straight into the fire of the Light Horsemen, many of them were also killed or wounded. But as soon as the Light Horsemen stopped one line of charging Turks, another immediately replaced them. Idriess reported: 'Our patrols send word that at least two thousand Jackos have appeared' and 'Fighting has been severe all night and apparently very uncertain'. Even though they were charging into point-blank gunfire, the Turks seemed to think they could win through sheer weight of numbers. The desperate Light Horsemen were not only using rifles to defend their positions but also heavier arms, as Idriess reported, 'Heavy machine gun fire broke out. It is terrific now'.

The outnumbered Light Horsemen did well, considering this was their first desert battle. But they began to buckle under the relentless assault, and as they weakened, their commander ordered them to make a fighting retreat.

Sensing victory, the Turks charged with greater passion. They broke through some parts of the retreating Light Horsemen's line, killing many of the troopers, especially those whose horses had been shot or who sank into the soft sand, slowing their escape. Idriess reported, 'There were big bayonet charges at Romani' and 'the Australians suddenly sprang to it as thousands of throats yelled, "Allah, Allah, Allah, Allah. Finish Australia! Finish Australia!"', and 'there is bitter fighting now' and 'the Australians are slowly falling back'.

4 August, dawn

As dawn broke, the determined Turks realised they had successfully pushed back the Allied defenders of Romani. Once they gathered even more numbers, they attacked the retreating 1st Brigade with great gusto.

As daylight lit up the bloody battle, Chauvel, watching from a vantage point, could see his outnumbered 1st Brigade still struggling against massive odds as it continued to retreat. Riding with the 1st Brigade, Macfarlane wrote: 'The battle of Romani commenced at midnight last night when the 2nd and 3rd regiments engaged the enemy on our line of outposts. We soon moved out to reinforce. At daybreak the main attack began. Our infantry (Scotties) reinforced our line so that we could retire. As it was necessary to do so to save our horses. Which were being heavily shelled and bombarded by Taube (planes). We retired out of range of enemy guns and camped for the day. We were heavily shelled and machine guns were used on us during our retirement. At dusk both the 1st and 2nd Brigades moved around the right flank and reinforced the "Tommy" infantry'.

Chauvel could also see massed waves of Turks attacking the New Zealand Brigade's lines. The battle was going exactly as he had imagined, and he held back his reinforcements. Idriess, for once unusually respectful of senior officers, wrote that Romani 'proved that the predictions of the Heads in charge were spot on'.

Chauvel still had his 2nd and 3rd Australian Brigades up his sleeve, waiting behind cover on the flanks for his command to attack. The British, too, had reserve cavalry and also artillery units already moving up into position. Chauvel kept his nerve as the determined Turks routed the New Zealanders defending Wellington Ridge, and then infiltrated the Light Horse base. In the confusing, dim light of dawn, Idriess reported: 'The Australians could only distinguish Turks as shadow men', and in the frenetic hand-to-hand combat some Australians shot each other, and some Turks did likewise to their own men. In fact, one Light Horseman — a Queenslander 'who thought one of his men went down' — Idriess revealed, had 'wheeled roaring into the Turks — lifted that man straight up on to his saddle and galloped back unharmed only to find that his rescue was a Turk!' Another Australian managed to wheel back 'into a horde of Turks where four of his men's horses were bayoneted — two men leapt on the horse, one clung to each stirrup and they all actually got away'.

4 August: The Turks charge Mount Meredith

Suddenly, above the defending noise of battle, came a cry louder than before — 'Allah, Allah, Allah' — as 800 Turks charged the Allied strongpoint of Mount Meredith, convinced the Allied defenders were on the run and they could win. Their battle cry was like 'a terrible scream', Idriess thought, as 'their bayonets glinted in the starlight' as 'the men of Allah leapt up from the Romani bushes' to charge Mount Meredith. Before long, the Turks managed to capture both Mount Meredith and Wellington Ridge — at least for the moment.

But the Turks had not reckoned on more plucky New Zealanders, who suddenly arrived as reinforcements, leaping to the defence of this strategic position, Mount Meredith. These tough Kiwis drove the Turkish troops back off the mount, turning the tide of battle. The Kiwis gave as good as they got with a murderous rapid fire into the close-packed enemy ranks, sending the Turks face down in the sand in their hundreds. 'They shot the Turks down like Wallabies,' wrote Idriess, 'and they rolled over and over and over down the walls of sand'.

But then, in the chaotic fighting nearby, a large body of Turks also punched a gap through the Australian defenders and swept around the edge of a high escarpment nearby hoping to come in on the Australians' rear. Something had to be done.

Turning point

Fortunately, Chauvel had already stationed another reserve of Australians on top of this high escarpment as a trap to guard against such a move. Now, he ordered these men to spring into action.

Chauvel also ordered remaining 1st Brigade troopers to abandon their withdrawal and close ranks with the New Zealanders, holding a firm line. Then, a masterstroke: he personally brought the 2nd and 3rd Brigades in from the flanks, thus implementing his plan to funnel the Turks into an area covered by British artillery. As Idriess reported: 'Chauvel at dawn and in person came to the rescue, trotting into action with the 2nd Light Horse Brigade'.

The British artillery began to send down a barrage to soften up the Turks before the Light Horsemen reached them. Accurate salvos devastated enemy ranks, killing or wounding many and decimating the unified front they were using to counterattack the advancing Light Horsemen. In the mayhem, bloody Turkish body parts lay scattered across the sandy ground.

Now, 'with their blood up', as official war historian Charles Bean had often written in his Gallipoli dispatches about these men, the Anzacs launched such a frenzied attack on the enemy that they drove the defenders back down from the crest of Wellington Ridge. But even then most of these fearless Turks refused to retreat any farther, so the light Horsemen killed even more of them.

As well as winning their first major battle at Romani, the Egyptian Expeditionary Force had the satisfaction of capturing thousands of prisoners whom the Light Horsemen then escorted through the streets to POW camps.

4 August, 6am

Hubert Billings noted: 'Heavy firing masses of Turks — they cannot be stopped. Eight planes bombed hell out of this place and one of our planes was shot down. The planes dropped bombs all around us one falling within 50 yards of me and I had to dodge the bits. It is a funny situation when you run for your life at 6 to 7 miles an hour and kid yourself you can dodge the planes flying at 60 to 70 miles an hour'.

Billings continued: 'The phone line was cut in three places by bombs and

Jeff Playfoot and I rushed out and fixed it and got peppered all the way with one big shrapnel bursting right over us and splattered all around but missed'.

Before long, this greater show of strength turned back most of the Turkish advance, and the Australians captured large numbers of prisoners. There had been many great acts of valour, but Idriess singled out 'Brigadier Royston, "Galloping Jack" they call him. He wore out fourteen horses, galloping up and down the line to wherever the fight blazed thickest'. Brigadier-General John Royston could predict battle action pretty well, having fought as a teenager in the Anglo–Zulu War of 1879, and then leading the 5th and 6th Contingent of the Western Australian Mounted Infantry in the 1899–1902 Boer War.

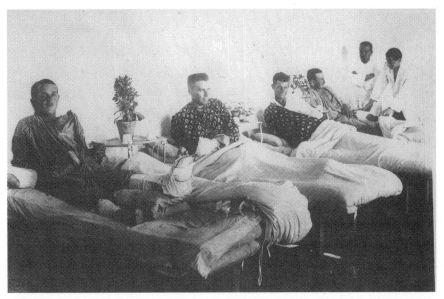

Although the losses were heavy, those troopers who suffered minor wounds from the Battle of Romani were taken to hospitals in Cairo to be patched up as soon as possible, so they could rejoin their units in time for the next battle.

4 August, noon

By the middle of the day on 4 August, under a hot, unforgiving sun, the two sides fought each other to the death on the sandy Romani tableland as the tide of battle swayed back and forth. Thanks to the 'sullen booming of the big guns' as Idriess wrote, the artillery barrages (hitting and killing the oncoming Turks) enabled the Australians to force their way forward, pushing back counterattack after counterattack as they repelled the enemy from one position after another. Even so, the Turks still charged forward in massed suicidal attacks, trying to break through the Australian ranks. But the Australian defence line held firm as troops rushed from one hot spot to another to plug the gaps.

Once they regained the summit, the troopers on Wellington Ridge had clear sightlines to shoot the Turks as they scrambled up the almost sheer sides of this highpoint. So finally, the surviving Turks retreated.

4 August, 2pm

A relieved Hubert Billings reported: 'Things are now rather normal, we have stopped the Turkish rush, and even have our artillery in position ready to pound them'.

4 August, nightfall

As darkness fell after that bloody day of 4 August, the fighting stopped and silence returned. Turkish and Allied soldiers collapsed from exhaustion, many lying down where they stood, crumpled on the bloody sand beside the dead and wounded.

William Fraser wrote: 'About dark the whole exhausted force bivouacked holding the line, sleeping over night when fortunately only a few shots were exchanged'.

5 August, 4am

But before the first light of dawn on 5 August, Chauvel, determined to keep the initiative, ordered his spent troops into action again. So, after sleeping where they had collapsed, these exhausted troopers got back on to their feet and led another fresh offensive against the Turks. William Fraser explained what happened next: 'Orders were given to advance at 4.a.m. But luckily at dawn the whole Turkish force was seen retreating towards Katia. And during the day — 5th August — the whole mounted forces pushed forward and linked up with the 3rd Brigade and made one big front engaging and pushing off the enemy. The 3rd Brigade engaged the enemy from the S. capturing many prisoners, machine guns, camels etc.'

Chauvel also ordered artillery to fire on the equally exhausted retreating Turks. He made sure that the shells did not land short, as they sometimes did on the Western Front, often killing Allied soldiers — mistakes known as 'friendly fire'.

Macfarlane, riding with the Anzac Mounted Division, wrote: 'The 1st, 2nd and 3rd Brigades and NZ Brigade moved forward on the right flank and we captured numerous prisoners and a complete mountain battery. And 250,000 small arms ammunition. A good day's work'.

5 August, dawn

Attacked by the 2nd Light Horse and two battalions of Scottish Rifles, the last of the Turks on Wellington Ridge surrendered at dawn on 5 August.

A relieved Hubert Billings confirmed that by early morning on 5 August, 'Situation now good. Not a shot being fired. Turks are surrendering in hundreds. All our troops now on the skyline watching Turks everywhere. Our 1st Brigade charged the Turks up on the ridges on Mt. Meredith and absolutely cleared the Turks out and got them running'.

Nevertheless, to keep up the momentum, the relentless Chauvel applied more pressure on his men to keep chasing the disorganised and retreating Turks to ensure they would not regroup and counterattack. His artillery alone killed so many of them that the survivors had no option but to turn around and retreat. A staggering 5,000 dead Turks lay on the battlefield. The killing only stopped when they reached their base to the east across the Sinai Desert.

They would not remain safe there for long, because the unstoppable Chauvel forced his weary troopers to keep the Turks on the run, pushing them back east towards the next significant settlements of Katia and El

Arish, which he planned to capture next. The Allied victory at Romani had put paid forever to the Turkish mission of capturing the Suez Canal.

Chauvel was, however, pushing his men to breaking point, as Idriess complained: 'The troops have been fighting day and night ... in fierce charges — attack and counter attack — galloping their horses to within point blank range of the Turks — scrambling on their horses when the Turks came raging around them only to gallop back to turn around and fight again. Men and horses are desperately in need of sleep'.

Apart from the fatigue, the combined British Empire forces had also lost many men killed in action, with Chauvel's own 1st Light Horse losing most of its officers. Idriess concluded: 'The Turkish attack on Romani is broken', but 'it was a very close battle as some of their battalions actually got to the railway line behind Romani', and for a while 'their main attacks captured Mt. Meredith, and Wellington Ridge'. It had been, he wrote, a 'touch and go battle' that the Allies had only just won — thanks to good leadership from Chauvel and great fighting by the Light Horse and other units.

Murray had been vindicated. It had been the right decision to ask the War Cabinet for the Australian and New Zealand Light Horse to stay in the Middle East to help the British defend the Suez Canal. Chauvel's leadership had also been demonstrated. As he concluded in a letter to his wife, Sybil: 'We have fought and won a great battle, and my men put up a performance which is beyond all precedent', adding, 'Our losses have been heavy. Of course, but absolutely nothing in comparison with what has been achieved'. The Light Horses's casualties in the hundreds were also 'nothing' compared with the 2,000 AIF soldiers killed in one afternoon at Fromelles on the Western Front a fortnight earlier for no territorial gain whatsoever; during August, the AIF would suffer 23,000 men killed or wounded during the hopeless Battle of Pozières in the same bloody theatre.

Breaking the stranglehold of the Turks in the western Sinai was also the first land victory for the Allies in World War I. After so many lost or inconclusive battles on the Western Front, Romani was a great morale booster. Victory also gave Murray and Chauvel the confidence to implement their plan of advancing east and driving the Turks right out of Egypt and beyond.

Trooper Dennis Rock from 6th Regiment, writing to his sister Hope, said, 'We had a scrap with the Turks here at Romani on the Sinai Peninsular [sic] and beat them and drove them back. Now we are having a spell, men and horses, and a couple of times we have been over to the Mediterranean and had a swim which the horses enjoy almost as much as we do'.

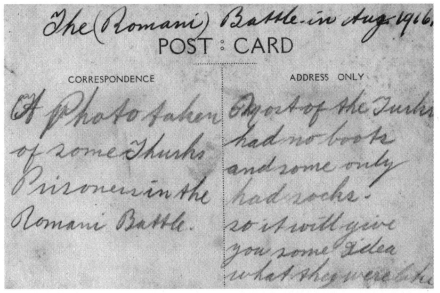

Sending a morale-boosting postcard home that pictured 'some Thurks' on the other side of the card, an unknown trooper was pleased to report that most 'had no boots and some only had socks'.

Aiming for the sky

General Murray now asked the British War Cabinet if he and Chauvel could lead their victorious warriors on a new offensive against the Turks, who they claimed they could now drive back across the Sinai, into Palestine, and then up north to Damascus. They got a good response. Nothing succeeds like success, and the War Cabinet approved the plan, signalling a major turning point in this Middle Eastern Campaign. The British were not just defending the Suez Canal now — they were embarking on a great offensive to liberate the Middle East from the forces of the Ottoman Empire, which had occupied the region for centuries. It was a tall order, but they were all game. And that was the main upshot from the Battle of Romani. The British war leaders also asked Chauvel to come to Britain to report on Romani and explain his tactics for the next stage of the campaign in the desert.

Chauvel's ruthless strategy continued to work. Although wrung out and dazed by lack of sleep, his equine steamroller had by 9 August advanced, basically unopposed, from Romani almost to El Arish (the next target) in the north-western Sinai.

MINOR BATTLES: KATIA AND EL ARISH

5 August, Katia

After Romani, Chauvel forced his exhausted forces to ride east, pursuing about 20,000 Turks towards the place where he and Murray believed the next big battle would take place — Magdhaba. On the way, the unstoppable Light Horse captured two fortified Turkish outposts, Katia and El Arish.

Katia was a small but well-defended outpost, to the south-east of Romani, an old Arab settlement established in a saltwater swamp spread out over a few kilometres. Taking this outpost would not be easy, as William Fraser reported: 'By 8am the Turks had got into prepared positions at Katia and fresh Turkish troops had arrived to cover their retreat'.

Yet despite the challenges of the heavily armed Turks, that afternoon the Anzac Mounted Division captured Katia.

Here, the loyal horse-loving Stuart Robertson Macfarlane recorded the worst experience of his life: 'At 3.15 the Mounted Division moved forward to attack Quatia [Katia] 2nd Brigade on the left flank, 1st Brigade next, then NZ next and 3rd Brigade on right flank. The Turks rear guard was in Quatia already and after fighting them for two hours we had to retire when the attack was on, the enemy tried hard to get our horses with shells. This was the worst experience I have ever had. We only had one bottle of water for 35 hours and we had an awful time from thirst, the horses were for 56 hours without water and for 44 hours in the saddle'.

But the Anzac Mounted Division won the battle, and 'Among the prisoners,' Macfarlane noted, 'was the Turkish commander and two complete German machine gun sections and some German officers. Our guns did great execution and our machine guns did good work'.

Chauvel's scouts had reported the Turks dug in behind palm trees and shrubs with their machine guns, rifles, and even artillery on the other side of the swamp. Chauvel lined up his riders in three brigades totalling 700 horsemen and ordered them to charge — old-fashioned cavalry style — across the hard ground of the saltpan towards the hidden Turkish gunners 1,500 metres away.

'At this point all our troops became engaged and kept in touch throughout the night of the 5th,' wrote William Fraser. It must have been an exciting sight as hundreds of horsemen with bayonets fixed, charged at a gallop. For the Anzac horsemen, this was a much better way to challenge Turkish machine gunners than it had been back at Gallipoli, when some of these riders had charged across open ground at The Nek on foot. Now at least they had their horses. The charge at Katia would also prove a useful rehearsal for the big charge against the Turks at Beersheba in Palestine the following year.

Not that they got the whole way, because the hard ground gave way to boggy swamp soil, making it necessary for them to dismount and run into the Turkish machine-gun nests. Even so, they succeeded in overcoming the Turks in what became a desperate hand-to-hand struggle with bayonets, and by nightfall the Turks had been displaced from Katia and the Light Horse were free to move on to the next obstacle to the east.

'Under darkness the enemy retired to Ogratura [Oghratin]', William Fraser wrote, 'and from there brought their long range guns into action and they held their position for three days in order to get away their heavy guns. They then retired to Bir el Abd while the whole mounted forces followed including the Camel Corps'.

6 August

Before long, Hubert Billings reported things had quietened down, both on the ground and in the air: 'All quiet again. Turks have evacuated Katia. Hostile planes overhead but no bombs'. The following day, this Gallipoli veteran noted in his diary: 'At 4am exactly a year ago I was landing on the beach at Suvla Bay (Gallipoli) how time flies!'

Although Katia was a victory, some paid the highest price, much to the consternation of their mates. Stuart Robertson Macfarlane reported that 'Russell Drysdale is reported missing. The 2nd Regiment had to retire at daylight and Russell was last seen trying to mount his horse; the 2nd Sergeant and the Lieutenant in his troop were killed' and 'they had to go straight on and did not recover any bodies'. He still held out hope for his mate: 'the ambulance followed later and picked up all the bodies they could find, so there is just a chance they found him and that Russell is in one of the hospitals', even though 'they found his horse dead'.

Lance-Corporal George Johnston from the 6th Regiment wrote: 'My dearest Mother, we have just been through a couple of days with the Turks but as this is supposed to be a private letter I will withhold details, suffice it to say that we have had a strenuous time but did good work as you will no doubt hear through the papers. I got a bullet through the crown of my hat which singed my hair but nothing more. I got it whilst six of us were bringing in a wounded mate. They asked for volunteers for the job as it meant going back through a heavy rifle fire to a position we had just left at the gallop. The Colonel asked for our names when we came in. Three of us had bullets somewhere — one was hit in the leg, one in the water bottle, and mine. However we are settling down again but we are kept busy and did not lose too many.' Johnston also had an eye for wildlife and added: 'You have heard of the chameleon — the lizard who changes his color. There are plenty over here, and one spent the day in our tent gathering up some of the flies. They have a tongue that springs out and grabs the fly even if he's a foot away, and whilst on the sand he will be quite white, and if you put him on a date palm he immediately turns green, a real hard case.'

In between battles, when their horses were being rested, troopers like George Johnston grabbed any means of transport they could as they searched for food and supplies from the local Arabs.

7 August

Although he now believed he had lost his mate, at least Macfarlane was able to confirm next day: 'A quiet day in camp and our infantry have now occupied Quatia'.

8 August, El Arish

After giving his troopers a rest, Chauvel ordered them further east to keep up the momentum and drive the Turks before them.

By 8 August, they had forced the Turks to abandon the little outpost of Oghratin, which the Turks had retreated to — although they failed to dislodge the Turks from the stronghold of Bir el Abd (because the Turks had twice their number defending it) and later at Bir el Mazar, which Chauvel refused to attack, fearing casualties would be too high. Instead, he wisely bided his time until, fortunately, the Turks retreated east to El

Arish. *They can wait*, the shrewd strategist thought, *we will drive them out of El Arish when the right time comes.*

That time would come after Chauvel, his men, and the horses were given a well-earned rest. Chauvel himself travelled to France and England to report the great news of the Romani victory, meet his family, and also consult with his superior officers. He would not return to the Sinai until December.

It was during this Light Horse rest period that T.E. Lawrence, 'Lawrence of Arabia', started to plan the Arab Revolt with Arab would-be leader Hussein, and his son, Feisal, to drive the Turks out of the Arab lands of Palestine, Jordan, and Syria. Lawrence hoped to install Hussein bin Ali, Sharif and Emir of Mecca, or his third son, Prince Feisal, as rightful Arab leader after the war. 'I believed in the Arab movement', Lawrence wrote subsequently, 'and was confident before I ever came, that in it was the idea to tear Turkey into pieces'. With Feisal as his co-leader, Lawrence moved into the Arab lifestyle, adopting appropriate Arab costume and setting up camp in the Hejaz region, which he used as his headquarters to plan the liberation of Arabic-speaking lands from the Turks. Lawrence wrote: 'Suddenly Feisal asked me if I would wear Arab clothes like his own while visiting his camp. I should find it better for my own part, since it was comfortable dress in which to live Arab-fashion as we must do. Besides the tribesmen would then understand how to take me'. As he explained: 'If I wore Meccan clothes, they would behave to me as though I really was one of their leaders and I might slip in and out of Feisal's tent without making a sensation'.

The tactics used by Lawrence and Feisal (who eventually provided 3,000 loyal Arab troops) were different to those used by the Light Horse; these Arab Revolt leaders specialised in guerrilla raids on strategic railway lines and bridges used by the Turks, blowing them up with explosives. Their strategies, approved by Murray (and Murray's successor later, General Sir Edmund Allenby), worked well, complementing the more conventional tactics of the British-led Light Horse — especially when the leaders met and coordinated their attacks.

The ride east from the Romani area would be risky, as although men could survive using the oases dotted throughout the desert, there were long stretches without water. From Romani heading east along the old caravan route, there was little water until Bir el Mazar (120 kilometres), then hardly any at all until El Arish was reached (150 kilometres), which the Turks were believed to hold. So before the advance to El Arish could even begin, the state of the water supply had to be thoroughly explored. By mid-December 1916, a British water pipeline and railway was under construction, making it possible to store sufficient water at points along the route to supplement the special camels that carried water for troops in support of an attacking force. These water considerations were critical, because if a trooper was left behind in the inhospitable Sinai, he might die in the burning desert sun during the day, or in the bitter cold at night. If a water bottle was accidentally tipped up or leaked, it could mean no water for its owner, for up to 24 hours in extreme temperatures.

These high temperatures could even break the local Arabs, as Lawrence wrote based on his own experience: 'It can be terribly hot' and 'the anxiety and constant movement makes it ever harder to bear for all of us. Some even of the tough tribesmen break down under the cruelty of the sun and crawl or have to be dragged under rocks to recover in the shade'.

But it was something other than the heat that made Trooper George Smith, who served in the 9th and 14th Light Horses and the Camel Corps, wish he was in France, as he wrote on August 12: 'To My Dearest Little Sister. Well Dot old Kid I'm as pleased as a boy with two tails. I've just this minute received a letter from my brother Mickie. He is in France which I suppose you know. He has been up in the firing line for 10 days. He said they hadn't been doing any shooting. They were only doing fatigue work. He said the bullets and shells make one screw up a bit when they landed close to you. He said they are going right into the front next time. Mickie says France is a lot better place than Egypt — plenty of cheap wine and beer and also plenty of nice 'Girls' — that's the place for me. I'll watch them.' He goes on: 'Plenty of fun here now Dot — aeroplanes flying over us every few hours. The Germans made an air raid over us the other day. They dropped 5 or 6 bombs right close to us — one was only 150 yards away from us — you ought to see the boys ducking their heads. I might tell you, I ducked mine too. I've got such a lovely little bay mare to ride. I'll give 'Mr Turk' some hurry-up with her. Plenty of fighting going on at a place called Katia. That's where we are going and we are going to fight on horseback — that will suit me. Well Dots this is a lovely little spot where we are camping right alongside of a big lake. We take our horses in for a swim every day … they get very tired travelling in the sand. I remain, Your affectionate brother George xxxxx. Kisses for Stan xxxxxxx [His baby brother.]

The studio portraits that troopers like George Smith had taken before they left Australia or in studios in Cairo became precious mementos for their families, especially if the trooper was killed in action.

Sadly, George's brother Mick (A.E.W. Smith) was killed in action in France the following April.

After the Romani battle, 6th Regiment Trooper Dennis Rock, a young country boy from New South Wales who had graduated from the King's School, was worried that uniform standards were slipping, writing to his sister Hope: 'There have been lots of arguments as to what our colours are, and it never seems to have been very clear as none of our Brigade ever wore colours; why I do not know. Some say its because we have the fir as a regimental badge, however lately a lot of the 7th Regiment have been wearing red and black and they claim ours should be red and green but I am not sure. But anyhow none of our fellows are wearing any colours'.

These 1916 campaigns against Romani and other objectives had been reported so badly in one newspaper that it made Trooper Rupert Fenwicke of Gunnedah angry. Writing to his parents, he complained: 'We never realised what mistakes a paper could make until we read the report of the latest stunts. I'll never take any notice of them in future'. He also revealed, 'It seems terrible to see the graves of our mates killed in these battles but it was the first chance we had so we visited some of them and took photos to send to their parents'.

David Laing Clark, writing to 'Dear Mother and the Girls' on 16 August, also guessed: 'No doubt you have heard all about it in the newspapers', saying, 'things have been a little mixed up here this last week or so but it has all passed over now' and he 'had quite enough of it'. In fact, he admitted, 'Our horses got a great amount of work in that attack and could do with a long rest like some of ourselves'.

December

By early December 1916, construction of the British pipeline and railway had reached the wells at Bir el Mazar, the last water sources available to the Egyptian Expeditionary Force before El Arish. Bir el Mazar was about halfway between Romani and El Arish, which Murray and Chauvel wanted to capture, and to then advance as soon as possible towards Magdhaba. British intelligence had reported Ottoman Army plans to strengthen the garrison at Magdhaba, by extending the railway south-east from Beersheba (and Hafir el Auja) towards Magdhaba. Mounted patrols to the outskirts of El Arish discovered 1,600 well-entrenched Ottoman troops holding the town, supported by forces based 40 kilometres to the south-east on the banks of the Wadi el Arish at Magdhaba and Abu Aweigila.

20 and 21 December, El Arish

On 20 December, a week after Chauvel returned from Britain, the Australian commander ordered the advance to El Arish. The Anzac Mounted Division left Bir Gympie at 9.45pm, ready to ride about 30 kilometres through the night. It was not only safer to ride at night but also less disconcerting, as Idriess wrote, because 'We sometimes ride across dead Turks. The wind has eddied the sand away and part of the half-dried bodies are exposed'.

They moved out without the 2nd Light Horse Brigade, which was in the rear assisting with patrolling the lines of communication stretching 140 kilometres back to Kantara on the Suez Canal. The force for El Arish consisted of the 1st and 3rd Light Horse Brigades, the New Zealand Mounted Rifles Brigade, the 5th Mounted Brigade, and the newly formed battalions of the Imperial Camel Brigade, with the mountain guns of the Hong Kong and Singapore Camel Battery.

The loss of valuable horses at battles like Romani — where they were either killed outright or, if badly wounded, had to be shot — undermined the strength of the Light Horse, which had to keep finding new mounts from the limited number of horses brought from Australia.

El Arish was a small village of simple dwellings and palm trees on the coast of the Mediterranean Sea north of the Turkish base at Magdhaba, which in turn was just short of the Palestinian border. Chauvel ordered his riders to ride around the whole settlement and surround it with their horses side by side before morning. Much to their relief, it seemed the Turks had already fled El Arish, and, just after 7am on 21 December, the advance party of the 1st Brigade easily occupied the town. They were welcomed by the locals, who surrendered their settlement to these Australians on horseback.

William Fraser wrote about the capture and also about unexpected dangers: 'Orders were well carried out during the night but after a long march it was discovered at dawn that the Turks had evacuated El Arish and gone to Magdhaba 20 miles [32 kilometres] south and also Rafa. For once there were no casualties apart from two keen Australian swimmers who were blown up by a sea mine when they went for a celebratory dip'. Idriess confirms the tragedy: 'Two 1st Brigade chaps, rushing to the shore for a swim were blown to pieces by a mine. A thumb was the biggest part of them found'.

Despite the apprehension and earlier intelligence report from their patrols, the Allied forces had had an easy victory — especially compared to Romani.

Trooper Jeff Holmes described El Arish as 'inhabited by half Gypos [Egyptians] intermingled with Turk and Bedouin. The huts are built of mud brick and some of clay only. There is only one decent house and that is the mosque'. But there *was* the all-important water. 'Water of the best variety is found at a depth of three to five feet only 100 yards from the sea. It is remarkable that such fresh water is found so close [to] the briny. It is so sweet the troops prefer it to the inferior water we are issued with.'

Australian airmen had, in fact, updated earlier reports revealing that the Turkish garrisons at El Arish appeared to have been withdrawn. The arriving troops took command, arranged badly needed water supplies, established lookouts, and fortified the village. By 4pm on 21 December, the 1st and 3rd Light Horse, the New Zealand Mounted Rifles, and the Imperial Camel Brigades were in bivouac at El Arish — enjoying a bloodless victory. Soon after, Lieutenant-General Philip Chetwode, the new commander of the Desert Column — of which the Anzac Mounted Division was a part — landed on the beach to take up his appointment opposite the division's headquarters, and British ships delivered supplies and rations. An upper class Englishman, Chetwode, 47, an old Etonian and 7th Baronet, was as keen as Chauvel was to attack Magdhaba as soon as possible.

The Turkish abandonment of El Arish for Magdhaba was a rare and lucky break for the Allied forces. Idriess exclaimed: 'Well, I'm blest — our troops have occupied El Arish. The Turks evacuated it — we thought hell would be played there'. Chauvel's troops had marched overnight ready to fight for El Arish, he wrote, 'but the Turks had just gone'.

It might have been an easy victory, but Chauvel had another conquest to add to his successes and they were now closer to Palestine — with one obstacle between them and that long-awaited border: Magdhaba.

2.
MAGDHABA,
23 DECEMBER 1916

DEFYING TOP BRASS ORDERS TO WIN A NECK-AND-NECK BATTLE

As well as the difficulty of negotiating the rugged terrain surrounding Magdhaba, as the Light Horsemen rode towards the village, they never knew where a deadly Turkish sniper or machine-gun nest was hiding.

The mounted men at Magdhaba had done what we had never known cavalry to do in the history of war: they had not only located and surrounded the enemy's position, but had gone down to it as infantry and carried fortified positions at the point of the bayonet.

LIEUTENANT-GENERAL PHILIP CHETWODE, COMMANDER DESERT COLUMN, 26 DECEMBER 1916

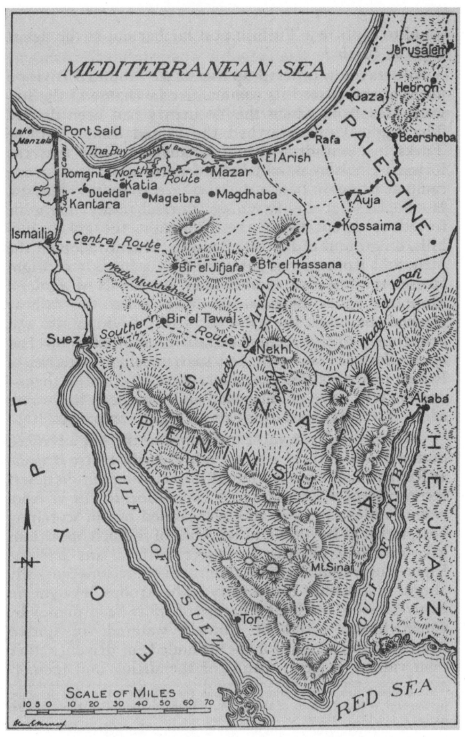

In order to force the Turks back east through the Sinai towards Palestine, after defeating them at Romani, Britain's Egyptian Expeditionary Force defeated them at Katia, chased them to El Arish on the coast, and then rode inland to fight them at their major stronghold — Magdhaba.

BACKGROUND TO THE BATTLE

The Light Horse had to win the battle at Magdhaba, about 35 kilometres south-east of El Arish, if they were to drive the Turks out of Sinai and into Palestine. By December 1916 this was the plan that had been approved — despite recent personnel changes at the very top.

The British War Office's policy in 1916 had initially been to mount offensive operations only on the Western Front and to stay on the defensive everywhere else. But when H.H. Asquith resigned as Prime Minister on 7 December, his successor, David Lloyd George, ordered the British War Cabinet to accelerate its plan of attacking the Ottoman Forces in the Middle East.

The commander of Britain's forces there, the Egyptian Expeditionary Force, General Sir Archibald Murray, was ordered to extend his eastern frontier, so that his advance would undermine Turkish forces in the southern Ottoman Empire, drawing more Turkish troops to resist the Desert Column and so slow the transfer of German and Ottoman units to other theatres of war. On 7 December 1916, Murray had appointed the newly promoted Lieutenant-General Sir Philip Chetwode as commander of the Desert Column. As a British major-general, Chetwode had been in command of cavalry on the Western Front, where he was involved in pursuing retreating Germans after the First Battle of the Marne in 1914.

Chetwode's Desert Column consisted of: the mounted force of the Anzac Mounted Division, commanded by Australia's Major-General Harry Chauvel; the 5th Mounted Brigade; and the Imperial Camel Brigade. His three infantry divisions included the 53rd (Welsh) Division, currently serving in the Suez Canal Defences and commanded by Major-General A.G. Dallas, the 42nd (East Lancashire), and the 52nd (Lowland) Divisions.

The British War Cabinet was more confident in the Sinai campaign after success at Romani and along the Suez Canal, where British forces had captured a number of Turkish positions right through to El Arish in the north-east corner of the Sinai.

While the railway line and water pipeline continued to be built, the British began to establish protective garrisons along their supply lines, which stretched across the Sinai from the Suez Canal. The garrisons patrolled the railway and pipeline, keeping them safe from Ottoman attack. These supply lines were marked by railway stations and sidings, airfields, signal installations, and standing camps where troops could be accommodated in tents and huts. By this time the EEF had a strength of 156,000 soldiers, plus 13,000 Egyptian labourers.

Meanwhile, after their retreat from Romani, and while the Allies were treating their wounded and burying the dead, the routed Turks regrouped. Over the next few months, they travelled back east with their wounded, setting up a new base at Magdhaba. Using the momentum of the Romani victory, the Anzac Mounted Division, under the command of Major-General Sir Harry Chauvel, had driven the Ottoman Army's Desert Force, commanded by the German General Friedrich Kress von Kressenstein, out of Bir el Abd and across the Sinai to El Arish and beyond. By mid-September 1916, the Anzac Mounted Division had also pursued the retreating Ottoman and German forces from Salmana about 30 kilometres along the northern route across the Sinai Peninsula to the outpost at Bir el Mazar.

The Ottoman Army's Desert Force, which had occupied the Sinai for so long and opposed the British forces, had established its principal desert base at Hafir El Auja, located on the Ottoman side of the Egyptian–Ottoman frontier. Linked to Beersheba, Gaza, and northern Palestine by road and railway, this major German and Ottoman base in the central Sinai desert supplied and supported smaller garrisons in the area with reinforcements, ammunition and rations, medical support, and places of rest away from the frontline. Turkish troops at Magdhaba and Hafir el Auja blocked the advance of the EEF along the northern route towards southern Palestine

The first target under this newly confirmed policy of driving the Turks back east and out of the Sinai towards Damascus had to be Magdhaba. It was essential to drive the Turks away from Magdhaba because they were blocking the route north to Palestine that Chauvel wanted to open up.

Magdhaba was only 30 kilometres west of the border with Palestine — tantalisingly close.

Of course, the Turks understood the strategic importance of the village, too, and here they decided to make a stand against the pursuing Allied forces. Intelligence reports from patrols convinced Chauvel — who wanted to keep the pressure up against the Turks — that his forces now had the strength to attack.

Once supplies for the Egyptian Expeditionary Force were brought ashore by local sailing vessels, they were loaded onto the most reliable and hardy form of transport, camels, which served the EEF throughout the entire campaign in Palestine.

Trooper Roy Dunk reported: 'At 10 o'clock on the morning of 22nd [December] Sir Philip Chetwode landed on the beach at El Arish having come by sea from Port Said. After consulting with Chauvel he decided to take up the pursuit at once.' In fact, the Desert Column had done so well so far that Chetwode had been preparing a simultaneous advance towards both Magdhaba and another Turkish strongpoint, Rafa, but then decided to send all his available mounted strength against Magdhaba, suspending operations further to the east for the moment.

Now Chauvel committed his Anzac Mounted Division, with the Imperial Camel Corps attached. Once again, Chauvel used his own 1st Light Horse Brigade, commanded by Brigadier Charles Cox, to spearhead this attack and do most of the fighting. Like Romani, this was to be a bloody battle — both on horseback and then on foot, with much bayonet work.

It certainly was bloody hand-to-hand killing. For 5th Regiment Trooper Ion Idriess, 'Magdhaba was full of thrill. When redoubt after redoubt was falling to the bayonet the troops got wildly excited'.

THE BATTLE OF MAGDHABA
22–23 December

On the night of 22 December, General Chetwode ordered Chauvel to attack Magdhaba from his new base at El Arish, meaning the troops would start the battle after a long night march.

Employing the latest technology, prior to the battle Chetwode ordered planes from the newly formed No. 1 Squadron, Australian Flying Corps (AFC), to fly low over Magdhaba to see exactly where the Turks were based in their series of redoubts. Apart from reconnaissance, the planes also took part in bombing raids. On 22 December, one British and ten AFC planes dropped a hundred bombs on Magdhaba, although targets were difficult to locate.

Chauvel led his men out of El Arish in the early hours of 23 December towards Magdhaba, after reconnaissance parties had established the size of the Ottoman force from El Arish that had travelled along the Wadi el Arish into Magdhaba.

Patrick Hamilton scribbled in his diary: 'Sent back to El Arish to bring up the Camels. Exciting ride finding the way. Returned back again with the camels. Got on the move as soon as we returned and travelled all night towards the battle'.

'No time was lost', William Fraser wrote in his diary. 'The whole force was ordered to make a forced march under Chetwode and Chauvel to attack Magdhaba arriving at 4 in the morning.'

As this was going to be a fight to the death, Chauvel also took his best fighters: three brigades of the Anzac Mounted Division — 1st Light Horse Brigade (1st, 2nd, and 3rd Light Horse Regiments), the 3rd Light Horse Brigade (8th, 9th, and 10th Light Horse Regiments) and the New Zealand Mounted Rifles Brigade (Auckland, Canterbury, and Wellington Mounted Rifles Regiments) — together with three battalions from the Imperial Camel Brigade in place of the 2nd Light Horse Brigade. These nine regiments and three British infantry battalions were also supported by the Inverness and Somerset Artillery Batteries, Royal Horse Artillery, and the Hong Kong and Singapore Artillery.

It was a gruelling ride, as Patrick Hamilton noted on Saturday 23 December in his diary en route to the battle: 'After an all night ride sitting [in the saddle] we only stopped for half an hour for breakfast'. Trooper George Smith from Echunga, SA confirms: 'After riding all night and supplied with only a quart bottle of water, we fought from daylight to sunset in the heat of a foundry. Tanned as we were, our elbows became blistered from the scalding sand as we gripped our hot rifles'.

Claude 'Dennis' Rock, 6th Light Horse Regiment, (left) posing with comrades outside their tents, kept a photographic record of his service, later compiling a comprehensive album of his Palestine campaign.

23 December, pre-dawn

They reached the plain about 6.5 kilometres from Magdhaba at about 5am on 23 December, sighting the enemy-held village by first light. Idriess reported that they 'dismounted within four miles of their bright campfires. Jacko never dreamed that the Desert Column, after a thirty mile night ride could possibly carry on with the business', but 'it was an epic fight'.

The Turkish defences consisted of six well-situated, fortified redoubts arranged around the village, which protected the only available water supply in the area. A series of trenches linked the redoubts, so that the Turks did not have to put their heads up when moving from one to another. These redoubts were almost impossible to locate on the seemingly flat ground on both sides of the Wadi el Arish. The whole Turkish position, extending over an area of just over 3 kilometres from east to west, was narrower from north to south.

Magdhaba's defences had been inspected the day before the attack by Kress von Kressenstein, who'd expressed satisfaction with the garrison's ability to withstand any assault. As well as the redoubts, Magdhaba's remoteness made it difficult for the enemy to amass forces against it: Magdhaba was about 65 kilometres from the British railhead and 40 kilometres from El Arish.

Using the information gained by aerial reconnaissance about the ground best for horses and/or camels, Chauvel decided to surround Magdhaba. He sent his main brigades to attack around the northern flank where the ground was more solid so that they could charge from the north and north-east. The ground was sandier on the northwest, and therefore more suited to camels, so he ordered his Imperial Camel Corps to attack from that direction. As Allied pilots reported the Turkish positions were just east of the Wadi el Arish, Chauvel also cleverly sent one regiment on a wide circling movement to the east and then south, to cross the wadi and take up positions in the rear of the enemy position and block their retreat. The Turks' positions were, as Idriess confirmed, 'Entirely surrounded'.

23 December, 6am

Once these intelligent strategies were followed, Chauvel's forces were well placed to start the battle. Capitalising on surprise, Chauvel's men opened up with withering fire over the open desert before the Turks spotted them. That triggered the battle, as Idriess reported, selecting some highlights: 'When redoubt after redoubt was falling to the bayonet, at Magdhaba the troops got wildly excited. Two West Australian troops of only forty men charged a redoubt of four hundred Turks! They galloped yelling straight over the trenches', and then: 'Soon afterwards a squadron of the 2nd Light Horse galloped shouting at the same redoubt, leaping over the dead and wounded men' and 'pounding into the trenches with their horses, firing through the dust from the saddles. They shot up the Turks and took the redoubt even though the Turks were four times their number and were supported by German machine gunners'. Idriess concluded: 'It must have been a mad few moments; the chaps even got wildly excited as they tell us about it'. By now there was no doubt that the battle-hungry Anzac Mounted Division loved old-fashioned cavalry charges, no matter how bloody the ensuing battle would be.

But as Trooper Roy Dunk added, the enemy resistance could be very stiff: 'For a minute or more we enjoyed the excitement of a cavalry charge as the horses fought for their heads and the quart pots and other gear pounded against the saddle. But the rush was brief ... after half a mile we charged into heavy machine gun fire and rifle fire from a strongly defended redoubt directly in front of us so we turned around and galloped off to take cover in a deep blind tributary of the Wadi where we could size up the situation'.

23 December, 6.30am

From the start, Chauvel's plan to encircle the enemy worked well, although his men met stiff resistance everywhere. Major-General Edward Chaytor led the New Zealand Mounted Rifles Brigade, in the main attack on the Turkish garrison, from the flat, featureless north and east, supported by a machine-gun squadron armed with Vickers and Lewis guns, and the 3rd Light Horse Brigade. Even though Chaytor had started his attack outside Magdhaba near Wadi el Arish, and was supported by British forces, he met such heavy Ottoman fire that his mounted troops had to find cover and dismount. Some of the New Zealanders got as close as 370 metres from the redoubts and entrenchments; others were kept at bay about 1,500 metres away.

23 December, 7.30am

Soon after these early charges, the units of the Imperial Camel Brigade moved straight on Magdhaba, in a south-easterly direction, following the telegraph line, and by 8.45am had come close enough to the Turkish defenders to advance on foot. Behind them in reserve was the 1st Light Horse Brigade.

23 December, 9.25am

At 9.25am, Chaytor ordered a regiment to circle the entrenched positions and move through a strategic outpost, Aulad Ali, to cut off a possible line of retreat to the south and south-east. Soon, the eccentric Brigadier-General J.R. Royston — who had distinguished himself at Romani wearing out a series of horses as he galloped up and down the frontline — now led the 10th Light Horse Regiment in capturing Aulad Ali and hundreds of prisoners.

Idriess reported: 'Royston's men are chuckling over their prized brigadier. In the big charge where the 10th captured seven hundred prisoners Royston as usual was galloping all over the battlefield and suddenly found five Turks peeping from a trench with levelled rifles. The brigadier instantly raised his cane and shouted furiously at them in Zulu, and I'm blessed if the puzzled Turks didn't drop their rifles and hold up their hands'.

23 December, 10am

The attackers achieved another breakthrough by 10am when the persistent New Zealand Mounted Rifles Brigade advanced close towards the firing line, even though the Turks' artillery batteries and trenches were difficult to locate.

William Fraser reported, 'Moved into position at the gallop. Attack on enemy position at Magdhaba commenced at 10am'.

After flying over the battle, pilots reported that some Turks were beginning to retreat already. Ever the optimist, Chauvel ordered his beloved 1st Light Horse Brigade to charge the town, passing the dismounted Imperial Camel Brigade battalions on their way. But that was a premature move, and they were repulsed by heavy shrapnel fire as they trotted over the open plain, and were forced to take cover in the convenient Wadi el Arish. Despite constant enemy fire, battalions of the Imperial Camel Brigade continued their advance over the flat ground, thanks to covering fire provided by each section in turn.

William Fraser wrote: 'Later in the morning the 3rd Brigade were told to storm and take trenches. The 8th and 9th regiments (Col. Maygar and Scott) were ordered to carry out this operation. The 10th (Col. Todd) was sent around — mounted — to get behind enemy's position and cut off their retreat. Col Todd ordered "Fixed bayonets and charge!". Our aeroplanes also bombed the Turks'.

Temporary progress aside, both sides fired at each other relentlessly hour after hot sweltering hour. Idriess admitted that 'The Turks fought stubbornly all day'. During the day, pilots and their observers provided frequent accounts of estimated positions, strength, and movements of the Ottoman garrison. These were reported verbally by the observer, after the pilot landed near Chauvel's headquarters.

23 December, noon

By noon, all brigades were hotly engaged, as the 3rd Light Horse Brigade's 10th Light Horse Regiment continued their sweep round the garrison's right flank.

23 December, 1pm

By 1pm, the right of the Imperial Camel Brigade battalions had advanced to reach and link up with the 1st Light Horse Brigade, but they could not advance any more against the withering fire from the Turks hidden in their trenches.

Having secured the enemy village of El Arish, General Murray's forces found it faster and safer to transport by sea, from Egypt, the supplies that they needed for the assault on Magdhaba .

23 December, early afternoon

Unfortunately the Turks, Idriess noted, 'were snug in their deep trenches supported by machine guns', making it difficult for the Desert Column forces to dislodge them. The situation was not helped by the enemy breaking all the rules of war. William Fraser reported: 'Three times the Turks held up the white flag pretending to surrender but after each display when our men believed that the Turks did want to surrender the Turks treacherously poured lead into our men when our men approached them to accept their bogus surrender'.

As the Turks still held fast right through the scorching heat of midday and into the hot afternoon, Chauvel suddenly lost his nerve and feared his attacking force would lose. Knowing only too well how badly his parched men and horses needed water from Magdhaba's wells, the normally unflappable leader now feared the worst and made one of his few mistakes of the 1916–18 campaign. He issued an uncharacteristic order to the dispatch rider to tell the officer leading the attack, Brigadier Cox, that he must give up and tell his men to retreat!

Dispatch rider Trooper Roy Dunk recorded this order: 'As the enemy is still holding out and horses must be watered the action will be broken and all forces withdrawn. Each Brigade will be responsible for its own protection during the withdrawal'.

Luckily, Chauvel's subordinate knew better. As soon as he was given this written order to withdraw, Charles Cox refused to obey; he reckoned his men were on the cusp of victory. Dunk, who was watching, said Cox handed the order back to the dispatch rider who had delivered the written message and spat out the words: 'Take that damn thing away. And let me see it for the first time in half an hour'.

This insubordination was almost unprecedented. It was a brave move, but Cox was right — unlike Chauvel, he was on the frontline and knew better. Cox at that moment ordered his men to fix bayonets and charge the main enemy defences. He also knew that reinforcements had just arrived and would help turn the tables. Commanded by Brigadier-General 'Galloping Jack' Royston, those troops, the 10th Light Horse Regiment, had just captured Aulad Ali and advanced over the Wadi el Arish, and around Hill 345, to link up with Cox. Their fresh mounted charge enabled the Light Horsemen to defeat the remaining Turks and secure the vital water supplies.

Idriess reported that the men of the Desert Column 'fixed bayonets and regiment after regiment charged the redoubts. Only one crowd of Turks stood up to the steel,' although other Turks 'fired right up to the moment that the Anzacs jumped down into the trenches'.

Within the half hour, Cox's men had conquered that stronghold, put the Turks on the run, and turned the tide of battle. Those much-needed wells were theirs for the taking. Cox had won the day and captured Magdhaba — disobeying his superior officer's order in the process.

Although they had only been invented shortly before the war, motor vehicles played a key role in transporting men as well as supplies, and provided work for a range of people, as this transport compound in Egypt shows.

23 December, 2–2.15pm

By 2pm, the tide had well and truly turned, and most of Chauvel's attacking units had captured the No. 2 redoubt and were making more progress against the rest of the Ottoman garrison; in fact, the first reports confirmed even more Ottoman troops retreating.

At 2.30pm, Royston's 10th Light Horse Regiment advanced to attack the rear of No. 4 redoubt.

23 December, 2.55–3.05pm

Just before 3pm, the frontal attack by the Imperial Camel Brigade, fighting together with Cox's 1st Light Horse Brigade, reached a position within about 500 metres of the final Ottoman defences.

A relieved Stuart Macfarlane was certainly surprised at the speed of the Allied victory: 'The Anzac Mounted Division and Camel Corps engaged about 2,000 Turks 25 miles up the Wadi and this engagement lasted until 3.30pm. Then our C Squadron got the order to move and we rode over very rough country and then dismounted ready for action — only to find that the Turks had surrendered! About 1,500 prisoners were taken, a corresponding number of small arms and one mountain battery ... Our losses were light'.

23 December, 3.15pm

The New Zealand Mounted Rifles Brigade, with fixed bayonets, then attacked the trenches to the east of a collection of Turkish houses. Royston's 10th Light Horse Regiment, by now advancing from the south, captured two trenches on that side, effectively cutting off any retreat for the Ottoman garrison. The Imperial Camel Brigade and Cox's own 1st Light Horse Brigade attacked No. 2 redoubt.

23 December, 4pm

The 1st Light Horse Brigade finally captured No. 2 redoubt by 4pm. Chaytor also reported capturing more buildings and redoubts on the left. After a telephone call between the greatly relieved Chauvel and Chetwode, the two leaders decided the battle had been won. Chauvel later told Cox how grateful he was that Cox disobeyed his orders.

Roy Dunk wrote with some surprise about the Turkish surrender: 'Now, when you are in a show like this and being fired on at point blank range and there are fellows falling after being shot — perhaps your best mate — you don't feel like kissing the enemy when you get there even if they have got their hands up; but that is almost what happened on this occasion. Within seconds of reaching the trenches our blokes were shaking hands with the Jackos and handing around their cigarettes. The Turks got the greatest surprise they had ever got because they thought they were about to be killed'.

Dunk was not supposed to be in the charge on No. 2 redoubt, but when he delivered a dispatch to Major Lewis, his squadron leader asked him: '"The boys are just about ready to attack No.2 Redoubt with the bayonet, would you like to be in the fun?" So I said "Too right" even though a bayonet fight was the last thing I would have chosen at that particular time for enjoyment. "Well" he said "if you are quick you will just be in time" directing me to the trench from where we were to charge.'

Dunk was glad he took part, because 'This successful capture of No.2 Redoubt was the turning point in the engagement which made Chauvel realise he had been wrong ordering a retreat'.

By mid-afternoon, William Fraser noted: 'Todd's men [10th Regiment] cut off the fugitives from escaping. The trenches were stormed and carried. This action was successful. Many Turks were killed in the trenches' and all forces performed well, and 'even the Hong Kong Battalion did splendid work. The battle lasted till 4 pm until the white flag went up.'

23 December, 4.30pm

One final Turkish stronghold was still holding out. Finally, at around 4.30pm, the dismounted attackers got to within 20 metres of it.

The Ottoman garrison had no option but to surrender, and as darkness fell, random firing petered out, the victors rounded up prisoners, collected horses, and at last watered at the captured wells — enjoying the biggest prize of all. William Fraser wrote: 'After the 1st Brigade pushed on the right flank the whole Turkish garrison surrendered and we took 1,200 prisoners many were killed or wounded and much material was captured before our force returned to El Arish'.

Jeff Holmes described the prisoners as 'the most non-descript lot you ever set eyes on. They had no regular uniform, some had puttees others none; some boots, some bootless and some hatless and some wearing German leggings. There were a lot of lads who appeared to be no more than 16. Their officers included Turks, Austrians and Bulgarians but I could not see any Germans'. That was probably why, according to Roy Dunk, 'a Light Horseman seized the French Military attaché Count St. Quentin who was wandering about looking at the Turks and — despite his excited protests — just bundled him in with all the captives'.

From an elevated position, Holmes had 'watched the fight all day'. Big guns helped win the battle, he explained, as fortunately, 'The Turks had very little artillery and what they did have did very little damage. Our artillery done very little in the morning but in the afternoon the right guns opened up of the Turkish redoubt doing great damage and by late afternoon made the trenches untenable so our fellows just advanced and took them'.

Afterwards, the conqueror Chauvel rode into Magdhaba and gave the order to clear the battlefield and collect the wounded. William Fraser wrote: 'Kept under cover from place to place until 8pm looking for and collecting wounded. Under fire plenty of bullets and shrapnel. Picked up wounded till dark. Took them to Turkish hospital'. Then: 'Dressed the wounded till 10.00pm 85 of them. Took night shifts in turn, work very hard but interesting talk with Turkish Doctor'.

The Allied forces had fought on that hot afternoon — despite Chauvel's momentary loss of nerve — attacking the garrison, driving the Turks back and defeating them, with little loss of life on the Allied side (only 22 dead), but hundreds killed on the Turkish side. Another great victory!

An elated Holmes wrote: 'The fight was over by night and as long as I live I don't think I will ever get such a panoramic view of a fight as we were on a hill overlooking the valley and followed the fight through glasses all day. Even though there were 2,000 Turks entrenched in a good position we outflanked them and cut them off capturing 10 guns, several machine guns and twelve hundred prisoners. It was a complete victory for us and losses were light under the circumstances, the total casualties numbering 108'.

There was nothing more rewarding for the Light Horsemen after defeating the enemy than to capture and parade the flag of the vanquished, seen here hanging from the tip of their bayonets, as proof of their victory.

At 11.30pm, in the cool of the night, the exhausted sleep-deprived attackers left Magdhaba for El Arish, where they did not arrive till dawn on Christmas Eve. They did so having left El Arish only the night before.

Roy Dunk revealed that 'This was the third, and for many of the Regiments the fourth night without rest and many of the officers and men slept as they rode back to El Arish'. That was bad enough for the able-bodied men he said, but for the wounded 'A hideous night followed as the long column of 150 camels each bearing its burden of two jolted groaning wounded men moved through the intense darkness to El Arish' during which 'extreme suffering was inflicted upon the wounded'.

It was just as well Chauvel's men finished the fighting as soon as they did, because as Idriess reported: 'The troops when riding back the thirty miles [about 50 kilometres] from Magdhaba were enveloped in blinding clouds of dust'. And in their exhausted state, this dust storm affected them in strange ways as they rode sleeplessly across the barren and featureless desert.

'Nearly the whole column was riding in snatches of sleep no one had slept for four nights and they had ridden ninety miles [about 150 kilometres]. Hundreds of men saw the queerest visions — weird looking soldiers were riding beside them, many were mounted on strange animals. Hordes walked right amongst the horses making not the slightest sound. The column rode through towns with lights gleaming through shuttered windows of quaint buildings. The country was all waving green fields and trees and flower gardens.'

And as they sat 'smoking under the palms', Idriess continued, 'Numbers of the men are speaking of what they saw in a most interesting queer way. There were tall stone temples with marble pillars and swinging oil lamps — our fellows could smell the incense — and white mosques with stately minarets'.

Light Horseman James Williamson, a Dispatch Rider with the 2nd Brigade who came from New South Wales, only met the South Australian Maude Clayfield once before sailing off to war; yet, after writing to her throughout the war, he won her hand in marriage on his return.

In an address to the troops after the battle, Chetwode expressed his appreciation for the mounted rifle and Light Horse method of attack. He said that in the history of warfare he had never known cavalry to not only locate and surround the opponent's position, but also to dismount and fight as infantry with rifle and bayonet.

Roy Dunk complained of 'stifling dust and extreme cold' the night after the battle, but even so, claimed 'the unqualified success of Magdhaba supplies a classic example of the right use of mounted riflemen. In just over 24 hours the desert Column had ridden 50 miles [80 kilometres] and had fought mounted and dismounted 23 miles [40 kilometres] from their water supply and 50 miles from their railhead and had surprised and annihilated a strongly placed enemy. This engagement brought out all the best qualities of the Light Horsemen: the excellent discipline of the silent night ride, the rapid approach before dismounting; dashing leadership of junior officers; the cleverness of the men taking cover during their advance, and above all else the eagerness of the troopers for bayonet work as they got to close quarters'.

William Fraser added: 'The whole move was successful because an abundance of water was found in the enemy camp and on the way back we were met with water supplies brought out on camels from El Arish'.

But private reports on these battles were restricted, as 2nd Brigade Sergeant James Williamson wrote to his girlfriend, Maude: 'Orders have come out that no military matters can be mentioned in letters otherwise — finish letters! So I have to cut military information out and that leaves very little else to write about except sand, wilderness and flies, which I am sick and tired of writing about. With best wishes for a Bright and Happy Christmas, and a Prosperous New Year, Your sincere friend, Jim Williamson.'

Christmas Day

'And this is Christmas Day! Caesar! Great Caesar! Which reminds me: we are very near to the land which gave Christmas to the world', Idriess wrote, anticipating the next exciting Light Horse advance from Sinai into Palestine.

Jeff Holmes did not expect much on Christmas Day, saying: 'After watering and feeding the horses we had slept all day and night and never did we need sleep so much before but woke up to find that today is Xmas Day and I expect it will be the tamest ever that I put in, but we will have to make the best of it. We did however get a double issue of cigarettes and eight pounds of pudding between 11 of us so we will live high. We also got some tins of sardines and a couple of tins of milk'.

Stuart Macfarlane felt they deserved a Christmas break, saying: 'After being on the go for 62 hours during which time we only managed to get 5 hours sleep we celebrated Xmas'.

It was just as well the Australians captured Magdhaba in that one day, otherwise they would not have had water for their horses or for themselves.

As George and Edmée Langley write in their book *Sand, Sweat and Camels* (1976): 'Magdhaba was the first real taste of a pitched battle for the Camel Corps. Riding as a parallel column to the Light Horse, the Imperial Camel Corps was able, without pushing their beasts, to keep to the march schedule set for the operations. This was the first occasion when the two types of mounted infantry had covered the same distance under the same conditions.' But later the camels had to be left well back from the fighting, because they were such huge moving targets.

Trooper John (J.E.) Hobson, from Boulder, WA, had already fought in the Boer War, but enlisted in the 10th Light Horse in time for the Battle of Magdhaba. In February 1917, he wrote this grateful letter to the Theatre Club in Boulder: 'I received one of your parcels … for which I thank you all very much. I enlisted in Boulder 17 months ago, and lived with my wife and family in King Street previously … Our work has been very victorious considering we had long night rides over the desert. Very often our horses never had their saddles taken off for 48 hours at a stretch. A few weeks before Christmas we had a pretty severe days fighting and finished up with charging the enemy's position over very open country with fixed bayonets at a gallop, taking the whole positions and capturing all guns and enemy prisoners who numbered nearly 2000. Since then we have had still another great victory. I might add that Archbishop Riley, the Chaplain General of the Australian forces was present with us when your gifts were distributed. We are camped near the Mediterranean Sea which enables us to have a cold bath whenever we like, but it is winter here, and I can assure you that the water is quite cold enough for any body.' Trooper Hobson despite the cold temperatures survived to return to Australia.

This victory opened the way for the final expulsion of the Turks from the Sinai into Palestine. But to break into Palestine, the Desert Column still had another obstacle, one that was on the border itself — the village of Rafa. So now Murray and his generals had to work out how to capture this formidable enemy stronghold, ideally while they still had momentum.

There were many sick and wounded troopers after the Battle of Magdhaba, just before Christmas 1916, who would have appreciated receiving this 'Xmas Card' from Australia as they recuperated in hospital.

PART III
PALESTINE
1917–1918

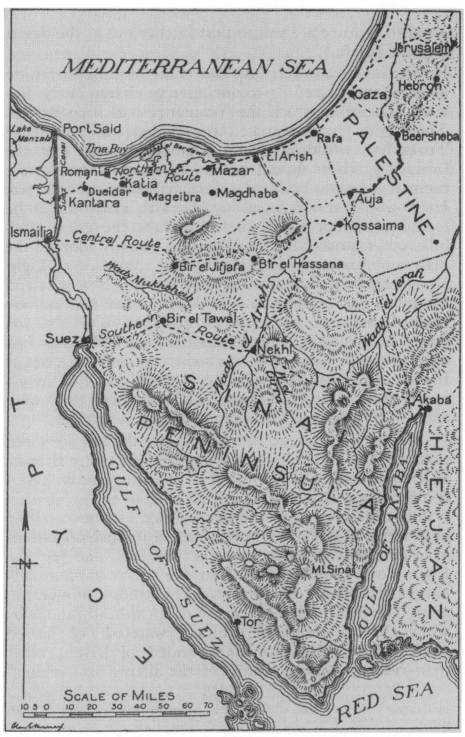

Having driven the retreating Turks out of the Sinai, and back east into Palestine, the Egyptian Expeditionary Force (with its Australian Light Horse in the lead) now had to break into Palestine itself; and to do that, they had to defeat the Turks in the next enemy fortress town of Rafa, which straddled the border between the Sinai and Palestine.

3.
RAFA, 9 JANUARY 1917

KIWIS IGNORE ORDERS TO RETREAT, DEFEATING TURKS HANDS DOWN

Before their attack on Rafa — which was surrounded by sandy hills — the Light Horse Regiments took advantage of the terrain by sheltering behind one of the hills close to their objective.

It was a very good performance from our first attack at dawn. There was a stubborn resistance right up to the evening from the Turks but just as our people were about to retire and give the job up, the New Zealanders charged forward and the Turks surrendered. We had a great advantage because for the first time our aeroplanes were in cooperation with the artillery by wireless during the engagement.

TROOPER ARTHUR MILLS, JANUARY 1917

BACKGROUND TO THE BATTLE

The first battle in Palestine started on 9 January 1917, and the Desert Column won this battle in ten hours. The course of the battle was almost identical to the previous one at Magdhaba. Again, the commander lost his nerve and ordered a retreat (mainly to get life-saving water) and once again the order was ignored; and this time a timely charge by courageous New Zealanders won the battle.

But where Magdhaba was an inland desert settlement in a wadi, Rafa was near the coast of the Mediterranean Sea (like El Arish) and right on the border between Sinai and Palestine. It had served as an Egyptian police post but was now a fortified Turkish stronghold. If the Desert Column were to enter Palestine, they had to destroy the Turkish defences there. Instead of deserts and sand dunes, the Rafa region featured more fertile country with grassy pastures, which the horses certainly enjoyed. As the biblically minded 5th Regiment Trooper Ion Idriess noted, 'We are beginning to think with all this grass and water and now hens eggs that we will soon be entering the land of "milk and honey"'.

Trooper Stuart Macfarlane also liked what he saw, writing: 'The country across the border is fairly good and evidently improves from the border onwards and there are thousands of acres of barley around Rafa, which itself is just a small village'. The battle for this ancient staging post was half in Sinai and half in Palestine, and Ion Idriess noted, 'We are not the first because this has been a holy battleground for different religions from ages past'.

Having been keen to push on anyway, the Egyptian Expeditionary Force commander, General Sir Archibald Murray, decided to attack the Turks at Rafa. Murray assigned this task to the Australian and New Zealand Mounted Division, led by Major-General Sir Harry Chauvel, accompanied by Brigadier-General Edgar Wiggin's 5th Mounted Brigade as well as the Imperial Camel Corps Brigade led by the highly decorated Brigadier-General Clement Smith, VC.

The Australian and New Zealand Mounted Division now included a formidable line up — the 1st Australian Light Horse Brigade (comprising 1st, 2nd, 3rd, and 4th Australian Light Horse Regiments) and 3rd Australian Light Horse Brigade (comprising 8th, 9th, 10th, and 11th Australian Light Horse Regiments) and the New Zealand Mounted Rifles Brigade (comprising the Auckland Mounted Rifles, Canterbury Mounted Rifles, and Wellington Mounted Rifles). The Imperial Camel Corps also included two Australian battalions, one British battalion, and a mixed Australian/New Zealand battalion.

The British commander of the Desert Column, Lieutenant-General Sir Philip Chetwode, planned the battle based on innovative aerial reconnaissance by British and Australian airmen, who confirmed that 2,000–3,000 enemy troops defended Rafa. And the Turks were expecting the British to attack. Chetwode carefully established his command centre several kilometres behind the attacking troops, but ordered Chauvel to position himself closer to the action. For the first time, they communicated by newly developed wireless transmitters and receivers, and with the airmen acting as 'eyes in the sky' — giving them a great advantage. They also communicated with each other by radio-telephones in the field.

This air-to-ground communication suffered a few teething troubles, as an airman from country New South Wales, James Traill, reported. When he was given a wireless set — the first used from an aircraft in Palestine — to test, he took it up in the plane and then lowered a lead weight from the aircraft on 100 feet (30 metres) of wire, which Traill hoped would act as an aerial to send his first test messages. But this had a devastating effect on his lightweight aircraft — the plane suddenly started an out-of-control dive. Desperate to avoid crashing, his pilot, Captain Peters, sitting in front tried to stop Traill from lowering the heavy weight any further through urgent gestures and loud curses. 'What the bloody hell are you doing?' The pilot shouted, 'I cannot keep her flying anymore — we are going down!'. But calmly ignoring this dire forecast, Traill just tapped out in Morse Code the routine training message to test the wireless: 'Now is the time for all good men to come to the aid of their country.' Then he finally pulled up the wire, enabling Captain Peters to avert the nose-dive and avoid crashing into the sand dunes below. When they landed, Traill asked some officers who had come to meet their plane, 'Did you receive my message?' 'Yes, yes,' they replied angrily, 'and so did all the enemy in the neighbourhood who think we must be in a very bad way to send out a message like that (calling for reinforcements) and the Turks will now use that for their propaganda purposes!' Needless to say, Traill perfected his technique before long, and air-to-ground communication played a helpful role in the battle.

Pioneering Australian Flying Corps aviator Captain Peters and his navigator, Lieutenant James Traill (who won the DFC), provided such useful aerial intelligence and dropped so many well-placed bombs that they helped the Light Horse defeat the Turks at Rafa and break into Palestine.

Not that flying was by any means straightforward, as Arthur Mills wrote to his father just before the battle: 'Flying is off today. There is a high wind and a frightful sand storm. The wind is doing about 40 miles an hour [65km/h]. One machine tried it but had to come back. It tipped over after landing and broke the propeller. It's not often we get these winds and this is the worst. I am trying to write this with three fellows talking loudly in my tent which is an awful nuisance'.

A relieved Stan Broome from the 12th Regiment wrote to his mother: 'At Rafa, the whole countryside is one big barley field and here it is better still, with villages scattered about. The country is like a Garden of Eden after the desert (Sinai), but strange to say, the water is scarcer here, although there are wells everywhere, but we are not allowed to touch them. We may have to ride 5 or 6 miles from camp to water our horses. The people here are an altogether different stamp to the Egyptian, being almost fair, although the hair is dark. The villages consist of mud huts with flat roofs and are mostly in a very bad state of repair with broken walls and roofs. There are miles of orchards, but the fruit is not as yet ripe, unfortunately. Pomegranates, dates, figs, almonds, peaches, apricots, guavas, grapes, water melons and other fruits are all prolific. We are experiencing a taste of the Khamseen, a hot desert wind, and I am writing this under ground level in a dugout, but even here it is stifling'.

Even though some Australian stockmen found it difficult to swap horses for camels in order to serve in the Imperial Camel Brigade, they then found it so much easier to ride across the soft sand as they rushed into battle that many were reluctant to go back to their horses when ordered to do so.

THE BATTLE OF RAFA

8–9 January

The enemy was also active in the air, according to Trooper Stuart Macfarlane. He described an air raid at El Arish prior to the Allied attack on Rafa: 'Three taubes [German aircraft] came over dropping bombs. As it was a full moon they were able to fly low. One bomb landed amongst our Egyptian Labour Corps — it killed about 30 and wounded about 50. I was in bed when the first bomb landed. They also shot off their machine guns at our horses but missed. Our anti-aircraft guns then fired back driving them away'.

Trooper Jeff Holmes could not wait to break camp and get on the move because of that bombing: 'Jacko is lively with his Taubes and bombs and today just dropped 10 bombs around El Arish and several near the line killing and wounding a score of niggers'. Hoping that might be the end of it, Holmes wrote: 'I just got to bed at 8.30 when boom, boom, boom. My God I said they are bombs and sure enough they were. They flew around for half an hour dropping 16 bombs and also turned their machine guns onto us, then our aircraft guns fired a few shots but could not find the Taubes without searchlights. Only a couple of mules were casualties'.

Then Macfarlane wrote that the orders had finally come to advance towards Rafa: 'The Desert Column is going out tonight to attack Rafa. We are taking four guns as evidently a "dust up" is expected'. Holmes added: 'We had been expecting this for a week or so and it did not surprise us. But just as we all lined up on the beach to get ready to move Jacko came over, but our guns kept him away'.

It was a bit of a rush, Trooper Patrick Hamilton complained: 'We were ordered to move out quick smart at 11.00am and had to pull down everything and pack up in a great rush! All the while hostile planes flew above'.

Having considered different attacking routes and researched Turkish defences from the air, Chetwode now ordered Chauvel's troops to advance from El Arish, at dusk on 8 January, the 40 kilometres to Rafa. Worried by possible Turkish reinforcements, Chetwode also made plans to fall back to El Arish. But his men quickly got to Sheikh Zowaiid, an Arab village 16 kilometres short of Rafa that Chauvel's men captured and surrounded, preventing locals from retreating and telling the Turks about the Desert Column's plans to attack Rafa.

Hamilton recorded his big day crossing from Sinai to Palestine: 'We crossed the historic border into Palestine! There is a real change of country from desert to grasslands'.

So overnight the men headed for Rafa, which would be 'a tough nut to crack', Trooper Ion Idriess reported, because 'it is dominated by a hill El Magruntein, which is tiered by trenches surveyed by German engineers. The other low hills around El Magruntein were all converted into redoubts'. To make matters worse, Idriess wrote, 'there is not even a bush for cover and there was only one tree visible and that was on top of a Turkish hill'.

It was very dangerous for the Light Horse to charge across open ground towards Palestine against Turkish defenders who had the latest machine guns and a clear line of sight; so when possible, they did so under the cover of darkness.

Here the 2,000-strong Turkish force had constructed a defensive position, on a rise known as Hill 255. Approaching Rafa on the morning of 9 January, the Australian and New Zealand Mounted Division and the 5th Mounted Brigade, together with three battalions of the Imperial Camel Corps Brigade, isolated this enemy garrison by cutting the telegraph lines to Gaza — the sort of guerrilla hit-and-run warfare advocated and later perfected by Lawrence of Arabia. The New Zealanders were sent to the south with instructions to attack the Turks from the east and north. Meanwhile, the 5th Mounted Brigade moved in from the west.

There was no shortage of men, Jeff Holmes wrote: 'When we joined up with all the other troops there were more troops than the Magdhaba stunt. As we moved off I hoped we would not have to ride through anymore [sic] wadis full of water because when you cross them you get your feet wet which proves very uncomfortable when night comes. But the road was not as bad as Magdhaba because it is the main road to Jerusalem'.

Wasting no time, and under the cover of darkness, Chauvel's keen troops rode silently forward and surrounded Rafa. They were now poised to charge the high ground in the centre of Rafa. But Chetwode and Chauvel hesitated to give the order because they now realised the enemy had cleverly blocked the approach to this high ground, creating a network of trenches rising in tiers around an earthen redoubt on a central hill, and although these works were not protected by barbed wire, they provided obstacles for the Light Horse, blocking their charge up the long, bare slopes leading up to them.

9 January, dawn

Yet as dawn broke on 9 January, the men themselves were keen to charge. They included some formidable fighters, especially Chauvel's Anzac Mounted Division (1st and 3rd Australian Light Horse brigades and the New Zealand Mounted Rifles Brigade), reinforced by three of the four battalions of the Imperial Camel Corps (which also contained many Australians), and the 5th Mounted Brigade, a British yeomanry outfit.

William Fraser's breakfast was certainly interrupted: 'We stood to and managed to eat breakfast at least till the attack commenced on the outposts, redoubts and trenches at Rafa'. Fraser needed a good breakfast because, among his other duties, he served as a medical orderly with the Field Ambulance.

Holmes reported: 'We had arrived at our position by 11 o'clock then were ordered to camp in a hod for the rest of the night near a native village surrounded by hedges of prickly pear. Although we are still well away from the firing line we can hear the artillery banging away and our planes are buzzing over. Earlier this morning there was a sharp burst of rifle fire so our boys must have struck an outpost. Then we could hear the rifle fire as well as machine guns so the artillery must be having a warm time of it. Armoured cars are participating in this scrapping for the first time.'

Initially, the wounded were taken away from the battlefield by horse-drawn ambulances — far better than the next generation of camel ambulances, which were so rough that patients sometimes died in agony on the way to hospital.

New Zealander Stuart Macfarlane, who enlisted in Sydney, was pleased to see his fellow Kiwis in action as they crossed the border into Palestine: 'The Anzac Mounted Division are to attack Rafa. We had crossed the Egyptian border just after daylight and cantered into action just on the left of the N.Z. Brigade'.

Although Chetwode decided to take the risk and order his men to advance in the dawn light, they could not get very far because of the well-defended Turkish trench system ringing the central hill. Chetwode pulled out all stops, ordering his aircraft, via their new radio network, to direct the fire of artillery, but despite this pioneering use of technology, he did not have enough heavy guns to dislodge the Turks, and he feared his mounted force could run out of ammunition and water. But from the ground, Stuart Macfarlane thought the big guns were doing their stuff: 'Our artillery did splendid work'. William Fraser also confirmed this: 'After we had crossed the border into Palestine for the Rafa stunt we saw and heard intense bombardment by our artillery'.

Jeff Holmes certainly thought they were in a strong position: 'We heard there were 3000 Turks strongly entrenched in this well defended Garrison but they were not effective with their guns and by first thing in the morning our troops were completely surrounding the enemy and cutting off their retreat. With our artillery firing on the Turks from all sides'.

9 January, 4pm

Suddenly, Chetwode's airmen spotted 2,500 Turkish reinforcements, approaching from the north-east and east. Jeff Holmes thought that there were even more Turks on the way: 'One of our aeroplanes dropped a message in the afternoon to say that the Turks were fetching 4000 reinforcements'. Not surprisingly, Chetwode lost his nerve. With such a strong network of trench defences blocking the attack, his men unable to advance, and also starting to run short of ammunition and water — and now enemy reinforcements on the way — he did what Chauvel had done at Magdhaba: he called off the attack and ordered an immediate retreat.

Unbelievably, however, this order to retreat was ignored by the troops themselves — who thought they knew better, like 1st Brigade commander Charles Cox at Magdhaba. The mounted troopers wanted to keep fighting because they thought they could win! Typical of independently minded Anzacs, the troopers seemed to be challenging their own commanders, becoming a law unto themselves. Disobeying orders was a serious offence, but if you won a battle by doing so, you could get away with it — as Cox had done.

Ion Idriess commented: 'The Rafa battle, like Magdhaba was almost given up at sunset because of the lack of water by Chetwode, the new English general, but just when he had given up all hope, the Turkish redoubts all fell to the bayonet. As the New Zealand Brigade was charging one redoubt the Cameleers charged another. Both Brigades at the same moment saw the Turks in their trenches fixing their bayonets and a loud and simultaneous roar swept all over the battlefield. The 1st Light Horse Brigade also then charged in the midst of the excitement and every Turkish trench was overrun'.

Jeff Holmes added: 'The N.Z.s charged with fixed bayonets and took the trenches quick smart. They charged over 1000 yards with no cover in front of the Turkish trenches with only our machine guns covering them to stop the Turks wiping them out. The Imperial Camel Corps then joined the fray and after them the 1st Brigade attacking on the flank with the 3rd Brigade in reserve waiting to greet any Turkish reinforcements. So the fight was soon over. Needless to say those Turkish reinforcements just vanished into thin air!'

William Fraser had this to say: 'All our units had been told to push on — take care — take cover and when ordered to advance and storm the Turkish trenches. But by 3pm after advancing our casualties were heavy. By 4pm things were looking rather black as though this business was impossible especially for Chetwode and Chauvel who heard that a large body of troops were advancing, which caused great alarm so the generals gave orders for all forces to retire. But by then the NZs had stormed the trenches and gone too far to retire especially as the unit commanders had already given them final order to charge. Soon after the 1st and 3rd Brigades charged so had also gone too far to retire'.

Stuart Macfarlane added: 'About 5pm just when a retirement on our part seemed imperative the New Zealanders charged and took the redoubt immediately in front of them; and before long the Turks were ready to surrender'.

These tenacious New Zealanders had broken the Turkish defence by charging into and through the redoubts at breakneck speed, yelling defiantly as they did so. Charging in from the north, three New Zealand regiments first attacked the main redoubt on Hill 255, charging up a 700-metre slope with their bayonets bared, which terrified the Turks, who either threw up their hands, fled, or were dispatched on the New Zealanders' steel blades. They were covered by machine guns and Lewis guns. Stuart Macfarlane reported: 'The Lewis gun worked splendidly … We managed to keep her right up with the line and only had one stoppage. We went forward with the line but the Turks surrendered so the guns were not required'.

If that was not enough to terrify the Turks in the fading light, the Imperial Camel Corps also called out with a blood-curdling scream and then charged. Their men overcame the main redoubts that remained, killing any defending Turks, while some regiments of the Australian Light Horse charged into the fray, crashing though the defences and killing any Turks who did not surrender. Macfarlane again: 'The First Brigade which had started to retire under orders then reformed and charged also'.

Arthur Mills wrote: 'It was a very good performance from our first attack at dawn. There was a stubborn resistance right up to the evening from the Turks but just as our people were about to retire and give the job up, the New Zealanders charged forward and the Turks surrendered. We had a great advantage because for the first time our aeroplanes were in cooperation with the artillery by wireless during the engagement'.

Shocked that their 'impenetrable defences' could be breached, most of the Turks surrendered or fled by nightfall. Stuart Macfarlane explained: 'The Turks fought for a while but surrendered before the bayonet work commenced'. Not all escaped, however, and (although the casualty estimates varied between participants) the Desert Column killed approximately 200 and took about 1,602 prisoners (including 168 wounded); those few that did escape got away because it got dark soon after. By contrast, the Desert Column casualties only totalled 486, including 71 killed. Macfarlane reported: 'Our casualties were fairly numerous but C Squadron was fortunate with only one man killed and about 15 wounded'.

Ion Idriess summed it up more passionately than most: 'The artillery opened out, then the troops galloped up close until their horses were being slaughtered, then dismounted and fought on foot getting closer and closer all through the day, until at sunset they were within bayonet distance. The whole crowd charged and stormed redoubt after redoubt, then took El Magruntein with the steel almost in the dark'.

Stuart Macfarlane added: 'There were more mountain guns used in this attack on Rafa than I have ever seen in action before. We captured a complete mountain battery and a couple of field guns also somewhere about 2,000 prisoners including a good number of Germans'.

Thanks to the troopers who had defied the order and acted so fast, they had captured the Rafa garrison before those 2500 Turkish reinforcements arrived. In fact, a relieved Chauvel ordered his men to fire long range at the approaching reinforcements. He then wisely withdrew, initially to Sheikh Zowaiid, where water and supplies had been stored in anticipation. Chauvel was also concerned that the Turkish reinforcements could pursue his men, so he decided it was safer to fall back towards El Arish with his men and the field ambulances that carried the wounded. William Fraser helped with this ambulance work: 'We picked up as many wounded as we could under fire before the Turks gave up at 5.00pm and we took 1,600 prisoners'.

Overnight, the Desert Column's defence of the newly won Rafa went unchallenged, and when dawn broke, they still occupied the village.

Surprising as it must have seemed to one and all, the Desert Column had notched up yet another victory — thanks to colonial troops like the Kiwis refusing to take no for an answer and despite the 'nervous nellies' in command. It was another example of the value of initiative at the level of ordinary troopers — they had won their first victory in Palestine. And because it was over the border, it was a victory that also ended the Sinai campaign of 1916. Nevertheless, as Ion Idriess concluded, 'it was a very close go'.

Close or not, Stuart Macfarlane wrote hopefully in his diary: 'I don't think there will be any more fighting now for some time'. Rafa was a big milestone. 'Are we to invade Palestine?' Ion Idriess asked excitedly. 'With the taking of Rafa,' he speculated, 'we have cleared Egypt and the Sinai of the Turk. So what next? Only the desert answers, which seems all whispers — in this land which was ancient when Christ was a child'.

As there was always a water shortage, troopers could only wash their clothes when they discovered a deep well with enough water for them to fill up their water bag for this luxury.

But, as always, the answer to such questions could depend not just on political decisions made in London but also on water supplies, as the advance from the Suez Canal had so far only been possible because of the availability of water along the route. The British and Commonwealth forces under General Murray had only been able to push eastwards across the Sinai Peninsula, from their defensive positions adjacent to the Suez Canal, and through the harsh desert because of the construction of this water pipeline to support the troops.

10 January

William Fraser's medical work began in earnest after the fighting was finished, as he explains: 'We were collecting the wounded all day up to 10pm then cleaning up till midnight before going on to the Light Horse Field Ambulance Casualty Clearing Station at 4am. Then had tea, a "bosca bath", breakfast before burying the dead and taking more wounded to the Anzac Casualty Clearing Station before travelling eight hours back to our base'.

The tireless Patrick Hamilton, who also served as a medical orderly, continued working very hard and long for hours after the battle: 'Collected the wounded until 10pm tending them till midnight. Moved off at 1.00am and reached the 1st Light Horse Casualty Clearing Station 4.00am. Breakfast then buried the dead. Started for home 1pm then travelled steadily carrying wounded to our Anzac Casualty Clearing Station then got home and went straight on Piquet duty till 1pm the following day. I went 65 hours without any sleep!'

After surviving the battle, Stuart Macfarlane wrote: 'I am going to give this diary and some snaps to a wounded friend to take home for me. I am writing this in haste and must start for the Field Ambulance immediately'.

11 January

Patrick Hamilton reported: 'Our casualties at Rafa known to be killed 68, and wounded 361 and the Turks suffered — killed or wounded 600 with 1,300 prisoners'.

Captain Jack Davies of the 12th Light Horse was among those who scored booty from Rafa, a practice that Chauvel allowed in the same way Lawrence of Arabia allowed his Arabs to take booty after their raids.

'It was a great go and I am glad I was there', he wrote to his wife Millie (who was conveniently based in Cairo), 'and my part of the show went off swimmingly. I had no trouble at all. I got two mules with pack saddles and 3 camels (with 2 humps) with four good leather pack saddles as booty for my little show. These things all help me to travel around in comfort'.

The 12th Regiment's Stan Broome, writing to his mother, said: 'I suppose you will have the report in full of the operations the other day and you could tell me more about it than I could. But I can tell you we had a very strenuous time and were just about knocked up when we came out of it. We were in the saddle day and night for nine days and the night riding was particularly tiring. Our casualties were rather heavy I think, but I believe we attained our objective.'

The Light Horse were also in danger of suffering casualties between battles, as Trooper Dennis Rock, wrote to his sister Hope, 'Last week we had a bit of excitement and amusement at least for the onlookers as our dugout was burnt; John Bell and I were down the line playing cards and Arthur Dorney was lying in the dugout reading and smoking and his cigarette ash must have got onto the sacking and started it going and took all the side and roof of our dugout but luckily did not hurt the framework much. None of our personal things were damaged'.

Using the local Egyptian word for a present (or bribery), Rock soon cheered up when he said he received a 'buckshee' sent from Australia (officially known as 'a Gift Issue Parcel'), saying 'and I got a singlet, shirt, socks and fruit chutney and cigarets [sic] for our section of four men'.

14 January

Aware that his wife, Millie, was surrounded by handsome officers in uniform, Captain Jack Davies wrote: 'Poor old Darling, did you think I'd think you would fall in love with anyone else? You just bang along as you feel inclined. I wont worry over much or lose much sleep over that danger, I can assure you'. Out in the desert it seemed he had more pressing needs, writing two days later, 'The chocolate and toothbrush came along OK.

Thanks old Dear but most of the chocky is now gone. We used a lot on the Rafa stunt. It's great tack and "I WANT MORE".'

Meanwhile, 12th Regiment Corporal Colin Bull was more worried about the effects of chocolate, or rather, *biscuits*, as on 16 January he wrote, 'Received a parcel from Mother with biscuits etc', and then on 24 January he said, 'Dr. Single came over and inspected our teeth and recommended me to the Dentist.' Bull then 'Had to visit the camp dentist who put a filling in one of my teeth but said I had to come back in two days to have more holes filled'. The dentist must have repaired his teeth well, as he then enrolled in the local military school, embarked on an intensive studies course which included subjects like 'Stoppages', and, when he sat his examination, got marks in the high 90s, peaking at 98 per cent.

Although the thousands of Turkish prisoners the Light Horse captured in battles like Rafa reduced the enemy numbers for future battles, these prisoners swelled the ever-growing ranks in the POW camps.

Despite the Egyptian Expeditionary Force's victorious entry into Palestine, the British War Cabinet decided to postpone the full invasion of Palestine until later in 1917 because of their massive commitments on the Western Front. The British needed to throw all their manpower and resources into Flanders and France to stop the Germans from advancing further west. Notwithstanding this policy, the British commander in Egypt, General Sir Archibald Murray, decided to make an early attempt to capture Gaza, to clear the way for his planned advance towards Damascus. This led to bloody battles for Gaza in both March and April of 1917.

The Rafa victory was another feather in the cap for Desert Column commander Sir Philip Chetwode, who watched and directed the battle from afar, and also for his commander in the field, Chauvel, whom Chetwode recommended for a knighthood as a Knight Commander of the Order of St Michael and St George.

Despite recurring rumours suggesting the Turks were about to attack with poison gas, this never happened — unlike on the Western Front where the Germans used gas to deadly effect — and so rather than practise putting on their gas masks day after day, the troopers had fun putting one on a visiting Bedouin child.

Enter Lawrence of Arabia

Despite their expectations of advancing north into Palestine, the Desert Column now had to bide its time and wait for orders. Out of the blue, the Desert Column got the best news. Ion Idriess and his fellow troopers captured some Bedouins in January, and in the pocket of one of the Bedouin's robes was a note in Turkish. When this was translated, Ion Idriess said, 'it was a proclamation informing the Bedouin that the Sharif of Mecca [Hussein] had revolted against the Turks, and taken the town of Medina and gone on the side of the Christian dogs. The proclamation exhorted all true Mussulmans [Muslims] to fight against the Christians lest they overrun the land and kill all the Bedouins in the hills'.

This was the first the men had heard about Lawrence of Arabia's timely Arab Revolt, which would turn out to be a game-changer, coming just in time for their next mission impossible — the assault on the heavily fortified Gaza.

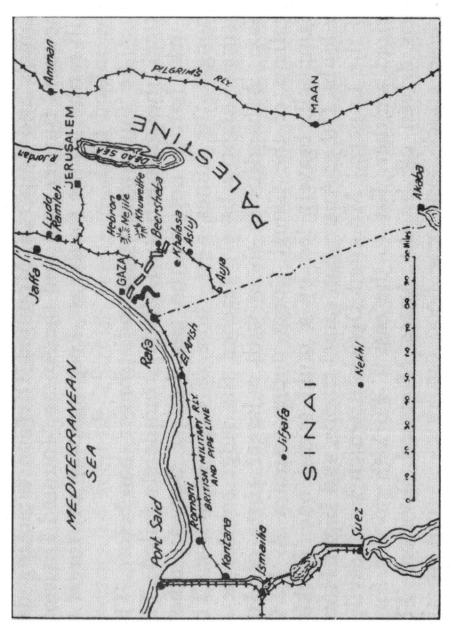

If they were to advance into Palestine, having defeated the Turks at Rafa on the Sinai/Palestine border, Britain's Egyptian Expeditionary Force now had to capture the heavily fortified town of Gaza, which blocked their way north and had a reputation for being unassailable.

4.
FIRST GAZA,
26–27 MARCH 1917

PANICKY BRITISH GENERAL SNATCHES DEFEAT FROM JAWS OF VICTORY

As they attacked Gaza, the Light Horsemen had to negotiate the worst terrain so far: before they could even get to the stone fortifications surrounding this Turkish stronghold, they had to fight their way through walls of prickly cactus, planted long before to provide an outer defence for the ancient town.

Never will I forget the utter amazement of all our troops when after taking Gaza we were ordered to retire! We simply stood gazing down the empty street of the town with officers shrieking for signallers to confirm that unbelievable order, lest it be the work of spies.

LIGHT HORSE TROOPER, ION IDRIESS, 5TH REGIMENT
26 MARCH 1917

BACKGROUND TO THE BATTLE

Having captured Rafa, which his forces and supplies had then reached by railway, the Egyptian Expeditionary Force commander, General Sir Archibald Murray, now developed plans for the Desert Column to attack Gaza to clear the way for an invasion of Palestine itself. But first he had to get British War Cabinet approval. Things were going well for Murray because his victory at Romani had put paid to any Turkish dreams of capturing the Suez Canal; his victory at Magdhaba had secured the Mediterranean port of El Arish and the supply route, water pipeline, and railway stretching eastwards across the Sinai Peninsula, and he had also captured Rafa, thus entering Palestine, and so bringing his Egyptian Expeditionary Force within striking distance of Gaza.

Gaza was a well-fortified Turkish town just beyond the Sinai Peninsula, which the Desert Column had crossed, and even deeper inside Palestine than Rafa. Murray wanted to take Gaza because it was the next domino heading north that he hoped would fall. It was such a massive Turkish stronghold, with a population of 40,000, and the main gateway to Palestine. Also, its position on well-protected high ground gave it commanding views. Once established there, the Desert Column would have a firm base from which they could see for miles and mount attacks on other towns en route to Damascus.

For the historically minded Ion Idriess, it was 'Samson's city', the place in the Bible where this giant 'tore down those city gates' and 'when chained to the Temple of Dagon, he pulled the roof down on top of 3,000 Philistines. Delilah was his girl'. Gaza may have been the site of an amazing victory for one biblical strongman, but it was now defended by another 3,000 opponents who were going to be harder to defeat for the EEF, even though they had thousands more troopers themselves. This estimate of 3,000 defenders came from British spies, so Desert Column commander General Sir Philip Chetwode advised his forces that 'It is believed that Gaza is not strongly held'. As it turned out, however, the spies were wrong or were lying, as later intelligence revealed as many as 18,000 enemy troops in the area. The exact number was not critical, however. With his infantry divisions standing by, Murray would have double the number, even if there really were 18,000 Turks defending Gaza.

Despite those superior numbers, what became known as 'First Gaza' was an example of poor British leadership. After the initial bumbling of this first battle, it would take another two bloody attempts throughout 1917 by Murray's British and Dominion forces before they captured Gaza.

It took these three attempts because the 'nervous nellies' in charge had very poor communication skills, lacked the courage, vision, and experience to push on, and, losing their nerve, just blindly ordered a withdrawal — as they so often had before. Unfortunately, this time officers and troopers in the frontline did *not* disobey the order to retreat, as they had at Magdhaba and Rafa. Once again, soldiers were killed because of incompetent officers leading from kilometres away from the frontline. Some Anzac troopers were reminded of the incompetent British leaders they had experienced at Gallipoli, who had sent so many Australian and New Zealand soldiers to be slaughtered on suicide missions.

Keen though the Australian Light Horsemen were to play a leading role in the attack on Gaza, charging forward on their wonderful Walers, the British infantry ended up leading the assault on this well-defended Turkish stronghold.

But as the British launched their attack on the key Turkish fortress town of Gaza, with the objective of capturing the great fortress of Ali Muntar — just outside of the town — the problems of leadership at the top became more obvious. Yet further down the chain of command, Lieutenant-General Harry Chauvel of the Light Horse had recently been knighted for his leadership to date. At the Battle of Romani, he had kept in touch with the battle on horseback, often under heavy artillery fire, and he was not too far back from the frontlines at Magdhaba and Rafa, while some other senior British officers stayed by telephones, kilometres from the action — so he was a better communicator than most. Even so, at First Gaza, Chauvel would be well behind the action, and Chetwode, who was in charge, was even further back. The attack would be delayed by fog and the attackers lost precious time, but ultimately it failed because of poor communication between British officers and their Australian subordinates.

With their horses tethered in the background while they waited for orders to advance against Gaza, these Light Horse troopers, each with their quart pot of billy tea, stopped for lunch out of the enemy's firing range.

Fortunately, there was a moment of quiet before the storm, quite literally for Corporal Colin Bull, 12th Regiment, who wrote on Sunday

4 March 1917 that he 'Went to a Church Parade in the morning', but then 'had to spend the day inside my tent because we had a dust storm all day. The worst experience I have had for some time'. There were also points of interest in this inhospitable desert, however, and later, on reaching the well in the desert at Bir-el-Abd after the storm, he was amazed to discover that 'it was erected by the Turks back in 1333!'.

There were other moments of light relief as well as drama: 'There was a football match between the 2nd Light Horse Brigade and the 10th Manchesters and the 2LHB won 9 to 3. An airplane smashed just near the field. And I went to a Concert given by Lena Ashfield at night.'

THE FIRST BATTLE OF GAZA

26 March, pre-dawn

This battle started very early on 26 March 1917. Henry Bostock, a Scout of the 3rd Brigade, wrote: 'Reveille at 3.15am and the Division led by a couple of scouts proceeded to Gaza to attack'.

This would be the biggest battle the Desert Column had ever fought, Ion Idriess forecast. He had heard two or three British infantry divisions were to attack the position from the south while the mounted troops of the Desert Column would attack from the flanks and north. He noted 'the boyish-faced cheerful lads arriving' and also the sounds of the infantry: 'For there floated to us, music — Bands! Masses of horsemen but then the Infantry. Brigade upon brigade battalion upon battalion, column upon column, growing rapidly spreading all over the plain, crushing wide lanes through the barley — the vanguard of the British Army!' Which inspired Idriess to boast, 'We feel that Constantinople is ours!'

For this battle, Murray had a very impressive line up of forces. The recently arrived English 7th Baronet, Sir Philip Chetwode, once again commanded the Desert Column. Within the Desert Column, Chetwode had the British infantry, including the 16,000 foot soldiers of the 53rd Division (led by Major-General A.G. Dallas), plus two mounted divisions — which included Chauvel's Anzac Mounted Division and the new Imperial Mounted Division led by Britain's Major-General Henry Hodgson. Meanwhile, Lieutenant-General Sir Charles Macpherson Dobell commanded the Eastern Force in the Sinai. Unfortunately, despite his important leadership role, Dallas made the mistake of staying back well behind the action which meant he was out of touch. Chetwode also had some air support.

The British should have won. They were in a much better position than the Turks, who, led by Germany's Kress von Kressenstein, only had 3,500 defending the Gaza garrison — as well as seven artillery batteries — although there were a total of 16,000 enemy troops in the area. The enemy did have some advantages, however, because they had more modern German planes and a formidable 'wall' of prickly cactus that had been planted over the centuries to block invaders attacking Gaza.

The British side's big and well-armed force certainly impressed Ion Idriess, who waxed lyrically over its firepower. 'An army is advancing and we are excited' with 'Battery after battery, limber after limber, swinging past and we gazed down on the guns! What numbers. What calibres. We thrilled as we watched those guns. What things we could do with them. I smiled at the thought of our own precious little guns that had stood us through the Desert Campaign. But these — why these are GUNS!' And as a relieved Idriess added: 'The Infantry were to take Gaza not us'.

Chetwode planned for the British infantry to attack from the south and south-east of the Turkish garrison, which was near the coast, aiming for the highest fortress on Ali Muntar ridge on the east of the town. He ordered the Welsh 53rd Division to spearhead this attack, with the 52nd and 54th Divisions to form a screen around the southern end of Gaza, while his mounted troops would form a protective screen around the east and north of Gaza to block any Turkish reinforcements that might turn up.

Having moved into position progressively, troops of the Desert Column were soon within reach of Gaza before dawn. 'We hurried to encircle the city to prevent the Turks from escaping their garrison', wrote Ion Idriess. Unfortunately, as the first light of dawn finally lightened the scene, the troops realised that Gaza was surrounded by a thick fog, which meant that the British artillery had insufficient visibility to fire off barrages to soften up the defending Turks. As Ion Idriess confirmed: 'all a man could do was lean back in the saddle and hold his breath as his horses ears disappeared into the fog'.

26 March, 9am

By 9am, the fog had lifted, enabling Ion Idriess to see 'the curious square built houses peeping among the hills with a fine minaret looming high above the roofs where we bet the Turkish artillery observation officer would be'. He said they then advanced, and 'The Australian cavalry were soon galloping hell for leather and we raced shouting boisterously as our cavalcade whipped up the dust'. Having set out on 'an exhilarating canter we turned in behind Gaza making straight for the broad white road that leads out to Beersheba'. Then other troops of the Anzac Mounted Division were able to reach and secure the main road the Turks used for getting reinforcements and supplies from their important inland base at Beersheba, thus cutting off Turkish reinforcements from that direction. To show they meant business, Australian Light Horsemen captured German pioneer workers, a convoy of wagons carrying supplies for Gaza, and then a Turkish patrol and the Turkish general in charge, who was then escorted to prison with other captives.

Idriess described the captives who were 'in two funny little coaches that might have come out of Queen Anne's reign' in which there was 'a Turkish Divisional commander moving into Gaza to take up his command. I shall never forget that disgusted general though. His a la mode Kaiser moustache was continually a-twitch as he twirled his cane and vainly turned his back on the unkempt troopers who threatened him from all angles with every breed of cameras'. Later, when delivered to Chauvel, the Turkish general demanded 'at least some of us be shot for not respecting his rank'. But Chauvel just sent him off to his army headquarters.

But there were rewards for capturing high-ranking Turkish generals, and Major Thomas Bird of the 7th Light Horse Regiment, leading the Advanced Squadron of the Advance Guard in the Anzac Mounted Division, won a Distinguished Service Order on 26 March for just that.

His citation confirmed: 'It was largely due to his dash and the skilful handling of his Squadron that a Turkish Divisional Commander was captured. Major Bird's steady and determined advance also brushed aside all opposition until the country to the north of Gaza was made good as far as the sea and it was due to his handling that the subsequent withdrawal was unobserved'.

Major Thomas Bird, 7th Light Horse Regiment, won the Distinguished Service Order at First Gaza because, as his Citation confirmed, 'It was largely due to his dash and skilful handling of his Squadron that a Turkish Divisional Commander was captured.'

Other troops also made good progress, thanks to modern navigational equipment, as Henry Bostock of the 3rd Brigade reported: 'Despite very thick fog our 2nd Division circled right around Gaza on the right and held in reserve. To help us we had been issued with a prismatic compass set on glycerine which kept the compass steady enough to take a bearing on horseback using a star in the night sky'. It was just as well that Henry Bostock had such good navigational equipment, because he was upset that for 'this stunt the High Command had reorganised our units and my 3rd Brigade was taken out of the Anzac Mounted Division and put into the Imperial Mounted Division and so we of the 3rd Brigade rather resented this change as we lost our old name of Anzac'.

Soon after the fog lifted, the attack proper began from units positioned at most points of the compass — not only by the Anzac Mounted Division but also by the Imperial Mounted Division and the Imperial Camel Corps

— whose men had almost surrounded Gaza by mid-morning. Henry Bostock thought it was, 'ideal cavalry country as it was gently undulating country and the Turkish defences were initially negligible'.

The attack was proceeding well, from the mounted troops' point of view. They were in position, ready to charge the town as soon as the British infantry eventually arrived from the south to subdue the Turkish defenders and the 40,000 residents.

Henry Bostock could not believe the Turks were such slow learners: 'Although the battle of Rafa must have been fresh in the Turks mind they still had not guarded against our enveloping tactics which allowed us to manoeuvre very widely and strike quickly at an exposed flank'.

Like many Light Horsemen, Major Bird carried a photo of his girlfriend back home, although in his case, this discreet officer did not write her name on the back of the photo.

26 March, noon

The only problem was that the British infantry was dragging the chain, and badly. Idriess described the infantry 'Toiling across the exposed country at the base of their objective Ali Muntar we watched these little toy men in the distance of the British 53rd Division plodding in waves towards the grim fortress, suffering under its machine guns'. Senior officers blamed poor light during the night, then the thick fog, which prevented their artillery supporting them, and also exhaustion. But the troops had marched so slowly that their leader, Major-General Dallas, revealed they were taking far longer than Chetwode had allowed; in fact, the British infantry did not even get close enough to Ali Muntar to start fighting the Turks till after noon.

Meanwhile, Ion Idriess commented: 'When the Infantry got closer to Ali Muntar they were steadily advancing under terrific fire. Every yard must have seemed like Death to them. Some thousands of the poor chaps bled on Ali Muntar that day. And the pity of it was they should have got there earlier and advanced in the protective fog'.

26 March, 1pm

Because the infantry were taking so long to get close enough to Ali Muntar to start fighting, a worried Chetwode (kilometres back from the action) now told Chauvel to order his Anzac Mounted Division to attack Gaza from the north.

26 March, 4pm

Because of bad communication, Chauvel, who was positioned closer to the action but a long way from Chetwode, took until 4pm to get the Anzac Mounted Division and Camel Corps to start their attack.

Trooper Stanley Parkes reported: 'We galloped into action with the Brigade over about five miles [8 kilometres] and it was very exciting'. They met fierce resistance. Henry Bostock wrote: 'Got under heavy fire and Bob's horse was shot while I was leading him'.

Watching from nearby, Brigadier-General Granville Ryrie wrote: 'Our men did splendidly I never saw anything like it. We had to attack through a perfect maze of narrow lanes and high cactus hedges, a perfect hideaway in which the Turks were hidden. I saw our men and the Turks firing at each other through the cactus not more than six feet apart. Some of our fellows were shooting off their horses, like shooting rabbits, they could see the enemy better from up on their saddles. Our mounted men also charged the Turks with their bayonets and killed a great many. But it was simply extraordinary how few casualties we had. I only had five killed and sixteen wounded — two officers, one was bayoneted'.

Ryrie was a pastoralist whose family owned Michelago homestead in the Monaro country in New South Wales and who had also fought in the Boer War and at Gallipoli. Henry Gullett, the official correspondent in Palestine, heaped praise on him: 'Of all our Australian leaders fighting this war, perhaps none stands level with Granville de Laune Ryrie, of the 2nd Light Horse Brigade, as a true representative of the Australian countryside'.

Meanwhile, Henry Bostock reported: 'Turkish troops approached our position but we held them all afternoon'. Eventually, the mounted troops took the advance into their own hands, and, without support, succeeded in capturing high ground to the north of the town and advancing into it. Some of the forces of the Desert Column eventually got right through to the central streets of the town.

'One of the amusing incidents', Henry Bostock said, 'was when some of our Anzac Mounted killed the Turkish gun crew and captured an 18 pound field gun and decided to destroy a two story enemy building full of Turkish marksmen'.

Ion Idriess takes up the story: 'These houses were full of lively snipers and this particular house only 70 yards away was furiously blazing with machine guns. The New Zealanders swung the captured gun around, a corporal quickly swung open the breech lock and pushed his face there instead of gazing down the barrel, the boys manhandled the wheels and to roars of laughter twisted the gun until the corporal could see the house through the barrel. They shoved in a shell, slammed home the block, fidgeted with the mechanism until suddenly unexpectedly bang crash up leapt the gun its wheels spinning men were flung among the dead gunners but the shell had gone clean through the house exploded and out came 28 Turks with their hands up coughing from the shell fumes! We all laughed delightedly before turning the gun on other houses with similar results until one of our officers caught up with us bellowing that he didn't want any of his own men killed with that "damned Krupp play-toy".'

Ion Idriess and his comrades turned their attention to another 'trench only 200 yards away' and, teaming up with the New Zealanders, 'rushed this trench with our bayonets, four machine guns spraying the trench with lead as we charged. It was blood-boiling work, but our charge was over quickly because the Turks could not stand up to our cold steel for more than the first dreadful minute. And as the sun went down a great shout came rippling faintly then swelling from man to man, "The Tommies have taken Ali Muntar! Hurrah! Hurrah! Hurrah!" We pressed right into the town with wild enthusiasm. But not 20 minutes later there came a staggering surprise — the order to retire!'

This ridiculous order sent a shock wave through the panting, blood-covered troopers. Exasperated, Ion Idriess complained: 'Everyone was mad. We knew that at sundown the British 53rd Division had actually taken Ali Muntar and linked up with the New Zealanders. We knew that the troops had really taken Gaza. We just could not understand what the "Big Heads" were doing. Our officers swore that we should all now collect together and march straight into the town with our bayonets, especially if we could not find our horses for the retreat'.

But even though Chauvel's unstoppable mounted men reached the centre of Gaza, Chetwode started to think it was a lost cause and began to panic. All he could see were problems. First, the slow British infantry had let down the mounted troops, who he imagined were now unsupported and in danger. Second, as this infantry got closer to Gaza and the fog lifted, they were sittings ducks for the Turkish artillery and rifle fire; many men were killed or wounded when the Turks opened up. Chetwode suspected the Light Horse would not be able to advance anyway because he believed the Turkish resistance was so strong. The troopers would also have to ride through a defensive barrier of cactus plants.

Nevertheless, as they were Chauvel's formidable Light Horse troopers — the same riders who had captured Romani, Magdhaba and then Rafa — and had very sharp bayonets, they overcame both spiky cactus plants and Turkish defenders. Despite Chetwode's fears, these mounted troopers had by evening surrounded the town almost completely, cutting off retreat by the Turkish defenders — much to the delight of Chauvel, directing them from a high point. Before long, they had not only invaded the northern outskirts of Gaza but had also linked up with the infantry's right flank. The Turks were all but defeated.

Ion Idriess reported on some of that incredible fighting: 'The fighting was all in scattered groups, we could only see a few yards around us because of the cactus pear so I can't tell all that happened, only in small groups. Poor Sergeant Gahn met his death by treachery, he and three other Light Horsemen rushed a Turkish officer with 15 Turks who all dropped their weapons and threw up their hands to surrender. But realizing how few our men were they snatched up their rifles again shot Gahn, and bayoneted one of his mates before the other two Light Horsemen with their blood now up shot six of the Turks quick and lively forcing the remaining nine to surrender'.

'Lieutenant Graham emptied his revolver and had a lonesome bayonet duel with a huge Turk,' Idriess continued, 'the giant Turk thrust his bayonet into Graham's stomach but as the Turk lunged to finish the wounded man off one of Graham's mates blew the Turks brains out. The Turks simply became terrified and ran. No wonder! It was they who were being killed not us as we carried on hacking our way through the cactus hedges and simply killing or capturing any Turks who resisted'.

Before dark, Idriess claimed: 'Our squadron penetrated through the thinnest wall of the cactus and with the New Zealanders advanced right to the suburbs of the town. The New Zealanders reached a final trench rattling with rifle fire right up until the Light Horsemen jumped in. The Turks tried to meet steel with steel but the New Zealanders killed 32 of them before the rest fled'.

When these bloodthirsty New Zealanders got into the town, Idriess reported: 'Turks swarmed to counter attack yelling, "Allah! Allah! Finish

Australia" waving their steel pointed rifles and things looked desperate. Then men of the 7th Light Horse burst through the prickly pear reinforcing us. One horseman knelt down in the open, an officer leveled a Hotchkiss over his shoulder and blazed away, at the advancing Turks who fell in writhing masses sprayed by the Hotchkiss bullets or melted away under the added crossfire of the New Zealanders'.

The Light Horsemen were wary of the local Bedouins they captured — these nomadic tribesmen occasionally stole food, clothing, and equipment from their camps or from badly wounded troopers, and reported their movements to enemy Turks.

26 March, 6pm

By 6pm, it was common knowledge among the frontline troops that just as the mounted men had achieved great breakthroughs, the British infantry had — against all odds — finally reached Ali Muntar, fought their way up the slopes, and captured the Ali Muntar ridge. They had, well before dark, won their battle — unbeknown to the doubting Chetwode. At a price, however, as Henry Bostock wrote: 'The English and Scottish regiments were severely dealt with and suffered very heavy casualties — it was reported 6,000'.

The German commander also certainly knew. Faced by certain defeat, Kress von Kressenstein sent wireless messages to the Turkish reinforcements marching towards Gaza, ordering them to stop, and to his commander on the ground, Major Tiller, telling him to surrender. Tiller duly smashed all his communications equipment so the British could not use it.

But none of this great news got back to British Divisional HQ. The only news they had was from their aircraft feeding them partial information. The planes had earlier spotted those Turkish reinforcements on the march, but had not seen the enemy troops stopping a little later. So with out-of-date information, and despite the heroic achievements of the infantry and the breakthrough of Chauvel's men from the Desert Column, Chetwode (and Lieutenant-General Sir Charles Macpherson Dobell commanding the Eastern Force), who was only aware of all the problems, lost his nerve. To make matters worse, these jumpy generals also feared that the Turkish commander, Tala Bey, might call in more reinforcements in addition to the troops British planes had spotted form the air. These two remote commanders, Chetwode and Dobell, consequently panicked and ordered a total retreat of all forces.

They ordered the British infantry leader Major-General Dallas to retreat from his hard-won Ali Muntar ridge. Having won his battle, Dallas protested, in vain, as the generals did not believe he could have conquered the ridge. Dallas had to force his troops to go back down the ridge, stepping over the bloodied bodies of their mates who had been killed as they conquered that formidable high point. The generals also ordered Chauvel, by phone, to call off the attack, even though Chauvel protested that his mounted troops had now practically taken Gaza with many already in the town. But Chetwode and Dobell did not believe Chauvel's mounted men could have achieved success against such odds: entrenched Turkish defenders and the ring of prickly cactus plants protecting the old town. But these great Australian warriors had succeeded. It all came down to shocking communications between the frontline and backline generals.

Sadly, this was indeed premature panic, as it turned out, because even before nightfall, Tala Bey had advised his German superior that the British had won and so confirmed with Kress von Kressenstein the cancellation of

Turkish reinforcements. Tala Bey told Kress von Kressenstein he planned to surrender Gaza, now that he could see the mounted troops in the town and the British infantry conquering the high point Ali Muntar. In his mind, he had conceded defeat and was preparing to surrender his Gaza garrison to the British. Not realising this, the British generals feared their plan had failed and ordered all their troops to withdraw at dusk. Those remote generals did indeed snatch defeat from the jaws of victory.

Reluctantly, the distressed Chauvel ordered his subordinates — the New Zealand Mounted Rifles Brigade commander Chaytor and 2nd Light Horse Brigade commander Ryrie — to order their mounted men to retreat. Neither wanted to obey; in fact, Chaytor demanded the dispatch rider go back to Chauvel and get the order in writing! After all, that order could have been sent by English-speaking Turkish spies, he thought. These leaders did not want to retreat because most of their men had broken through the outer defences; many could see the town centre and reported it was now deserted. The Turks had given up, stopped defending Gaza, and many had fled.

But when Chetwode confirmed his order to retreat was indeed real, Chauvel angrily passed this order down through his subordinates from officer to disbelieving troopers, who all reluctantly accepted it. At the same time, Major-General Dallas had been ordered to halt his British infantry, even though they had already captured Ali Muntar and were now within striking distance of Gaza. Ion Idriess reported some Light Horsemen suspected the retirement order was an enemy trick, until it was repeatedly confirmed by their officers.

So with feelings of great resentment, frustration, and anger, all the forces retreated, going back to where they came from, and, well into the night, criticising the British generals who had lost the battle they had so painstakingly just won.

'It seemed the day had been won', Henry Bostock commented on this order, 'and both the Anzac Mounted Division and Imperial Divisions wondered why we were surrendering particularly as a motor dispatch rider had just reported that Gaza had fallen!'

Brigadier-General Ryrie was not going quickly, though: 'I told the Heads I would not leave till all of my men are accounted for and I had a very anxious time for about three or four hours when we got the orders to withdraw — much to our surprise — because we thought we had taken the Gaza and by then it was getting dark'.

Astounded at what was happening, Henry Bostock noted: 'We were still holding out in Gaza when retirement was ordered! Yet we had no options and commenced to withdraw at midnight'. Not that this retreat would be easy either, as 'the enemy were still on all sides of us except one small outlet which we rushed and retired under rifle and gunfire at the double'.

Stanley Parkes blamed the British infantry: 'We had got into Gaza ourselves fighting in different stunts but the Tommies took so long to break through it slowed down the taking of Gaza'. Even retreating was an ordeal for Parkes: 'Having been on the go all night we were by then very tired. No sleep, hungry, and our poor horses were also hungry and thirsty. So we retired from 2.00am and at 4.45am ran into a party of Turks in a gully so galloped for miles with bullets flying everywhere and also shrapnel until we got out of their range. We were extremely lucky. But if the full Anzac Mounted Division had attacked Gaza using all of our units we would have taken it'.

Some officers did not believe the order to retreat. Henry Bostock said, 'I told an officer at 2 am that we were retreating and pointed out the direction for our retreat. But because I had no written order he refused point blank. So I showed him my Scout badge and numerals and after explaining the reasons he finally believed I was fair dinkum so reluctantly agreed to retire'. At least the retreating Allies would get away from 'enemy aeroplanes dropping bombs on us', as Bostock wrote, 'although to little effect as far as I know'. It was just as well they also had the protection of the newly formed armoured car unit, because pursuing Turks fired at them through the night.

As they were retreating, Ion Idriess reported, some of the mounted men were nevertheless pleased to be leaving Gaza that night because, out of the blue, or rather out of the black, as night fell they got the fright of their lives when they heard 'blood-curdling screams' — not from dying Turks among the cactus, but from scavenging hyenas that had come into Gaza from the hills: 'That was an awful night. It was our third successive night without sleep too and our days had been busy too and under continuous excitement. So that frightful scream, that suddenly pierced the air in a vibrating crescendo ringing through the cactus hedges terrified one and all. Sleepers sprang erect their hair on end. My hands clenched the rifle. It was heart-choking seconds before I could breathe. Hyenas! We knew no man even in agony could make that frightful sound'.

This retreat may not have been as long as Napoleon's infamous 1812 retreat from Russia, a century earlier, but for Brigadier-General Ryrie it still had its epic moments: 'It was very dark and we had 18 miles [barely 30 kilometres] of enemy country to ride through where big Turkish forces could cut us off at any moment. Three of my officers guided our column and I think it was a wonderful piece of work as it was difficult country, no roads, and quite dark and to go wrong meant disaster'. Sleep-deprived, many of the retreating riders fell asleep or just hallucinated in their saddles as the horses followed each other back to base. 'I think it is one of the longest nights I have ever put in and it was hard to keep awake as it was my second night without sleep', Ryrie recorded. 'I wish I could draw all the funny things I kept seeing. In the dark the men on their horse ahead of me looked to be riding huge buffaloes as big as elephants with enormous tails.'

Ion Idriess was also hallucinating: 'Everything seemed to dream away to nothing the steaming smell of the horses, the murmur of the gun wheels, the sway of a comrade's body on either side, the pressure of the horses belly against my legs, became part of me, all one with the night. The liveliest parts of us all — something within me insisted — were the bodies of our dead strapped to the limbers. The crash of the shells that was really only in my mind vanished; the terrified eyes of a man and the clash of steel, the cackle of a hyena and the howls of a jackal and the cries of our wounded men among those cactus pears faded away. The strangest feeling of peace then filled me as I swayed sleeping in the saddle. I could see all of our thousands of men at once and all their dear patient horses'.

During the retreat, Henry Bostock, who was still mounted, reported he 'felt a thud' when one of the horses he was holding, for his comrade Bob Louden, who had dismounted, 'was shot in the neck several inches from my knee. The bullet had hit an artery

Although it would be a rough ride, two wounded troopers could be carried from the battlefield in a camel ambulance like this one, which is being led by a local recruited to mind the camels till they were needed.

and blood squirted out as thick as a finger. I galloped with the weakening horse to cover. With blood still squirting from the horse's neck so I tried to stop it by inserting my finger in the hole but to no avail. Just then an 8th Light Horseman was killed for Bob took the dead man's horse, swapping his saddle from his wounded horse to the dead man's and we escaped, later delivering the bleeding horse to the veterinary sergeant and we all wished that gallant horse good luck'.

The wounded horse had more chance than some of those retreating, as Henry Bostock reported: 'In the pitch dark we lost one of our men, "Bullocky" May from the 9th Regiment who just disappeared'. Although months later, much to Henry Bostock's surprise, 'We got a postcard from him as a prisoner of war and he explained that in the dark his horse had fallen into a large hole and the following Turks grabbed him before he could clamber out. I suspected it was "Bullocky's" loud bad language which attracted the Turks as he had been a bullock driver in outback South Australia'.

27 March

As 'the Heads' expected a counterattack, an exhausted Henry Bostock reported: 'The Mounted Division took up a new frontline position and started to dig shallow trenches. We had no tools to dig with only bayonets and hands which was much harder in this hard ground than back in the Sinai where there was soft sand. But the counter attack never came in our position anyway'.

Unbelievably, the next morning, with the exhausted infantry still close enough to give it a go, Lieutenant-General Dobell — who was a long way back at Divisional Headquarters — tried to make amends. He told Major-General Dallas, who was still down on the ground with his troops, that he had had second thoughts and realised it had been a mistake to retire, so he asked Dallas to resume the battle with his infantry, exhausted though they were, ordering them to take Ali Muntar again. But this was a mistake. It was too late (and Dobell should have known this), as the clever Turks — who could not believe their luck when the British retreated after winning the battle — had by then changed their minds and ordered those 4,000 reinforcements to come and defend Gaza. So this fresh British attack floundered, and many of the infantry were killed or wounded before they gave up and retreated during the day.

Trooper Lloyd Corliss commented on this failed new attack: 'The Turks got more reinforcements and counter attacked inflicting heavy losses on the British and capturing many prisoners. When our side tried to attack again later to take the position [Ali Muntar] we lost it three times and many more casualties occurred on both sides. Seven tanks were also used in the attack but were a failure and caused many men to become casualties by their slow travelling. The men had to linger too long on open ground to allow the tanks to keep up with them'.

The tanks were hopeless, Henry Bostock claimed: 'The tanks that went into battle with the infantry made no impression on the famous Ali-Muntar fortress. One tank got close to the Turkish trenches but was then destroyed remaining there with its crew inside. Other tanks did not get far at all. In fact we had 12,000 estimated casualties over the last four days. It was a great victory for the Turks and their first!'

28 March

By 28 March, the remnants of the beleaguered British infantry managed to withdraw from the outskirts of Gaza, their tails between their legs.

After the decisive victories at Romani, El Arish, Magdhaba, and Rafa, this First Battle of Gaza went down in the history of the desert campaign as one of the worst-led battles, plagued as it was by poor communications and generals too far from the action — even though the generals had wireless contact with each other and were by then talking to their pilots in the air by radio phone.

Ion Idriess considered Gaza 'a tough nut to crack' first time around, and when he started thinking about the next attack on Gaza, he said astutely: 'I hope its not going to become another Gallipoli all over again. Why on earth', he asked his diary, 'don't they mount all the troops and rush in and finish the war? Infantry fighting is too indecisive and one battalion lost eight hundred men out of eleven hundred'.

Their German masters had issued the Turks with 'a new style of bayonet, an awful looking thing, broad steel blades, the backs of them armed with a double row of edged teeth, frightful weapons,' Idriess reported. Yet, as a great champion of the charging bayonet-wielding Light Horse, he continued: 'Horses are better than foot soldiers because we galloped right into them and within a few short minutes the individual Turk was terrified, fighting for his life against our steel and he went down paralysed with horror at the madness of our rushes. Even their biggest men were like schoolboys against us when we got amongst them'.

Still puzzled, he concluded his account of First Gaza: 'We just cannot understand why our own Heads made us give Gaza back to the Turks'.

Murray, in his official report to British War Cabinet, played down the heart-breaking and unnecessary defeat, creating the impression that it had really been a victory and all he needed to do to finally capture Gaza was to rush back in. But by trying to look good, Murray ignored the massive Turkish reinforcements. He was also signing his own death warrant and would soon be dismissed for incompetence. Not surprisingly, the disappointed British prime minister and his impatient British War Cabinet ordered Murray and his desert forces to try, try, and try again to capture Gaza; they still wanted their armed forces to invade and conquer Palestine and then capture the jewel in the crown — Jerusalem — if possible, David Lloyd George was to say, by Christmas, 'as a Christmas present for the British people'.

But as Murray and his men would find out, Gaza was an even tougher nut to crack second time around, because the Turks would now be forewarned and so forearmed. So by stupidly retreating from victory at First Gaza (when the British had such a great advantage outnumbering the enemy two to one), many lives were lost for no gain, and then the second time around, even more so and also for no gain. It was all a case of bad military management.

Let's give Ion Idriess the last word on the battle. In early April, he wrote that the *Egyptian Gazette* was headlining its report of the First Gaza battle with the boast: 'Defeat of 20,000 Turks near Gaza' — much to his disgust. 'When we read such lies as this', he commented, 'how can we believe the news of our victories in France?'

5.
SECOND GAZA,
17–19 APRIL 1917

'THE NUTTY' BRITISH TANK LEADS HUNDREDS TO THEIR DEATH ON A SUICIDE MISSION

[Lieutenant-] General Dobell's scheme for the second battle of Gaza which was a plain frontal attack against the full strength of the Turkish position at Gaza commended itself neither to Chetwode not Chauvel the two most experienced leaders on the Front Line.

HENRY GULLETT, AUSTRALIA'S OFFICIAL CORRESPONDENT,
PALESTINE 1917

BACKGROUND TO THE BATTLE

Not long after the British generals had lost First Gaza through bad communication and jittery nerves, Britain's commander of the Egyptian Expeditionary Force, General Sir Archibald Murray, with the enthusiastic support of the British War Cabinet, renewed his attempt to capture this strategic Turkish coastal stronghold just three kilometres inland on the edge of the desert. But Murray had hoodwinked the British War Cabinet with his glowing report of First Gaza, which Charles Bean, Australia's official war correspondent, then based on the Western Front, said Murray described as 'a most successful operation' which 'has filled our troops with enthusiasm'; so the ill-advised Cabinet urged him to

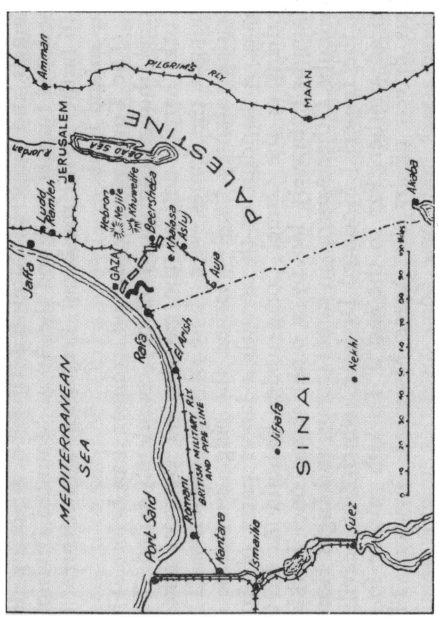

Although they failed in their first attempt to capture the strategic fortress town of Gaza, Britain's Egyptian Expeditionary Force had to try a second time — if they could not defeat the Turks in this coastal stronghold, they could not advance any further into Palestine. Despite their failure, in a turning-point battle, Lawrence of Arabia captured the Turkish port of Aqaba ['Akaba' on map] on the gulf of Aqaba, shown to the south of Palestine, near the end of the Sinai–Palestine border.

attack Gaza again and finish the job. But rather than being a successful operation, Second Gaza became a bloody mission impossible.

While the British casualties at First Gaza of 4,000 were reported accurately, Murray dishonestly inflated Turkish losses and trebled details of Turkish casualties, which, at 2,400, were actually lower than his own. Yet in reality, Gaza, although open and vulnerable on its west to the Mediterranean Sea coast, had a defensive fortress-style wall around its three landward sides: north, east, and south, right to the coast. So to attack successfully, the British forces had to get inside that defensive perimeter. Not only that, but to get through the defences from the east (their main point of attack), the invaders had to conquer the dominant Gaza high point of the dreaded Ali Muntar on a ridge towering above the eastern approaches — a ridge that had already claimed so many British infantry lives in First Gaza.

To help with the second attack on the well-fortified Gaza, British and French war ships stationed in the Mediterranean Sea were able to shell the Turkish town because it was so close to the coast.

Hoping the Turks would still have the inferior numbers they'd had for First Gaza, Murray's subordinate, Canadian commander of the Eastern

Force, Lieutenant-General Sir Charles Macpherson Dobell, who had also ill-advisedly aborted First Gaza, now prematurely planned this new attack as an old-fashioned, no-frills, direct frontal assault. He had no idea that the Turks knew the British would attack again, and had called in massive reinforcements and added to their fortifications, guns, and ammunition. Naively, Dobell and Murray believed they could capture Gaza if they hurled three infantry divisions at the Turkish defences, supported by the Imperial Mounted Division and the Imperial Camel Corps. As the official war correspondent assigned to Palestine, Henry Gullett, wrote later: 'This time it was to be a straight-out frontal attack by the infantry, with the Camels and Imperial Mounted Division attacking dismounted further east and the Anzac Mounted Division still farther to the south-east, just keeping away any threat to the inland flank'.

Unbelievably, the Anzac Mounted Division was not going to play a central role in this bigger battle, despite their having performed so well at the battles of Romani, Magdhaba, Rafa, and First Gaza. Instead, Chauvel was simply ordered to block any more Turkish reinforcements that might travel up the road from Beersheba in the south-east to help their comrades in Gaza. As Chauvel's most gung-ho trooper, Ion Idriess, 5th Regiment, wrote resentfully after Second Gaza failed: 'They wouldn't let us gallop in as mounted troops and finish this battle — all because some English general wanted the honour of taking Gaza by infantry!'

Although Dobell's simplistic strategy did not impress the more sophisticated generals, Chetwode and Chauvel, unfortunately Murray — back in his luxury hotel in Cairo — authorised Dobell to proceed. Yet it was doomed from the start, because the Turks had not only strengthened their fortifications, brought in more weapons after First Gaza, and marched in thousands more troops, they had also obtained the latest German fighter planes with a new arsenal of deadly bombs — all ready and waiting for this obvious British attack. Once again, thousands of lives would be wasted because of shocking leadership — stupid decisions by incompetent British generals — the same ones who had withdrawn from First Gaza when victory was imminent. Idriess moaned: 'Turkish reinforcements are pouring into Gaza day and night. And to think that one little Light Horse brigade and one little New Zealand brigade had galloped right into the back doors of the town and driven the Turks to their very mosque, three weeks earlier!'

Nevertheless, once again the battle-weary British infantry would try to assault Ali Muntar, even though it was a heavily fortified highpoint and their approach would be on exposed open ground. Not surprisingly, they would suffer many casualties failing to capture this strong point, which was still littered with the bodies of their comrades who had been killed on the bare slopes a few weeks earlier.

As it turned out, the Light Horse were lucky not to be supporting the British infantry during their advance over open plains, as they would also have had many casualties. Even so, the 10th Light Horse, which was closely involved in this attack, did suffer greatly. Gallipoli had been bad enough — many of their troopers had been killed in the insane dismounted charge at the Nek, which had also taken place in broad daylight — but even here at Second Gaza, the 10th would lose half its strength, either killed or wounded.

The only breakthroughs they would manage this time were temporary and cost many lives. The infantry with the Camel Corps, which included some Australians, would capture only a single redoubt, and the Imperial Mounted Division, which also included Australian troopers, and Light Horsemen would capture another. Chauvel's division would also succeed in blocking reinforcements from Beersheba in the south-east — defeating enemy units such as the 3rd Turkish Cavalry Division in the process.

But overall, the Turks would easily defeat the British forces attacking Gaza, killing or wounding thousands. The British gained no territory at all, confirming the stupidity of Dobell's frontal attack during broad daylight. Having snatched defeat from victory at First Gaza, the British generals had now rubbed salt in the wound by confirming that defeat at Second Gaza, and at the cost of many more wasted lives.

It may have been a curiosity for these troopers afterwards, but one of the great disappointments in the second battle for Gaza was the failure of the 'newfangled' British tank, known as the Nutty, which travelled too slowly, got bogged, was shot to pieces, and eventually exploded, killing the crew trapped inside.

THE SECOND BATTLE OF GAZA

The ill-fated Second Battle of Gaza was fought between 17 and 19 April, although preparatory troop movements and artillery shelling started some days earlier.

Backed up by Murray, Lieutenant-General Dobell prepared to launch his frontal assault. Murray and Dobell believed they could succeed if they had enough men — three British infantry divisions (52nd, 53rd, and 54th), the Imperial Mounted Division, and Imperial Camel Corps, with Chauvel's Anzac Mounted Division just hanging back on the south-eastern side of Gaza to stop Turkish reinforcements from Beersheba. The British forces would, in fact, outnumber the Turks by two to one. They had even been reinforced by troops from their European Allies, France and Italy. Dobell also reckoned he would have a big advantage because he planned to deploy a new weapon, the tank; he would have six of these machines. This was despite the fact that tanks had failed in battle that very month on the Western Front at Bullecourt, where they had become bogged, hindering Anglo-Australian forces, who were badly defeated in a battle that Australia's most decorated soldier, Harry Murray, described as, 'Murder! sheer bloody murder!'

Dobell also had new Hotchkiss light machine guns (replacing the old Lewis machine guns) to terrify the Turks. Thanks to the railway being extended by the British engineers from El Arish towards Gaza, Dobell was also able to take delivery of sixteen heavy guns to increase the firepower of his artillery brigades. They would complement the 92 guns he already had, including 18-pounders and 4.5-inch howitzers. This deadly arsenal should have been enough to blast the Turks to kingdom come.

But the Turks also possessed big guns, including 100 field guns, and had now built a 20-kilometre-long series of fortified outposts and strong points along the Beersheba-to-Gaza road, to stop mounted troops outflanking Gaza. This was like a new 'border' and also like the trench system on the Western Front, which had by now created a stalemate in Europe.

Unbeknown to the British, the Turks had reinforced their defenders dramatically during this period, with 18,000 men ready to repel any attack, and had also extended and improved their defences. So this second attack would be much more difficult than the first, especially now that the commander of Gaza's permanent garrison — General Kress von Kressenstein — knew the British would attack again and believed that he was effectively in the boxseat, with great aerial support from his own countrymen. Henry Bostock reported, days before the battle began: 'The German planes are very active and are bombing our horses and doing much damage which we cannot escape'.

James Williamson (who was a better signaller than speller) did escape, however, just before the battle, as he wrote to his girlfriend, Maude: 'I have been sent down to Alexandria to a special school in Telegraph work … I greatly enjoyed the train ride … leaving the desert behind us and entering the rich furtile country in the nile valley. It did my eyesight good to see the great fields of corn, oats, barley and coitton … as for the past 15 months Ive seen nothing but the worst that Egypt could offer — the desert.'

Even though these Light Horse troopers look relaxed in this posed photo in their camp, most of them were upset that the British leaders chose to use their infantry instead of the Light Horse in the Second Battle of Gaza.

13 April

Although the attack did not start officially till 19 April, the troopers had to be on the alert because of continuous enemy shelling, bombing, and isolated skirmishes. As early as 13 April, Idriess noted: 'There was thunderous bombing at the Gaza trenches last night. This is going to be just like the Gallipoli Peninsula all over again! Guns are muttering out in front and our mounted patrols are now clashing with the Turkish cavalry'.

14 April

'One big bomb ploughed right through a row of hospital tents', Idriess complained, 'but this was not Jacko's fault as some of our hospitals are located in amongst our ammunition dumps and artillery'. Then another bomb hit their camp, killing and wounding some of the local Egyptian

Labour Corps. Idriess wrote about the aftermath: 'there was smoke, earth and fragments of niggers — chaos then away across the plain stampeded the niggers followed by a convoy of lumbering camels — as these niggers always hung onto their camels'.

17 April

On 17 April, the preparations for the attack scheduled for 19 April escalated. The artillery batteries began shelling Gaza at 5.30am to 'soften up' the Turks. This bombardment was sent from artillery batteries on land and also from the sea into the open end of Gaza's three-sided fortress wall, which protected it from the land but not the sea. The French cruiser *Requin* and two Royal Navy monitors offshore fired a barrage of shells, although these caused little damage to the fortified earthworks or town. The British infantry then attacked at 7.15am, led by the 52nd and 54th Divisions, which approached Gaza across Mansura Ridge, sadly on open ground and in view of the enemy. They continued to edge forward towards Gaza and were closer by nightfall.

At last came the long-awaited order for Idriess, who said: 'We are marching out tonight — for a fight'. Thus the pre-battle plan got into gear on 17 April 1917 with men taking up positions in preparation for the fight, including the Desert Column, which moved into position at 2am.

Trooper Arthur Adams noted in his diary: 'General Action. I am in charge of the led horses. Getting the horses ready, watering them grazing them on the plentiful barley. We are reserves for the 3rd Brigade. Moved out to the outposts. Everything went off well today'.

Trooper Charles Pointon confirmed: 'The bombardment commenced at 05.30. We marched up into position and camped in the afternoon'.

18 April

Despite opposition from the Turks, on the 18th, the British infantry crept forward towards Gaza to get into position for the attack scheduled for the next day. Their first objective was to clear the area south of Ali Muntar of Turkish outposts, and to secure a start line for their main assault on that strong point, which they hoped to capture before consolidating their position the following day, and then moving into Gaza itself. Chetwode's two mounted divisions also moved into position.

The battle proper may not have started, but it was still dangerous. 'We moved out in the early daylight', Arthur Adams wrote, 'just had enough time to make a cup of cocoa. Snipers were giving us trouble with shrapnel also bursting over our heads. Moved out mounted at 12 midnight to a certain spot, dismounted, handed horses over to the handler and waited for dawn'.

Charles Pointon noted in his diary that, 'Our Regiment was camped just short of Gaza. We got ready to move forward in support of attacking infantry. After dark we moved up into position. Stayed awake all night waiting for order to advance'.

Idriess wrote: 'At about 7.30 pm our brigade filed out. Right across the plain we could hear the dull rumble of artillery, the murmuring of thousands of hooves, the tramp, tramp, tramp of marching columns, shouted commands. We filed past innumerable campfires then out beyond the outposts on our cold and sleepless night ride into the land of the Turk'. But it would not be much fun as 'we are not in this battle at all', he complained, adding on a lighter note: 'I watched a lark for quite a long time: he fluttered far, far up into the air singing almost joyously'.

This attack would be dominated by the infantry. The foot soldiers would, however, be aided — for the first time — by those six heavy Mark I tanks, plus 4,000 shells containing poison gas. But they were going to face challenging obstacles — the Turks had extended their formidable garrison defences south-east along the road to Beersheba so much that it would make any frontal attack very dangerous indeed.

19 April, pre-dawn

The attack proper began at 5.30am, when the British and French warships renewed their bombardment from the sea, targeting the centre of Gaza.

The British artillery also opened up from their land batteries, directed towards Ali Muntar. But these barrages did not silence the Turkish artillery. Nevertheless, at 7.30am, the British infantry moved forward in a big semi-circle, closing in on Gaza from the south and the east. It was indeed a large force, which included the 52nd, 53rd, and 54th Divisions together with the Camel Brigade, 3rd and 4th Light Horse Brigades, and the 5th Mounted Brigade; the Anzac Mounted was on the extreme right, to the east.

The attacking forces began to creep bravely forward during the morning, but before long they were being shot to pieces by the Turks; the attackers were out in the open, on bare ground with no cover. They were sitting ducks for the Turks shooting at them from Gaza's high ground. Trooper J.E. 'Chook' Fowler, of the 12th Light Horse, complained in a letter home: 'Many times we had to jump away from the nose caps of shells speeding along the hard surface of the ground, like a cricket ball hit at terrific speed, but I didn't see anyone try to stop them'.

Having been awake all night, Charles Pointon and his comrades came across patrolling enemy troops. He wrote: 'Action commenced 05.15. We drove the Turks back about a mile until they stood their ground and dug in new trenches. Our squadron casualties were 6 killed and 33 wounded but the regiment suffered 65 casualties. We took 62 prisoners'.

By around 9.30, when the Turks counterattacked, pushing back some of the attackers, the invading forces realised they were up against great odds.

The mounted forces then followed the infantry. But apart from limited fighting, the Light Horse itself played a marginal role, as a resentful Ion Idriess complained: 'Our regiment was ordered to be in reserve all day, and with other brigades our job is to prevent the garrisons at Beersheba from sending more troops to attack our forces attempting to storm Gaza'. He could not understand why the 'Big Heads' would not let the Light Horse gallop in as mounted troops and get the thing over and done with — was it just because some English general wanted the honour of taking

Gaza by infantry? But he argued that 'infantry cannot fight any faster than they can march. Actually when fighting they cover distance practically at a snail's pace. And if they meet opposition in trenches they have to dig trenches themselves and end up going nowhere'.

They may have appeared colourful, but the Light Horse troopers suspected the Bedouins whenever they appeared out of the desert, because they were never sure whose side these mysterious nomads were really on.

Idriess was certainly right for this battle. Despite Dobell's new, bigger guns and superior troop numbers, it was carnage for the British infantry, who were decimated carrying out his simplistic and outdated frontal-assault plan. The infantry could hardly even get a foothold, let alone advance against the Turks in fortifications like Ali Muntar, because the enemy had entrenched in much bigger numbers since the successful British attack of a few weeks before. Dobell had hoped his artillery shells loaded with gas would soften up the Turkish defenders, but they failed to make any impact because the gas just kept evaporating. He also hoped his new tanks would make all the difference, but they also failed because, as Idriess — citing one example — revealed, they were unpredictable and unreliable. 'A tank called "The Nutty" waddled along to give a hand when men of the British infantry and Camel Brigade advanced to attack a Turkish redoubt', he explained. 'She fought to the very last but got the British and Australians annihilated as well as herself. In only minutes she was enveloped by bursting shells; the men following her on foot fell in swathes under the terrific machine-gun fire.'

Mind you, that was a very difficult redoubt, as Idriess explained: 'enclosed by barbed wire and surrounded in smoke the advancing men could only see the fortifications in patches between drifts in the smoke.

The men panted on until suddenly the tank began to wobble in circles like an antediluvian monster shot through the stomach'. Then, after some of the infantry managed to take aim and fire at the startled Turks watching from the redoubt ahead, 'The tank righted itself, and under a tornado of shells again clanked straight for the redoubt. So inspired by this the Tommies and Australians fixed their bayonets and charged screaming towards the redoubt through clouds of smoke. The tank rolled on with her shell-pierced machinery, grating, and shrieking, fumes sizzling out from the shell holes in her sides. But it was a terrible charge. In the last few yards the struggling monster grew red hot and belched dense clouds of smoke but whoever was left of her crew had fastened the steering gear so that the great thing clanked on tearing up rows of barbed wire until it reached the very centre of the redoubt and burst into flames'.

Nevertheless, Idriess continued: 'The Turks who had lost their nerve at the blazing tank groaning upon them fled when they saw the glint of steel as 30 Australians and 20 British infantry maniacs broke into the enemy redoubt — all of them mad-men. No less than six hundred Turks fled'. These 'mad-men' who had followed 'The Nutty', and who were led by a 32-year-old Queenslander, Captain A. Campbell, then picked off some of the retreating Turks, took some prisoners, and secured the redoubt, at least for the moment. They then fought on with their machine guns and rifles, hoping to advance further up the slope, but there were too many enemy soldiers, and the Turks had many more big guns too, so Campbell and his madmen could get no further into Gaza itself. Capturing the redoubt had been a great moment for the British, but before long, the Turks counter-attacked even more fiercely and — with the tank out of action — the position in the redoubt was hopeless. So after fierce fighting that left many of the attackers dead or wounded, Campbell had to abandon the hard-won redoubt by mid-afternoon and retreat. He made it back to his own lines, but of the 102 men in his company he was one of only five survivors — so much for Dobell's full-frontal daylight attacks supported by tanks and gas shells!

In his post-war book, *Anzac to Amiens* (1946), official correspondent Charles Bean summed up: 'A handful of infantry with a larger party of Australians of the Camel Corps under Captain A.E.G. Campbell bravely led by a tank did seize one Turkish redoubt. And other Australian camel troops and Light Horse of the Imperial Mounted Division (which lost heavily) managed to seize another'.

The price for this second go at Gaza was proving insanely high and even the generals must have realised their mistake by now. Idriess blamed the tanks for that debacle: 'We, but especially the infantry, expected great things of the tanks. Well the tanks may do great things in France, but they are death traps to us here'.

Trooper Lloyd Corliss added: 'When our side attacked Gaza again we used six tanks in our attack but they were a failure and caused many men advancing with them to become casualties because these tanks travelled so slowly. The men had to linger too long in the open ground waiting for the tanks to catch up with them'.

Arthur Adams, who was wounded and lucky not to be killed, headed his diary entry for 19 April 1917 with the words 'Attack on Gaza'. He said they 'Moved out over the fields of barley, were showered with shrapnel with bullets flying past very thick. Foley was the first man hit. I helped him get up. It was HELL. Men were being knocked down all around me. I got hit in three places myself at 8am. Not many of our troops were left. The enemy was very strong. I made it back to the Australian Hospital tent. Was given a brandy'.

It was certainly hell for Trooper Vince Connolly of Coffs Harbour, New South Wales, who was shot through the throat and left to die on the battlefield. His mate Keith Booth Halloran, who served in the Camel Corps and was promoted to sergeant in the 4th Light Horse Brigade, explained what happened later: 'The 4th Light Horse were advancing towards a rocky outcrop. Unknown to them the Turks were behind that outcrop anticipating their advance in that direction. Nearing the outcrop of rocks the Turkish soldiers opened fire. Caught by surprise some of the

Light Horsemen were sitting ducks and were killed outright by the well-concealed Turks, before the main body of Light Horsemen retreated to cover some distance in the rear.

'Connolly's horse was shot dead from under him and he was stranded in no man's land so all he could do from a lying position was open fire from where he was stranded. But within a few minutes he was shot through the throat. The bullet entered at the base of his ear lobe and made its exit at the very same place on the other side.'

'I was doomed,' Connolly himself added later, 'with blood spurting out from either side of my throat I knew all I could do was keep firing at the enemy. As I was losing consciousness, my last thoughts were, what a God forsaken place for my life to end. But I became conscious a couple of days later in a hospital tent and could not believe how lucky I was to have survived and how I had been rescued. Our troops had fought the troops off so were able to rescue those of us wounded. So I had indeed cheated death.'

Unfortunately, some of those wounded in the attack were hit by 'friendly fire'. Henry Bostock reported: 'After riding all night to get to the battlefield and dodging bullets from our *own* outposts who were firing at us in the dark we eventually reached our new positions. Our artillery bombardment started at sunrise on the 19th April and the engagements started soon after'.

The attack on Gaza was indeed a suicidal advance. 'There was very heavy battle all day but we were on bare flat ground with no cover', wrote Bostock. 'As the Turkish trenches were so well positioned we had no cover in our advance.' This desperate situation inspired some rash decisions, even by a hero, Hugo Throssell, who had won a Victoria Cross at Gallipoli. Bostock again: 'When B Squadron was lying pinned down on the ground, Lieutenant Throssell, V.C., told the Sergeant to order his troops to fix bayonets and charge over about 300 yards. But the Sergeant (I've forgotten his name) told Throssell not to be so bloody foolish and to go to hell'.

But Throssell (whose reputation had grown since he won the sole Light Horse VC at Gallipoli) must have been under great pressure himself because Bostock — a scout who served as a dispatch rider — said later on, 'After I delivered a message to Throssell after he had retired from that action, I noticed blood on his trousers and boots and so I said, "You have been shot in the leg Sir". "No" came the answer "I don't think so". But he had been shot in the calf of his leg and did not know it. That is how V.C.s is won I suppose'.

Idriess reported other skirmishes that achieved little: 'The brigade mounted hurriedly towards the Hareira redoubts where the 6th and 7th Light Horse opened fire on the garrisons. Heavy fighting rolled in thunderous waves right across to Gaza'. But by then, an unusually pessimistic Idriess did not think the British forces could defeat the newly strengthened Turks and invade Palestine any further, because the 'Turkish defences now stretch right across Palestine from the sea coast at Gaza to Beersheba'. As enemy planes were now dropping bombs everywhere, he speculated on this new form of warfare: 'God help the nation or rather the civilians who experience war without having protections against planes — they would be hell for the defenseless'.

Breakthroughs

Before the battle was over, the British attacking force only managed to achieve minor gains because of the complex and effective Turkish defensive lines generally, their new, bigger guns and planes, and especially the dominance of the Turkish defence from Ali Muntar.

The infantry was certainly unable to repeat its feat at First Gaza due to the improved Turkish artillery, as 3rd Light Horse Brigade trooper Henry Bostock wrote: 'The tremendous roar of guns indicated the Ali Muntar was under attack; but the enemy artillery fire was the heaviest we had ever experienced, with shrapnel and high explosives. In fact it was reported that the Turks now had 250 big guns in action'.

Even after hours of trying, and despite heroic efforts, the British infantry was never able to fight its way right up to the Turkish frontline. The 52nd Division did manage to capture Outpost Hill for a while on the way to the objective of Ali Muntar, but then the Turks counterattacked and the British lost it again. The 53rd Welsh Division briefly captured Samson's Ridge by a bloody bayonet assault, which cost them hundreds of casualties, before they too were forced back.

On the other hand, the Light Horse — mounted most of the time — performed well, and stopped reinforcements marching up from the Turkish base at Beersheba to join their comrades at Gaza.

Despite the challenges, Bostock reported: 'Our troops by short sharp rushes got to within striking distance until the heavy casualties made it impossible to go any further. Our 10th Light Horse lost 14 officers alone almost half the regular strength in other ranks killed or wounded. The 5th Brigade also suffered severe losses'.

Nevertheless, the Imperial Camel Corps, with the Imperial Mounted Division, stormed and briefly took several redoubts with their bayonets in their advance on another strongly held system of redoubts called Atawineh, which was also an objective. Before long, though, they too had to retreat.

The 8th Light Horse distinguished itself in a number of skirmishes to the east, where their job was to block Turks coming up from Beersheba on the road to Gaza. The 7th Light Horse, under Major-General J.D. Richardson, held off the Turks in a series of confrontations. Richardson wrote: 'The day was full of interest and the work was ideal for mounted troops. Few will forget the excitement of hanging on to positions for as long as possible in order to hold up the enemy's cavalry division. Our Regiment's casualties were not heavy because moving troops in shell formation present poor targets for either field or machine gun except at close range'.

Far to the east, a Turkish cavalry force was driven off by other troops of the Anzac Mounted Division. But these successes did not scratch the surface of the impenetrable Turkish defence — so much stronger than at First Gaza. Idriess had once boasted about the big guns the British had before First Gaza; now, he and the other troopers were overawed by the big guns the Turks were using. The Turkish guns stopped the infantry's advance in its tracks and also damaged the British artillery batteries trying to shell Gaza. Meanwhile, the latest German planes had a great advantage in the air.

Overall, the infantry — the main attacking force — failed miserably (and at great cost to lives) on its mission impossible to storm Ali Muntar, and retake Gaza. The troops could make little headway against well-sited Turkish redoubts, and the tanks and gas were both dismal failures. So the attack was called off, having gained no significant ground.

Trooper Colin Bull, writing home from 'a Tommie hospital' said, 'We got right into a hornets nest of machine guns and shrapnel and I reckon all those who got out alive should send off for a ticket in Tatts. All of our officers were knocked and most of the NCOs. I stopped a bullet in the fleshy part of the left leg and some shrapnel in the back but the bullets have been taken out and I am only waiting for the flesh to heal. Then I will be able to go back and give a little in return. I cannot tell you too much in this letter but I will be able to tell you when I get back home'. Sadly Bull was killed in the next battle at Beersheba.

Trooper Bruce McColl of the 12th Regiment — a country boy from New South Wales who was also wounded in the battle — managed to write home from hospital, much to the relief of his father who then wrote gratefully to the Ministry of Defence, 'We thank you for your three telegrams. We have also heard from Bruce who is in Cairo. He is doing well and writes in good heart. He says it is a good spell for him. The first he has had in two years fighting'. Fortunately, McColl recovered in time to charge with the 12th Regiment and capture Beersheba.

Retreat

Things had certainly gone badly, according to the arm's-length official correspondent Bean, who concluded later: 'The Turks were ready and stronger than before. The attack though continued all day completely failed. The Turks hardly noticed the gas shell — a German officer thought the fumes were those of a high explosive. The British infantry barely reached ... Ali Muntar'. In other words, Second Gaza was a disaster.

Lieutenant-General Charles Dobell, by the night of 19 April, could only see problems (as he had at First Gaza). It was getting dark, he feared his men and horses would run out of water, and he feared his artillery batteries would run out of shells (they had certainly fired off all of their gas shells) and the infantry would run out of bullets; which was actually true of the Turks, who were down to their last shells (although Dobell did not know this). He was also worried by reports of massive Allied casualties — an estimated 6,000 — and the collapsed morale of his men.

As Dobell could see no sign of let-up by the Turks, he felt justified in calling off the patently unsuccessful attack. At first, he just said he was postponing the attack till the next day; when he realised how badly his side had been defeated, though, he admitted defeat. That meant two straight victories to the Turks — Gaza round one (which the Turks won by mistake) and Gaza round two.

Like the retreat from First Gaza, this retreat was not only hard on men but also on horses, as Bostock reported: 'After delivering a message a Scout galloped off when a big H.E. shell landed and exploded with a big noise and a lot of black smoke right under his horse. We thought, "There goes poor old Mick". The horse kept galloping with its stomach hanging out the further he galloped the more his stomach fell out. He then fell, squealed loudly and kicked madly until someone rushed up and shot him. To our astonishment Mick crawled out from the smoke and dust untouched but badly shaken of course. After a couple of days in the field hospital he returned to the Scout Unit'.

Things were getting too hot for comfort, Bostock reported: 'Enemy aero planes bombed the brigade horses before sunset and did much damage. Also heavy howitzers got to us. We suffered much loss of life'. Bostock also had to look out for his own side's artillery during the retreat. 'We retired at Sunset under fire from both Turkish cavalry and also a few shells from our own British gunners but fortunately with no casualties,' Bostock wrote. 'I was up all night and went on patrol at 2am. We saw some Turks and shot some of their snipers. We had good sniping conditions ourselves but I only shot a camel. But when we Scouts were a long way out in front of the general line we often came under fire from our own Brigade. We would signal back desperately, "Scouts" and if they could read the signal that was O.K. but if not they would fire a few more shots at us'.

20 April

Arthur Adams, who had been wounded in three places, wrote: 'I arrived at the Casualty Clearing Station after a camel ride from 1am to 6am. My name and particulars taken. I was taken in an open truck train on a terrible ride. Arrived at El Arish, got wounds dressed and to bed at 2pm in a second Clearing Station. My wounds are very sore. I got inoculated again for Tetanus'.

Bostock was busy: 'I was on observation duty and well out in front again and a thin line of Turkish cavalry advanced towards us. So I had some good sniping again and on my second shot I dropped my man and as his mates just left him there I suppose the poor devil had died. After a few more casualties they all retired'.

Charles Pointon was pleased to be retiring from the flat, open, cover-less ground. Although British forces had been 'digging trenches for shelter', he could see all around him that the attacking troops had suffered casualties in the hundreds.

21 April

Wounded and impatient, Arthur Adams was disappointed to 'see many of my mates lined up' to leave the Casualty Clearing Station 'by cattle truck', saying, 'I missed out and have to stay but I may have to go tomorrow'.

In the aftermath of the British defeat, the German commander of Gaza, Kress von Kressenstein, favoured a counterattack against Murray. Fortunately for the British, he was overruled by the more cautious Turkish commander at Gaza, Djemal Pasha.

Back at their base, Bostock said the men and horses were eating properly again after a few days on short rations: 'we bought fruit, eggs to go with our tins of salt bully beef and large hard biscuits and we also found some good grazing for the horses. We seldom get stew and the only fresh meat we get is what we buy ourselves or steal'.

Having been given a day off, these scouts headed for the beach, 'and both men and horses had a good swim,' Bostock said.

Back at his base camp, Idriess confirmed that it was a disaster: 'We know now that the Second Battle of Gaza has meant a second hiding for us'. The 25,000 Turks must have their tails well up, he continued: 'Our infantry attacked Gaza, Sheikh Abbas and the Mansura Ridge with Lowland and Welsh Divisions going into action with 20,000 bayonets strong. But we hear there are few of the poor chaps left now — they suffered terrible casualties. Even the Light Horse Brigades, Cameleers and East Anglia Division troops were cut to pieces trying to break through the Turkish redoubt system between Atawineh redoubts and fortifications on Hareira'.

The fight had developed into a great battle, Idriess wrote, raging for miles. 'What in the hell happened to the infantry at Gaza?' he asked. 'For their mission was impossible. They took Sheikh Abbas Ridge but then were beaten back elsewhere. Every man from the Imperial Mounted Division and Camel Corps went to help them but were all beaten back. The Light Horse and New Zealanders helping lost fifty percent of their officers. The Yeomanry Brigades galloped almost to the fortifications and fought in a way that has made our crowd accept them as brothers.' Summing up Second Gaza, Idriess wrote that the mounted troops went into battle towards the end in many places, but 'when it was too late just as in the First Battle of Gaza'.

Major Thomas Darley of the 9th Light Horse Regiment spoke for many when this seasoned Boer War veteran noted in his diary after the battle: 'To say all ranks were disappointed at the failure of the attack hardly describes the feeling which existed — but that failure was not due to any lack of determination or bravery on the part of the troops engaged. The policy of passively allowing the enemy to build a long line of strong positions on ground previously taken by our own troops could never be understood but seemed to be a repetition of the mistakes made at Gallipoli!'

Idriess wrote admiringly that 'the Tommies were wonderful — wave after wave annihilated by machine gun fire but other waves came steadily on to be destroyed by the artillery blazing away at those tanks'. But a Turkish atrocity angered him: 'One of the Light Horsemen badly wounded was stripped of his clothing and bayoneted to death by the Turks!'

And there were other dangers, too, he wrote: 'Some of our chaps brought in some Staffordshire Yeomanry this morning. They had been lying out all night putting up a fight against Bedouins who were trying to cut their throats'.

Unnerved by the battle, James Williamson wrote to Maude: 'There has been a dust-up here since I wrote to you last. It was at Gaza where we met the Turks ... Nearly every letter I get now wants to know when I'm going to England or else Australia on furlough. Well it is not at all likely that I will leave here for many a long day and if I should go to England I don't think it is likely that I'll be tying myself up with a matrimonial knot. If I can't find her Ladyship in Australia I don't I think I'll import her. It's no good saying these things now. One of these days I'll lose my top piece and then I wont care where she comes from. We're having a beautiful day here, I don't think, sand and dust flying everywhere with flies in abundance and I feel like a piece of roast pork in the oven. Another summer here will send me balmy. Well Maude I have reached the end of my tether so will close.'

24 April

Although it was a disaster for most of the British forces, some Australians came out of Second Gaza well. A bushman from New South Wales, Major Thomas Bird, who had only recently been recommended for a decoration for capturing a Turkish general at Gaza and helping with the withdrawal, now received another citation, which would add weight to his superior's recommendation that he be awarded a DSO: 'On the night of the 19th/20th April Major Bird did very good work on the Outpost Line. Again on the 24th April owing to the skilful handling of his Squadron a troop of Turkish cavalry was captured in another action in which he took a leading role consistent with his good work since joining the A.I.F and serving with his Regiment at Gallipoli'.

AFTERMATH: HEADS ROLL

Summing up this disaster later, Bean wrote: 'The whole attack cost some 6,000 casualties, mainly in the infantry. The Turks were confirmed in their belief that they could hold southern Palestine, and accordingly strengthened their line there'. To win future battles now, the British would need a Herculean effort, or at least better leadership.

Idriess compared Second Gaza with the Western Front, although he had wrong information about total casualties: 'Officers from France say that in point of numbers engaged in the Second Battle of Gaza it has been one of the bloodiest in the whole war. We have lost 18,000 and gained nothing. I hope that estimate is incorrect for 18,000 is a terrible number of men for a little army like ours to lose. It would be a dreadful loss for a much larger army'. Murray, aware of the likely reaction in London to the attack's failure, quickly found a scapegoat and relieved Lieutenant-General Dobell of his command on 21 April. Too late, Murray now realised that his and Dobell's battle plan of a full-frontal attack in daylight never had a chance of succeeding.

Murray appointed the Desert Column cavalry general Sir Philip Chetwode, the English 7th Baronet, in place of the incompetent Dobell as commander of the Eastern Force (British infantry). He then put the Australian bushman Chauvel in charge of the Desert Column, which Chauvel organised into the Anzac Mounted Division, Australian Mounted Division (instead of Imperial Mounted Division), and a Yeomanry Division. But this 'window dressing' did not save Murray's skin.

In London, the War Cabinet was not pleased. One of its members said at the post-Second Gaza meeting in London, 'Gaza appears to be a second Gallipoli'. As this was Murray's second major blunder — and a bloody one at that — before long, these shocked political leaders took the opportunity to purge the high command: Murray was recalled to London.

Corporal Colin Bull, 12th Regiment, who managed to score two days leave in Cairo, made the most of it writing in his diary: 'Arrived midnight at Metropole Hotel. Went to the bank in morning, had a general look around, visited Abassia in the arvo. Met Belle Crawford. There was a dance on at the hotel that night. Had a splendid time. Won first prize in lottery and presented prize to best looking girl in the room'. Returning to reality just days later, he wrote, 'General attack all along the line. Heavy artillery bombardment then we charged across open plain. Many killed and wounded. I was wounded in leg and back myself. Brought to CCS railhead sent to CCS El Arish by cattle train. Arrived about 1AM. Tucker not too good.' Not long after discharge from hospital, Bull's last entry in his diary — 11 July 1917 — before being killed at Beersheba reads, 'Promoted to temporary Sergeant. To complete establishment posted to 4th Troop'.

While on leave in Alexandria at the end of April 1917, Sergeant James Williamson wrote to his sweetheart, Maude: 'There has been a good deal of heavy fighting going on lately out at Gaza, no doubt you have heard of it or seen it in the papers ... I'm nearly Stoney Broke already its as bad as being in prison as being in a city with an empty purse. Last Wednesday being Anzac day we were invited to some English peoples home where we had a great afternoon and enjoyed ourselves A1. All the Australian and New Zelanders [sic] in Alexandria went. The majority coming from the hospitals. About 80 to 100 were present. Well Maude I can't find anything else to write about, letter writing is one of my failings. Will try and do better next time. Best wishes and kindest Regards, Yours Sincerely Jim.'

On May 18 1917, Stan Grant of the 12th Regiment wrote to his father: 'You may be wondering how I fared in the big stunt. As it is now over a month since it took place I don't suppose there is any harm in giving you a little information. We were 7 days on the job altogether, although we were only in touch for about 3 days ... It was mostly night riding and we shifted our positions in a most bewildering fashion with our horses saddled all the time and practically no rest. You know the country here looks just like the Queensland Downs, but it has this difference, that it has deep washaways and creeks cut here and there, not noticeable at a distance, but very awkward at night. There is one main wadi, as they call them, and we attacked up this one after being bombed the day before by aeroplanes. I was a horseholder and was out of the main scrap, although we had an anxious time for the Turkish guns fired all the time to get the lead horses. We were galloping from place to place dodging shrapnel most of the time.

'We had one good raid ... and had been out on patrol all night ... when we were told to saddle up again. We were cantering most of the time, driving the Turkish cavalry in front of us, and pulled up 16 miles within the Turkish lines. My squadron went the furthest and the Captain had just given the order to attack when the call came to withdraw. It was just as well because they were 600 strong and we hardly had 50. Also the sun went down and we didn't know where they were and could have had a bad time ... They didn't have enough gumption to try and cut us off and we arrived home without any casualties barring a few horses shot. It was the only real light horse work we did. It was all rather enjoyable.'

Williamson had had enough of shelling, writing to Maude (who had recently posted him a pair of pyjamas): 'A couple of nights ago there was a terrific bombardment with artillery on our left by the "Tommies". It only lasted for a few minutes, but what happened in that few minutes is more than I can describe. The flashes from the guns lit the whole of the heavens up and the roars from the heavy guns were deafening. It is no wonder that the Germans, Turks and even our own men get demoralized and suffer from shell-shock with great shells like iron foundries bursting and exploding all around them, coming down as fast as raindrops.' He goes on: 'Sorry to say that your parcel has not arrived. Three mails have come in since you first advised me but I have had very bad luck with parcels, especially yours.'

June: Allenby replaces the dismissed Murray

In June, the War Cabinet took some dramatic political decisions. They appointed General Sir Edmund Allenby as the new British commander-in-chief to replace the disgraced Murray, who had approved Dobell's hopeless plans.

Once the brilliant General Sir Edmund Allenby, aka, 'The Bull', replaced the disgraced Murray as commander-in-chief of the Egyptian Expeditionary Force, they would start winning more battles at less cost, starting with the great charge at Beersheba.

Allenby had been serving on the Western Front, where he'd clashed with the commander-in-chief of the British Expeditionary Force, Sir Douglas Haig. A big, stubborn, energetic cavalryman who quickly earned the nickname 'The Bull', Allenby would bring some fresh ideas with him. The Bull's appointment would turn out to be a good move — Allenby would engineer a spectacular revival of the Egyptian Expeditionary Force's fortunes, managing a series of comprehensive British victories in Palestine that featured the Desert Column, now commanded by the more appropriate horseman Chauvel, in particular the Australian Light Horse.

For one thing, Allenby wanted to be near the action. As British headquarters had been at the Savoy Hotel in Cairo, Allenby announced: 'We're a bit too far from our work here. I'd like to get up closer where I can have a look at the enemy occasionally'. So he moved everything 240 kilometres nearer to the frontline. He then inspected everything from cookhouses to flying schools, visiting different units in his Rolls Royce staff car. Signallers warned of his whirlwind approach by transmitting a cryptic 'B.L.', for 'Bull Loose'.

The Australian bush poet, Andrew 'Banjo' Paterson, who was in charge of a Light Horse remount depot, wrote about 'a great, lonely figure of a man, riding silently in front of an obviously terrified staff'. Allenby, whose son was killed on the Western Front, told the poet: 'I am afraid I am becoming very hard to get on with. I want to get this war over and if anything goes wrong I lose my temper'.

To start with, Allenby formed all his mounted units into the Desert Mounted Corps under Chauvel to improve efficiency. Before long, the Australians in the Light Horse took to Allenby, and he took to these unruly but great fighting bushmen; having commanded a squadron of Australians in the Boer War, he knew how fast, fearless, and capable they were — all the qualities needed to drive the Turks back to Damascus.

But not long after he arrived, he hatched a secret plan that would make world history — and it was *not* to attack Gaza again.

Lawrence of Arabia

As well as Chauvel's outstanding Australians, Allenby also wanted to use the local Arab forces, who sought independence from the Ottoman Turks. Not long after his arrival, he announced he was keen to work with Lawrence of Arabia and help this British intelligence officer, who was leading the Arab Revolt against the Turks.

But Allenby wanted better communications with Lawrence. He selected an experienced aerial observer, a New South Wales countryman from the Tamworth region, James Traill, to fly missions for T.E. Lawrence. When General Allenby ordered the airman to report to his headquarters for new duties, Traill wrote later about how surprised he was to be introduced to the legendary Lawrence, who was with Allenby. Lawrence told Traill he needed an airman to fly back and forth between his moving desert camps and Allenby's headquarters, carrying messages, equipment, and supplies whenever Lawrence needed support. Recalling this conversation privately, Traill noted that he was 'amazed by Lawrence's magnetism and commanding presence yet at the same time this engaging leader seemed so easy going'.

When Lawrence of Arabia led the Arab Army to victory at the southern port fortress of Aqaba, he won the full support of General Allenby, and from then on the two worked closely together.

His work leading Feisal and the Arabs in sabotage missions against the Turks was so secretive that Lawrence wrote nothing down, and simply told Traill how to find his camp. Traill, himself an experienced aerial observer, wrote: 'Lawrence had the most extraordinary ability to impart his knowledge. The way he told me how to find his camp was like drawing a whole picture of a huge relief map showing the most minute amount of detail from the air. Lawrence did not forget to tell me anything!'

Apart from the challenges of aerial navigation based on landmarks, these flights turned out to be both long and hazardous, as Lawrence and his Arabs moved from camp to camp. Sometimes, Traill had to stay the night in the Arab camp, as it was too far back to base and he did not want to fly by night. One night, when a gale hit the camp unexpectedly, Traill had to leap up, rush out, and, with his fellow airman, and the pilot of his plane, Captain Peters, hold on to the plane for dear life to stop the light aircraft blowing away into the desert, never to be seen again! The contrast between the sand-based camel-riding nomadic Arabs in the camp and Traill's high-flying plane must have seemed astounding.

After many flights to Lawrence's camp, Traill realised Lawrence also had a good sense of humour. Having delivered two carrier pigeons on an earlier trip, for Lawrence to use for carrying messages back to Allenby's headquarters, Traill asked, 'How did you get on with the pigeons?' To which the mischievous Lawrence replied with a smile, 'Excellent — they made a delicious stew'.

Lawrence may have been able to harness the unpredictable Arabs for his Arab Revolt, including some nomadic Bedouins, and the British commander Murray had earlier issued orders to protect the Bedouins, but Ion Idriess had little time for what he called these 'treacherous creatures of the desert night'. In one of his mid-1917 entries, Idriess wrote: 'These people cut the throats of our wounded, they dig up our dead, they snipe us; they steal everything they can lay their hands on and they are the Turks best spies; in fact German and Turkish officers dressed in filthy Bedouin's rags are often undetected as they wander freely throughout our big camps'.

Even as he wrote, he said: 'There were 14 of us on guard to prevent the Bedouins robbing our precious stacks of grain; yet 200 of them rushed from all sides. While we were driving off one lot, 50 others appeared from behind the stacks ripping open the sacks and carrying off the grain as fast as they could bag it and run'.

July: Arabs capture Aqaba

The Light Horse got a boost to their morale when they heard Lawrence and his Arabs had taken the Turkish occupied port of Aqaba on the northern end of the Gulf of Aqaba, a waterway running off the Red Sea. Against extraordinary odds, this force captured Aqaba, with its well-armed Turkish garrison, in the most dramatic manner. They rode south from the inland across the Negev, one of the most inhospitable deserts in the world, and emerged unobserved behind the port's guns, which were fixed and pointing out to sea in the expectation of a naval attack. The Arabs were, as Lawrence later wrote, 'very fierce because the slaughter of their Arab women by the Turks just the day before had revealed a new and horrible side of warfare to them. So they brutally killed most of the Turks defending Aqaba leaving three hundred dead and dying scattered over the open valleys and only took one hundred and sixty prisoners many of them wounded'. Now Lawrence's Arab Army were a force to be reckoned with, especially when their blood was up, as they fought their parallel campaign towards Damascus at the same time as the Egyptian Expeditionary Force, including Australians, fought their way towards the same goal. The British forces took the coastal route north along the Mediterranean Sea, while Lawrence's Arabs fought more inland to the east, north from Aqaba, towards Maan, Petra, the Dead Sea, and Amman.

Despite what Idriess said, Australians in the Desert Column were pleased to hear that Lawrence had conquered Aqaba and was stepping up his parallel campaign on behalf of the Arabs to dismantle the Ottoman Empire. Their spirits were lifted when they heard his Aqaba conquest had enabled him to consolidate his command of the Arab Revolt, teaming up with Feisal, the most active son of King Hussein, Sharif of Mecca. Now the Light Horse had another mounted ally, one who was working outside the conventional military system and was on the move the whole time; and, surprisingly, one who also sought help from Australians from time to time.

By mid-year 1917, with Lawrence planning to blow up vital Turkish railway lines and trains with his untrained Arab forces (starting with the vital Hejaz railway lines), he was looking around for assistance. If he were to succeed in this sophisticated work of detonating explosives, his inexperienced Arabs would need some instruction from explosives experts — like those serving with the Desert Column. For training, Lawrence was assigned a well-recommended Australian sergeant-instructor named Charles Yells of the 3rd Machine Gun Squadron, who was commissioned to teach Lawrence's Arabs how to set up and then detonate explosives. In his apparently whimsical way, Lawrence nicknamed Yells 'Lewis' from the start, because of the Lewis machine gun the Australians used at the time.

'Lewis was an Australian, long thin and sinuous,' Lawrence wrote respectfully, 'his supple body lounging in unmilitary curves. His hard face, arched eyebrows and predatory nose set off the peculiarly Australian air of reckless willingness and capacity to do something very soon'. Lewis 'was an admirable man', Lawrence concluded, and with the help of an English comrade, Stokes, he soon taught the Arabs how to destroy the Turkish communication and transport lines. 'In a month without a common language, or interpreter, they got on good terms with their classes and taught them their weapons with reasonable precision.' Not only that, after their teaching was over, Lewis and Stokes volunteered to accompany Lawrence on the next raid to help them blow up their target near Mudowwara (even though neither instructor had ridden a camel before, nor travelled under the hot desert sun). Nevertheless, they certainly pulled their weight — once they derailed the Turkish train with their explosives, Lewis shot thirty Turks and Stokes twenty using their own machine guns, 'helping win the battle for which Allenby gave them a medal each', Lawrence reported.

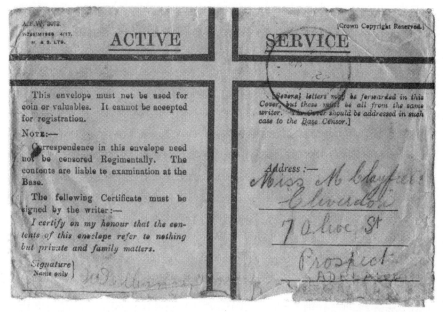

To maintain top security, the Australian Imperial Force ordered soldiers to use standard envelopes containing 'nothing but private and family matters' that they could censor — like this sample sent by James Williamson to his sweetheart Maude.

Writing to his sweetheart, Maude, Sergeant Williamson dropped a bombshell: 'There is great rumours afloat here that Russia is trying to cry "quits" and draw out. If they turn "dog" on us when victory is in sight they ought to be gassed, bombed or torpedoed. In fact the worst would be too good for them. All we can do is hope for the best and that the rumours are foundless.'

Williamson told Maude he was now a Dispatch Rider, warning her, 'a lot of Dispatch Riders in other units have come to grief. Parts of country are covered with disused trenches and one can't see till he is right on top especially when it is night time. I had my first smash yesterday when our division was out stirring "Jacko" up. I was travelling at a good speed when lo and behold I sighted three or four holes ahead and before I could shut off steam I hit the first hole, bounced into the air and landed into the second. That ended my day's outing — had to count myself out of action and retire to camp with a twisted wheel.'

September: Colonial forces overlooked

After so much hard and mostly successful fighting by his own Australian men, Chauvel was not happy with their treatment by the British. On 28 September 1917, Chauvel, who by this time had been promoted by Allenby to command the three mounted divisions of the Desert Mounted Corps, wrote to General Headquarters: 'The point is now that, during the period covered by Sir Archibald Murray's Dispatch of 1–3–17 [Battles of Rafa, First and Second Gaza], the Australian and New Zealand Troops (with the exception of the 5th Mounted [Yeomanry] Brigade and some Yeomanry Companies of the I.C.C.), were absolutely the only troops engaged with the enemy on this front and yet they now see that they have again only got a very small portion indeed of the hundreds of Honours and Rewards (including mentions in Dispatches) that have been granted. My Lists when commanding the A. & N.Z. Mounted Division, were modest ones under all the circumstances and in that perhaps I am partly to blame but, as you will see by attached list, a good many of my recommendations were cut out and in some cases those recommended for decorations were not even Mentioned in Dispatches'.

This British deceit was blatantly biased; especially as the Australians had fought so bravely and with such skill, and had sacrificed so many lives to help the British succeed with their objectives (lives so often sacrificed on the altar of stupid decisions by incompetent British generals). Thanks to Chauvel's protest, in time, the British would listen, and the Australians would be given more recognition for their great fighting.

Many Light Horsemen were also disillusioned with the way they had been used at Second Gaza. They now hoped for a chance to meet the famed Turkish cavalry. But after ambushing some small Light Horse patrols and being ambushed in return, the Turks avoided major clashes and retreated to their base at Beersheba.

From then on, for five months, the British and Turkish armies would face one another along a 50-kilometre line from Gaza on the coast to Beersheba in the inhospitable desert country between the Sinai and the Dead Sea. But so as not to waste a moment, the Light Horsemen researched and mapped the arid lands on the Beersheba flank — rolling brown country with eroded wadis, or creekbeds, somewhat like the Australian outback. They also manned lonely outposts around the clock, watching the Turks through field glasses, dug trenches, collected wood to boil their billies, and learned the position of every well and waterhole needed for their horses' and their own survival.

There were minor fights with the Turks, as 6th Regiment Trooper Dennis Rock writing from 'Somewhere in the Desert' told his sister Hope: 'A couple of days ago we went out on a bit of a stunt and had a bit of excitement before the day was over as the Jackos were sniping at us with shells fairly frequently and some were pretty close; going home we had to cross some open country and we went at the "igree" (Gypo for hurry) and a couple of our Troop got wounded but not seriously I think'.

17 September

Perhaps to compensate for their lack of official recognition in the honours list, Chauvel gave his men time off and encouraged sports and entertainment events like musical chairs performed by Light Horsemen — with a twist! It gave the great general some light relief as he wrote to his wife: 'I have never seen anything so funny as the musical chairs on camels'.

Meanwhile, Sergeant Hunter Edmunds, of the 1st Light Horse, who had been shopping while on leave in Port Said, continued his long distance courting of Hilda Reed, his girlfriend in Newcastle, New South Wales, who would become his wife, sending her a parcel and a business card from the Emporium of Mohamed Osman. Edmonds said: 'Dear Hilda, Hope you like this blouse material and also the Maltese lace'. In a follow-up letter he said: 'I enjoyed my three days in Cairo. I still have the camera & put most of my time in at different places taking snap shots. What do you think of this photo. Do you think it is anything like me, you will notice I am trying to cultivate a moustache. I hope you don't pull me to pieces too much when you comment on it … I am in the best of health but don't know when I will be able to write again as I hear our regiment is on the move again so will conclude with heaps of love from Hunter xxx'

Hilda may have been pleased to receive his gift and photo, and been looking forward to welcoming him home to Australia, but it was his mother who missed him most of all, poorly-educated though she was. Writing to her 'Loven son' from England, she said: ' I have been verry pooly and just feele as if I do not see you soon I will be passing off before I see you. I am just longing fore you and Dear you will have to try and get home fore a bit as you are wanted badly hear Dear. You know I am getting old and Daddy is failing to and I am fretting about not seeing you coming. Do try fore you are badlly wanted Dear. I cannot remember things and the paines is bad they are worce in my leg now and I cannot hardly hold the pen fore my fingers is so numb … am sending you a parcel and papers but there is no sweets to get and all papers and postage stamps is rissen up. Dear this is a very dollfull letter but I cannot help it fore it is just as I feele. I am under the Dockter and as been fore a good bit now so Dear tell me you are coming the next letter you rite ... Dear excuse this short letter but the papers will make up fore it so good Night and God Bless you and keep you all safe, from Mother to her loven son xxx Dear I hop you are liven neear to God and asking his to help you.'

Although he sustained a bad shrapnel wound at Romani and was pronounced dead by one surgeon, a second surgeon saved his life, enabling Hunter Edmunds (standing) to return to the Hunter Valley, New South Wales — still carrying some shrapnel — marry his sweetheart, Hilda, have a family, and live to 93.

Unfortunately, due to war rationing, Edmunds' mother said: 'I cannot get cholate so I have just sent wat I can get the things is a tabarill price the store manager will send you the toboco and sigs straight from the factry and they will come cheeper. I hope the Ginger cake will keep untill you geet it Dear. I am not getting the australian letters verry reglur fore it is taking a long time fore them to come Dear. I had a nice letter from Miss hilder Reed she is a nurse now I am keeping every letter I get from australia so there will not be any mistakes ... The nabours is sending their love to you so good Night and God Bless you and keepe you safe from mother to her loven son xx God is Love.'

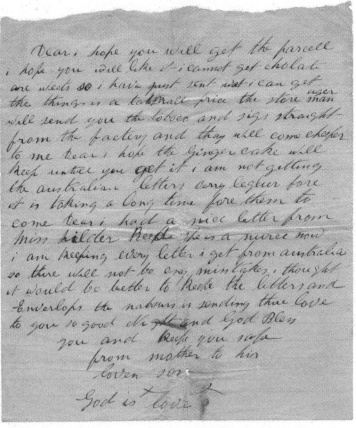

Light Horseman Hunter Edmunds would have been pleased to hear from his mother (bad speller though she was) that she had received a letter from the girl he would eventually marry — Hilda Reed.

Writing later to Hilda, Edmunds' mother said: 'Dear Girly i received letter and photo of you and was very proud to received it. Was begen to think i was not goin to get one from you. i told the girls it was not right them getting one but Florry just said Mother allways wants all the photos so wen i rite to hir i will tell her i have got one. Is it not a pittey all of my children is a long way from me. It make it bad wen you have just to rite ensted of goin to see them ... it makes the home lonly when thay have been and then go away again Dear. I often Wounder if Hunter will ever have the plesshure of bringing you to England to see yous all fore a trip. I think your mother would spare you for a wile and I know that Hunter would take grate care of you cumming across and then thay would be no fear of you when you did land hear. We are not verry fine people nore a grand home but you would fine it home so you quite know wat is before you if Hunter get safly landed, so good day and god Bless you and Keepe you safe Dear Girley from Mrs Erickson. All send their love.'

The British forces would need all the rest they could get before the next battle on their way north to Damascus. The Turks were now the winners and, after their victory at Second Gaza, Kress von Kressenstein was reinforced with two more divisions. By October 1917, his expanded Eighth Army was ready to defend any attacks by the British, with its headquarters at Hulayqat, north of Huj. At the same time, the EEF's numbers — which at full strength could have supported an advance to Jerusalem — were too reduced to risk mounting fresh attacks.

With the Turkish defences in Palestine suddenly looking so strong, and the British forces so weak, the march towards Damascus now looked impossible.

But rather than focus on far-off Damascus, let alone Jerusalem, or the elusive Gaza for that matter — all difficult nuts to crack — Allenby secretly switched his attention towards the Turkish stronghold of Beersheba, where he planned to fight the next major battle — a battle that would become enshrined as history's last great, successful cavalry charge.

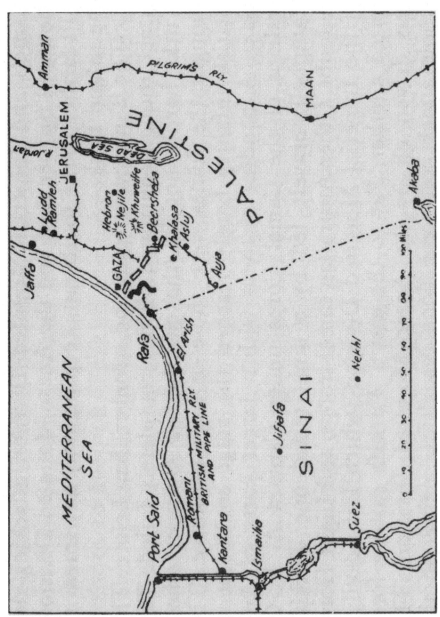

As the Egyptian Expeditionary Force had twice failed to capture Gaza near the coast, General Allenby now turned his attention to the inland Turkish stronghold of Beersheba, believing that a victory there would shatter the Turks' southern defence line, which stretched from Beersheba back to Gaza. So he set his mind to come through the back door. To fool the Turks, this cunning fox 'lost' a secret plan near Gaza that 'revealed' he was going to pretend to attack Beersheba, but in reality, he would be attacking Gaza for a third time — and this ruse worked.

6.
BEERSHEBA,
31 OCTOBER 1917

HISTORY'S LAST SUCCESSFUL CAVALRY CHARGE

The Light Horsemen knew well that the fate of the battle — and probably the campaign — depended on this charge at Beersheba; they also realized that, for the first time, Australian cavalry were actually to charge! For this time the Light Horse were to act purely as cavalry, although with only their bayonets as shock weapons.

CHARLES BEAN, OFFICIAL WAR CORRESPONDENT,
Anzac to Amiens, 1946

BACKGROUND TO THE BATTLE

The next major battle in which the Australian Light Horse fought — Beersheba — was a stunning victory that established the troopers and their wonderful horses as the best cavalry force in the world. It also became a turning point in the battle for Palestine, opening the door towards the final goal of Damascus; and since 1917, the battle has been enshrined in history, especially in Australia, where it is considered one of the nation's greatest military achievements.

It was also a great achievement of the new commander-in-chief of the Egyptian Expeditionary Force, Sir Edmund Allenby — a descendant of the 17th-century English Civil War leader Oliver Cromwell — who employed an exceptionally creative strategy he had devised while fighting in the Boer War, where he had learned great tricks to deceive the enemy. In South Africa, he was taught to 'inform' the enemy that he was about to attack from one side, but while they defended that side, he attacked with the advantage of surprise from the other side. In Palestine, Allenby also teamed up with a highly imaginative Cairo-based staff officer, Colonel Richard Meinertzhagen, a 39-year-old head of military intelligence who liked to employ Machiavellian tactics against the enemy. Meinertzhagen had already installed a radio receiver antenna on the tallest of the pyramids at Giza so he could intercept and decode messages from the Germans and Turks. Working with the receptive Allenby, who was open to all bright ideas, Meinertzhagen would achieve wonders in the coming battles.

As well as dodging enemy artillery shells, machine gun, and rifle fire, when they were charging across the open ground towards Beersheba, the 4th and 12th Light Horse Regiments had to ride their horses across the most uneven terrain, hoping their horses would not trip and fall, leaving them an easy target on the ground.

Allenby also had a highly skilled and experienced subordinate in Australia's Lieutenant-General Sir Harry Chauvel, the newly appointed commander of the Desert Mounted Corps. Chauvel now commanded nine brigades (of 1,500 men each), including four British, four Australian, and one New Zealander; along with two Australian mounted camel battalions (of 1,000 men each) and one British mounted camel battalion, not to mention all the supporting artillery. The Desert Mounted Corps was at that point history's largest mounted force.

Then there was Chauvel's man down on the ground, Brigadier-General William Grant, commander of the 4th Brigade. It was he who would lead the charge of the two regiments (of 500 horsemen each) at Beersheba — the 4th and the 12th (both from his 4th Brigade). Others, like Sir Philip Chetwode, commander of the XX British Army Corps infantry, also helped with his foot soldiers in the overall campaign of driving the Turks back up north before and after the Battle of Beersheba. The British heavy artillery that shelled the enemy in and around Beersheba before Allenby's forces attacked also softened up the Turkish resistance.

When the Desert Column commander, Lieutenant-General Sir Harry Chauvel, decided to charge Beersheba, he just said, 'Put Grant straight at them', thus ordering the 4th Brigade's Brigadier-General William Grant to order his 4th and 12th Regiments to charge. (AWM H00020)

Allenby was determined to sweep the Turks clean out of Beersheba. A hardened Western Front veteran, Allenby wanted to surprise the Turks when he attacked Beersheba, so his first move was to deceive them. Meinertzhagen and Allenby devised a very clever and secret trick, through which Allenby ordered a British officer to 'lose' some faked papers with false instructions for attacking Gaza again in October 1917, just to convince the Turks to prepare for this attack; and to thicken the plot, he put fake instructions in the lost saddle bag pretending he would mount a mock attack on Beersheba (included in these fake instructions was the explanation that this mock attack would deceive the Turks into thinking Allenby's main target was Beersheba, not Gaza!).

Apart from this and other creative strategies he developed with Meinertzhagen, Allenby also planned the battle from each point of the compass and in great detail. He organised a series of secret night marches in which the British infantry prepared to attack Beersheba from the west and south, while Chauvel's Desert Mounted Corps, with the Australian Light Horse, would sweep out wide to the waterless east and prepare to attack from the desert, from where they were least expected.

Allenby had to be smart to capture this stronghold in one day, because Beersheba contained wells that were the only source of water in the region, and vital for the parched Light Horse coming in from the eastern desert, not to mention thousands of other men and animals involved in the attack, all of whom would be desperately short of water by the end of that day.

Echoes of the Light Brigade

Allenby and his subordinates grew up hearing stories of Britain's infamous Charge of the Light Brigade, which had taken place just 63 years earlier, in 1854. This disastrous charge mounted during the Crimean War was one of Britain's darkest hours. Allenby, Chauvel, and Grant would have been determined not to make the same mistakes as the commander of the 1854 Light Brigade, Lord Lucan, and his subordinate in the field, Lord Cardigan, who led his men into the valley of death at the Battle of Balaclava (in today's Ukraine) where they came face to face with a wall of Russian canons from which the only escape was retreat under murderous fire.

Later immortalised in romantic fashion by Britain's poet laureate Lord Tennyson, the charge was a fiasco. Facing 5,240 Russian troops, which included both artillery batteries and riflemen, the Light Brigade suffered 245 casualties, of whom 118 were killed — out of a total of 673 cavalrymen. As Cardigan said later: 'When we were 50 yards from the mouth of the artillery which had been hurtling destruction upon us we were surrounded and encircled by a blaze of fire in addition to the fire of the riflemen upon our flanks. As we advanced further the oblique fire of the artillery poured upon our rear, so we had strong fire upon our front, our flank and our rear'.

Then when retreating, 'We had to run the same gauntlet and incur the same fire as we had encountered before'. So men and horses were killed, and many of the soldiers who had lost their horses were also shot down while trying to escape.

That disaster motivated Allenby and his subordinates to make this attack on Beersheba history's best charge of a light cavalry: a clear-cut victory and with as few casualties as possible.

It was to be the Australian Light Horse's role to make historical amends with that tragic 1854 charge. They nearly lost this opportunity, though, as Idriess revealed: 'We heard that a British yeomanry

The Light Horse troopers had to capture Beersheba by nightfall in order to get the badly needed water from the wells there, because they and their horses had gone for so long without water, travelling through the desert, and that was the only water for many miles.

General pleaded with Chauvel just before Beersheba for the honour of the charge to take the town. These Yeomanry could have succeeded as they are armed with long swords, a terrible weapon on horseback at close quarters whereas our Light Horse have no cavalry weapons at all'. But Chauvel refused their offer, selecting his mounted Australian horsemen instead of the British.

The planned Beersheba breakthrough

Their charge on Beersheba was part of the wider British offensive collectively known as the Third Battle of Gaza. Turkish forces still held the line from Gaza to Beersheba, about 46 kilometres to its south-east. The Allied forces, meanwhile, held the line of the Wadi Ghuzzer from its mouth to El Gamly in the east. The positions were not continuous trench lines but rather a succession of strong posts. Both sides kept their strength in front of the city of Gaza.

Beersheba had been developed over the centuries by the Ottoman Empire from a camel-trading centre on the northern edge of the Negev, halfway between the Mediterranean and the Dead Sea, and was now an important military post. Major Wilfred Kent Hughes of the 3rd Light Horse Brigade reported that, 'Many months before our troops arrived the town of Beersheba had been evacuated by the civilian population as it was regarded by the enemy as an important military post'. It was also on a minor railway line, which branched off a major line from Jerusalem, and so it was linked to the outside world. The capture of Beersheba would allow the subsequent advance to Jerusalem. Attacking it would be especially difficult as, when approaching Beersheba, the men and their horses had to traverse the desert sand at night as the terrain had limited cover. After watering for the last time, it would be 48 hours before the horses could drink water again. But Allenby believed the wells at Beersheba could contain 400,000 litres of water — if they had not been poisoned or blown up.

The military leaders hoped the capture of Beersheba would be the biggest breakthrough yet — and fortunately, as it turned out, it was. Their victory at Beersheba would give British forces control of a large collection of wells and the best supply of water in the area; it would break that previously impenetrable Ottoman line between Beersheba and Gaza, eventually enabling the capture of Gaza itself and then the long-awaited advance into Palestine. This would open the way to Jerusalem, which the British Prime Minister David Lloyd George had demanded be captured before 25 December as 'a Christmas present for the British people', who would be celebrating the birth of Christ, born in that same Holy Land.

This political request carried obvious overtones of the Christian Crusaders who in medieval times had fought in vain over Jerusalem, which was still in the hands of the Muslims whose mosques dominated this holy city. The feeling was that the British would strike a blow for Christianity by driving the Turks from the Holy Land, before going on to clear Jordan and Syria en route to Damascus.

But as we will see, this British-led EEF would not have succeeded in this overall quest without the Australian Light Horse, who would actually liberate this longed-for destination themselves — even though Lawrence of Arabia had demanded he and his Arabs liberate Damascus first, so they could take control and establish the Arab government the British had promised as a reward for the Arab Revolt. But in the end, the Australians would arrive at the final destination ahead of both Lawrence and Allenby, who had also planned to be first into Damascus so that he could take control of this heartland city and divide up the territorial spoils between the British and French — even though this meant breaking the British promise to Lawrence in the process. But it was at Beersheba that the Australians first demonstrated the remarkable skills that enabled them to reach the Damascus winning post first.

Preparations for battle

Allenby insisted that Beersheba be captured on the first day of operations, and he left nothing to chance. Even trooper Ion Idriess, who was stationed nearby, was impressed: 'General Allenby visited us. We all thought quite a lot of him coming out all this distance and seeing with his own eyes what is being done'. As Idriess explained: 'As our operations were now extending right away to Gaza — well everything was now on such a vast scale that we simply knew our Desert Men had to take Beersheba on the very first day, else the whole overall battle would be lost'.

After the Second Battle of Gaza, the mounted troops had spent the summer of

The victory at Beersheba was General Sir Edmund Allenby's first breakthrough in Palestine, and vindicated his clever strategy of tricking the Turks into thinking he would attack Gaza by planting false battle plans in their territory.

1917 in constant reconnaissance and in preparation for the offensive to come. These horsemen — especially the Australians — got to know the terrain backwards.

Having listened to his subordinates on arrival, Allenby built on the plans to attack Beersheba that had been developed by Chetwode. This was the plan to have mounted troops attack from the less-expected east, while Chetwode's infantry attacked Beersheba from the south-west. But Allenby created the great advantage of surprise by adding the trick of deceiving the Turks with those false plans to attack Gaza as the main event. This would be the opposite of that last big battle, when Dobell stupidly made a frontal attack on Gaza in broad daylight, even though the Turks knew they were coming. Various deceptions were employed to keep the enemy thinking the attack was going to be at Gaza, including keeping the infantry's main strength there until the last minute.

But as Chauvel was going to ride out into the desert, the greatest problem would be finding sufficient water east of the Beersheba area for his mounted troops. Information from reconnaissance revealed that there was none, other than at Esani, which was too far to the west to be of any use for a surprise attack. Chauvel, through studying the nineteenth-century records of the Palestine Exploration Fund and after questioning local Arabs, knew that the larger ancient towns in the area to the south and south-west of Beersheba must have had water supplies at some point. At Asluj, about 50 kilometres from Beersheba, the old wells were found, and a fortnight's work put them into working order. This made the attack on Beersheba a feasible operation.

Enemy opposition

Beersheba's strong and long-standing defences presented another big obstacle for Allenby. The town's Turkish commander, Ismet Bey, had at least 28 artillery field guns, nine machine guns, and two modern aircraft, as well as at least 4,400 men, including 1,000 experienced Turkish riflemen. Most worrying of all, Allenby feared the Turkish commander would ask his superior, Kress von Kressenstein, for more reinforcements. As it turned out, he would do just that, telling the German that Beersheba was being attacked by greater numbers than he could fight off. But fortunately, Kress von Kressenstein did not believe him and so refused. Thanks to the 'secret plans' a British officer 'lost' in Turkish territory, the German commander-in-chief believed to the last minute that Allenby's attack was just a pretence and that the real attack would be against Gaza.

At Beersheba, a series of trenches and redoubts placed in commanding positions had good zones of fire. But unbelievably, reconnaissance patrols reported that on the east and south the trenches were not protected by barbed wire. The Turkish forces on that side were solely relying on the forbidding open terrain, as well as the absence of water, to defend the town. They never dreamed horsemen could ride in out of the desert from the east. In any case, the Turks were convinced that the attack would be on Gaza and that any movements by British forces towards Beersheba were fake.

Chauvel's orders when he left the last water wells of Asluj, before the battle, were for Major-General Chaytor's Anzac Mounted Division to close the Beersheba Road at Sakati (almost 10 kilometres north-east of the town) in order to prevent Turkish reinforcements from coming in, and also to cut off any Turkish escape from the town as Chauvel — thinking ahead — wanted to take as many prisoners as he could once he had captured Beersheba.

29 October

One of those preparing for the battle was New South Wales bushman Guy Haydon, who wrote a letter home describing the uncertain build-up to the attack: 'We left our Camp at Tel-al-fara on the night of the 29th at 5 p.m. and marched to a place called Essani reaching there about 11 p.m. and camped there the night and all next day. About 3 p.m. an enemy Plane came along but was driven off by our planes. At 5 p.m. we moved off again and marched to Khalassa reaching there at 10.30 p.m. and camped. At 2 p.m. the following day the enemy plane again endeavoured to fly over our lines but was attacked by two of our Bristol Fighters and much to our satisfaction they succeeded in shooting her down with their machine guns.

'At 5 p.m. we were off again and marched all night and on until 9 a.m. next day when we halted in some broken country 4½ miles [7 kilometres] east of Beersheba. The previous instructions were that the mounted troops were to attack Beersheba at 10 a.m. and we all quite expected to do so as the infantry were due to attack on the other portions of their line at that time, but 10 a.m. came and went and nothing.'

30 October

But on the night of 30 October, about 40,000 Allied troops moved silently towards Beersheba, including most of Chetwode's XX Corps and Chauvel's Desert Mounted Corps, in a night march of over 40 kilometres. After trekking since 28 October via Esani, members of the 12th Light Horse Regiment (who would play a major role) arrived at Asluj on 30 October.

Lieutenant Philip Tod, a South Australian of the 9th Light Horse Regiment, wrote in his diary: 'It is the eve of my 22nd birthday and we have orders to set out on an all night ride in complete silence, even our stirrups and bridles are muffled. Rumour is we are to attack and capture the Wells of Beersheba'.

The author of the 12th Regiment's official diary, Eric Keith McGregor, confirmed the long hard ride just getting to Beersheba, writing: 'We left Assani at 5 a.m. rode all day arriving at Khalassa at night. In the morning we watered at wells as other supplies had been blown up by the enemy. We moved out that evening and rode all night. We halted a few miles N.E. of Beersheba behind some hills. Everybody anticipated our Regiment would bivouac here for the night but after a conference of the Generals it was decided for the 4th Brigade to attack Beersheba mounted. The 4th Regiment (A and B Squadrons) and 12th Regiment would lead the attack'.

One of these Light Horsemen, Corporal Harold Gleeson, who complained he got no water at Asluj, wrote that at 6pm on 30 October, he had to move on, parched with thirst, towards Beersheba, marching all night on a 'very weary and dusty ride of 30 miles [nearly 50 kilometres]'. Another, Private Hunter, wrote in his diary: 'The dust was terrible. One could not see beyond his horses head. The horses braved the journey which was about 36 miles [58 kilometres]'. But he said he kindly dismounted and 'Walked at my horses head for about 10 miles [16 kilometres] of flat country giving him a rest'. The horses were carrying heavy packs, on average of about 120 kilograms, and their riders knew that there was no water available until — and if — they captured Beersheba against the odds. The men were also half-starved, as Private Keddie added: 'On this stunt we have been told we would have to live on what rations we had for a few days'.

31 October, morning

But then the big day came, and from dawn on the morning of 31 October, as planned by Allenby, General Chetwode's corps bombarded the Turkish line west of Beersheba, while three British infantry divisions attacked and stormed the outer defensive Turkish positions around Beersheba from the west and south, supported by the sustained artillery bombardment of over 100 guns — to soften up the Turkish defenders (who still thought this was just the start of a fake attack by the British who were really attacking Gaza again). Later, Major Wilfred Kent Hughes of the 3rd Light Horse Brigade claimed this enabled the success of the cavalry charge, as although, 'the greater share of the honour and glory for the capture of Beersheba fell to the mounted forces who executed the most spectacular part of the fighting, it was in part due to the Infantry capturing the defensive works on the ridges to the south and the south east of the town on the early morning of the 31st October that the way was opened for the cavalry to rush the northern defences and thence onwards into the town'.

Chauvel established his command headquarters for the Battle of Beersheba about 6 kilometres away, to the south-west of the town on a high hill called Khashim Zanna, which gave good views of the battlefield.

31 October, 1pm

By 1pm, the British artillery and infantry had dislodged some of the besieged Turks from their defences to the west and south-west of Beersheba, but the forces in the main garrison of the town were still holding firm.

Meanwhile, some of the horsemen who would be the stars of the charge, the 4th Light Horse Brigade, waited to the south-east of the town, scattered over a wide area as a precaution against bombing. Private Hunter wrote later: 'The Turks immediately started shelling us with heavies. But good cover and tact on our part prevented casualties'. In order to rest them before the charge he said their horses were unsaddled, watered, and fed (with the little supplies their riders carried).

Then the 4th Brigade's commander, Brigadier-General Grant, told his water-short men that the wells of Beersheba were vital for the survival of the brigade, let alone the Desert Mounted Corps' horses, many of whom had been without water for days. He reminded them that the horses would be so keen to get to the water in the Beersheba wells that they would gallop fast towards the town.

31 October, 3.15pm

It was not until 3.15pm that units of the Desert Mounted Corps were able — en route to Beersheba — to defeat enemy forces strongly defending Tel el Saba, three kilometres to the east of Beersheba. It had taken a tough day's fighting to capture this redoubt protecting Beersheba's eastern flank. Once they got control of Tel el Saba, the 1st and 3rd Light Horse Brigades were free to get ready to attack Beersheba from the east. They could be told to charge at any moment because none of the troopers knew at that stage which brigade or regiments would be ordered to take part in the charge.

31 October, 3.30pm

With only a few hours of daylight remaining, and both horses and men desperately needing water, orders were issued at 3.30pm for the final phase of the struggle, the charge against Beersheba. It was then that Chauvel decided to order the nearest brigade, Grant's 4th Light Horse Brigade — with its three regiments: 4th (Victoria) 11th (Queensland) and 12th (New South Wales) — to charge Beersheba and defeat all the remaining Turks in the trenches who had not been driven away by Chetwode's British artillery barrages. Chauvel knew the best route would be the open path from the south and south-east, where there was no barbed wire. Chauvel also knew that he must take the town before dark to secure the wells for Allenby's large force.

31 October, 4.30pm

By 4.30pm, the two leading regiments of the 4th Brigade, the 4th and 12th, were assembled behind rising ground around seven kilometres south-east of Beersheba, ready to go. The 11th Regiment, mainly horsemen from Queensland but also some from South Australia, was standing close by in reserve. The official Australian World War I historian Charles Bean later wrote: 'The Light Horsemen knew well that the fate of the battle — and probably the campaign — depended on this charge; they also realized that, for the first time, Australian cavalry were actually to charge! For this time the Light Horse were to act purely as cavalry, although with only their bayonets as shock weapons'.

But even then the troopers did not know what was going to happen, as a disappointed Trooper Keddie reported: 'We began to talk among ourselves saying Beersheba will be taken by others without us doing anything — when suddenly about 5 o'clock our major came and said that Beersheba had not yet been captured and that we were the ones going in'. But as Chauvel himself later explained, it had taken a while to line up the horsemen for the planned charge, 'owing to the constant attacks from aeroplanes, which had devoted a good deal of attention to my own headquarters, it took some time to assemble them and push them off'.

31 October, 4.45pm

Then, at 4.45pm, Chauvel made up his mind, saying, 'Put Grant straight at them!', meaning that the commander of the 4th Brigade, Brigadier-General William Grant, had been selected to capture Beersheba with whichever regiments he chose. The long-awaited moment came when Grant gave the 4th Light Horse Regiment the order to charge, initially saying: 'Men you're fighting for water. There's no water between this side of Beersheba and Esani. Use your bayonets as swords. I wish you the best of luck'.

Equipped with rifles, the Light Horsemen would hold their bayonets as swords, which would have been more suited to a cavalry-style charge (the Light Horse was really mounted infantry rather than full cavalry). Of course, they were not real swords — long, thin, and razor sharp — but luckily Major-General Hodgson, who had commanded the Imperial Mounted Horsemen, had on 26 October ordered his men to sharpen their bayonet tips. Grant knew this, and he also understood the desperate need for water and that they were running out of time and had the advantage of surprise, so, on the spur of the moment, he decided to order his men to charge cavalry-style, staying on their horses when they would normally have ridden close to an objective then dismounted to fight. It was pretty impetuous and could have gone terribly wrong — as indeed it had in 1854.

A mounted charge at the gallop by Light Horsemen across four miles [6.4 kilometres] of open ground carrying only rifles with bayonets against entrenched infantry supported by artillery, machine guns, and planes dropping bombs in the sky — this had never been done before. It would be old-fashioned cavalry skills against deadly modern mechanised weapons.

But Chauvel and Grant both felt certain it would succeed. With the sun low in the sky, and many of the horses without water for nearly 48 hours, they had no other option. The sun would set at 4.50pm. So Grant ordered the 4th and 12th Regiments (approximately 1,000 men in total, 500 in each regiment) to form up behind a ridge, ready to move off on a classic, three-line charge formation, going from walk-march, to trot, then canter and gallop. These men would become the envy of troopers in the rest of the Australian Light Horsemen serving in the Middle East.

The battle

The troopers sat in their saddles in silence at their assembly point, about 6.4 kilometres south-east of Beersheba. The 4th Regiment of Victorians was led by Lieutenant-Colonel Murray Bourchier, and the 12th Regiment of New South Welshmen by Lieutenant-Colonel Donald Cameron, supported by a legendary officer and New South Wales pastoralist, Major Cuthbert Murchison Fetherstonhaugh. Meanwhile, the disappointed troopers of the 11th Regiment were told to just stand by in reserve — 'so near and yet so far', as one trooper complained later. As the evening shadows lengthened, they waited patiently for Grant's order to charge, their thirsty horses desperate for water.

Through their binoculars, the commanders could see Beersheba. Idriess, who as a member of the 5th Light Horse did not take part in the charge, nevertheless reported: 'Hiding in a depression behind the hills was Beersheba, the white dome and minaret of the great mosque and the railway station, barracks and numerous buildings, growing plainer to us'. In the extreme heat of the day, Idriess wrote that the men thought longingly 'of the cool wells of Beersheba, and by Jove I know I experienced a choking feeling of these senses on remembering that we *must* take those wells'.

The men knew their main objective was to capture this Turkish stronghold, the Yildirim Army Group garrison, with its vital water supplies. They also knew that the fate of their horses and the future of their Palestine campaign depended on their charge being successful, because if they won, it would be the real beginning of the Southern Palestine Offensive. They also had to get to that water in the wells at Beersheba before the Turks poisoned the wells, as they had often done before. The horses on which they depended for everything had not had any water for 48 hours — time was running out. They had to take those wells by nightfall before the horses started to die of thirst, and before any Turkish reinforcements crept in overnight. Allenby's orders from back behind the lines were clear: 'Take Beersheba before nightfall!'

After the charge, the Light Horsemen were lucky to reach the main well in the town of Beersheba in time — when the first troopers arrived, they captured a German officer who was about to detonate explosives that the enemy had planted in the wells to blow them up so they could not be used.

From the crest of the ridge in front of the hidden troopers, Beersheba was in full view. Luckily, the Turks could not see them — anyway, the Turks would have discounted the idea of a charge, especially from the east out of the desert. It was lucky, too, that their route lay down a long, slight slope that, although devoid of cover, was free of obstacles. Yet before the town, there were certainly some formidable enemy defences.

The Charge

Finally, Grant, mounted on his horse in front of the 800 horsemen, gave the order: 'Forward!' Immediately, the Light Horse leapt into action. As they rode off at a walk, the 4th was on the right; the 12th was on the left — all were riding with bayonets in hand, like swords. Within each regiment, the troopers were riding in a traditional squadron frontage (two squadrons wide and three lines deep but with spaces between them).

Captain Jack Davies then shouted at the top of his voice: 'Come on boys, Beersheba first stop!' The boys replied, 'You'll do us, Jack!' Then suddenly, the commanders of both the 4th and 12th realised that only a wild, desperate charge could seize Beersheba before dark. Although, as Bean wrote: 'Australians had never ridden any race like this'.

Yet Cameron, leading the 12th Regiment, said later, 'It was clear to me that the job had to be done before dark, so I advised galloping towards the place as our only chance. I had some experience of successful mounted surprise attacks on the Boer camps in the South African war.'

As soon as these charging horsemen came over the top of the ridge — which had been hiding them from the Turk's view — and were riding down the long slope towards the Turkish garrison and trenches, the enemy woke up and began shooting at them. It may have been frightening for some of the troopers, but as the battle-hardened Idriess wrote: 'I think all men get scared at times like these; but there comes a sort of laughing courage from deep within the heart of each, or from some source he never knew existed; and when he feels like that he will gallop into the most blinding death with an utterly unexplainable, don't care, shrieking laugh upon his lips'.

When they were only three kilometres from the first of the Turkish trenches, the Turkish machine-gunners started firing at them. But the Turks could not find their targets, as the Light Horse were still too far away, and the watchful British batteries were too accurate for the gunners and soon silenced most of them with great accuracy.

Thankfully, the brilliant British batteries had already weakened the enemy's resistance by long-range shelling the Turkish artillery earlier in the day, making it even harder for these enemy gunners to do much damage. The Royal Horse Artillery had worked out the distance between their batteries and the Turkish gunners, and had, with great accuracy, put many of them out of action.

Despite that earlier 'softening up', remaining Turkish machine gunners and infantry in trenches now increased their rifle fire as the Light Horse charged towards them. But the troopers' speed meant that the remaining Turkish artillery and machine gunners, as well as their riflemen, rarely hit their targets because the horse's pace was soon too fast for the gunners to

adjust their sights. For after breaking into a trot and spreading out to create five-metre spaces between each horse (to minimise casualties), the Light Horsemen began accelerating to a canter.

Then, 2.5 kilometres from the first Turkish trenches, Bourchier ordered his 4th Regiment to 'Charge!' So the Light Horsemen immediately spurred their horses from a canter into a gallop, yelling at the top of their voices, thrilled to be galloping at last full pelt for the enemy. The leading squadron on the left of the line was led by the brave Bourchier himself, who would shoot six Turks once he reached the trenches and had dismounted. All officers inspired their troopers. All the horsemen broke into a gallop within minutes, deploying at once

The Commander of the 4th Light Horse Regiment from Victoria, which led the charge at Beersheba, was Lieutenant-Colonel Murray Bourchier, who personally rode out in front, ordered his men to charge, and galloped off ahead towards Beersheba. (AWM HO1371)

into artillery formation. Seconds later, the lead squadrons galloped forward in a wide, breaking wave over the ridge and down the gentle slope towards Beersheba, where they saw, straight ahead, the Turkish trenches of the garrison spread out in front of the town. The leading squadron on the right of the line was led by Major James Lawson, who would be recommended for a Victoria Cross for fighting so hard in this battle.

Watching from a vantage point was Major Wilfred Kent Hughes of the 3rd Light Horse Brigade. He described the scene: 'As the horses advanced at a hard gallop a cloud of dust enveloped the arena through which the rearmost lines could be seen heading towards Beersheba until they too disappeared into the wall of dust over which could just be seen the minarets of the mosque thrown into relief by the setting sun. This golden reflection then turned to red, before the red faded into the grey mists of the night which rapidly enshrouded the field of battle ... In the still evening air the thick pall of dust hung listlessly over the plain, enfolding beneath its cloak the result of the fight, which we watchers on the hills waited eagerly to learn'.

By now, with only two kilometres to go, the remaining big Turkish guns were aiming and firing as the galloping Light Horsemen charged towards them. But as they had been caught by surprise, these remnants of Turkish artillery just sent random shrapnel high into the air. Because the horses were spread out widely rather than bunched up, the big guns could only hit a few of the horses.

Watching through binoculars, Idriess reported: 'We laughed with delight when the shells began bursting behind the men as that revealed the Turkish gunners could not keep their range, then suddenly the riders ceased to fall and we knew instinctively that the Turkish infantry, wild with excitement and fear had forgotten to lower their rifle sights and the bullets were flying overhead'.

'Next came the rifle fire from the Turkish trenches,' Bean picked up the story, 'dangerous at first but also wild and high as the Light Horse approached'. In fact, the charging horsemen were galloping right underneath the Turkish guns' set range, which was calibrated for long-range firing, as the rattled Turks fired over their heads! The Australians galloped closer and closer with surprisingly few casualties. Within minutes, they reached the outlying Beersheba trenches, well before any remaining Turkish batteries could lower their sights.

Enemy mistakes

Luck was also on the side of the charging Australians. For right to the last, the Turkish officers wrongly identified the advancing horsemen as mounted infantry, and so instructed some of their riflemen in the trenches to hold their fire until the Light Horsemen reached the trenches and dismounted to start the fight. The Turks did not realise the Light Horse would ride straight over the top of them and on into the town.

And even when the charging horsemen were only one kilometre from the trenches, the Australians could not believe how little opposition there was. Suitably inspired, the Light Horsemen spurred their horses on to a furious gallop with wild bush yells, egging each other on, drawing their bayonets as they closed in on the first trenches and waving them in the evening sunlight. Turkish artillery intensified as the panicking gunners increased their fire and shrapnel exploded, but above the lines of horsemen. Some horses were hit and also their riders, but the frightened Turks still could not wind down their guns fast enough; soon, the shells were bursting behind the charge.

Gunner Len Hall, a sergeant with the 10th Light Horse supporting the charge at Beersheba, was wounded when a German plane dropped a bomb into his gun position, killing some of his men and his horse. He was patched up so well he lived to 101, becoming the last survivor from his regiment.

Although two German planes attacked the Light Horsemen from above, firing machine guns and dropping bombs, they failed to have much impact; the horses were too spread out and the bombs exploded harmlessly between the widely spaced lines of horses. However, one of these bombs did hit 10th Regiment Gunner Len Hall from Western Australia, who was carted off to hospital in a camel ambulance. His wounds were not too serious, though, and he lived to become the last 10th Regiment trooper to die, aged 101, in 1999. Nevertheless, as the charging Australians approached to within a kilometre of the first trenches, the Turks had more success with rifles and machine guns, as their targets were now larger, closer, and more bunched together.

Idriess reported that, 'The last half mile was a berserk gallop with the squadrons in magnificent line'.

Bean continued, 'Next the foremost troops were over the front trench and jumping the main one, dismounting and turning upon the Turks from the rear with rifle and bayonet. The bewildered garrison quickly surrendered. Other Light Horsemen galloped ahead to the rear trenches, where parties of fifty Turks surrendered to single men. Other squadrons galloped straight for Beersheba. The day was won.'

It was too late for the Turks. Now the Light Horsemen were literally on top of them, jumping the trenches, dismounting, and taking on the Turks in bloody hand-to-hand fighting. Other troopers rode on towards the town itself.

Idriess again: 'It was a heart throbbing sight as they plunged up the slope, the horses leaping the redoubt trenches with Turkish bayonets thrusting up for the bellies of the horses. We heard the mad shouts as the men jumped down into the trenches'.

During the charge, Squadron Quartermaster Sergeant Alfred Richard Townsend and his comrade from New South Wales, Sergeant Harry Peard, just 17 years of age, decided to silence one of the enemy redoubts, winning Distinguished Conduct Medals in the process. 'Heavy enemy fire was being brought to bear on a large number of the men who were assaulting Beersheba,' the citation later explained. 'This fire was coming from a Turkish Redoubt situated a few hundred yards to the left of the attacking party.' Townsend and Peard joined forces and 'quickly

Although only 17, Harry Peard from Benowa, New South Wales, won the Distinguished Conduct Medal when, as his Citation said, he helped 'shoot 10 of the enemy, captured two men and routed the remainder, thus silencing the enemy fire' and 'this clearance of the redoubt allowed the charge of the horses, clear passage to the town'.

wended their way up to the Turkish Redoubt, shot 10 of the enemy, captured two men and routed the remainder, thus silencing the enemy fire'. As the citation concluded: 'This clearance of the redoubt allowed the charge of the horses, clear passage to the town'. The DCMs were awarded because, 'Many lives were saved due to the action of these men'.

Later, during a ceremony in Palestine, they were presented their medals, which were 'for conspicuous gallantry and devotion to duty in the field'. Although four Light Horsemen received this honour at Beersheba, this was an especially great achievement for the teenager Peard, from Benowa, New South Wales, whose father was a dairy farmer who had raised the boy alone after young Peard's mother died when he was just two years old. In January 1915, Peard enlisted, aged only 15, but claiming to be 25 (not just 18 as most under-age youngsters did). Young Peard would also bring another trophy home from the war: when he went on leave to England, he met the love of his life, Elizabeth, whom he married and brought back home to Australia, settling down on a farm near Wagga.

Reviews of the charge

As Idriess explained, looking back after interviewing prisoners of war, the enemy never suspected their fortress stronghold would be overrun: 'Captured Turkish and German officers told us that they never dreamed that mounted troops would be madmen enough to attempt rushing infantry redoubts protected by machine guns and artillery. Yet despite roaring machine guns and rifle fire the 4th Brigade just galloped on. And no wonder the enemy had taken fright at the sight of the troopers charging. At a mile distant their thousand hooves were stuttering, coming at a rate that frightened a man — they were an awe inspiring sight galloping through the red haze knee to knee — horse to horse — the dying sun glinting on bayonet points'.

Looking back over the day's action, Guy Haydon, of the 12th Regiment, who had brought from Australia his own beloved horse, 'Midnight' —

later to be celebrated in a book written about him — reported what he saw while charging up until he was shot:

'We trotted for the first 2 miles then the Turks opened fire on us from a line of redoubts about half a mile out from the town and we could hardly hear anything for the noise of their rifles and machine guns. As soon as their fire started we galloped, and you never heard such awful war yells as our boys let out, they never hesitated or faulted for a moment, it was grand.

'Every now and again a rider would roll off or a horse fall shot but the line swept on. As we neared their trenches, our men were falling thicker and thicker and the pace became faster. 30 yards from their trenches were some old rifle pits and as soon as my eye lit on them I wheeled my horse round and yelled to the nearest men to jump off, let their horses go and get into the pits and open fire. Just previously I had seen Major Fetherstonhaugh's horse go down killed, the Major get up and run for cover only to fall again shot through both legs. A few seconds afterwards a bullet hit me high up in the left buttock, just under the belt, lifting me clear off my horse and dropping me sprawling on a heap of dirt that had been thrown out of a rifle pit, and I rolled down into the pit and into safety.

'But all this time, really only a few seconds, the charge went on, men raced their horses through and over the trenches and while some of us were still engaged in hand-to-hand fighting in the trenches, the remainder had charged through the town and went on to the high ground a mile beyond. The town was ours.

'It is impossible to describe one's feelings, but for myself although it is the heaviest fire I have been under, I never felt less afraid, and I was terribly disappointed in being shot before reaching the town.

'After being wounded, I lay in a hole for about 2 hours listening to poor devils groaning all round me, and then an M.O arrived with a lantern and some sandcarts, he planked the lamp down near me and the stretcher bearers brought in the wounded from all points of the compass to be dressed, after being dressed the worst cases were loaded into carts and sent off to the Ambulance, 4 of the poor chaps died there within a yard or two of me, but it did not worry me, I had got past worrying.

'At last there was only myself and 1 man left and we had to lie there all night. One of the boys got me a blanket off a dead horse but it was terribly cold, and I shivered all night long and in the morning my wound was so stiff that I couldn't move. About 7 a.m. a sandcart arrived and I was taken to the Field Ambulance where my wound was carefully dressed, then, we went per car to Beersheba then on to the rail head to a big casualty clearing station, where we spent the night. At 9 a.m. we were loaded onto the Hospital Train and reached El-Arish about 2.30 p.m. that afternoon. We spent the night there and left the next day at 12 a.m. for Kantara which we reached about dusk. The next day at about 11 a.m. we boarded the train for Cairo and finally reached the 14th A.G.H. (The best spot on this side of the water). At 4 p.m. today I was X rayed and the bullet was located about half way up my back and about an inch to the left of my spine, it must have hit a bone and turned at right angles, otherwise it must have gone right through my belly a wonderful streak of luck, am not suffering much pain and don't know when they will operate on me, but hope it will be soon as I don't want to be stuck in here any longer than I can help. I can't get any correct estimate of the killed and wounded in the 12th yet but may hear in time to put it in this letter yet.'

Haydon then added a postscript:

'Was operated on the day before yesterday and bullet removed, am sending you the bullet for a Christmas Present by the same Officer who takes this letter. Am having very little trouble with my wound except at night when it aches a lot, but it is nothing to what some of the poor devils have to suffer. Poor old Nearguard was killed, I was awfully sorry about him, he was such a good Soldier, absolutely fearless. Roy Whiteman and Maclean both have commissions. Roy did splendidly, so well in fact that he was paraded to the Divisional General Hodson and actually promoted on the field of battle. Major Fetherstonehaugh got a D.S.O. He is the bed opposite me. His wife nearly went mad when she heard about it. As far as we can gather, there must have been about 27 12th L.H. killed in the charge and about 15 wounded.

'It is impossible to describe the charge, I was talking to a British Cavalry Officer in Hospital who had arrived 3 days previously from France, he went to France with the first batch of English Cavalry and had been there ever since, and he said "I have seen every action in which the British Cavalry have taken part, but the charge of the L.H. at Beersheba yesterday, is the finest thing that I have ever seen mounted troops do." Our Brigadier received a wire from the G.O.C. congratulating him on the brilliant work his Brigade had done.

'We took 2,000 Prisoners and their trenches were full of dead. Two Regiments of the first Brigade also had a charge, but they were further round on our right and we didn't see them, anyway we had the town before they got there.'

The author of the 12th Regiment's official diary, Eric Keith McGregor, also concluded that it was one of history's greatest cavalry charges. 'The mounted charge of our men rivals any other in the annals of military history. At some trenches many horses were brought down but this did not deter the men, who followed on foot and finished off what the mounted men had missed in their hurry.'

So despite having the advantage of heavily defended trenches, the Turks were not able to stop this khaki wave — especially once the first Australians got among them. Because many of the Light Horse were country blokes used to jumping wombat holes, not to mention shooting wild pigs from the saddle of a galloping horse, they had little trouble jumping the trenches surrounding Beersheba nor jumping into the trenches and fighting the Turks there hand-to-hand.

The extraordinary bravery and skill of these Light Horsemen was well demonstrated by the leading officer of the 12th Regiment, Major Cuthbert Murchison Fetherstonhaugh from Coonamble — a standout hero at the battle, who won the Distinguished Service Order (DSO) for his bravery and fighting skills. After charging most of the way to the Turkish trenches, he felt his horse shudder under him as a Turkish bullet ploughed into the charging steed just 40 metres short of the first enemy trench. Fetherstonhaugh slipped his feet out of the stirrups and leapt off the crashing animal. It was every trooper's nightmare, to lose his mount in a charge against heavy enemy fire. But he knew he must not be crushed underneath the horse, in which case he would become a sitting duck for enemy machine guns. So he jumped well clear of the groaning horse, now writhing on the ground, then pulled out his revolver and put a bullet straight into his beloved animal's head.

This senior Light Horseman had never lost his mount in the Boer War, nor been so exposed before, even at Gallipoli. But, keeping his head, he knew he had to continue demonstrating courage to his comrades in the 12th by example — even if most of them were still mounted. So quick as a flash, he sprinted through the hail of Turkish bullets to the nearest trench that he had been riding towards. Reaching the edge, this bushman-warrior jumped in among the startled machine gunners and riflemen and emptied his revolver into the nearest group of Turks who fell at his feet. Then, tossing his now empty weapon aside and with his blood up, he clenched both fists for hand-to-hand combat, but as he lunged forward towards the last remaining Turks, his legs would not carry him. Collapsing to the bottom of the enemy trench, he saw that he had been shot through both legs. Luckily, the frightened Turks fled. But now he had to hope and pray the stretcher-bearers would find him. 'I got a bullet through both thighs, it made a clean hole through the left but opened out a bit and made a large gash through the back of the right which will take a little while to fix up', he reported later.

Meanwhile, Fetherstonhaugh's comrades of the 12th Regiment rode through a gap between the trenches and on into the town. The 4th Light Horse had earlier dismounted at the trenches and tackled these first objectives on foot — stabbing to death any resisting Turks with their bayonets. Although outnumbered, they killed or captured so many Turks with their bayonets that they soon took control of all trenches. Overpowered and shocked by the carnage in their trenches, the Turkish garrison then also surrendered. So the 4th Regiment took the trenches while the 12th secured the town of Beersheba, with the entire enemy in the trenches and the town surrendering well before dark, as Allenby had ordered.

Reviews of capturing the town with its vital wells

Fortunately, because the 4th distracted the Turks in the trenches and the 12th were able to ride straight through the town centre, troopers were able to secure the all-important wells before the enemy damaged them. And so, men and horses quenched their thirst — after all, they had earned it many times over. As it turned out, they were just in time. The Turks, and their German masters, were about to poison then blow up all the wells and retreat to a safer position.

Captain Jack R. Davies of the 12th Light Horse, who took command after Fetherstonhaugh was wounded, won an MC and was one of the very first men into Beersheba (with 13 others) and the first to find the wells. With drawn sword, no hat on, and at full gallop, he charged the Turks, his men using their bayonets.

He commented gratefully: 'Providence guided me that day as I rode into the town as if I knew all the roads leading into it! I think I can say quite without fear of contradiction, that I was the first officer, or man into the town, but really it was just easy going once we passed the trenches'. But the charge, he said, 'was the best run I ever had, from start to finish it was just about 6 miles'. Looking back over the charge, he wrote: 'We rode the first half mile at walk and slow trot, getting into line. Two squadrons each in line with five yards between each man and 300 yards from A Squadron back to B (my squadron). The next mile I should say was a trot, then the Turks spotted us and enemy fire started to hit us and we went at it hell for a split, then we struck the trenches one and a half miles from the town, some of the troopers jumped clean over them ... some went round them ... but we were the lucky ones who rode practically straight through.

'I've seen some surprised people but those Turks were certainly not expecting us, just then. Though I have no doubt they thought we'd be along *on foot* sometime that night. The greater majority were evacuating the place and we were rounding up as many as we could handle ... where we got through past the mosque ... The 4th Light Horse got about 350 prisoners on the right of the town, we in the 12th also took many prisoners after the charge was over and I counted my little lot of prisoners and sent them away under escort (it was a beautiful moonlight night) and I counted them like a lot of sheep ... reaching 647 privates and 38 officers!'

But the Light Horse was still very lucky with those wells. Within minutes of galloping into the town, one of the Light Horsemen who dismounted at the nerve centre captured the young German officer in charge of blowing up the wells. According to some of the troopers who made it to these wells, most of the senior German officers had saved their skins by retreating from Beersheba and heading north or north-west away from the Light Horse attack, along with the Turkish commander of Beersheba, Ismet Bey. They had ordered one junior German engineer to stay behind on his own and blow up the wells, around which demolition charges had been laid. But the Australian trooper — with just seconds to spare — saw what was about to happen and captured this lone German as he was about to set off the charges. As soon as he pointed his rifle at the German — poised to press the lever down and detonate the explosives in the wells — the German just raised his hands, preferring to live rather than die for a lost cause. As Bean confirmed: 'It was found later that the Turks had decided to make an orderly withdrawal from Beersheba after blowing up the wells upon which everything depended. But the charge forestalled them; nearly all the wells were intact and a storm had filled the pools'.

Nevertheless, the wells could easily have been sabotaged, as Captain Davies wrote: 'I began to think it was time to go home, then I sighted another Light Horse troop that had come around the right of the town, so we just grafted as many as we could and made back to the wells, which was what we were really after as the whole troop engaged were depending on them for water. Johnny (the Turks) got out in such a hurry that though he had the wells and the Railway Station and the approaches to the town already mined and ready to blow up, he forgot to detonate the charges, or when he tried they failed to explode properly — so he did not try again!'

Secrets of success

The charge — which was a success because of its shock value and the sheer speed with which the troopers took the town before it could be destroyed by a retreating Turkish force — turned out to be history's last successful mounted cavalry charge.

The commander of the successful 4th Light Horse Regiment, Lieutenant-Colonel Murray Bourchier, said after the charge, 'I consider that the success was due to the rapidity with which the movement was carried out. Owing to the volume of fire brought to bear from the enemy's position by machine-guns and rifles, a dismounted attack would have resulted in a much greater number of casualties. It was noticed also that the morale of the enemy was greatly shaken through our troops galloping over his positions thereby causing his riflemen and machine gunners to lose all control of fire discipline. When the troops came within short range of the trenches the enemy seemed to direct almost all his fire at the horses.'

The commander of the Desert Mounted Corps, Lieutenant-General Sir Harry Chauvel, claimed it was continual movement rather than speed which won the day: 'If there was one lesson more than another I had learned at Magdhaba and Rafa, it was patience, and not to expect things to happen too quickly. At Beersheba, although progress was slow, there was never that deadly pause which is so disconcerting to a commander'.

It was certainly a good haul, as the 12th Regiment's official diary reported: 'We captured in all 9 guns, 1080 prisoners, 180 animals and much other war material'. The town's military storehouses were well stocked, but there were dangers too, as Harry Langtip found: 'The town is small but has some very nice buildings with tiled roofs. The water scheme is grand. We got into the army stores and helped ourselves to grain for the horses & got bivy sheets and peg posts. We got all the Turkish stores, there was everything from a telephone to a pack saddle. We got lots of horses and bullocks. There was rifles and gear lying everywhere. But the Turks left bombs and if you kicked one up it went. One Tommie got both his eyes blown out by a bottle. He just kicked it out of the way and it must have been full of explosives.'

Yet even after the Australians secured the position, there were still pockets of resistance. Sergeant Charles Doherty wrote: 'The first party sent across to the large cement troughs had just finished, when from the east came an unexpected fusillade of bullets. Though this assault made it appear that we had been cleverly ambushed, we retained control over the prisoners and secured what cover there was until further support arrived. Between 8 & 9:30 pm the 11th LHR arrived and the 4th MG Squadron came in. Then a complete chain of outposts was established while the main body of prisoners, together with many scattered lots from the various redoubts were taken back to Brigade HQ'.

But there were also pleasant surprises, including an unexpected reminder of home. Major Wilfred Kent Hughes of the 3rd Light Horse Brigade reported that: 'A small park of Australian gum-trees was perhaps the most familiar sight that the light horse saw the following morning'. And, 'Several times at a later date further north Australian gum trees would be encountered rearing their heads high above any native trees in the vicinity and apparently quite at home in their foreign surroundings'.

For a while, the Germans also hit back from the skies above, as the 12th Regiment's official diarist, Eric Keith McGregor, attested: 'Whilst in Beersheba the 4th Field Ambulance and our 12th Regiment suffered casualties from enemy aircraft from bombs'.

Eventually, however, Beersheba was secured, and the dehydrated horses and men all quenched their thirst in peace. The field ambulances also helped the wounded and counted the dead. Thirty-one Light Horsemen had been killed, an amazingly low figure when compared to previous battles. Those killed included some of the 'Originals' from the 4th Brigade (as they called themselves), who had enlisted in 1914, such as Edward Cleaver and Albert 'Tibbie' Cotter, the famous Australian cricketer. Sadly, Cotter was killed while serving as an unarmed stretcher-bearer, when he was shot in the back of the head. Cotter, who had dismounted to collect wounded Australian troopers, came across a stray Turk, who put his hands up and surrendered. But when Cotter turned away for a second to get something from his horse, the treacherous Turk pulled out a hidden revolver and shot Cotter from behind. Angered by this, six of Cotter's mates then rounded up ten of the killer's comrades and shot the lot of them dead, along with the killer. Once again, Light Horsemen realised that white surrender flags meant nothing to Turks. Another notable death was that of VC winner Leslie Cecil Maygar (who had fought well in the Boer War and at Gallipoli), who was found bleeding on the battlefield that night after he was shot in the charge; he died in the field hospital soon after.

They did not die in vain, however, because this great victory now paved the way for penetrating southern Palestine, advancing towards Jerusalem and Damascus, and defeating the Turks and dismantling their Ottoman Empire.

All credit to the horses

It was also a great victory for the young nation of Australia, where horses were still a part of everyday life. Many Australians lived and worked in the bush, where they had developed a formidable culture based around the horse. Some of the 4th and 12th Regiments were country stockmen, very skilled in all kinds of horse work, such as chasing runaway cattle, so the charge at Beersheba was exactly the sort of horse-riding they had enlisted for, and which was a long overdue event — especially for those riders who had had to put their horses aside (leaving them in Egypt) and fight on foot at Gallipoli.

The last surviving rider from this battle, Gunner Len Hall, told the author during a filmed interview in 1997 that he had been looking forward to riding in a charge like Beersheba since the start of the war: 'That was what we had been trained for — that's why we enlisted and what the Army promised us; and we had been so disappointed when the top brass ordered us to leave our horses in Egypt when we sailed to Gallipoli. I felt quite naked without my horse, which I had got from the cattle baron Sid Kidman. And although we fought well at Gallipoli and survived that bloody massacre at the Nek — we could not wait to show what we could do once we were reunited with our horses'.

Like Fetherstonhaugh, Hall lost his horse. 'Oh, the charge went well enough at Beersheba, we won that stunt hands down; but it was just very sad for me because my horse, Q6, was shot as I approached the Turkish trenches and when he fell under me I jumped clear, quick smart to see if I could save him but he was a goner — so I had to shoot him through the head. Even in the middle of the battle with blokes dying all around me I broke down and wept for Q6 — as I'd lost the best friend I ever had.'

Lieutenant-General Sir Harry Chauvel's daughter, Elyne Mitchell, told the author the following story in 1995 at her Towong homestead, near Corryong, Victoria. When the astounded Allenby first met Chauvel after hearing about the success of the charge, he asked his subordinate: 'But how did your troopers get across the enemy trenches?' To which the Australian bushman replied: 'We just jumped the bastards'.

But they could not have done so without those horses. It was those great-hearted Walers that carried the brave young men to victory in this turning-point battle; the attack would have failed if they had faltered. Some Light Horsemen reported later that the horses 'galloped in a wild frenzy' because they were mad keen to get to the water in Beersheba. Those courageous horses certainly jumped those 2.5 deep x 1.2-metre wide trenches in great style. Many horses received terrible injuries when the Turks lifted their bayonets to the horse's bellies as they jumped over them. And there were the bullets. One Light Horseman recounted that, 'there was nothing more sickening than the sound of bullets thudding in to the belly of your horse' as they charged in to the enemy lines. The toll was also sickening to the riders, as 44 horses were killed and 60 horses were wounded or became sick after the attack.

The horses certainly paid a high price for the victory, as the 12th Regiment diary reported: 'Our horses are in a woeful state at present as the night before the attack we rode 40 miles [64 kilometres] and then charged full gallop for five miles [8 kilometres] — they had no water for 36 hours then we lost over 50 horses in our squadron alone, during the charge and those that are left are in a sorry state at present'.

Sadly, just a year later, most of these survivors would be shot by their owners or given to the Egyptians because the Australian government refused to transport the horses home.

Writing home

With the town taken and secured, and time on their hands, many troopers sat down and wrote letters home describing their part in the great charge.

Looking back over his ride, Sergeant Charles Doherty wrote that the horsemen who cleared all the trenches had come up to an open plain, which 'was succeeded by small wadies and perpendicular gullies, surrounding which scores of sniper's nests or dugouts each were holding seven or eight men. After progressing another quarter of a mile, we turned to the right at an angle of 45 degrees to converge on Beersheba. The enemy's fire now came from the direction of the town and a large railway viaduct to the north. The limited number of entrances to the city temporarily checked us but those in front went straight up and through the narrow streets. Falling beams from fired buildings, exploding magazines and arsenals and various hidden snipers were unable to check our race through the two available streets that were wide enough for 2 to ride abreast'.

Remembering the excitement, Trooper Keddie wrote: 'We were all at the gallop yelling like mad, some had bayonets in their hand others their rifle then it was a full stretch gallop at the trench ... the last 200 yards or so was good going and those horses put on pace and next were jumping the trenches with the Turks underneath ... when we got over the trenches

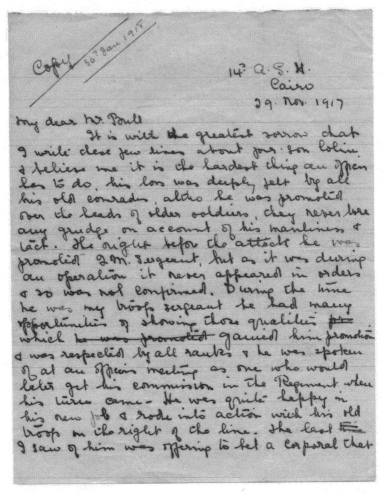

After Colin Bull was shot dead while charging Beersheba by a Turk in a concealed trench, the letter his commanding officer wrote to his parents may have comforted them a little when it said, 'his loss was deeply felt by all his old comrades' and that he was 'respected by all ranks'.

we went straight for the town'. But Keddie had also had a near miss: 'I felt a bullet go past my ear and thought if that bullet had been a few more inches to one side …'

Keddie was not the only one who escaped lightly, as Trooper Eric Robertson, of the 1st Regiment, wrote home about his mate, Tom Hicks, who 'got a slight wound in the seat of the pants, and as he was lying down facing the Turks at the time, it will tell you how the lead was flying'.

The officer confirmed that the young trooper was happy charging Beersheba, writing that Bull was 'offering to bet a corporal he would beat him in the gallop for Beersheba' and that he had 'died instantly and without pain' dying 'as he lived, a true soldier and a gentleman.'

Robertson went on to describe the charge to his parents: 'It was absolutely the prettiest thing I have ever seen in my life. I looked back and there were about eight lines of galloping horses and about four miles long!'

Trooper Edward Dengate wrote that it had been a challenging ride from start to finish: 'We got mounted, cantered about a quarter of a mile up a bit of a rise lined up along the brow of a hill paused a moment, and then went at them, the ground was none too smooth, which caused our line to get twisted a bit … Captain Davies let out a yell at the top of his voice … that started them all we spurred our horses … the bullets got thicker … three or four horses came down, others with no riders on kept going, the saddles splashed with blood, here and there a man running toward a dead horse for cover, the Turk's trenches were about fifty yards on my right, I could see the Turk's heads over the edge of the trenches squinting along their rifles, a lot of the fellows dismounted at that point thinking we were to take the trenches, but most of us kept straight on, where I was there was a clear track with trenches on the right and a redoubt on the left, some of the chaps jumped clear over the trenches in places, some fell into them, although about 150 men got through and raced for the town, they went up the street yelling like madmen'.

With their handsome faces of youthful innocence, troopers Colin Bull (left) and his mate Gerard Digby could not have known when they enlisted together in the 12th Light Horse that Bull would be killed in action at Beersheba, and Digby would return to farm land in New South Wales, marry, and raise a family.

Trooper Dengate, who was also wounded, wrote home saying: 'I suppose you heard about the capture of Beersheba by the 4th Brigade, well I was right in it, and came through safe, and with my skin intact, I got a bullet through the leg of my breeches, just above the knee, grazed my leg but didn't make it bleed'.

Obituary

Sergeant Colin Bull was one of 31 troopers killed in action, and the letter his superior officer, Lieutenant E.B. Ralston, wrote on 29 November 1917 was typical of many letters of condolence. 'My dear Mrs. Bull, It is with the greatest sorrow that I write these few lines about your son Colin' who 'died instantly and without pain. It will be a relief to know he never had to go through that most awful horror of a battlefield lying crippled and praying for death. His loss was deeply felt by all his old comrades. Although he was promoted over the heads of older soldiers they never bore any grudge on account of his manliness and tact. He was respected by all ranks'. Ralston continued: '[Colin] rode into action with his old troops in the right of the line. The last time I saw him he was offering to bet a Corporal that he would beat him in the gallop for Beersheba. I had just told the troops that we were to charge the position and take it at all costs. The town was about 3 miles away across the open, my troops after going a mile came on to a concealed trench & it was there your son met his death'.

And Ralston concluded: 'He died as he lived a true soldier and a gentleman'. In a postscript, Ralston added: 'I was unable to write before as I was wounded in the same action'.

A week after the battle, on 7 November, a brother officer from the 12th Regiment (whose identity is unknown) wrote home about Colin: 'We have had some hearty action since I last wrote' as we 'attacked and captured Beersheba', but 'The horror of it is a bit too fresh for me to care to write more fully about it, especially as my pal Colin was shot dead while we were charging a redoubt. It has almost broken my heart to see him go under, and it will be an unbearable blow to his mother, you can tell her he died like a soldier with a rifle in his hand and could not have suffered as he was shot through the heart. We have buried him with the other brave fellows on a rise not far from Beersheba well in sight of the minarets of the mosque — May he sleep well there. God rest him'.

Luckily, in one of his last letters home, after apologising for not writing more often, Colin Bull reported: 'I had a great time while on leave in Cairo. It was great sleeping in a bed again. I had three days leave and thoroughly enjoyed the trip after roaming around the desert for about eight months'.

Guy Haydon was also among the casualties, writing home: 'You will know from my Cable that I am in Hospital here with a rather nice wound, a bullet about 2 inches to the left of the crupper bone. I will write soon and try and give you an account of exactly what happened from the start of operations until I was knocked out'.

Postscript: Decorations for heroes

Among the many decorations handed out at Beersheba, two other officers won a DSO — Lieutenant-Colonel Donald Cameron ('Long Don from Rouchel') and Major Eric Montague Hyman, who, Captain Jack Davies explained, 'Fighting with a few others accounted for 60 dead Turks — which was not bad seeing that Hyman and his mates were out in the open and the Turks were in a beautiful trench'.

Captain Jack Davies really inspired the boys of the 4th and 12th Light Horse Regiments when he galloped bravely out in front of them, turned back to face them, and shouted, 'Beersheba next stop'.

But of all those decorated on the day, perhaps Major Cuthbert Fetherstonhaugh's DSO was the hardest won. The citation to the award states: 'This officer was with his squadron when it came in touch with the enemy trench which formed the main defences obstructing the attack. The enemy opened a very heavy rifle fire and machine gun fire. Major Fetherstonhaugh quickly summing up the situation with great gallantry charged full at the trenches, mingling with the leading squadron and thereby making the pressure so heavy as to quickly overcome the enemy and so enable the assault to be carried forward successfully to Beersheba. This officer's horse was shot from under him about 40 yards from the trench but he continued to lead his men forward using his revolver with good effect until wounded in both legs'.

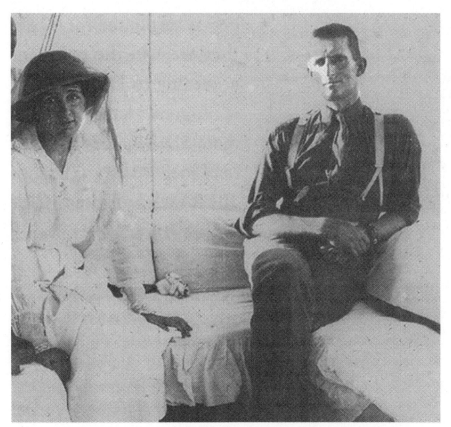

One of the greatest heroes to emerge from the great charge at Beersheba was the never-say-die Boer War veteran with the unforgettable name of Major Cuthbert Fetherstonhaugh, aka 'Fethers', from a property near Coonable, New South Wales, who fought on even after the Turks shot his horse and then his legs from under him — seen here with his supportive wife.

In his report, Charles Bean wrote this about Fetherstonhaugh: 'A South African veteran and fine soldier, his first thought was for his wounded horse and he quickly put the animal out of pain with a shot from his revolver before he rushed on to the trench and emptied his weapon into the nearest Turks before falling, shot through both legs'.

Beersheba was just one achievement in a lifetime of achievements for Major Cuthbert Fetherstonhaugh, grazier from a property near Coonamble, who grew up with horses and was well equipped to play a leading role at Beersheba. He served in the Boer War and then at Gallipoli, where he was promoted to captain before joining the 12th Light Horse in Palestine, where he was promoted to major on 24 April 1917, before helping lead the charge at Beersheba. He was awarded the DSO for this heroic action and later was 'Mentioned in Dispatches'. In 1919, he returned to Australia suffering from malaria, and went back to his property until, aged 63, he enlisted for World War II, serving with the army as lieutenant-colonel until he died in 1945. His Beersheba comrade Captain Jack Davies described him: 'A great old bird, son of the old man who drove horses four in hand in the old days. Winning a DSO for his heroism a thoroughly deserved recognition for the splendid cool way he deployed the Squadron in action at Beersheba'.

Aftermath: Next day

The next morning, Private Keddie rode over the ground to see if any of the horses could be found roaming, but he only saw dead animals. He wrote: 'We were sent looking for the horses whose riders were killed so we made for the other side of the town where several other light horse regiments were … met some friends in the first light horse and yarned for a while they asked me what it was like in the charge gave them a full account. At least 70 horses died …'

So now Beersheba was in the hands of Allenby's Egyptian Expeditionary Force. Mounted infantrymen and their superb Walers had carried out one of the most successful cavalry charges in history — against what seemed impossible odds. Certainly 31 Troopers had made the ultimate sacrifice, but the rest of the 800 Light Horsemen had survived to tell the tale.

The fall of Beersheba swung the tide of battle against the Turks in Palestine. It marked the beginning of the end of Turkish rule in Palestine and opened the way north for the eventual destruction of the Ottoman Empire, 11 months later. But to achieve that victory, Allenby still had to attack that stronghold of Gaza, which the Turks had successfully defended twice already.

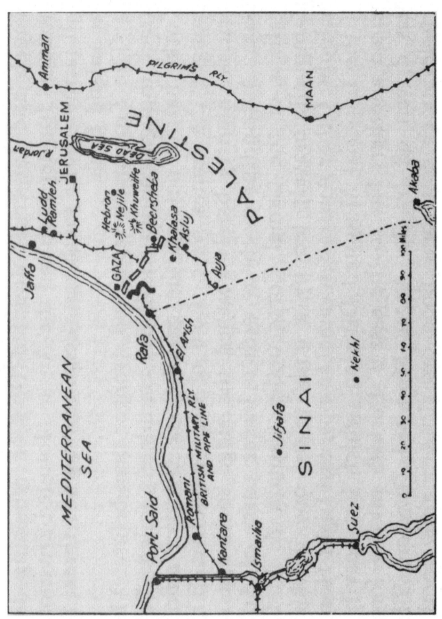

Once the Light Horse had achieved the impossible and captured Beersheba, some of the frightened Turks began to retreat from Gaza itself, fleeing north along the coastal strip — which would make it a lot easier for Allenby's Egyptian Expeditionary Force to attack the poorly defended Gaza from Beersheba in the east and from Rafa in the south. Allenby's strategy of capturing Beersheba first rather than the more fortified Gaza had paid off: his forces had successfully begun demolishing the Turk's southern frontline of defences in Palestine (the Gaza–Beersheba line) by entering through the back door.

7.
THIRD GAZA,
1–8 NOVEMBER 1917

THIRD TIME LUCKY

General Allenby's plan was to capture Gaza so that he could move his Egyptian Expeditionary Force down onto the coast, from where they could advance northwards along the edge of the Mediterranean Sea towards Jaffa and eventually right up to Damascus.

We have captured the Turkish garrisons at Gaza at last and the Turks are finally retreating down the Jaffa Road; we must now fight our way through miles of Turkish flank-guards and try and cut the Garrisons off. So we rode out straight for the tail of Turkish rear-guard. Under shrapnel, our bellies empty, but we almost cried for our poor horses. They had nothing to eat for forty-eight hours and again no water.

ION IDRIESS, 5TH LIGHT HORSE REGIMENT,
NOVEMBER 1917

BACKGROUND TO THE BATTLE

Poring over his map of Palestine, after winning the Battle of Beersheba on 31 October, General Allenby, commander-in-chief of the EEF, discussed with his officers the best plan of attack to drive the Turks back up north to their base at Damascus. By capturing Beersheba, Allenby had started to dismantle the old Turkish frontline across Palestine from Beersheba to Gaza on the Mediterranean, opening up a pathway north towards Jerusalem and beyond — but to proceed, he now had to capture the elusive Gaza.

Even before he ordered the successful charge at Beersheba, Allenby had been planning his attack on Gaza. From 27 October, his artillery batteries at sea and on land began delivering a heavy and almost continuous bombardment against Gaza. Determined to win on this third attempt, Allenby mustered as many forces as he could. These included from Australia the Desert Mounted Corps, commanded by Lieutenant-General Sir Harry Chauvel, with 745 officers, and 17,935 other ranks in the Anzac, Australian, and Yeomanry Mounted Divisions; the British XX Corps, commanded by Lieutenant-General Philip Chetwode, with 1,435 officers, and 44,171 other ranks in the 10th, 53rd, 60th, and 74th (Yeomanry) Divisions; and the British XXI Corps commanded by Lieutenant-General Edward Bulfin (which would have a key role at Third Gaza), which had 1,154 officers and 34,759 other ranks in three infantry divisions, with 35,000 rifles in the XXI Corps (which also had its own cavalry).

The XXI Corps infantry troops lined up to attack Gaza included 52nd (Lowland) Division; 54th (East Anglian) Division; 75th Division; 25th Indian Infantry Brigade; a West Indian battalion; French and Italian detachments; and, finally, the unit that would ride into the old city first, the Imperial Service Cavalry Brigade — with 1,000 sabres!

Although these EEF forces could have been opposed by the large enemy forces of the Turkish Yildirim Army Group — which was, under the command of Field Marshal Erich von Falkenhayn, responsible for the defence of Palestine — many of the Turkish forces, fortunately, were redeployed elsewhere before the battle began. It was just as well, because the Ottoman Eighth Army was initially composed of their XXII Corps' 3rd and 53rd Divisions defending Gaza itself — which were separate from their XX Corps' 26th and 54th Divisions defending the line stretching to the east of Gaza, under the command of Kress von Kressenstein.

Lawrence of Arabia, now working closely with Allenby, had mustered large bodies of Arabs like these on both horseback and camels, strengthening his Arab Army for the advance north through Palestine once Gaza had been captured.

But the Turkish defence of Gaza was mainly the responsibility of XXII Corps, which had two divisions in the frontline — the 53rd Division (which had helped win the Second Battle of Gaza) and the 3rd Division (which had helped with the First and Second Battles of Gaza) — as well as two divisions in reserve (the 7th and 19th).

The XXII Corps boasted a total of 4,500 rifles, which, when reinforced by its two divisions, had a total of 8,000 defenders. And they had plenty of big guns, including the 116 guns of the Ottoman XXII Corps artillery, six large naval guns, and several batteries of 150mm howitzers.

Steeped in ancient history, and a devout Christian, Allenby was also well aware of the religious significance of the Ottoman towns he now identified standing in the way of his path to Damascus. Many of them had been fought over in the Crusades. These towns included, in geographical order: Gaza, Ashqelon, and Ashdod on the coast; Hebron, Bethlehem, and Jerusalem inland; Amman and Es Salt in Jordan to the west; and Megiddo and, finally, Damascus.

Although developing his battle plans almost simultaneously, Allenby decided to capture Gaza first, launching the Third Battle of Gaza, just before starting his advance on Jerusalem. He needed to neutralise the heavily fortified city as soon as possible so that he could advance north with safety. Allenby had plenty of men now, so he developed a broad moving frontline that stretched west from Beersheba across to below Gaza. If he could capture Gaza, he would at the same time break the last of the Turkish defence line from Gaza to Beersheba, which was overseen by the recently arrived German commander, Erich von Falkenhayn, the former German army Chief of Staff.

Once General Allenby's forces had captured Gaza and secured the port town of Jaffa, the great leader planned to increase the maritime support for his forces by ordering British ships to deliver men, equipment, and supplies from across the Mediterranean Sea, without the Turks shooting at these vessels.

As it turned out, the Third Battle of Gaza (also referred to as the Battle of Beersheba — Gaza Turkish Defence Line) was fought almost simultaneously with the unplanned sub-battle for Tel El Khuweilfe (the main Turkish stronghold inland from coastal Gaza, just north of Beersheba and between Beersheba and Hebron). As this Tel El Khuweilfe battle was being fought, Allenby's troops were also advancing north to capture Jerusalem — these three battles all overlapped and affected each other. In fact, the British only succeeded in capturing Gaza because the Turks sent some of their defending troops away to defend other Turkish strongholds such as Hebron, north-east of Gaza, en route to Jerusalem.

The Turks believed Hebron, not Gaza, was Allenby's main target. Charles Bean wrote: 'Once Chauvel's mounted troops and also Chetwode's infantry started thrusting into the deep hills of southern Palestine' along with 'the Arab army led by Lieutenant-Colonel T.E. Lawrence' as well as 'Colonel S.F. Newcombe's detachment pressing ahead on the extreme right towards Hebron ... the Turks apparently thought that Allenby would thrust northwards first through Hebron, and they accordingly withdrew their troop reserves from Gaza'. Allenby had tricked the enemy again.

Allenby had been persuading Lawrence of Arabia (in whom he had great faith) and his Arab Army to join forces ever since he took command in July 1917. By Third Gaza, he had them well and truly in support, as long as Allenby could advance himself. As he advised his superiors back in England: 'They, naturally, won't and can't do much unless I move; and it is not much use their destroying the Turks' communications unless I take immediate advantage of such destruction ... If I bring them into the fight and do not make progress myself, this will also expose them to retaliation — which to some tribes, such as the Druzes, S. of Damascus, may mean annihilation'.

Even before Third Gaza, Allenby, writing on 3 October 1917, had revealed to his wife: 'The Arab rebellion is spreading well, and the Turkish communications will be difficult to guard against their raids. The enclosed photograph of the Shereef of Mecca, and the proclamation by him, is one of the means we have of inducing the Arabs to desert the Turks. We drop these papers and packets of cigarettes over the Turkish lines from aeroplanes. The proclamation is an appeal from the Shereef to the Arabs to leave the Turks and join in the war against them for the freedom and independence of Arabia. A good many come in, as a result of our propaganda'.

And 'propaganda' it would certainly turn out to be, because despite Allenby's promises, when Lawrence and the Arab Army helped him liberate these Arab lands from the Turks, they were refused 'the freedom and independence of Arabia', as Britain and France took control of Palestine.

Allenby launched the Third Battle of Gaza on 1 November, determined not to suffer the bloody losses of the shockingly managed First and Second Gaza battles. On the same day, Allenby also ordered some of his other forces to begin the advance on Jerusalem.

The embittered Gallipoli and First and Second Gaza veteran Ion Idriess reported with great glee that, 'The navy and land batteries are putting Gaza under a terrific bombardment as the Turks never dreamed of — even in their worst experiences of Gallipoli'.

Despite this bombardment, the Turks did not realise this was part of a major assault on Gaza. For once again, Allenby and his intelligence advisers had misled the Turks into thinking they were thrusting north as their main offensive. If Dobell had lost Second Gaza through stupidity — attacking full frontal in daylight — Allenby would win Third Gaza by pretending to attack elsewhere and then suddenly attacking Gaza. It was a case of brain not brawn.

THIRD GAZA

1 November, midnight

During the night of 1–2 November, Allenby ordered a series of assaults by XXI Corps to be mounted against the Gaza defences. Charles Bean wrote: 'Just then on the night of November 1st 1917 the XXI British Corps struck Gaza attacking between the sea and the town which they outflanked'. This softened up the resistance, although the attackers were only partially successful due to the strength of the garrison.

Yet as Allenby had also sent some of his forces straight up north towards Hebron, rather than sending all his troops west to nearby Gaza, the German commander Kress von Kressenstein switched some of his troops from protecting Gaza to protecting Hebron (which was en route to the Turkish stronghold of Jerusalem) from a British attack that was virtually non-existent!

Allenby had committed far fewer troops to this northern advance towards Hebron than he had to Gaza. His northern thrust included Colonel Newcombe's Arab detachment of only 70 camels, along with the 2nd Light Horse Brigade, which soon gained control of the road heading north to Hebron at Sakati. But that nevertheless inspired Kress von Kressenstein to transfer a total of three divisions from Gaza inland to the east; and this left Gaza open to attack with 60,000 fewer men defending it.

Wasting little time, Allenby began his attack on Gaza by moving his real advancing force into position, with British Lieutenant-General Edward Bulfin attacking with his XXI Corps. Lieutenant-General Sir Philip Chetwode's XX Corps also captured a great part of the Turkish line between Beersheba and Gaza.

Riding towards battle, the Reverend Nigel Backhouse of the 2nd Brigade's 7th Light Horse did not think there would be many casualties during this third attempt to capture Gaza, writing: 'I was given a number of wooden burial pegs but I told the officers that I would be using them to boil my quart pot; and as it turned out there were no fatalities or serious casualties in the first few days of the stunt in our 7th Light Horse Regiment'.

The Australians certainly had the upper hand, Backhouse continued, against half-hearted resistance. 'Four of our troopers galloped up to a party of 40 Turkish engineers and captured the lot; winning four Military Medals although the Turks seemed pleased to be captured.'

Apart from tending his own flock, the Reverend Backhouse took a great interest in other flocks, reporting: 'It was interesting to note the

Bedouin dodging the shells, clearing out with camels, donkeys and all. Under heavy fire on the first day of the battle Bedouin children guided their goats into safety. One goat gave birth to a kid which a Bedouin child kissed affectionately'.

Both the Imperial Camel Brigade and Lawrence of Arabia's mounted Arab Army needed a continuing supply of hardy and strong camels in order to increase the size of the force that Allenby was gathering to drive the Turks north once they had captured Gaza.

2 November, early hours

Then four EEF infantry brigades of 10,000 rifles attacked four Ottoman regiments of 4,500 rifles — which were reinforced by two divisions to over 8,000 men. Both sides suffered heavy losses. The attacks were to be carried out by well-prepared troops, with overwhelming artillery support and six Mark IV tanks. These attacks were designed to keep the Gaza garrison in place and not cause the British any trouble after the capture of Beersheba and during preparations for the main EEF advances north.

Allenby used planes dropping bombs, heavy artillery, infantry and tanks, the latter not performing much better than at Second Gaza. A

British signaller, R. Loudon, from the 52nd Lowland Division, wrote a vivid account of the first stage of the bloody attack:

'A man who obviously had been able to get more than his allowance [of rum] started singing loudly, and was removed. We then set off in a long line, and passed through our front line trenches into "No–Man's–Land". I saw a man breaking the ranks, and dodging back towards our lines, obviously his nerves having given way. An NCO dashed out, got hold of him, and took him away. I was with Hq. sigs. [headquarters signals] in the "fourth wave". Four parallel lines of white tape, had been laid out, and I and the others spaced ourselves out along the fourth tape, and lay down, facing the enemy lines, to await the signal to advance. Two tanks came rumbling up from behind, and a few of us had to jump up and get out of the way to let them pass ... Our shelling increased in volume, and at 03:00 the 4th RS [Royal Scots] advanced in four lines on a front of 300 yards [270 metres] towards the El Arish Redoubt. Two Turkish contact mines exploded as our 'first wave' approached the redoubt, blowing many of the men to pieces. We were not, of course, aware of this at the time. As I got near the Turkish trenches the enemy shell and machine-gun fire became so intense, with shells bursting all around, that I and several others decided to stop in a large shell or mine crater for a few minutes till the shelling eased somewhat. When the barrage moved forward we resumed our advance'.

Nevertheless, the Turks and their German officers were surprised: first of all, they had been tricked into thinking Allenby was going to attack Gaza back on 31 October, because that was 'confirmed' in the fake battle plan the Turks had discovered inside the lost briefcase dropped by a British officer in no-man's-land before the Battle of Beersheba. So when Allenby attacked Beersheba instead of Gaza, the Turks believed he would bypass Gaza on his advance north towards Hebron and Jerusalem. So now they were totally confused — which is why they did not believe this attack on Gaza was real and why they had diverted their troops from Gaza up north. Like a clever chess player, Allenby had outwitted Kress von Kressenstein and his Turkish subordinates once again. They certainly could not guess Allenby's next move on this Palestinian chessboard.

After their stunning success at Beersheba, and having rested in their makeshift camps, the Light Horsemen were disappointed that General Allenby used British infantry forces instead of Australian mounted troops in the Third Battle of Gaza.

Allenby also knew from the Second Gaza disaster that a frontal attack would fail. He resolved instead to focus on less-defended areas, where an attack would be least expected.

Both earlier attacks at Gaza had also been hampered by water shortages — an ever-present concern in desert warfare — and Allenby understood that establishing command of water supplies was critical.

Allenby took no chances. Apart from providing Bulfin's XXI Corps with a big enough force to defeat any remaining Turkish resistance in Gaza, Allenby also insisted the British artillery bombard Gaza relentlessly, forcing Turkish forces to start abandoning the town and flee north.

Allenby later confirmed his progress to his superior, General Sir William Robertson, who was back in Britain: 'On the morning of the 2nd, Bulfin put in an attack, by the 54th Division and part of the 52nd Division, on the S.W. of Gaza. He got all his objectives, with the exception of a few yards of trench here and there ... The navy have given us great help. They are making splendid practice on the Gaza defences, and the railway bridge and junction at Deir Sineid. This is the result of careful preliminary work and close collaboration between land and sea'.

In fact, before nightfall on 2 November, the British infantry forces had succeeded in subduing serious resistance. The main work now was to eliminate any remaining pockets of opposition.

'The Turks did not put up much of a fight', James Wight Williamson, a despatch rider from Sydney for the 2nd Brigade, wrote to his sweetheart, Maude, in Prospect, South Australia, 'for within a few hours a large number of prisoners and guns and the town had fallen into our hands'. After four years of winning her over with these upbeat letters, Williamson would return to Australia and marry Maude Clayfield.

It had been a good start, as Allenby confirmed on 2 November in a letter to his wife: 'This morning, at 3 o'clock, I attacked the SW front of the Gaza defences. We took them; on a front of some 6000 yards, and to a depth of some 1000 to 1500 yards. We now overlook Gaza; and my left is on the sea coast, NE of the town. The Navy cooperated with fire from the sea; and shot well. We've taken some 300 prisoners and some machine guns, so far'.

Allenby, who was fighting on many fronts at once, had hoped to trap Kress von Kressenstein's Eighth Army at Gaza, but the Turks got away too fast and retreated in some haste further up the coast.

Battle of Tel el Khuweilfe

1 November

Allenby had his hands full because, on the same day he had ordered Bulfin to attack Gaza, some of his other forces had to fight an unexpected battle on their great drive up the Plain of the Philistines towards Jerusalem, at Tel el Khuweilfe, a prominent hill 18 kilometres north of Beersheba in a dry, arid, rocky landscape. The battle lasted about a week. The main Australians involved were the 1st Light Horse Regiment from New South

Wales and the 8th Light Horse Regiment from Victoria, although they were later relieved by Britain's 53rd Division, and also the Camel Brigade.

This was also an important battle for Allenby to win as this position had great strategic value as a vantage point; it also had a plentiful supply of water. Neither Allenby nor Chauvel had actually planned this battle because they were focused on capturing Gaza, then Jerusalem.

As they won battles, the Australian Light Horse troopers captured more and more Turkish prisoners, who they then had to shepherd back behind their lines and into POW camps — where most of the Turks were happy to go, knowing they would get a good feed.

The battle began with a Turkish attack on a 70-man detachment of the Desert Mounted Corps, who were searching for water towards Nejile beside the road to Hebron. The Turks were now convinced that the British had started a massive advance north to Jerusalem via Hebron, which was the headquarters of the Turkish Seventh Army. The Turks called for reinforcements, and six battalions (of 1,000 men each) were brought across from the forces defending Gaza.

Idriess wrote: 'Von Kressenstein is rushing columns of motor-lorries packed with men to Tel el Khuweilfe for there lies the water for an army; and now the British 53rd Division, Londoners and also Camel brigade along with the 1st and 8th Light Horse and New Zealanders are fighting bitterly around Tel el Khuweilfe. For that place is an important junction seven miles west of Dharayet. But above all else it holds the life-giving water which is needed by great bodies of troops.'

Idriess's account included the fact that the 8th Light Horse of Victorians (who had also fought at the bloody Nek at Gallipoli) 'have been fighting for forty hours without any rations and their horses without water'.

Yet there was a silver lining. By diverting these troops away from Gaza, the Turks inadvertently helped the British capture Gaza at the same time, since they had weakened Gaza's defences. As the enemy reinforced their troops at Tel el Khuweilfe, the leader of the Desert Mounted Corps, Lieutenant-General Sir Harry Chauvel, was ordered to drop everything and tackle the Turks there as quickly as possible.

Needing all the troops he could get for this sudden battle, Chauvel used his own Light Horsemen, British Yeomanry, and New Zealanders, along with infantry from the British 53rd Division and men of the Camel Brigade, to start pushing the Turks off that Tel el Khuweilfe ridge. But even the crafty Chauvel, who was on a winning streak, made little headway during that time, as the fighting in the waterless and rocky country was extremely difficult, and at times the attackers found themselves under immense pressure. Brigadier-General Ryrie, Commander of the 2nd Brigade, who was also fighting there was so committed to the battle that he wrote to his wife, 'I have not even taken my spurs off for three days'.

Idriess, who was also fighting nearby, was ordered with his comrades to capture two large Turkish guns, which were supported by machine guns and rifles. They did this successfully, although not without great difficulty for both riders and horses, facing at one point a precipitous gully as dangerous as the 'terrible descent' faced by the mythical 'Man from Snowy River', written 20 years earlier by the man in charge of their horses, Major Banjo Paterson.

'We galloped straight for the guns, horses reefing for their heads, three blood boiling miles with the screeching air blast of the shells in our faces

... We waited until two shells exploded crash crash! We spurred up into the cloud of smoking dust, horses pawing the bank, and were racing for our lives. Crash crash! A blinding flame tore the ground in a whirlwind of dust and fumes. We strained hold of our maddened horses then, Christ! A precipitous gully in front — the awful sensation of a void — a breakneck swerve horses berserk ... we lined the ridge and opened out on the Turks. They would not stand and they steadily retired before us but still blazing with their guns as they retired.'

Idriess and his fellow horsemen had forced the Turks back, but 'Pools of blood were now forming there; an old chestnut horse I had often ridden hung its head pathetically bleeding from the nose and its rider Lieutenant Webster lay dying at its feet and his men liked him very much'. Nevertheless, Idriess said, 'our casualties were, as almost always, extraordinarily light'.

4 November

Nearby, the keen-eyed Reverend Nigel Backhouse recorded in his diary: 'We were ordered to stand to at 4. a.m. and heard very heavy bombardment in the Gaza direction'. He said he could 'see our reinforcements coming up the valleys'. He had also seen 'Two shepherds herding at least 100 beautiful goats, dark brown and black in colour with light brown tints'. Apparently fascinated by the stock, he wrote: 'I took some photographs of Bedouin with their sheep and goats. The sheep and goats actually recognised their shepherds, for quite a large flock went single file through another flock and followed their own shepherd. One goat ran beside the shepherd and kept looking up at him like a friend. The shepherd boys who were clad in sheep skins looked after the kids when they were born'.

This nature lover also reported seeing a fox and also 'a large dark coloured snake which we killed immediately'. And there was something grimmer: 'there are plenty of dead Turks scattered about lying unburied from earlier battles. But we are all covered in dust and are dirty and have slept without tents for a week now'.

6 November

On 6 November, Chauvel, needed for other operations in the area, handed over the fight to Major-General George de Symons Barrow's Yeomanry Division, who then fought on with the help of troops of the British 53rd Division.

Meanwhile, as part of these overlapping battles, Bulfin's bombardment of Gaza intensified on 6 November, and during the night of 6–7 November, successful attacks were launched on several trench systems, which Bulfin's men captured, thanks to the Turkish troops who had left their post at Gaza. Bean also reported that 'Chetwode's 20th Corps captured a part of the Turkish line between Beersheba and Gaza leaving Gaza open to attack from both sides'.

Idriess was lucky to survive: 'We were all sitting down eating bully beef and biscuits on a hill above the Plain when a screeching hail of iron and splintered rock smashed throughout the regiment. Men went down, some horses went down, others were rearing — one poor brute balanced on its head for seconds before it collapsed and rolled down the hill'. He 'rushed to help the wounded men' but before long 'many of their horses were stone dead' and 'one horse had its neck cut clean in halves by a single fragment'. He said the men were soon 'Shooting the poor brutes that were too badly hurt to save. I saw men nearly cry today — we love our horses'. Then, 'On the rocky crags above, the Bedouins like black vultures had stood all day watching us and waiting. We hate the Bedouin. It makes us think what a miserable thing war is!'

Allenby then struck north at Tel es Sheria at dawn on 6 November, splitting the Turkish Seventh and also the Eighth Armies, which had been tricked once again by another diversionary attack to the east by the camel company that was only 70 strong. The Turkish defenders now fled from what they thought would be a large-scale flank attack, thus leaving the flank of their Seventh Army exposed. The Seventh Army then retired to the stronghold of Tel es Sheria, which was under the control of German commander Kress von Kressenstein's Eighth Army.

7 November

As Bean reported, once Chetwode's XX Corps had opened up a gap in the Turkish line of defence between Beersheba and Gaza, the British were able to attack on both sides of Gaza on 7 November. Here, they found 'the resistance was feeble'; largely because 'so many Turkish troops had been withdrawn to fight other imagined battles or had already fled. So Gaza fell.' The Imperial Cavalry Brigade then entered Gaza to take control on behalf of Allenby's conquering forces. They were followed by the Desert Mounted Corps assigned to chase the retreating Turks.

The leading forces of Allenby's EEF advancing through Gaza during the morning of 7 November found the town abandoned. British artillery had destroyed nearly all the homes of the 40,000 people who had lived in Gaza before the war. The conquering troops advanced through gardens and fields to the main road northwards unopposed, and so began chasing the Turkish Seventh and Eighth Armies as they fled.

Idriess wrote about the ground around Gaza being littered 'with many dead and decaying Turkish corpses and even the bodies of some of our boys who died in earlier battles for Gaza'.

Meanwhile, Turkey's Eighth Army established itself in Jerusalem preparatory to the next big stand against the British. For, having concluded the successful capture of Gaza and Tel el Khuweilfe, the Turks suspected Allenby would next turn his attention to the capture of the Holy City itself.

8 November

The Reverend Nigel Backhouse wrote that at 7am, 'There was terrific gun fire in the direction of the Khuweilfe hills with the enemy shelling pretty heavily and a great interchange of rifle fire'.

But as Bean reported, 'In the end on November 8th as a climax to the stubbornness and dash of the Camel Corps and 2nd Light Horse Machine Gun Squadron — the hill at Khuweilfe was seized by Britain's 53rd Division' and the British Yeomanry.

Although they were British forces, Idriess overcame the traditional Anglo-Australian rivalry, exclaiming, 'These British Yeomanry fought so well we now see them as our brothers!'

Most importantly, water supplies were now assured. A jubilant Idriess reported: 'When the news came through that the forts of Khuweilfe had fallen that thrilled the whole brigade not only because of the victory but there was water, water, water!'

By nightfall on 8 November, all Ottoman positions of the Gaza to Beersheba line were captured, Gaza itself was captured as well as Tel el Khuweilfe, while Turkey's Eighth Army was in full retreat. The easy occupation of Gaza, without much of a fight, facilitated Allenby's swift direct advance northwards, chasing the retreating Turks. In fact, they were not actually defeated at Gaza, because they had organised a skilful retreat from the town, demonstrating both operational and tactical mobility.

Now, with both Gaza and Tel el Khuweilfe behind him, Allenby was at last free to press northwards towards Jerusalem.

9 November

The victory brought relief, as Reverend Backhouse reported: 'The night of the 8th and early morning of 9th was absolutely quiet, and we finally reached a position where there was water supply and were able to water our horses for the first time for 50 hours. We drew no rations all day and horse feed was pretty short except for some grain we got from Bedouin dumps'.

Trooper Leslie Taylor, who was just 17, of the 8th Regiment had helped with this victory, and subsequently won the Military Medal because, according to his commanding officer, he 'gallantly volunteered and rode in under exceptional heavy fire at close range to try and rescue two wounded comrades. He was wounded himself in doing so. I considered his action very brave as there were no stretched bearers available and he volunteered'. Taylor was a butcher's apprentice from South Australia who had enlisted under age; he not only survived the war but also went on to father eight children, one of whom, Lea, contributed this extract.

He might have been riding a camel here, but the enterprising trooper Victor Dignam made sure he got the best horse when he had to go into battle: he stole a good horse belonging to a British officer one dark night and swapped its horseshoe number with his own inferior horse.

One of Taylor's British comrades, Sergeant-Major Herbert Mason from the Warwick Yeomanry, who won the Distinguished Conduct Medal, had also helped greatly — as according to his citation, 'During the charge he showed great gallantry, killing several of the enemy with his sword including a German officer and his example helped make the charge a success'.

Others like Trooper Victor Dignam, from Menangle, of the 12th Regiment, only survived the battle by taking things into their own hands, according to his daughter, Lorna Roberts: 'Victor was allotted a horse that used to bolt when the gunfire started as it was a badly behaved gelding. So having spotted a lovely mare that an English officer had, he decided to do a swap. One dark night he filed the number off his gelding's hoof, took this over to the officer's stables, and stole the number off the hoof of the officer's mare and stuck the number of his gelding onto that hoof of the officer's mare, then put the mare's number onto the gelding's hoof — thus swapping the horses. So Dignam passed the bucking gelding over to the unsuspecting English officer, telling his mates he wanted to make sure none of our boys got stuck with the rogue gelding. So he was certainly a bit of a lad.' From then on, Dignam rode happily into battle on his new quiet mare, leaving the unsuspecting British officer to cope with the bucking gelding.

A victory worth waiting for

The Third Battle of Gaza was more successful than imagined, and, as it turned out, it was well worth postponing the attack till this later stage of the war. Allenby had only planned to keep the garrison in check after the capture of Beersheba. He had only expected to capture the first line of Ottoman trenches, which had been the objective of Bulfin's XXI Corps, which used new infantry tactics, tanks, and massed artillery organised in accordance with standards on the Western Front. But as two regiments of the Ottoman 7th Division reserve had actually retreated, the EEF advanced further, driving the Turks before them. As Allenby's determined forces had forced the enemy to retreat as they advanced, it seemed this attack on the western defences of Gaza had achieved the objectives. The EEF had also inflicted severe losses on the Ottoman defenders; more than 1,000 of whom the EEF buried in the captured trenches. During the fighting, the Corps infantry had advanced about 2 miles (3.2 kilometres) on a 5,000-yard (4.6 kilometre) front, and held their gains against repeated Ottoman counterattacks; the frontline defensive system on the south-west side of Gaza had been captured, so the

After capturing Gaza, the deeply religious General Allenby realised he would now be advancing into the Holy Land, so advised his generals that, although he was planning to capture Jerusalem next, he did not want to damage this Holy City site by shelling it unnecessarily because it was so sacred to Christians, Jews, and Muslims.

infantry were able to occupy a position from which they could threaten the dreaded Ali Muntar (which had claimed so many Allied lives in the First and Second Gaza battles) and the rest of the defences in front of the town.

With renewed confidence from having bagged Beersheba and Gaza, Allenby now set his sights on the Holy City itself.

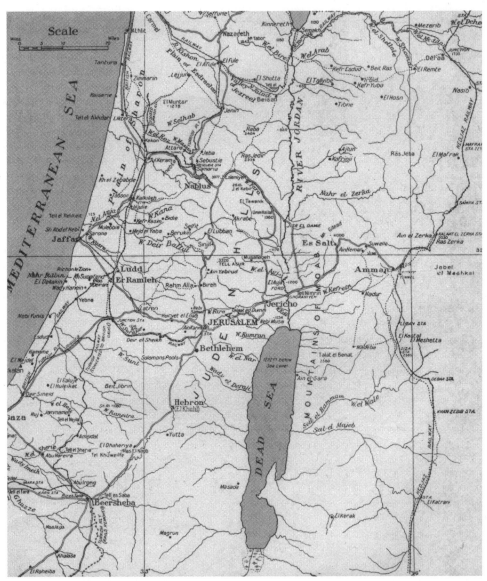

As the Holy City of Jerusalem was his next major objective, General Allenby ordered his forces to advance north from the recently captured towns of Gaza and also, most directly, from Beersheba, travelling via Hebron and then Bethlehem into the Holy City itself.

8.
JERUSALEM,
17 NOVEMBER–
11 DECEMBER 1917

FIRST CHRISTIANS TO CAPTURE HOLY CITY FOR 650 YEARS

Although the approach to Jerusalem itself over the rolling hills did not present any great military challenges for the troopers ordered to capture the Holy City, those brought up as Christians faced the prospect of invading this religious icon with some trepidation.

The capture of Jerusalem would be a wonderful Christmas present for the British people and a great boost to morale for the British Empire.

BRITISH PRIME MINISTER, DAVID LLOYD GEORGE,
SEPTEMBER 1917

BACKGROUND TO THE BATTLE

Confident that Gaza was no longer a threat, the God-fearing commander-in-chief, Sir Edmund Allenby, turned his attention to capturing the Holy City of Jerusalem. He had little choice, actually, as his ultimate boss, Prime Minister David Lloyd George, had asked him to capture Jerusalem before Christmas as a 'Christmas present' for the British people — most of whom were, of course, Christians aware that they had lost this Holy City to the Muslims more than 650 years earlier. Lloyd George wanted his war-weary people to have something to celebrate after suffering the worst year on the Western Front. Thousands had just been slaughtered in the muddy quagmire of the pointless Battle of Passchendaele in Belgium. Christians, Lloyd George believed, would rejoice at regaining control over the Holy City of Jerusalem and its neighbour, royal David's city, Bethlehem, where Christ was born. For Lloyd George, entry into Jerusalem would be worthy of the bells of Westminster Cathedral pealing joyfully all Christmas Day, along with St Paul's Cathedral and churches around Great Britain. It would certainly help him get re-elected.

If Allenby's 'onward Christian soldiers marching off to war' were victorious, they would be the first Christians to win back the Holy City of Jerusalem. Looking back through history, that would also put a long overdue end to the earlier series of Crusades mounted by Western Europeans from the 11th century to the 13th century. It would also be a reversal of the Battle of Hattin, when Saladin (1137–1193) led his ferocious Muslim warriors into Jerusalem. Saladin's greatest triumph was to defeat the European Crusaders at this battle in 1187, as this paved the way for the Islamic re-conquest of Jerusalem and other Holy Land cities. After the subsequent Third Crusade, Saladin also negotiated a truce with Richard I (the Lionheart) that secured continued Muslim control of Jerusalem.

Holy City or not, Trooper Ion Idriess thought the whole business of capturing this religious icon was pretty unholy. 'The mounted men are pushing the Turk fast towards Jerusalem. Jerusalem the holy city of peace and hope! But its byways are now all roads of hell'.

However, some of the more devout Christians among Allenby's troops also believed their success was inevitable because of the writings of the ancient prophets, who had claimed that the forces of good would capture this Holy City from the forces of evil at about this time. Always acutely aware of the historical and religious significance of the Holy Land through which they were fighting, Idriess wrote as they reached Esdud, just north of Gaza, where they were chasing retreating Turks towards Jerusalem:

British Prime Minister David Lloyd George put a lot of pressure on Allenby to capture Jerusalem before Christmas, believing it would boost the morale of his Christian nation after British forces had suffered such terrible losses fighting on the Western Front during 1917.

'Our Bible enthusiast is bubbling over, for Ed Dud [sic] is the ancient Ashdod of the Old Testament, the Ashdod of the Philistines … Cox's brigade has just saved the bridge at Jisr Esdud and are defending it by a bridgehead. Our troops have galloped over Ascalon, and the Bible enthusiast has balanced himself on a German beer-barrel (empty) and got this off his chest: *"O man savage, ferocious, what desolation hast thou wrought on the earth! They have stretched out upon Ascalon the line of confusion and the stones of emptiness. Thorns have come up in her place and brambles in the fortress thereof and it is a habitation of dragons and a convert for owls"*.

'So we cheered our bible enthusiast: he bowed and gave us a lecture. It appears that Gaza and Ascalon, Ashdod, Gath and Ekron were five capital cities. Some old Prophet cursed them and the prophecy came true. Ashdod the Proud defied the siege of Psammetichus for 29 years. An old Crusader castle, ruined like the city, still guards the forlorn harbour. At Ascalon city, Herod was born. Gaza is the only city of them left. But a shell has just burst above the Bible enthusiast and he ended his lecture abruptly — five shrapnel bullets whizzed right through the barrel.'

Much later another 'Bible enthusiast', Andrew Adams, revealed in his 1993 book, *As Birds Flying,* biblical prophecies that he claims had foretold the capture of both Beersheba and the Holy City of Jerusalem in 1917 'by the forces of good' — written by prophets quoted in the Old Testament, including Isaiah, (31: 5) Daniel (12:12) and Haggai (2:18–20), thousands of years earlier.

Adams, whose book title derives from the biblical text of Isaiah 31:5, claimed that, according to Genesis 21:33, Abraham — the prophet of all three monotheistic religions and the Hebrew patriarch — dug a well there thousands of years ago and swore an oath to God that the well would only be used for good not evil. He named his new well Beer-Sheba, 'The Well of the Oath'. Adams claimed that this original well and a Tamarisk tree Abraham also planted in Beer-Sheba could still be located in 1918, providing inspiration for good to triumph over evil, and he saw the Light Horse victory as a fulfilment of God's will. Adams went on to claim that biblical prophecies had also predicted that the forces of good would capture the greatly contested holy city of Jerusalem, which the British would liberate from the oppressive Ottoman Empire in the final year of the war.

Back down on the ground, Idriess took notes about the response of the locals to these 'forces of good' liberating the Holy Land from those 'evil' Muslims, claiming they also told him about these Prophecies. Taking notes in his saddle, riding through villages that his 5th Regiment was liberating, he remarked: 'The inhabitants all wearing queer garments lined the roads and shady lanes and stared at us brown sleeveless soldiers. We must have seemed queer fighting men to them for they stared as if they had expected to see supermen not rough clad Australians. I don't think they could believe that we were actually the men who had driven back their taskmaster of centuries. They also seem to be on the verge of something they cannot believe, cannot understand: they tremble when they whisper of Jerusalem. It appears there is some Prophecy, centuries old, that foretold that one day Jerusalem will fall and be taken from the Turk or whatever infidel holds it'.

Jerusalem is, in fact, a Holy City to all three monotheistic religions. Judaism (the oldest at more than 2,000 years old) claims the prophet Abraham travelled to Jerusalem to found their religion, and Moses led the escaping Jews on an exodus from Egypt to Jerusalem. Christianity, the second oldest, was founded in Jerusalem on the claim that Christ was crucified there in 30AD. Islam, the third-oldest religion, claims that their prophet Muhammad founded their religion at nearby Medina in the seventh century, and, in a vision, flew his winged steed to Jerusalem, where he taught his followers how to pray to Allah. So all three faiths had great and competing claims to Jerusalem by the time Allenby's forces liberated the ancient city.

But when Allenby did enter Jerusalem on 11 December, the Jews were just as thrilled as the Christians, because their religious scholars claimed that one of their most heroic warriors, Judah Maccabee, defeated his enemy at Jerusalem on the 'same date' more than 2,000 years earlier. In fact, their texts recorded that Judah Maccabee 'drove the heathen oppressors from the Holy City' — in his case, these oppressors were the leaders of the Seleucid Empire; for Allenby, the oppressors were the leaders of the Ottoman Empire. He declared he was 'liberating Jerusalem for all the peoples of Palestine — Christians, Jews and Moslems — from the tyranny of the Osmanlis'. To confirm this fair deal, he installed a neutral British official from the Egyptian service, Borton Pasha, as military governor. Notwithstanding the many changes to the calendar over the centuries, this historical coincidence of the date of liberation still gave the Jews great joy.

Ironically, although Allenby and his Christian soldiers kept on marching off to war to liberate these holy lands — occupied by the Ottoman Empire for centuries — in the name of Christians, it would be the Jews who would benefit by 'inheriting' this territory, first by political decree, then by military might. No wonder the Jews were so pleased to welcome the British and

Anzac forces. As Idriess reported from a village near Jerusalem, which he helped liberate and thought was called Richon, the Jews welcomed them with open arms, offering them plentiful supplies of food and drink as long as the hapless troopers were prepared to pay — including wine 'which made things a bit lively'. He wrote: 'The inhabitants are very fair skinned mostly Jews. They are by far the most clean people we have met. They are very hospitable although they do charge a hefty price for brown bread, honey and tobacco. Lots of them have had a hard time from the Turks. They seem to live between two devils — the Turk and the Arab. Apparently the Turks prevent the Arab from massacring them outright because the Jews are a very handy people to squeeze taxes from'.

General Allenby, a devout Christian, was well aware that capturing Jerusalem from the Islamic Turks would transfer the Holy City from Muslim to Christian rulers for the first time since Muslims captured it from the Christians more than 650 years earlier.

The Jews saw the Allied dismantling of the Ottoman Empire and the withdrawal of the Turks as the first major step towards them getting control of their Holy Land. Over the centuries, the Jews had experienced domination by the Seleucids, Romans, Byzantine Christians, then Muslims, who won the last Crusade after centuries of fighting against Christians, and lastly the Muslim Turks of the Ottoman Empire. It had been a long wait, but now that Christian forces had liberated their coveted Holy Land, they planned to create a Jewish homeland. Unwittingly, the simple blokes from the bush, the Australian Light Horse, would play a pivotal role in paving the way for the future state of Israel.

But unbeknown to troopers like Idriess or any other well meaning Light Horsemen from Australia, behind the scenes in London, big international political changes were being planned. The Foreign Secretary, Lord Arthur Balfour — a deeply religious Scotsman who grew up reading the Bible every day and singing psalms honouring Zion — was the author of the Balfour Declaration, which pledged British support for a 'national home for the Jewish people'. The British Zionist Federation, with supporters in many countries, had been lobbying for years to get Britain's help to create a new nation state for the Jews — in Palestine. Predicting the British military forces would liberate the Holy Land from the Ottomans, Walter Rothschild, 2nd Baron Rothschild, a leader from the Federation who was one political jump ahead of everyone else, had sent a letter to Britain's Foreign Secretary in late October (as Allenby's forces were making their momentous breakthrough by capturing Beersheba).

In his letter, Rothschild asked Balfour to help him create a homeland for Jews in Palestine, where Rothschild felt they belonged historically. Sympathetic to these ideas, Balfour replied to Rothschild in early November 1917 — just as Allenby was advancing towards Jerusalem — confirming that not only he but the British War Cabinet (which had now discussed the request) liked the idea of the Zionists creating a nation state for the Jews in Palestine and had formulated a position statement: 'His Majesty's Government view with favour the establishment in Palestine of a national home for the Jewish people, and will use their best endeavours to facilitate the achievement of this object, it being clearly understood that nothing shall be done which may prejudice the civil and religious rights of existing non-Jewish communities in Palestine, or the rights and political status enjoyed by Jews in any other country.'

Balfour asked Rothschild to 'bring this declaration to the knowledge of the Zionist Federation'. The declaration was a game-changer, one of the biggest in history, and would in time change the shape of politics in the Middle East, fuelling wars for years to come.

The British Prime Minister, Lloyd George, who had a Welsh Protestant background, also supported Balfour's Jewish homeland. Well-schooled in the Old Testament, which he said he loved more than the New Testament, he claimed he knew the names of the towns Allenby was capturing in Palestine much better than the towns Haig was fighting for on the Western Front just across the English Channel. Lloyd George also wanted to curry favour with and win votes from the powerful British Zionist Federation headed by Dr Chaim Weizmann, who lobbied the prime minister to support a homeland. Jews like Weizmann claimed it was predestined anyway, as the Old Testament prophets like Isaiah had prophesied that the gentiles would one day bring the Jewish people back to their land, as foretold in Isaiah 49. Jewish people around the world had for centuries expected this to happen, and a popular greeting at their annual festival of Yom Kippur was, 'Next year we celebrate in Jerusalem!' Lloyd George also hoped to win political support for Britain from powerful Jews in the diaspora throughout Europe and America, who all wanted this homeland.

Eventually, the Balfour Declaration became a foundation stone for the creation of the state of Israel. Once Allenby captured Jerusalem, the British would establish a military administration there, and this would be headed, in reality, by Weizmann and other powerful Zionists, including Major James de Rothschild, a military officer who was also a billionaire. The establishment of a Jewish state was later accelerated, when Jews desperately needed a homeland after they were so cruelly persecuted by Nazi leader Adolf Hitler, who murdered them using gas chambers in his concentration camps in the Second World War; Israel came into existence in 1948.

If the secret Sykes-Picot Agreement of 1916 promised the conquered Arab lands to the English and French great powers — marginalising the indigenous Arabs (and their leader Lawrence of Arabia) — the Balfour

Declaration offered the Holy Land itself to the Jews, without consulting the Arabs who had lived in Palestine for centuries.

Meanwhile, of course, the British — with their innocent Australian Light Horsemen — still had to liberate this Holy Land from the Turks. Not that these men were ignorant of the Old Testament, as Idriess explained while liberating villages west of Jerusalem: 'We are convinced the Bible has gone to our enthusiast's head. He says the New Zealanders crossed the Naha Sukereir river by an old stone bridge built by the Crusaders! The Naha Sukereir is a real river flowing with water. We don't believe it. There is one thing we are certain about though, the New Zealanders have been furiously opposed by the Jaffa Turks. All one day too, at Ayun Kara they were fighting with the bayonet, charging and being charged. Ayun Kara is the place where Samson fought with the jawbone of an ass. I'll bet the En Zeds found the cold steel a deadlier weapon'.

Allenby, a devout Christian himself who considered he was performing a religious duty (although initially for the Christians as much as the Jews), knew it would take some very hard fighting indeed to drive his forces north for the advance on Jerusalem, and he would need skilled tactics to secure the city; after all, it was so well fortified by the Turkish army. A hardened veteran of the Boer War and the Western Front, he would employ all the tactics he had used successfully in the past. That is why he bolstered his forces with a fresh new division of British troops to supplement his other three divisions; and he did this while he could because he knew the British War Cabinet wanted some of his troops to fight on the much bloodier and more urgent Western Front, where he knew from bitter experience how intense the fighting was.

Trooper Nigel Backhouse claimed the fighting was also pretty intense as they rode towards Jerusalem: 'Had a stunt at 4am moving rapidly into action against intense rifle fire, intermittent shell fire, shrapnel from heavy guns and a burst of machine gun fire. The machine gun bullets were singing about our ears. But our men gained possession of the country near a railway arch where there was a good supply of water in a wady.'

That intense fire claimed many victims, Backhouse said: 'Where we can now see the Tommies collecting some of the dead killed in yesterday's battle. We also notice dozens of motor lorries bringing back wounded'.

Apart from bringing back wounded, Trooper Fred Cox said the advancing Light Horsemen also had to escort increasing numbers of prisoners back behind the lines after successful stunts: 'Although the enemy shell fire from both flanks was very persistent our dashing move was carried out at a gallop until our objective was obtained.' But then he said, 'We captured 1,230 prisoners, officers, medical officers and other ranks and had to leave men behind to guard them till they could be taken behind the lines'.

Yet there would be more prisoners to come, as Allenby deployed his increased aircraft support to help capture more villages en route to Jerusalem. Idriess reported: 'Hearing a tremendous buzz in the sky I looked up and there flew a great sight — twenty eight roaring birds going to bomb the Turks along the Jerusalem road! Soon we heard explosions that thundered along the Shephelah Road. What hell those close-packed batteries must have got, hedged in by the cliffy hills. Presently, back they flew again in clockwork formation, very businesslike, roaring through the sky. An hour later they returned and again we listened to detonation after detonation as they helped spread demoralization among a retreating army'.

Later, he saw, 'Miles ahead along the road blazed fires like street after street of burning houses where the plane bombs had ignited the Turkish supply-dumps'.

Trooper Lloyd Corliss from Boggabri, New South Wales, who was riding towards Jerusalem with his Regiment, was also dodging bombs, writing, 'A Taube flew over us and bombed and killed several men and wounded others. One of those killed was Karl Hargraves from Gunnedah. But we had to push on as our orders were to take the next position at all costs because we could not get any water elsewhere'.

Planes attacking from the safety of the skies were one thing, but Allenby did not want to sacrifice his own men on the ground as they advanced towards this heavily fortified, well-defended stronghold with its high and impenetrable city walls. After all, he had lost his own son, Lieutenant Michael Allenby, killed in action with the Horse Artillery on the Western Front. Yet as it would turn out, Christians among the British forces had many reasons to believe God was on their side. The night before they attacked Jerusalem, for example, the heavens opened and an unexpected deluge poured down, flooding the Turkish trenches and forcing the enemy to flee. The storm also gave Allenby's men and their horses much-needed water, too.

Notwithstanding this answer to prayers, securing the main long-term objective — Jerusalem — would not be easy. For one thing, Allenby's men were nearing exhaustion, as Idriess wrote: 'So Australia's mounted army rode into the Plain of the Philistines, half paralyzed by the longing for sleep', but on and on they rode with 'mounted troops pouring onto the Plain', and 'we are all waiting now for our own turn to attack. The waiting is nerve-wracking and there are such a lot of dead men lying about too'. Desperate for a smoke, he revealed: 'Our nerves are so raw and we so keenly feel the loss of our tobacco that our men are now smoking horse manure, tibbin, dried tea leaves, grass — anything!'

Writing to Maude, Sergeant Williamson said: 'The worst thing of all is the thought of going down to Jericho and the Jordan Valley because the heat in that place is nearly unbearable. No wonder people say "Go to Jericho!". In the House of Commons, (England) Lloyd George said that only black troops would stay in the Jordan Valley and white troops were all withdrawn. If it is any news to him the Australian Light Horse has been down there the whole time, but perhaps we are all counted as blacks with him and his crew. It is a hundred times hotter than the Sinai desert knows how to be.' Reserved to the last, Williamson signs off, 'Your sincere Friend Jim.'

Battle plans

Allenby was optimistic about capturing Jerusalem, especially as Bulfin and Chetwode's XXI and XX Corps had captured Gaza so soon after

Chauvel's stunning Beersheba victory. Apart from having the Turks on the run, Allenby also enjoyed troop numerical supremacy in Palestine. He was much more hands-on than his predecessor, Murray — having relocated his GHQ from a first-class Cairo hotel to the moving frontline in order to boost the flagging morale of the British troops — and he was in a much better position to direct operations. For this advance on Jerusalem, he amassed unprecedented troop reinforcements, artillery, gas shells, tanks, and planes, and was adamant that he would not proceed until certain of victory. By mid-November 1917, his forces were formidable, with seven infantry divisions plus the Desert Mounted Corps, consisting of both horses and camels, numbering 88,000 men.

As they captured biblical town after town, some of the Christian Light Horsemen who recognised the ancient names said it was like riding through the pages of the bible they had studied since childhood.

This would give him the edge over his opponents. The declining Turkish forces now retreating north through Palestine included only the

Turkish Seventh Army under General Erich von Falkenhayn and the Eighth Army under General Kress von Kressenstein, totalling just 35,000 men stretched out along a 40-kilometre line.

After their success on the Gaza–Beersheba Defence Line, Chetwode's XX British infantry had been advancing into the steep hills of southern Palestine from early November 1917, chasing the Turks as they went. The mounted troops also began advancing north towards Jerusalem, along with Lawrence of Arabia's Arab Army — which was increasingly respected now the news had got around about their July 1917 capture of Aqaba.

8 November

After capturing both Gaza and Tel el Khuweilfe through deception, the canny Allenby wanted to distract the Turks from his real purpose: seizing Jerusalem. He made sure the Turks could not work out which of his two moving frontlines was the most important: the troops marching up the Plain of the Philistines along the coast — which included both British infantry and the Australian Light Horse led by Chauvel — towards Jerusalem; or the mounted men and other troops riding through the Judean Hills inland to the east of Hebron.

En route, Allenby wanted to destroy or capture the retreating columns from Gaza and Tel el Khuweilfe. But when the mounted troops tried to intercept the columns, the retreating Turkish flank guards often fought too stubbornly for the horsemen to get through. Turks, guns, and equipment were captured, but these were largely the stragglers, with the main Turkish forces getting away. A continuing problem for the mounted troops was the difficulty in watering horses, which sometimes went without a drink for more than two days. Idriess reported that some horses rode without water for 70 hours.

The defending Turks were also a major problem, as before they retreated they fought back. Trooper W.G. Murray from the 12th Regiment, who had fought at Beersheba, recorded in his diary: 'As soon as we started out towards Jerusalem, the Turks came out of nowhere and attacked us.

Although we beat them back before us they came out again and again trying to block out progress towards Jerusalem. We had several attacks but they left behind large quantities of war material'.

Allenby wanted to minimise the number of defending Turks who could stop him entering Jerusalem, so he ordered Chetwode's infantry and Chauvel's Desert Mounted Corps to strike even harder north-westwards, to cut off the Turks retreating from Gaza, thereby reducing the size of the Turkish fighting force for future battles. He sent the 60th British Division along with the Light Horse to capture strongholds to the north, including Tel el Sheria, inland between Gaza and Tel el Khuweilfe. He ordered the Anzac Mounted Division to advance further inland to the east, capturing positions like the Ameidat railway station just north of Sheria. Chauvel's Australian Mounted Division also drove away a Turkish force repelling the advance of the 60th London Division. But these Light Horsemen did not always drive the Turks further north, and in one battle the Turks defeated Lieutenant A.R. Brierty and the mounted men of his 4th Brigade — by trickery. As Charles Bean later explained: 'Some Turks held up their hands and the party galloped over the enemy trench and dismounted to attack (and accept the Turkish surrender). But the Turks however rallied and, despite a brave effort of another troop, annihilated them'.

In another battle, British infantry went to the support of the 8th Light Horse Regiment. Second Lieutenant Boughey of the Royal Scots Fusiliers rushed forward alone with bombs, right up to the enemy, killing many and causing the surrender of a party of 30. But as he turned to go back for more bombs, he was mortally wounded, just as the Turks were surrendering. He was posthumously awarded the Victoria Cross. Over and over, as the mounted men tried to cut through the lines of retreating Turks, the Turkish rearguard fought back and stopped them. One gallant attack by the Warwickshire Yeomanry succeeded, but only at a great loss of life.

Yet Allenby's advance continued — despite the shortage of water — with the mounted troops watching the Turks from Gaza fleeing near the coast in long columns to the north.

9 November

Although some of the horses had gone for more than two days without a drink and their riders were on short water rations, the moving frontline pushed on. The mounted troops — including Idriess's 5th Regiment — then cut right through the lines of retreating Turks to reach the coast near the town of Esdud (formerly Ashdod) between Gaza and present-day Tel Aviv, and captured many more prisoners of war. They also captured guns and military vehicles and horses — although, as Bean reported, 'men and animals were in a dreadful condition as they were largely the weaklings straggling behind the Turkish army as the main forces had gone clear'.

This was a big breakthrough. Having cut the large column of retreating Turks in half, Allenby's men not only captured many prisoners but they could also now attack the tail of the Turkish retreating force. Having broken through on his left flank, Allenby's moving frontline driving the Turks back could now concentrate on the western side near the coast. Now the British Yeomanry Mounted Division and the Anzac Mounted Division drove up the Philistine Plain more rapidly, with the infantry in a seemingly unstoppable parade of force. The Turks did not have much hope, because inland to the east the Australian Mounted Division were riding faster and faster through the Judean Hills, forcing any Turks in that area to go north. So while Allenby's frontline stretched from the coast to the Judean Hills, his main aim was to advance rapidly up the Philistine Plain, through the Jewish settlements, vineyards, and orchards.

The battles continued in the rocky Judean Hills, which of course was crowned by the Holy City. By mid-November, it was also bitterly cold and chill rain swept across bare ridges. Then when the rain came, it turned every gully, creek, and road into a quagmire.

The Light Horse scrambled across this bleak battleground dismounted, as infantry, as they were at Gallipoli, with no shelter but their waterproof sheets, no food but army biscuits and tinned bully beef — and very little of these. One regiment moved into the Judean Hills with orders to relieve a unit of British infantry for a single night, but were then ordered to stay for five weeks, rain-soaked, frostbitten, and half-starved.

The ground was too rocky to dig trenches, and the men sheltered behind 'sangars' — walls of loose rock, about a metre high. They were often pretty miserable. But one of the Light Horsemen, Trooper Red Hutchinson, recalled that he and his outnumbered mates were crouched behind their flimsy rock barricade one freezing night, waiting for a big Turkish counterattack, when suddenly they heard the sound of bagpipes as a Scottish regiment came marching to relieve them in the frontline. 'I like the bagpipes', he wrote, 'but they never sounded as they did in the hills that night. It was the most beautiful sound I'd ever heard. It was salvation'.

12 November

The Turks, believing the inland eastern thrust was the main British advance, then mobilised as many troops as they could to fight a rearguard action. They then mounted a surprise attack at Summeil, forcing back the Australian Mounted Division and stopping their advance through the Judean Hills.

Meanwhile, down by the coast, Allenby's moving frontline pushed on successfully through the central plain past Wadi Hanein, and then Richon le Zion, and then Ramleh, on the coastal side of Jerusalem, before progressing on to Jaffa further north on the coast and then Ludd. By now, the Turks would have felt surrounded.

13 November

Following the successful Battle of Mughar Ridge, Allenby marched eastwards towards Jerusalem.

While his right flank headed north through the Judean Hills, his left force adopted a defensive posture at Jaffa, newly secured by the British. Allenby now geared up to face an expected last-ditch stand by General Erich von Falkenhayn's Yilderim Force, which had markedly strengthened the Turkish lines from Jerusalem to the sea.

Von Falkenhayn lost little time in launching attacks by his Seventh Army, succeeding in greatly slowing Allenby's advance. Allenby now realised he would be unable to secure Jerusalem's fall without first consolidating his force. To make things more complicated, both rival commanders had been specifically instructed by their respective governments (for religious reasons) to avoid fighting either in or immediately around the Holy City itself.

15 November

Lieutenant W.H. James led 40 Light Horsemen against a column of 300 retreating Turks at Ludd, capturing them all and winning the Military Cross. However, once again, Bean reported, the main Turkish fighters were away up north where they were regrouping for a last stand and 'these captured enemy were still only the belated elements of the escaping Turks'.

Riding north along the Plain, Idriess reported: 'Two miles ahead of us is the roar of rifle and machine gun fire, it spreads far away to the left towards the sea, we can hear its faint echoes far to the right amongst the grim Judean foot-hills.

'The magnitude of these operations has long since gone out of my focus but the officers say that as the Desert Mounted Corps sweeps right up Palestine, the Anzac Mounted Division is now spread from the coast inland, with its right flank joining the Australian Mounted Division which spreads out with its right flank touching the foothills of the Shephelah. Thus Australians and New Zealanders stretch right across Palestine from the coast to the Judean Hills riding in a face right up the country packing the Turks along every road back towards Jerusalem.'

But these Australians forces could have done better against the Turks with better weapons, according to Idriess: 'the 3rd Light Horse Brigade were wishing for swords — they broke through the Turkish flank guard killed hundreds and took a long column of prisoners. But if they had had swords the men swear they could have cut the retreating column up in such a way that the division would have taken thousands of prisoners. Nevertheless if we can only keep on winning like this the war would end soon'.

Swords or no swords, some of the Light Horse did not even have horses. 'We passed by Bamleigh and on to the strong and rugged ranges where we parted with our old Gees and started advancing north on foot', wrote Trooper James Gordon Murray, a country boy from Cumuoek in New South Wales serving in the 12th Regiment of the 4th Brigade Light Horse. Murray, who had charged with the mounted forces at Beersheba, was not reunited with his old 'Gee' until 5 January 1918, when he reported: 'We came out of the Front Line and took over our horses on the same day'.

And so the British frontline continued to advance until December, by which time the demoralised Turks had been pushed back so consistently that the time had come to move on Jerusalem.

1 December

By the start of December, it was clear to Allenby that the Turks could no longer advance south, let alone win any ground as a result of their counterattacks. Not only that, but the Turks were running short of men while Allenby's new British troop reinforcements were successfully replacing their tired comrades and entrenching themselves close to Jerusalem.

2 December

On 2 December, Chetwode's XX Corps also relieved Bulfin's XXI Corps. These new arrivals then improved their frontlines, and Allenby increased the number of soldiers in their line to create a powerful concentration.

3 December

British troops then recaptured the strategic village of Beit Ur el Foqa, attacking from the head of the Wadi Zeit and taking 17 prisoners and three machine guns. This position, however, proved impossible to hold, as it was overlooked by Ottoman positions on higher ground. Bombing and hand-to-hand fighting continued all morning, and the battalion withdrew, suffering 300 casualties.

Fortunately, by nightfall, the remaining Turkish defenders abandoned their counterattacks, and fighting in that part of the Judean Hills ceased.

4 December

Meanwhile, on the Hebron to Bethlehem road south of Jerusalem, the British infantry were making great progress snaking up to Jerusalem from a south-easterly direction — from Bethlehem, in fact, 'Royal David's city', which Allenby hoped would be a back door into Jerusalem. The 53rd (Welsh) Division (which had fought so well at Second Gaza and was known as Mott's Detachment) had continued their tentative advance to arrive about seven kilometres south of Hebron on 4 December. After two Australian light armoured cars of the Light Armoured Motor Battery drove in from the north, reporting no Ottoman units in Hebron, these Welsh warriors continued on to the Dilbe valley that night.

Christian Light Horsemen rode into Bethlehem with great respect and reverence because this was where the bible told them that three wise men had ridden in from the east, bearing gifts for their Saviour, Jesus Christ, who was born there in a humble stable.

Chetwode then ordered Mott to advance as quickly as possible to get into a position three miles (4.8 kilometres) south of Jerusalem by the morning of 8 December. Mott's advanced guard again moved tentatively during the night of 5 December to about five kilometres north of Hebron.

7 December, morning

Mott's Detachment reached the Turkish frontline defending Bethlehem, which was only 6.4 kilometres from Bethlehem itself, but bad weather prevented any advance. Mott's Detachment was meant to have marched northwards in time to cover the right flank of the 60th Division (Londoners) and to cut the road from Jerusalem to Jericho, preventing any Turkish soldiers escaping that way to the east. Instead, Mott's Detachment managed to capture Solomon's Pools to the south of Bethlehem by the evening of 7 December, so at least the Turks could not put up a fight from there.

It was little wonder the Turks began to retreat or desert in increasing numbers when they saw Brigadier-General Ryrie leading thousands of Light Horsemen in the 2nd Brigade across the Esdud desert and along the Philistine Plain.

Meanwhile, Allenby's relentless drive up the Philistine Plain now forced the two main Turkish armies to separate. In fact, to protect Jerusalem, Kress von Kressenstein's Turkish Eighth Army had already headed east, inland, to surround the Holy City, which was still at least 40 kilometres north-east of Allenby's main moving frontline. By now it was difficult for the Turks to move around, because Allenby's forces had already captured the railway line they used to transport men and equipment. Meanwhile, von Falkenhayn's Turkish Seventh Army retreated to Jaffa, north-west of Jerusalem on the coast, ready to block the British forces on their anticipated drive north, closer to the coast.

Tricky as always, Allenby ordered some of the forces on his left — on the western side of the moving frontline — to drive back the Turks on this coastal side and make a big show of their advances. This was just to fool the Turks, because he was not really using this coastal thrust as the main attack at all. Instead, Allenby next decided to strike from his right flank, which was further inland, north-east, to cut off and surround the Turks defending Jerusalem — which the Turks did not expect. His main infantry marched into the Judean Hills with his mounted men and began driving Turkish defenders back through this difficult terrain. He also ordered more mounted troops to support the infantry riding about over the hills and down through the valleys, driving back hidden pockets of Turkish defenders. The 3rd Light Horse Brigade did some of the hardest fighting as they stopped a Turkish battalion turning around, charging south, and breaking through Allenby's moving frontline at El Burj.

Allenby kept up the pretence of a coastal advance and, in fact, allowed the deceived Turks to push back some of his forces on the coast just to let them think that was the main battleground, and that they were winning on that side. Allenby hoped they would then divert more of their forces there, weakening the Turkish defences in the path of his main advance. Meanwhile, his frontline crept closer to Jerusalem.

7 December, afternoon

As the Turkish Seventh Army still controlled Jerusalem with its neighbouring town of Bethlehem, and still had their frontline running along to the south of these two major strongholds, Allenby paused before striking. The Turks also had artillery located on hills around the Holy City.

Allenby ordered his big guns from the south to send heavy artillery shells at both the Turkish frontline and the enemy batteries on the hills — but not to shell old Jerusalem itself. The Australian Light Horse had been unable to push the Turks back from these frontlines, so it was up to the big guns now.

Overnight, on 7 December, the heavens opened and down poured torrential rain. Some of Allenby's soldiers with a Christian bent saw this deluge as divine intervention. The Turks, on the other hand, shivered in their trenches and prayed to Allah for relief.

Idriess wrote: 'It rained last night over Jerusalem and very very heavily. That is great. There will be plenty of water in the wadi beds for our horses. It makes us a bit miserable though because we have no tents only a "wee" bivy sheet to each man — a strip of waterproof just long enough and wide enough for a man to spread on the ground so that he will not actually be inside the wet mud. If we tie four sheets together we can also make a roof held up by our rifles'.

This poor accommodation was the last thing Idriess and his comrades needed, as by December 1917, 'Eighty per cent of us men are now half rotten with septic sores', and it was not till his regiment was given 'a couple of days' spell' that Idriess and his comrades 'had a chance to dress our septic sores — so the flies wont get such a feed now. But the greatest of boons — a tobacco issue has just arrived'.

8 December

By 8 December, Allenby was ready to attack, but reluctant to do so. His infantry had fought its way, against all opposition, to a line threatening Jerusalem from the west and the south-west, and were poised to finish off the job and march on Jerusalem. But Allenby did not want that. He did not want any fighting to destroy the Holy City so dear to him and fellow Christians, so he paused. This campaign was the most delicate from a religious point of view, calling for extreme sensitivity. Allenby had ordered some of his subordinate commanders not to shell holy cities like Bethlehem in case they damaged them. Instead, they were ordered to wait till the Turks evacuated, allowing the British to enter the old streets and alleyways without damaging them.

A keen student of history, literature, music, and art, Allenby was also an authority on Crusader castles and religion, which he discussed often with fellow officers. A deeply religious man, he would consult his earmarked war-torn Bible for spiritual guidance. From time to time, he asked his staff officers to bow their heads and pray with him for the success of an attack with few casualties. He also used it for the historical and geographical insights it offered for his campaigning in Palestine.

A New Zealand officer, Colonel C.E.R. Mackesey, reported that: 'When Allenby came within striking distance of Jerusalem, he told his officers he did not want to fire back at the Turks for fear of damaging the ancient Holy City'. Mackesey said Allenby then cabled Prime Minister David Lloyd George for directions. But Lloyd George just cabled back saying the British Cabinet had advised that he Allenby 'should do whatever is deemed necessary'. Unsatisfied, the deeply troubled Allenby, who was on the spot looking across at the ancient and fragile Holy City through his field glasses, then cabled King George V. This time, the King replied more specifically, cabling back: 'Pray about it.' So Allenby did, praying with his officers

When asked by General Allenby how he could capture the Holy City of Jerusalem without shelling the sacred site to bits, King George V replied in a cable: 'Pray about it.' Allenby did, and the Turks stopped opposing his approach soon after.

for spiritual guidance, as he had done many times before. Soon after, the enemy stopped sending shells from Jerusalem towards the British. The Turks, it turned out, were prepared to surrender rather than risk their sacred Islamic places being destroyed by battle.

Turkish forces began to abandon their trenches outside Jerusalem. At the same time, refugees also fled, fearing the British shelling. Overnight, thousands poured out of the city, heading north away from the British.

Having reinforced his frontline, Allenby assigned the task of capturing Jerusalem to XX Corps under the highly experienced Sir Philip Chetwode. Chetwode's attack began on 8 December. The assault took two forms: a central thrust from Nebi-Samweil — a commanding series of heights some 13 kilometres to the west of Jerusalem — and a secondary attack south from Bethlehem.

Chetwode and his XX Corps launched the final advance, taking the heights to the west of Jerusalem on 8 December and forcing the Ottoman Seventh Army to retreat during the evening. The city surrendered the following day, although sporadic fighting would continue in the surrounding hills in the days following.

So, in the end, the city fell after a single day's 'fighting'.

Some of the refugees were a sorry sight to see, especially Arabs fleeing the fighting from Jerusalem and nearby villages. The British had shelled and conquered one Turkish village, forcing both Turks and Arabs to flee, as Idriess reported: 'Swarms of Arabs, men, women and children staggering under loads of loot, panting and struggling the sweat pouring down their swarthy faces in their greed to get it all away before more distant villagers should rush the spoil. I felt quite sick watching the greedy women, hysterical, shrieking, almost crying in their excitement as they clawed the contents of abandoned Turkish horse-drawn wagons not knowing in their envy and fear which of the stuff to take. They did not think to end the misery of the poor moaning beasts upon whose mangled bodies they climbed up onto the wagons'.

Even worse, he noted: 'Among the huge litter lay dead Turks, their dusty faces trodden on by men, women and children'. In fact, the women and children 'whose blood-stained feet were covered with dust' used three dead Turks huddled together under a wagon 'as a footstool'. Idriess 'wondered if the Bedouins had troubled to put the wounded quickly out of their misery in their hurry for loot. Feeling rather sick, we then rode on following the same trail, broken wagons, dead beasts, Turkish clothing, smashed men, greatcoats, baggage'.

The temptation to steal was too much for New South Wales country boy Stan Broome, from the plucky 12th Regiment that had fought at Beersheba: 'The boys sneaked out last night into the paddocks under the stars and keeping very quiet brought back five sheep — so many of us camped around the fire cooked up a great feast'.

Stan Broome had collected so many trophies that he thought it was now time to sent a parcel home to his unsuspecting mother, 'Containing a very old scored copy of the Koran, written in sanscript [sic], which I picked up in the Gaza Mosque, a toilet set I got at Beersheba, a curio made from a shell top and Turkish bullets.' The handsome Broome also received letters from 'Nurse Peterson who is a fine girl who often drops me a line. Also a Miss Evelyn Davies from South Australia, who has sent me three Christmas parcels also papers and books and writes often. She seems a very nice girl also and is very sensible and unaffected'.

9 December

Most appropriately, the liberating British troops entered Bethlehem before Jerusalem. With the last of the Turkish forces gone, the British 4th Battalion, Sussex Regiment, marched with due reverence through Bethlehem, well aware that it was the birthplace of Jesus Christ. The 53rd (Welsh) Division — which had suffered so much at Second Gaza and won one of the few battles — then occupied Bethlehem as the new controlling force.

The British infantry troops entered Bethlehem unopposed, setting up their local headquarters in Manger Square, in front of the Church of the Holy Nativity that had been built on the site where their saviour was born. By then, all soldiers would have been aware of the religious significance of their advance.

Meanwhile, just up the road to the north, the mayor of Jerusalem, Hussein Salim al-Husseini, attempted to deliver the Ottoman governor's letter surrendering the city to Sergeants James Sedgewick and Frederick Hurcomb of 2/19th Battalion, London Regiment, just outside Jerusalem's western limits on the morning of 9 December. But these two sergeants, who were scouting ahead of Allenby's main force, refused to take the letter because they did not have a high enough rank, and it was not their job — they were not even dispatch riders. So a more appropriate officer, Brigadier-General C.F. Watson, commanding the 180th (2/5th London) Brigade, accepted the governor's letter of surrender and delivered it to Allenby's staff.

Some of the more devout Light Horsemen attended services in churches like this one — the Church of the Holy Sepulchre in Jerusalem.

By then, Jerusalem was almost encircled by the EEF, although Turkish army units still held the nearby Mount of Olives until they were overwhelmed by the 60th (2/2nd London) Division the following afternoon.

The surrender note from Izzat Bey, governor of Jerusalem, is worth quoting in full: 'Due to the severity of the siege of the city and the suffering that this peaceful country has endured from your heavy guns; and for fear that these deadly bombs will hit the holy places, we are forced to hand over to you the city through Hussein al-Husseini, the mayor of Jerusalem, hoping that you will protect Jerusalem the way we have protected it for more than five hundred years.'

Largely deserted and mostly undefended, Jerusalem seemed to invite those 'Christian soldiers' onwards through its ancient gates into the old walled town and down its cobbled streets. Victory was something of an anti-climax — it seemed that rather than fight to the last man, the Turks had given up.

The 60th (London) Division entered Jerusalem then and there, led by the divisional commander, General Sir John Shea, confirming earlier reports of his scouts that it was safe to do so. Finding the Turks and Germans gone and no snipers left behind, he advised Allenby that it was safe for the commander-in-chief to enter as soon as convenient. Even though his entry was unofficial, Shea was welcomed by cheering Christian residents who had stayed behind. Well aware of the long historical wait, these Christian embraced the first Christian soldiers to have captured their Holy City from the Muslims for over 650 years. The Jewish residents also welcomed this first British conqueror.

At the same time, on the more important military side of things, three of the British infantry divisions moved swiftly into position around the city, taking no chances until they had encircled it completely. 'Jerusalem the golden' now belonged to the British.

James Wight Williamson, the dispatch rider with the 2nd Brigade, wrote to sweetheart Maude about 'a lecture we had the other day about Palestine and all the religious country we have crossed, where the City of David was, the River Jordan and where David slew Goliath with his slingshot and lots of other things'. As a result, he confided: 'Our Division had high hopes of being the first troops to enter Jerusalem. We were in sight of the Holy City but we were ordered away to the left flank to Jaffa where our services were more useful. But the real honour had to go to another more deserving unit anyway'.

Although the official entry by Allenby was still two days away, nevertheless on 9 December, the first Australians were allowed to enter Jerusalem, and they did so in a most symbolic way. Conquering Jerusalem meant so much to the Christian commander Chauvel, commander of the Desert Mounted Corps, that he selected the regiment that needed the most healing — the 10th.

The 10th had suffered most in the slaughter at The Nek, back in Gallipoli, where they had run (along with the 8th) across open ground into the murderous fire of enemy machine guns on 7 August 1915. They had also suffered fighting at Hill 60 on 29–30 August 1915, and it was in this last action that Lieutenant V.H. Throssell won the Victoria Cross — the only Australian Light Horseman to win a VC during the Great War.

Like conquering heroes, thousands of Light Horsemen ride past the outskirts of Jerusalem as they continue their conquest of the Holy Land, relentlessly heading north towards their final destination, Damascus.

After the withdrawal from Gallipoli, the 10th had also fought as hard as any other regiment as they defended Egypt from the Ottoman army advancing on the Suez Canal, and drove the Turks across the deserts of the Sinai, participating in the battles of Romani and Magdhaba, and then advancing with the Desert Column into Palestine where they helped fight in the bloody battles to break the Gaza–Beersheba line. Because they had sacrificed more than any other regiment and fought just as hard as any other regiment, they deserved to enter the Holy City of peace first, as a long overdue reward.

So the 10th Light Horse Regiment entered the city, where they were warmly welcomed and billeted in houses in which they slept in beds for the first time since sailing from Australia three years ago. It was indeed a fitting reward for the survivors of the regiment slaughtered so needlessly at The Nek.

10 December

After their one night of luxury, the men of the 10th Light Horse Regiment were then ordered to ride north of Jerusalem to engage with and push the new Turkish frontline further back north up the Nablus road.

11 December

General Allenby had achieved miracles in the land where miracles were celebrated by all religious faiths. Seven weeks after the capture of Beersheba, he had captured the Holy Grail — Jerusalem.

On 11 December 1917, General Sir Edmund Allenby finally entered Jerusalem: after dismounting outside, he and some of his officers walked in on foot through a minor gate, the Jaffa Gate, as a sign of respect for the Holy City.

But humble to the last, he entered on foot through a minor gate, as a sign of respect for the Holy City. This was in marked contrast to the pomp and ceremony of the German Kaiser, who in 1898 entered the city on horseback through ceremonial gates cut into the wall especially for his visit. By contrast, Allenby and his officers dismounted on reaching Jerusalem and entered the city on foot through the Jaffa Gate.

Allenby was the first Christian for more than six centuries to take control of Jerusalem, and the battle was a great morale boost for the people of the British Empire.

In taking possession of the city, Allenby wrote a Proclamation that was read to the citizens who gathered on the steps of the Citadel, by the base of the Tower of David. Addressed to 'the inhabitants of Jerusalem, the Blessed and the dwelling in this vicinity', and written in English, Arabic, Hebrew, French, Italian, Greek, and Russian, it created a Charter of Freedom for all faiths and protection for all holy sites: 'Since your Holy City is regarded with affection by the adherents of three of the great religions of mankind and its soil has been consecrated by the prayers and pilgrimages of multitudes of devout people of these three religions for centuries, therefore do I make known to you that every sacred building, monument, Holy Spot, shrine, traditional site, endowment, pious bequest, or customary place of prayer, of whatever form of the three religions will be maintained and protected according to the existing customs and beliefs of those to whose faiths they are sacred.'

And from the top rank to the bottom, these conquerors were excited by Jerusalem. Trooper James Gordon Murray, of the 12th Regiment of the 4th Brigade Light Horse, wrote that he camped just outside the Holy City, 'near the monastery of Foka where Christ broke bread with the two disciples and the old table is still supposed to be inside the Monastery'.

Writing to Maude, Williamson said: 'In Jerusalem I visited all the holy places which was very interesting indeed. All the holy places have a church built over them so you have to enter the church to see them. On the Mount of Olives the Kaiser has built a magnificent Cathedral and what do you think the hound has done on the ceiling? He has himself painted as a Saint. It would have been more like it, if he had painted himself as a devil.' Writing to his mother, an excited Stan Broome said, 'I have finally seen the Holy City Jerusalem, we rode right through the town, I took lots of good photos and will send them in the next mail. I hope you get them alright and thanks for the cake — it was a beauty'.

With
Kindest
Wishes for

Christmas
and
New Year.

1917–1918.

... To ...

You and all our Brave Australian Boys.

From *The Committee*

Newcastle & Hunter River District Citizens' War Chest Fund.

(N.S.W. FIELD FORCE FUND.)

Patriotic organisations around Australia sent Xmas cards to 'all our brave Australian boys' and this one was sent to Major Thomas Bird by the Committee of his local Newcastle and Hunter River Citizens War Chest Fund.

But not everyone respected these sacred sites, and Major-General F.G. Hughes, of the 3rd Light Horse Brigade, reported in his diary: 'Here at last we were in the Holy City but dirt and filth seemed to reign supreme everywhere and in this respect it was very little above the average Arab village. In fact, the holier the portion of the city the dirtier it seemed to become.' This devout Christian was impressed with 'The Mosque of Omar, or the Dome of the Rock which was one of the most beautiful mosques we had seen including those in Cairo'. Respectfully inspecting the mosque, he continued: 'Our first impression was one of awe and wonder at the magnificence of the building. The whole of the outer surface of the

Mosque except the roof of the dome was one mass of beautiful mosaic work executed in coloured tiles their brilliant colours of blue, green and gold undimmed by time standing out resplendent in the dazzling brightness of the midday sun'.

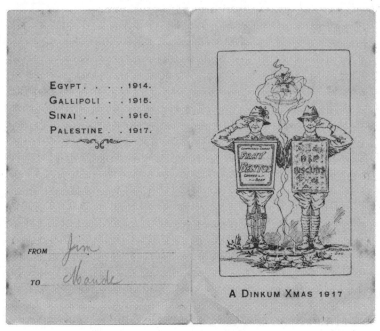

EGYPT . . . . 1914.
GALLIPOLI . . 1915.
SINAI . . . . 1916.
PALESTINE . . 1917.

FROM *Jim*

TO *Maude*

A DINKUM XMAS 1917

Proud of surviving his long war service in different theatres, James Williamson sent his sweetheart, Maude, a Xmas card celebrating the two main ingredients of army food — which he had also somehow miraculously survived — Fray Bentos tinned corned beef and H&P Anzac Biscuits.

On entering, 'wearing the usual slippers over our boots we found that the inside of the Mosque was even more perfect than the outside. Rich Persian rugs covered the tiled floor. Massive square marble columns in which the grain of each formed a different but perfect pattern supported the dome the inside of which was covered with exquisite mosaic work. Every window was of richly stained glass' and 'an iron grille about eight feet high, which was erected by the crusaders, surrounded the huge rock over which the Mosque had been built'. Sacred to different religions 'it was the threshing floor of Omar', and 'the rock on which Jacob slept when he had his dream' as well as 'the rock from which Mohammed is supposed to have leapt up to heaven'.

Christian though he was, Major Wilfred Kent Hughes, also of the 3rd Brigade, by contrast, found the Church of the Holy Sepulchre disappointing: 'We were shown Christ's tomb, Joseph of Arimathea's tomb, the hole the cross was put into and many other sacred spots all in an area of fifty square yards. The impression received at the time was that the whole place was faked to satisfy pilgrims and tourists which we afterwards found was more or less correct. Unlike the Dome of the Rock, which was scrupulously clean the Church partook of the filth and dirt of the surrounding city, and even the many candles and glittering decorations could not overcome this. We felt more disgusted than otherwise on leaving'.

Fortunately, out of respect for centuries of faith, neither the retreating Germans (Christians) nor Turks (Muslims) damaged any of the holy sites, despite laying explosive charges and threatening to blow some of them to kingdom come. Nor did they put up a fight within the streets of the old city walls, which could have damaged buildings.

To keep the peace, Allenby proclaimed martial law, but reassured the inhabitants of his intentions: 'Lest any of you should be alarmed by reason of your experience at the hands of the enemy ... every person should pursue his lawful business without fear of interruption'. Then Allenby met with the heads of all the religious and civil communities and other notables. He met the mayor and the mufti, the sheikhs in charge of the mosques of Omar and Aska, and the heads of all faiths — Anglican, Jewish, Orthodox, Greek Catholic, Armenian, Syrian, Coptic, and Abyssinian.

After receiving all of these leaders, Allenby walked back to the Jaffa Gate, and only after passing through it to the outside did he mount his horse.

François Georges-Picot, the head of the French political mission, made sure he entered Jerusalem just behind Allenby to position himself and France at the front in preparation for the liberation of Damascus, where he hoped his Sykes-Picot Agreement would be put in place. The agreement installed Anglo-French governments in liberated Ottoman territory, excluding Arabs from ruling their own lands — despite the earlier promises made by Britain and confirmed by Lawrence of Arabia. This secret agreement struck between Picot and British MP Sir Mark Sykes even contained a map making clear which areas would be ruled by which country: zones marked in red were for British control and those in blue for French control.

Conclusion

In the midst of a terrible war and Middle East campaign, Jerusalem passed as peacefully as possible from Ottoman Turkish rule (and German military command) to British military administration. And according to the face-saving German propaganda wireless announcement on 12 December: 'The most important reason for Germany's voluntary evacuation was the fact that no nation in the world that believes in God could wish its sacred soil to become the scene of bloody battles. The keeping of a town which is worthless from a military point of view was of no importance in comparison with this consideration.'

Prime Minister David Lloyd George was overjoyed when General Allenby cabled that he had won control of the Holy City; the bells did indeed peal for hours at Westminster Abbey, St Paul's, and in many places around Great Britain. King George V was also pleased, declaring that he 'joined with his people throughout the British Empire in welcoming the joyous tidings of this memorable feat of British arms'.

At Christmas services, many of the congregations sang the old favourite hymn 'Jerusalem', with its tantalising lines: 'And did those feet in ancient times walk upon England's mountains green, and was the Holy Lamb of God on England's pleasant pastures seen.' It raised British morale at a time of continued high casualties and ongoing stalemate on the Western Front. As well, many Christians rejoiced in the fact that Jerusalem was back in Christian hands.

The capture of Jerusalem was a major blow for the Turks and their German allies. Despite this, the Turks mounted a major counterattack towards Jerusalem, but this was defeated by the British on 26 December. British forces then advanced to establish a front securely beyond Jerusalem and on the Mediterranean coast beyond the Nahr Auja. Winter rains, which severely damaged roads, prevented any further advance.

Plans for an early resumption of operations in Palestine were quickly ended by the frightening German spring offensive on the Western Front in March 1918. Sixty thousand British troops, including the 52nd and 74th Divisions, 22 infantry battalions, and most of the Yeomanry, were sent to France as reinforcements. Allenby had to reconstruct his British divisions — except the 54th — with Indian troops, each with a British nucleus. The 4th and 5th Cavalry Divisions, also composed of British and Indian cavalry, were formed. In June, the Imperial Camel Brigade was disbanded and its Australian members formed the 5th Light Horse Brigade and joined the Australian Mounted Division, which was now equipped with swords.

At the same time, the British War Office called for the 54th Division and half of the Australian Light Horse to be sent to France as infantry reinforcements. But fortunately, Allenby (like Murray before him) protested, and with Australian help the proposal was dropped.

This victory at Jerusalem finished Britain's liberation of Palestine. Now Allenby turned his attention further north towards Jordan and, after that, Syria.

PART IV
JORDAN 1918

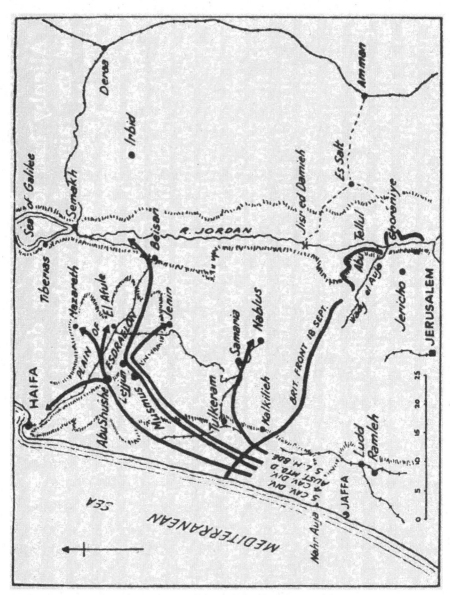

The next two towns General Allenby wanted to capture after occupying Jerusalem were Es Salt,
which was north-east of both Jerusalem and Jericho (but over the other side of the treacherous
River Jordan) and Amman, which was further inland to the east of Es Salt. Both were well-
defended fortress towns on inaccessible high ground.

9.
ES SALT AND AMMAN, 22 MARCH–4 MAY 1918

ALLENBY MEETS HIS MATCH

As Es Salt was built on well-defended steep hills, it reminded the Light Horsemen of Gallipoli, and, as it turned out, it would be just as difficult to conquer, as would its nearby sister town of Amman.

> The Jordan Valley in the parts around the Dead Sea is about the most desolate and God-forsaken country I have ever seen ... and the heat in the valley is very considerable ... around Jericho which is 1,300 feet below sea level no humans could survive living here most months of the year.
>
> TROOPER STAN BROOME, 12TH REGIMENT, 1918

BACKGROUND TO THE BATTLE

With Jerusalem now behind him and anxious to keep driving the Turks back north towards his ultimate goal, Damascus, capturing towns like Jericho along the way, Allenby now set his sights on two more Turkish strongholds en route.

These two towns, just north of the Dead Sea, which would prove so elusive, were Es Salt — the closest to the Jordan River and north-east of Jericho — and Amman, a little further east of Es Salt. Both were within reach of the moving British frontline, but very high up on a plateau behind foothills. In fact, Australia's official war historian Charles Bean, after his eight months writing newspaper stories from Gallipoli, claimed in his official history of the war that these fortress towns were almost as well fortified and inaccessible as the Turkish positions on the heights above Anzac Cove, which the Anzacs had been unable to capture. To make matters worse, the same leader who had stopped the Anzacs dislodging the Turks from those Gallipoli heights was commanding the Turkish here — the clever and dreaded General Otto Liman von Sanders, who was determined to repel the Australians from these heights as well.

But here, Bean's colleague, Henry Gullett — the Official Correspondent for Palestine, who covered these battles — tells most of the story, along with some of the troopers who fought there.

Historically the bigger of these two towns, Amman was the fabled and vibrant former Greco-Roman colony of Philadelphia, although now degenerated into 'a shabby town', as Bean described it, with little but a railway connection there. Allenby wanted to destroy that railway line, hopefully with the help of Lawrence and his Arab Army, which had been busy blowing up rail tracks and stations being used by the Turks to transport troops and supplies.

Thanks to continued fighting, Allenby's men had forced the Turks out of most towns along the way by early March 1918, so his frontline was now established from the coast, stretching inland across the desert north of Jaffa, Ludd, the northern tip of the Dead Sea, and the ancient city of

Jericho, and continuing east just south of Es Salt and Amman; he also had forces stationed to the west of the Jordan River, just above where it ran into the Dead Sea.

Not all troopers were happy to be advancing north up the Jordan Valley. The 12th Regiment's Stan Broome wrote home: 'The Jordan Valley in the parts around the Dead Sea is about the most desolate and God-forsaken country I have ever seen ... and the heat in the valley is very considerable ... around Jericho which is 1,300 feet below sea level no humans could survive living here most months of the year'.

Despite its great biblical associations and reputation as the world's oldest city, trooper Eric Robertson said Jericho 'is not much of a place and is a terrible hotbed for disease'.

Eric Robertson of 1st Light Horse told his parents riding was also difficult, as it was 'the roughest country I have ever seen' and to ride from Bethlehem to capture Jericho, 'We rode all day over a terrible track only wide enough to ride single file in most places and in some places it was so bad that we had to walk and lead our horses. The country was all hilly and one mass of rock. We had to stop at dark and sat down and held our horses all night on account of the country being too rough to travel across in the dark'. Not only that, 'We moved off at daylight and struck a Turkish Redoubt which held us up for a day. The Turks were kept busy all day and by night time we had cleared them out which left our road clear to Jerico [sic]. We moved on again at daylight following the Dead Sea and occupied Jerico with very little trouble and watered out horses for the first time for 40 hours.'

But it was worth the hardship, as 'We camped at the foot of Mount of Temptation where Christ was tempted and fasted for 40 days. There is a Monastery built on the side of the Mountain where Christ fasted and next morning we went all over it. It is a marvellous piece of work and enclosed you will find a picture of it. It is mostly hewn out of solid rock and inside it is a beautiful church.'

Stan Broome did not share Robertson's admiration, telling his mother that he rode straight past the Monastery of the Mount of Temptation, as all that stuff was 'purely imaginary of course'. But in Bethlehem, Robertson loved visiting the Church of the Holy Nativity. Robertson continued, 'The stable is exactly the same as it was when Christ was born.' In Jerusalem, he also loved visiting 'the Mount of Olives, Garden of Gethsemane, many other places of interest and the old ruins of the city. Jerusalem is a very beautiful place and there are some beautiful buildings and churches there'.

By contrast, 'Jerico is not much of a place, and is a terrible hotbed for disease. It is 1,200 feet below sea level and to get to Jerusalem about 2,000 feet above sea level we had to leave at 6 p.m. and ride all night arriving at 2 a.m. so you can imagine the climb our horses had from Jerico to Jerusalem. We camped at Bethleham [sic] after a 30 mile ride arriving 5 am in the rain. It was freezing cold so we just rugged our horses and pulled a blanket over us and slept in the rain till mid day. Although we have had a pretty rough time, I would not have missed this trip for anything'.

Allenby's forces still included the Australian mounted men, because he had refused a request from the British War Office to send his horsemen to the Western Front; he knew they would fight dismounted there, and be slaughtered in the muddy trenches where hundreds of thousands were being killed.

Allenby knew he had his work cut out for him because, in early March 1918, the German High Command had replaced the tired German commander Erich von Falkenhayn (who had been defeated by Allenby so many times) with the experienced General Otto Liman von Sanders, with his prestigious Gallipoli track record. Those officers who knew of Liman von Sanders feared Allenby could have met his match — and, in fact, in this next round of battles, that turned out to be the case. The Turks also had greater numbers of men in these battles, and had bigger guns protecting Es Salt and Amman, which were located high up on a plateau, making them easy to defend against invaders struggling up steep cliffs. Yet the Australians of the Light Horse, who had been defeated by Liman von Sanders at Gallipoli, were hoping for some bloody revenge in this rematch against their old foe.

With high hopes, Allenby worked out a clever plan for his advance north towards Damascus. He would create the impression that his inland forces were the main forces attacking. In fact, his real thrust would be along the coast just inland from the sea. Apart from capturing Es Salt and Amman, Allenby's raid on these inland towns was primarily aimed at cutting the Hejaz railway line running south from Damascus, and destroying a railway tunnel and viaduct at Amman. The Turks were using the line to move troops and supplies from the southern town of Ma'an (100 kilometres south of the Dead Sea) up to Damascus. He was confident his forces would succeed, as he now believed he could depend on Lawrence and his Arab Army; so Allenby ordered Lawrence to attack the Turkish garrison at Ma'an and destroy the railway line there — a feat they should manage by mid-April.

Before leaving Jerusalem to fight in his next stunt, Trooper James Currie Rathie of the 2nd Brigade attended a church service: 'We went to St. George's Cathedral. It was inexpressibly queer to be entering a church again after so long accustomed to open air life. This beautifully designed cathedral was the centre of the whole Christian faith. It was immense and really magnificent. Beside the door as we entered was a bell rope and our "roughs" could not pass it without pulling it so the bell tinkled continually — I could have killed them'.

Rathie, who had survived bloody battles and was leaving to fight more, said: 'My feelings during that memorable service cannot be imagined let alone described. We knew that for many of us it would be our last and so it was. Think of it, we were at church in Jerusalem an event in our lives we would not have missed for anything. When the familiar peals of the organ began I felt like crying like a girl. It seemed to touch all the home-land memory chords all at once. When the choir began to sing I was deeply and strangely touched and my thoughts were solemn. We were on the eve of battle and the hymns were well chosen — "Onward Christian Soldiers", "Fight the Good Fight with all thy might" and "There is a green hill far away without a city wall". My comrades and I sang with great gusto and the sound of our voices in that immense stone cathedral accompanied by the mighty burst of music rose to the heavens above. Some of then took the sacred sacrament (communion). We were the first Australian troops to attend church in that cathedral.'

22 March

Allenby decided to attack Amman first, and in the most adventurous way, on 22 March 1918. He ordered some of the bravest and fittest Anzac engineers, along with Britain's 60th Division (Londoners), to start the action by swimming the flooded Jordan River from the west bank to the east at its narrowest point and establishing a beachhead on the other side, where he ordered them to built a bridge at Hijla.

As so often in the Holy Land, this area was rich in biblical associations, which would have been well understood by the British and Australians. In the bible, this part of the river was where John the Baptist baptised Jesus.

But the men had been given a dangerous mission, because the river flowed so fast. Trooper Stan Broome would not like to have tried it — he wrote: 'As for the Jordan River we expected to see a half dry creek, it is a medium sized river at the bridge about 50 yards wide, very deep and running at an incredible pace. As a matter of fact 9 strong swimmers out of 10 could not swim it at this time of the year'. But undaunted the swimmers gave it their best shot.

Once the strongest engineers had swum across the fast-running Jordan River carrying a line, they were able to construct this pontoon bridge so that the Light Horsemen could ride across from the west to attack Es Salt and Amman to the east.

Australia's official correspondent covering Palestine, Henry Gullett, in consultation with Bean, who was on the Western Front, reported on this heroic act. 'At Hajla [Hijla] the actual bridging party was made up of "D" Troop of the 1st Field Squadron Australian Engineers, who were attached to Desert Mounted Corps Headquarters, under the capable leadership of Captain E. J. Howells. A squadron of the 3rd Light Horse Regiment, under Major Dick, acted as a working party to assist in the bridge building, but the driving force of the enterprise was the 23rd Battalion of Londoners, led by Major Craddock, a stock broker on the London Stock Exchange. Just before midnight a party made up of Sergeant E. S. Claydon, Lance-Corporal R. Strang, Sappers S. Dawson and H. R. Y. McGuigan, and a few Londoners approached the river bearing a raft about 300 lbs. in weight. Dawson volunteered to swim across the rapid, swollen stream with a light line and he made it.

'He was followed into the water by Lieutenant J.W.R. Jones and half-a-dozen others, both British and Australians. The infantrymen swam naked, but carried their rifles above their heads. Dawson who was first across, assisted the others to land. At 1.20 am, on the 22nd the first raft, with twenty-seven Londoners, reached the eastern bank. Considerable forces of infantry were at once concentrated on ground covering Howells' engineers and the light horsemen; the material for a pontoon bridge was steadily assembled; at 6 o'clock the construction was begun, and at 7.15 the river was spanned.

Because it was so essential to keep the Jordan River crossings open for the Light Horsemen who were coming and going during their repeated assaults on Es Salt and Amman, a permanent detachment of riflemen was positioned to stop the Turks capturing these vital lifelines.

'Meanwhile, the raft was busily employed carrying across small parties of infantry, and at dawn a company was in position on the east bank. However daylight enabled the Turks to open effective fire with machine-guns, and the load on the raft had then to be reduced to eight, the men lying flat on the bottom. Casualties were numerous; of one load of eight Londoners, seven were hit. But additional rafts were employed, and before

8 a.m. the 2/19th Battalion of the Londoners had been ferried over; by noon the 2/18th had followed. As the men landed they endeavoured to clear a bridgehead but were strongly resisted by enemy machine gunners on the mud-hills immediately beyond. The work of the bridge builders and the supporting parties was marked by coolness and efficiency, and was distinguished by individual acts of gallantry. Lance-Corporal F. Bell: of the engineers, repeatedly swam down stream under heavy fire, bearing the cables which were to hold the bridge in position. Meanwhile, further attempts to cross at Ghoraniye were beaten off by the enemy fire'.

After the engineers' bridge was built, Allenby's forces also worked out another way to cross the river. There was an established crossing on the same latitude as Jericho and just a little east, which was used by the Turks on the old road to Amman. After a full day of fighting the Turks guarding the river at Ghoraniye, Allenby's men also seized and bridged that crossing. Now they had two crossings of the Jordan to help them on the road to Amman.

23 March

With the bridges complete and free from enemy fire, the way was clear for the advance against Amman and Es Salt. Allenby's latest plan was for the infantry to capture Es Salt, due north, and then remain there to prevent the enemy from sending reinforcements across from Es Salt to Amman high up on the plateau. If necessary, Allenby needed to contain the Turks at Es Salt, so he could send reinforcements to help the horsemen and the Camel Brigade at Amman. It was a bold plan.

James Rathie of 2nd Brigade, 7th Regiment, said, 'The order came, just after we finished tea, "Get ready to move" sweeping over our camp like a wave, men rushed to gather up gear, grabbed saddle blankets, saddles and flung them on their horses, rolled swags and strapped them, everything done in a feverish haste and in twenty minutes we were standing holding our horses smoking and ready to move off. Soon we became a long winding black string of horses zig zagging down to the valley'.

Using the new bridges, and under cover of darkness on the evening of 23 March, the British infantry's 60th Division and the Anzac Mounted Division — which included the lumbering Camel Brigades — commanded by Major-General Edward Chaytor, a New Zealander, then moved from their open-air bivouacs over the raging river and advanced up the hills towards Es Salt and Amman.

The dust stirred up by their horses in the hot, dry, sandy Jordan Valley — which at hundreds of feet below sea level is the deepest in the world — irritated the Light Horsemen, who claimed it was far worse than the dusty Australian outback, where some of them had worked as drovers on arid cattle stations before the war.

That night the men of the Auckland Mounted Rifles, who had since the occupation of Jericho been patrolling the valley, marched to Hijla, and at 4am on the 23rd, the New Zealanders led their horses over the bridge. This crossing was not easy, as James Rathie revealed when his Regiment crossed: 'We led our horses over single file, the floating narrow bridge rocked and swayed and the horses staggered across thumping the planks and reeling like drunken men'.

Riding through the little ring of Londoners and setting the pace, the New Zealanders proceeded vigorously to enlarge the bridgehead, and then, moving north, fought back Turkish defenders at Ghoraniye.

The enemy had already decided to yield the river, and were falling back towards the foothills about Shunet Nimrin, where the main road from the plain follows the Wadi Shaib in its steep climb right up to Es Salt. The Aucklands made the most of the position, and, shooting at the gallop from their saddles, killed many Turks; before noon on 24 March they had captured 68 prisoners and four machine guns, and cleared the country opposite Ghoraniye.

24 March

Throughout the day on 24 March, the British infantry forces and Australian mounted men were pushing into the precipitous hills, which rose 1,200 metres to the plateau on which the objective lay. The 3rd Light Horse Regiment played a leading role as they rode towards Es Salt; the 4th Regiment remained back at the bridge, defending it from Turkish counterattacks.

Unfortunately for the men riding horses uphill, heavy rain then fell, making the going extremely difficult along the main tracks by which the raiding party moved. Nevertheless, riding relentlessly on, the 3rd Light Horse Regiment made progress, despite wind and rain, camping when night fell.

Gullett reported that advancing due east across the valley, 'Ryrie's 2nd Brigade met with no opposition. In fact glimpses were soon seen of a long enemy camel-train, moving across the Australian front towards the north: it seemed as if the Turks were concentrating the forces which had been scattered between Amman and Maan so as to prevent their isolation and capture'.

Gullett added, 'In fact no Turks were seen until Amman was reached three days later ... Suddenly a great shouting was heard, and a swarm of men and boys mounted on Arab ponies of many colours came galloping ... in the distance they were picturesque and imposing and expectation ran high ... here at last, thought the Australians, were the superior men of the east of Jordan, the true Arabs of Arabia. They raced down, shouting, and waving their rifles, and in flowing dress of many hues made a gallant show against the green countryside. Seeking the Australian leader, they reined up their Arab steeds in a clamorous throng round Ryrie and his staff. But at close range they were a disappointingly strange, motley lot of warriors. Physically beautiful men, some were admittedly with an easy, graceful carriage, but they rode miserable skinny, little ponies, greys and bays and chestnuts, some with rich saddles and trappings, but most of them with the leather in tatters. Many of the wretched ponies bore two splendid men; or an Arab with the native majesty of a Saladin — the 13th century [sic] Moslem Crusader leader himself — clad in robes of silk and with a great sword at his side and a richly jeweled dagger in his belt, would be astride an emaciated pony, his feet in rusted stirrup-irons attached to the saddle with pieces of rope'.

Gullett continued: 'To the Light Horsemen they seemed like some strange circus troupe caught in all its soiled bravery in the pitiless light of sunrise. They knew no leader, and, when asked questions by the Brigade interpreter, all talked in chorus. But if in appearance they were unconvincing as soldiers, they were demonstrative in their welcome, and seemed very anxious to serve the British interest. After a brief parley … they rode with Ryrie towards the foot-hills … soon a large Arab encampment was reached, where, despite Ryrie's protests against delay, the Arab sheikh insisted upon entertaining him — with some members of his staff — to coffee in a huge, black goat-hair tent, decked with barbarous Manchester cottons'.

Yet as Idriess and his fellow Light Horse troopers had so often written, these Arabs could not be trusted (despite this welcome en route to Es Salt and Amman) and were as likely as not to join the Turks, if the Turks looked like winning, or attack the Turks if they were losing. If Idriess's pet hate, the Bedouins, found wounded or dying British or Turkish soldiers, he claimed they would sometimes cut their throats, rob the dead of their clothing and possessions, and even dig up bodies from shallow graves to help themselves. Idriess had earlier seen other mounted Arab parties, different to those who feted Ryrie's 2nd Brigade — 'hordes of "vultures", hundreds upon hundreds of Bedouin men, women and children driving donkeys and camels, all horribly eager to loot the Turkish camps. Numbers of these Arab cutthroats carried sacks of little flat loaves of brown Turkish bread looted from the still warm ovens. We hungrily commandeered some of that bread. The Arabs snarled at us. We could have shot them with far greater pleasure than we shoot the Turks'.

James Rathie added, 'Treacherous and merciless and ever used to having to defend their lives, these Bedouins — with their old fashioned rifles and curved knives in their belts — we knew well would favour us just as long as they thought we were winning — if the Turks beat us they would get in with the Turks'.

BRIG-GEN. GRANVILLE DE LAUNE RYRIE

C.B. C.M.G. V.D.

Despite continuing challenges and setbacks the great leader Granville Ryrie, a member of parliament in peacetime, led his 2nd Brigade relentlessly onward in their advance against Es Salt and Amman, providing constant inspiration to his men.

25 March

Allenby's forces found the going increasingly difficult. Yet they moved steadily forward, despite increasingly steep and muddy tracks — not to mention continuing rain, especially for the camels slipping on the muddy hillsides — towards the twin objectives of Es Salt and Amman. It was bad enough for the mounted horsemen — many of whom dismounted— and worse for the camel riders, who all had to dismount and lead their camels along the slippery tracks.

The keen-eyed Gullett takes up the story: 'At 2 a.m. on the 25th. Rain began to fall heavily. The hillsides were already soaked with water, soon the wadis were flooded, and the sloping track and patches of flat rock gave but a precarious foothold to the horses. The night turned bitterly cold. Within an hour most of the men were drenched. But the climb, with the 6th Light Horse as advance guard, was steadily maintained. Working parties with shovels accompanied the leading squadron, and strove hard to improve the worst patches, but still the whole brigade was at times reduced to leading the horses in single file'. It was certainly no place for motorised transport, as James Rathie said, 'General Chaytor's Ford car got stuck crossing a stream with a rocky bottom as it could not drive over the boulders so we tied a rope to the front axle and began to heave. I was on the end of the rope when it broke and we went down on our backs on the stones, me with half a dozen chaps on top of me.' They finally pulled the car through 'but even motor cycle dispatch riders had to strip and carry their bikes across'.

With a preference for white horses and traditional flashy Ottoman uniforms, the enemy certainly knew how to mount a parade with great style when it came to putting on a show to convince the locals they were the rightful rulers of Palestine.

Gullett continued: 'The ascent of the light horsemen, however, was an easy task compared with the terrible climb being attempted by the Camel

Brigade. They jested about their sodden clothes and chilled bodies; with a resource almost miraculous they quickly lit hundreds of little fires with wood which, with the foresight of hardened veterans, they had carried up from the plain below.

'A large Bedouin encampment provided a few lucky light horsemen with eggs and camel whey, but most of the men were confined to their rations. They had ridden from the valley with one day's supply on their saddles and two on the pack-camels, which had not yet arrived. Already the "iron" rations were being eaten, and the position was giving concern to Chaytor.'

Although Amman, which was more of a natural fortress and better defended by the Turks, was proving difficult, at least by the evening of the 25th some of Allenby's forces rode into and captured the village of Es Salt, even though this was further north than Amman. So far, so good. Allenby's men had now reached first base; having captured Es Salt, they hoped this would help them capture Amman.

'But they had ridden hard for Es Salt', Gullett wrote. 'The Turks, startled at the swiftness of their approach withdrew with little fighting. Es Salt is a dark, crowded, mountain-built old town of 15,000 inhabitants. Of these about 4,000 are Christians, who, living isolated among the fanatical Arabs of eastern Palestine, were during the war even more fearful of massacre than were the Christians of western Palestine. As Allenby's men rode into the narrow streets, these hapless people were for a time too surprised and incredulous to be demonstrative. But as the Australians cleared the town of the Turkish stragglers, and pushed out covering patrols, and as the infantry battalions marched in a few hours later, the Christians saw in this dramatic intervention their deliverance from the sinister shadow of Moslem rule and from the desert raiders, and their satisfaction and joy were immeasurable'.

Meanwhile, Ryrie's 2nd Light Horse Brigade, along with the New Zealand Mounted Rifles Brigade, had joined forces and was also heading towards Amman.

26 March

Unfortunately, despite their good progress and Allenby's faith in Lawrence, the British forces were then let down. Having commissioned Lawrence earlier as part of this plan of attack, Allenby had absolutely depended on Lawrence's Arab Army destroying the railway line south of Amman at a settlement called Ma'an, where Lawrence was meant to cut the line once and for all and stop the movement of Turkish troops and supplies. But the Arab forces proved to be unreliable, failing to turn up, for reasons of their own, at the rendezvous point for this important sabotage assignment. As Idriess had warned many times in his diary entries, the Arabs just could not be trusted.

Lawrence agreed, and had written earlier: 'I went off down the valley and lay there all day in my old lair among the tamarisk where the wind in the dusty green branches played with such sounds as it made in English trees. It told me I was tired to death of these Arabs; petty incarnate Semites who attained heights and depths beyond our reach, though not beyond our sight. They realized our absolute in their unrestrained capacity for good and evil; and for two years I had profitably shammed to be their companion'.

Throughout the British attack on Es Salt and Amman, the Turks continued to use this railway line to move up large troop reinforcements, even after the British had captured Es Salt. Turkish reinforcements also began arriving by rail from the north, until the enemy troops far outnumbered the British.

27 March

Despite these setbacks, in the morning Chaytor ordered the advance on Amman. After all, he now boasted a force of some 3,000 rifles in his two mounted brigades and the Camel Brigade for his advance, supported by the single mountain battery of 18-pounders attached to the Camels. Meanwhile, the Turks held Amman with about 4,000 troops, who occupied carefully prepared and superior positions; the enemy also had fifteen big guns, and many deadly machine-guns. They also knew that their position — like the steep Gallipoli cliffs where some of these Turks had fought — was almost ideal for defence. Nevertheless, Chaytor's three brigades advanced across a number of wide, shallow valleys divided by ridges with stony outcrops.

But this dangerous advance on the formidable fortress of Amman was too difficult for some of the mounted men. Leaving their horses behind (as they had been forced to do at Gallipoli) when they reached the last of the ridges, about 2.5 kilometres from Amman, the 6th and 7th Regiments of Ryrie's 2nd Brigade advanced down the boggy slope. But the enemy had no difficulty in stopping them, and the attack failed decisively.

James Rathie from the 7th Regiment said, 'The delay caused by the rain had left time for Jaco to find out we were coming and for him to get reinforcements from Aleppo by rail and now he was defending his line strongly'.

Shortly before dark, the Turks stoutly counterattacked. Yet even before the attack at Amman began, 60th Division commander General John Shea had himself doubted the capacity of Chaytor's Anzac mounted brigades to achieve the purpose of the raid. It was inevitable that the delay in arriving at their objective must have greatly reduced the chance of surprise and, therefore, a quick, decisive action.

Things were not looking good. From the last of these ridges, the men looked down a long slope — criss-crossed by many water-courses, with intervening patches of boggy, cultivated land — to the foot of the dark hills which rise sharply behind the village. But so rugged was the ground that no glimpse could be had of the village itself. Nevertheless, although outnumbered, sinking deep at every stride in the spongy ground, and unsupported by artillery, the mounted brigades moved steadily towards their invisible foe.

James Rathie said, 'Even before the brigades reached the last crest and dismounted, the Turks from their heights across the wadi had a complete view of the advance. Their guns had been registered on every path by which the British must come, and their machine-guns were placed so as to sweep the whole area. As the troops rode into range of the enemy's guns they were lightly shelled; but it was clear, as it had been on the ride up the range, that the Turk was well satisfied with his position and disposed to let the raiders come to closer and more deadly quarters'.

Allenby's forces reached the outskirts of Amman and prepared to attack the old town. Chaytor ordered his Anzac mounted brigades to begin the attack on Amman itself, almost surrounding the Turkish town. The 2nd Australian Light Horse Brigade, under Brigadier-General Granville Ryrie, attacked from the north-west, while the Imperial Camel Brigade (which also included large numbers of Australians) came in from the west, and the New Zealand Mounted Rifles Brigade from the south. In total, the three brigades numbered about 3,000 rifles in the firing line, and were supported by a single battery of mountain guns.

Even so, the attacking Anzac forces were up against it, because the Turks continually reinforcing their numbers — thanks to the railway line Lawrence and his Arabs had failed to blow up — now had well over 4,000 men in well-prepared positions, well supported by machine guns and artillery. Realising Lawrence had let them down, Allenby's men took things into their own hands and blew up large sections of the railway line south of Amman, and also a two-span stone bridge on the track north of the town and so put a halt to Turkish reinforcements being transported to Amman by rail for the moment.

Then, things took a turn for the worse. 'As if in instant response to a single order', Gullett reported, 'guns, machine-guns, and rifles opened fire together, with a roar and a rattle which echoed and re-echoed from the hills and wadis that covered them. The Australians, although falling thickly with many wounded and unable to continue the assault, pressed gamely on until some of them were within six hundred yards of the place where they believed the invisible village to be located'.

So far, so good, the survivors among them thought. 'But as the enemy corrected his range the deluge of shells and hail of bullets became annihilating in intensity', Gullett continued, 'and the advancing lines were forced to take to the ground for cover. For a time they held on; but they had no targets, their losses continued heavy, and further advance was impossible; they were therefore withdrawn to positions of relative safety'.

28 March

Allenby's remaining forces in the frontline continued fighting hard all day on 28 March, trying in vain to attack Amman — all they could do was hold their own. Meanwhile, the Turks used the day to quickly repair the damaged railway to the south and get ready to send in more troops by rail. Evidently, Australian raiders were not as effective as Lawrence and his Arab Army, because when the latter actually did turn up and blow up a railway line, it was normally unsalvageable.

The Light Horsemen attacking Es Salt and Amman north of the Dead Sea, pictured here, found the terrain just as difficult as the unwelcoming hills and wadis surrounding this famous low-lying inland sea.

Before long, facing more Turkish reinforcements, the advancing Anzacs came under a devastating fire from all arms, and the vigour of their advance was destroyed by the sheer number of casualties they suffered. Some troopers still made great efforts to break through. As the attack developed, two squadrons of the 5th Australian Light Horse Regiment made a mounted dash down a large wadi between the Camel Brigade and the infantry. They rapidly covered about 800 metres; but, after dismounting, their attempt was halted by machine-gun fire, while their horses suffered many casualties from the enemy's shells.

Meanwhile, the fight had also been going badly with Ryrie's 6th and 7th Regiments. For about 1.5 kilometres, the men pressed steadily on in the face of heavy machine-gun and rifle fire and light shrapnel. Then, before reaching the ridge, Ryrie himself, a 'never say die' leader, was severely wounded in the head, and the command of the 2nd Brigade was passed on to Lieutenant H. Dickson. Dickson at once reported back to base that he was being heavily shelled and the prospect of success was small. Trying to set an example to his men, the new leader then bravely dashed over the crest with three troops. Wounded at once, he handed over command to Lieutenant F.L. Ridgway, who, followed by his men, made a heroic rush down the slope. But these charging troopers were instantly caught in bursts of machine-gun fire from the front and the left flank; many men fell before they cleared the crest, and, of those who went down into the valley, only one man, wounded in four places, regained the Australian lines. By now, the attempt to capture Amman really did look hopeless.

The 7th Regiment were stopped almost immediately by the intensity of the fire and were ordered to retreat. Then the Turks, always quick to counterattack, left their fortified positions and rushed the Light Horse. The Light Horse casualties were heavy; of the 58 men in Ryrie's squadron of the 6th Regiment, 40 were killed, wounded (including Ryrie), or missing, and the 7th Regiment had also been severely mauled. The outlook was bleak; but with that coolness and straight shooting that always distinguished the

Light Horsemen at the blackest stages of a fight, the retreating line was at once well organised, and, with the assistance of a machine gun and Hotchkiss guns, the enemy was checked and held while the wounded were carried back to safety. The retirement was then continued. Throughout the night of 28 March, the enemy still freely shelled Chaytor's positions.

29 March

This shelling continued from dawn and throughout the day. The British mountain batteries were never able to trouble the Turkish garrison seriously. The heavy rains and mists on the highlands hampered operations in the air, and aeroplanes which were sent out totally missed Amman, bombing villages to the north and south instead. The Light Horse regiments were not only reduced by casualties but also by troopers having to go on patrol and other duties. At one stage, the 7th Regiment was only able to put 50 men in the firing line, and the brigade became so strung out that it was unable to take any further part in the actual attack. As James Rathie from the 7th reported: 'We were all cold and wet with swelled and sore hands and tired and hungry'.

But in deciding on a further night assault, Chaytor had the support of all brave officers on the spot who had already engaged the enemy at close quarters. So they decided to give it another go. The two daylight attempts had made them familiar with the ground, and they believed that a swift advance in the darkness, when the effective use of artillery and machine guns would be denied to the enemy, had a fair chance of success. But rain, driven by strong and biting winds, ruined their chances. Constantly wet and cold, the men had suffered acutely, while the boggy ground made all movement very exhausting.

The night of the 29th was dark, wet, and intensely cold, and all ranks prayed for the order to move as they shivered in the wind; anything but stay still.

30 March

Soon after 2am on 30 March the advance was begun, and the irregular line, with many gaps caused by wadis and steep ridges, crept forward with bomb and bayonet. Fortunately, for a time they were not discovered; but at 3.10am, heavy rifle and machine-gun fire broke out in front of the infantry, and soon became general along the intricate, winding bed of the main wadi and on the dark heights beyond.

On his ride north from Jericho towards Es Salt, trooper Eric Robertson wrote home saying, 'We camped at the foot of Mount Temptation where Christ was tempted and fasted for 40 days. There is a Monastery built on the side of the Mountain where Christ fasted and next morning we went all over it. It is a marvellous piece of work.'

Although they captured the higher trenches first at about 4.30am, and at dawn easily compelled the surrender of the line of earthworks lower down, where they took prisoners and six machine guns, they were unable to occupy the whole of the hill, and at about 9.30am, they were strongly assaulted by successive waves of Turks, who charged to within 10 metres, and were forced to withdraw. Even in the darkness, the Turkish machine-gun and rifle fire, registered on the converging front of the British attack, was very effective. By 10am on 30 March, it was plain that the assault had failed.

As James Rathie complained, 'Having no artillery we could not face Jacco's strong positions guarding the vulnerable spots'.

The attackers might have been holding their own against the Turkish defenders, but when the Turks sent in even more troops on the repaired railway line to strengthen the garrison, Allenby's forces did not stand a chance; they were badly outnumbered. To make matters worse, Turkish resistance was then bolstered by a battalion of the German Asia Corps coming from another direction. Now, no matter how hard they fought, the British and Anzac attackers had no hope of winning their battle to capture Amman against such large numbers, even when more British infantry arrived and entered into the fight.

Despite increasing opposition, New Zealanders fighting from the south captured nearby Hill 3039, which gave them a commanding view over the battleground from the southern point of view. But although Light Horse regiments like the 6th charged towards the entrenched Turkish fortifications from time to time, they were beaten back by the greater number of defenders, with many troopers being killed by machine-gun fire.

Now it was only a matter of time before 'the Heads' acknowledged the situation, admitting Allenby's men were no match for the thousands of Turkish reinforcements who continued to arrive by rail throughout the day with the latest troops digging in at a high point east of the town in an old Roman citadel, where they stopped any British infantry or mounted men getting any closer.

As each day of the Amman fighting went by, the position at Es Salt had become increasingly disquieting. The enemy, steadily drawing reinforcements across the Jordan at Jisr ed Damieh from the direction of Nablus, pressed in on Es Salt from the west and north. The commander of the 60th Division, General Shea, had only two battalions of the 179th Brigade and Bell's Light Horse regiment to resist this encroachment, and to prevent a march against the rear of Chaytor's force at Amman.

Soon afterwards, General Shea, who was still over at Es Salt, asked Chaytor if he considered Amman could be taken that day. The New Zealander replied point blank, 'No!' Shea then ordered the withdrawal of the force. The decision was inevitable. Shea had sent to Amman every man who could be spared from Es Salt. The Turks had won, and won decisively, by their superior numbers and their position of extraordinary natural strength.

With no end in sight to Turkish reinforcements, there was nothing for it but to retreat, especially as Lawrence had also failed to bolster the British forces with his Arab Army as he had promised to do.

Rather than allow unexpectedly large enemy counterattacks to decimate his forces, Allenby now ordered them to withdraw both from Es Salt, which they had captured, and the outskirts of nearby Amman, which they had failed to capture. After confirming this difficult decision with his officers, he reluctantly ordered his attacking force to start pulling back, using the cover of darkness of the night of 30 March. As it was, the Anzacs and the Camel Brigade had suffered more than 670 casualties and the foot-weary British infantry had suffered nearly 500 casualties.

Had the Turks made a general counterattack on the day or night of the 30th, Chaytor's withdrawal could have been extremely hazardous; but, except for sporadic advances, the Turks remained on their ground, and soon after dark the British retirement proceeded smoothly.

The retreat may have put some of the more educated troopers in mind of Napoleon's infamous 1812 retreat through the snow from Russia, where hundreds of poorly equipped and starving foot soldiers died in the freezing cold, simply dropping in their tracks.

It was wet with continual, unforgiving rain, and extremely cold. Among the troopers marching away from Amman, many were unable to find, let alone ride, their horses on the sodden and rugged ground; they were exhausted, underfed, and miserable. Those wounded at Amman suffered even more as they were evacuated over the terrible terrain. During the operations, a number of motor-ambulances were in use between the

Jordan Valley and Es Salt, but they were unable to traverse the soft road between Es Salt and Amman. Every seriously wounded man had therefore to be carried from Amman to Es Salt on the rough and wobbly camel cacolets (hospital beds mounted on camels). As Gullett observed: 'It would be scarcely possible to devise a more acute torture for a man with mutilated limbs than this hideous form of ambulance-transport.

'Even when the camels travel at a snail's pace on level ground, the wounded are horribly jolted; on country with steep gradients made slippery by rain, where the camels, fearful of falling, move irregularly, constantly sprawl, and often collapse, the agony inflicted is indescribable. "I had a rough spin," said an anonymous Light Horseman who, with a shattered arm, travelled by cacolet from Amman to Es Salt, "but when it seemed unbearable I reminded myself that the chap on the other stretcher on my camel had a badly broken jaw".'

As well as dropping deadly bombs on camels, wrecking this vital means of transport, German planes continued to kill and wound Light Horsemen attacking Es Salt and Amman — until the Royal Flying Corps shot them out of the skies or disabled them, forcing them to land.

It was even worse for some of the camels, James Rathie reported: 'Three bombs landed on the camel camp and the butchery was awful.

They were lying skittled everywhere, one had no head, another no legs, some lying full length ripped and torn, others sitting and blood squirting everywhere. Not a murmur from any of the dumb brutes — one with his belly ripped open stood nibbling at a bush while he trod on his trailing entrails — 17 out of 30 killed or had to be shot and most of the others with holes in them'.

Henry Gullet's coverage of the retreat continued, 'Evacuation was complicated by the unhappy multitude of terrified Armenians and other Christian peoples who fled from Es Salt down the track with the horsemen and infantry. The rejoicing that had followed the British occupation of the town had been succeeded, as the indecisive days of Amman dragged on, by uneasiness, then by fear, and, when the British withdrawal became known, by panic. The Moslems of the town had watched with sullen disapproval the happy demonstrations of the Christians; and now that the Turks had prevailed, all those who had rejoiced and had shown sympathy with the Londoners and the light horsemen feared for their property, their women, and their lives. Up till then they had during the war been spared outrage'.

31 March

The retreat continued all day. The local Christian inhabitants — who had welcomed the troops and now feared retribution by the Turks — joined the fleeing throng. They had to leave fast, as in some cases the Turks slaughtered them without mercy for their 'disloyalty'. So using the cover of darkness, on the night of the 31st, a great many Christians packed up all that they could carry, and began to flee. Before dawn, the leaders of this tragic, motley throng of aged men and women, of parents and families — even babies in arms — of rich and poor, rough and gentle, were far down the road. Some had camels and donkeys of burden, some drove their sheep, but most walked, heavily laden, along the road, which was steep and narrow, flooded and rough. James Rathie admitted, 'We felt sick at heart, mean and small standing by the road watching them pass — Armenians, Greeks, Syrians and Arabs making a bid for freedom in feverish haste. One aged woman slowly walked supporting a crippled son who had to pause every few yards.'

1 April

The withdrawal continued to become even more difficult, as the wet, slippery tracks became impossible to ride down, let alone to transport all the gear on, including heavy guns on wheels.

By noon the whole force, with the exception of the mounted rearguards, was on the march. The 2nd Australian Light Horse Brigade moved by the road to Es Salt, while the infantry and the Camel Brigade, followed and guarded by the New Zealand Mounted Rifles Brigade, used the track from Ain es Sir to Shunet Nimrin, by which the New Zealanders had gone up. Early in the afternoon, small bodies of Turks approached the Light Horse rearguards, but were fought back without trouble. As the New Zealanders rode slowly through Ain es Sir in the night, though, they were followed by about 500 Turks. The Circassians of the Ain es Sir village, who had during the fighting been sulky and aloof, were fully alive to the British failure; picking up courage, they joined with a few Turks in the village and opened fire at close range upon the Wellingtons, commanded by Brigadier-General William Meldrum, and about a dozen of his men were hit by the first volley. The revenge of the New Zealanders was instant and decisive. The night was wild and dark, with sleet and wind, which chilled the men to their bones. Wet, sleepless, and almost worn-out with their prolonged fighting, depressed with the sense of failure and saddened by the thought of dead comrades, they were in no temper to reward treachery with mercy. As their friends fell from the saddles, they rushed the Circassian houses, drove the civilian riflemen out, and in a few minutes had killed 36 of them. Not surprisingly, their retreat was not again molested.

Riding along in the darkness to Es Salt, a Light Horse officer noticed a man with a spare blanket wrapped about his knees. 'Picked it up, did you?' he asked. 'You were luckier than I was. I saw one lying on the ground as we pulled out from Amman, and jumped off to get it. But somebody, as he passed, had laid it over a dead Londoner.'

2 April

All the surviving raiders returned safely back across the Jordan to the west side by nightfall of 2 April. British and Anzacs protected the stragglers retreating down the slopes and across the bridge. All had not been lost, however, because the British continued to guard the bridgehead at Ghoraniye on the River Jordan and to keep this as a reliable crossing point.

By the end of this first two-pronged raid on Es Salt and Amman, the venture had cost a total of 1,200 British casualties; 724 were in the Anzac Mounted Division, of whom 118 were killed and 55 missing. The Turks were estimated to have suffered an equal number of killed and wounded, a claim that may well be exaggerated, but in addition the enemy were known to have lost 615 officers and men who were taken prisoner.

Eventually, withdrawing forces retreated back to safety down into the lower Jordan Valley, licking their wounds. 'Thus ended our first Amman stunt,' James Rathie concluded.

Arabs on both sides had undermined Allenby's attack on Es Salt and Amman: Lawrence's Arabs and non-aligned Arabs. Explaining the British failure, Gullett blamed the seemingly two-faced Arabs for telling the Turks beforehand about the planned attack: 'News travels rapidly among these nomads, and the British designs, once communicated to the Sherifian leaders, were undoubtedly soon fully known to the Turks. And because the crossing of the Jordan was delayed for some days by floods; during that time the enemy concentrated around Amman 4,000 troops with fifteen guns and a large number of machine guns. Trenches were dug, and the approaches to the tunnel and viaduct safeguarded against anything but a sustained assault by a strong force. At the same time the enemy marched 2,000 reinforcements towards Es Salt from the north'.

This failed frontal assault was, in fact, like the disastrous frontal attack of Second Gaza a year earlier, when the Turks knew the EEF was coming, as Gullet explained: 'A raid which fails to take the enemy by surprise has but a slender chance of success, especially when, as at Amman, the raiding party is operating far away from its base ... the Arabs throughout played the safe game of waiting for decisive fighting by the British before becoming pronounced in their sympathies and assistance. Around Amman they were still friendly to the Turks'.

But after the retreat, General Shea made no attempt to disguise his failure. 'The objects of the raid on the Hejaz railway,' he said, in his report written a fortnight later, 'were the destruction of the tunnel and viaduct, of Amman station itself, and of the railway for some distance north and south of that place. But adverse weather conditions and the opposition encountered prevented these objects from being completely attained.'

So Liman von Sanders had defeated British and Anzac forces attacking his high territory — as he had at Gallipoli in 1915. Now he had led the Turks to their first victory since they had defeated British forces at that Second Gaza battle, back in April 1917.

11 April

Flexing their muscles, Liman von Sanders' emboldened Turks now ventured down from the heights to destroy that main crossing further south, the Ghoraniye bridgehead. The Turks were desperate to recapture and cut off this British pathway to Es Salt and Amman. But having fought hard to secure this vital bridgehead, Allenby's forces resisted them. On the same day, the Camel Corps also repelled a Turkish counterattack at Wadi Mellahah, near the British frontline.

24 April

Allenby now held a series of conferences with his fellow leaders, including Chauvel. Allenby was not going to give up. He still wanted his moving frontline to fight its way right up to Damascus, so he had to capture Es Salt and Amman and then move on to attack the well-defended town of Deraa, where there was a rail junction, south of Damascus. Having lost some of his British infantry, which he had to send to the Western Front, Allenby hoped Chauvel and his mounted forces (whom Allenby had hung onto) would now help him with this difficult mission.

Allenby planned to deploy his forces to create the impression that his main thrust would be against Amman first. The Turks, he hoped, would send more troops there, enabling him to attack in other areas more successfully.

30 April: The second round

Angry that Liman von Sanders had beaten him in round one, the 'never say die' Allenby then launched a second two-pronged attack through the foothills of Shunet Nimrin towards Es Salt, hoping to capture Amman after that. Surely, he thought, having learned mistakes from the first attempt, he could defeat Liman von Sanders this time. He wanted to get control of Es Salt again, because that commanding high point would help him plan his advance north towards Damascus. From the Es Salt heights, he could also plan the capture of the next big target — the vital railhead to the north at Deraa, on the way to Damascus.

As usual, he ordered the infantry to attack the foothills first, sending in the tired but dogged 60th Division of Londoners. With Lieutenant- General Chauvel in charge of the Anzac and Australian Mounted Divisions, he ordered all his forces to try even harder than before and capture Es Salt before dark. So Chauvel sent Brigadier-General William Grant into battle first, his commander of the battle-hardened 4th Brigade, containing the 4th and 12th Regiments (which had made history at Beersheba). Chauvel ordered Grant's 4th Light Horse Brigade to line up along the natural barrier of the Jordan River and block any Turkish reinforcements that tried to come across from the west towards Es Salt to help Turkish defenders there.

This was difficult, as Eric McGregor from the 12th Light Horse Regiment — a bank clerk in civilian life who eventually managed an Australian bank in New Guinea — confirmed. He reported how the two regiments that had charged Beersheba now fought together again, but in defeat not victory. 'The

12th Regiment were placed to prevent the enemy passing from E. to W. of Jordan. This they did with the remainder of the Brigade for 24 hours when the enemy attacked with great style and with very much superior numbers — outnumbering the 12th Regiment 5 to 1. Owing to the roughness of the country and the length of the line held by us we were forced to withdraw our Brigade. We fought a determined rearguard action during which we were repeatedly attacked and heavily shelled. But then the 1st Squadron of the 12th Regiment and the 4th Regiment met the enemy with the bayonet and denied him the positions (which if he had gained) would have closed the Es Salt road to our troops who were then still in Es Salt'.

McGregor continued, 'We had great difficulty in obtaining supplies and watering our horses from this position owing to the openness of the country and the observations the enemy had over us from the higher ground. But we held this position for 4 days under the most trying circumstances. On the eve of the fourth night when all our troops were clear from Es Salt we were ordered to withdraw to the west side of the Jordan to our old Bivouac but were heavily bombed by enemy aircraft there'.

Luckily for James Rathie, 'Two small black cows wandered into our camp from Jacco's area and Jack Watson from Narrabri herded them into our camp and a rifle and Jack knives did the rest. We all had fresh steak for tea'.

With the embattled 60th Infantry Division advancing again up the foothills of the plateau on which Es Salt was situated, and the Australian Mounted Division riding up on the east side of the Jordan River, Allenby hoped to capture and also hold Es Salt the second time around.

Chauvel also ordered Brigadier-General Lachlan Wilson's 3rd Light Horse Brigade to ride steadily up the hills and onto the plateau, supported by mobile artillery batteries that fired shells ahead of the riders to soften up the Turkish defenders. It was a 17-kilometre ride, rising 1,200 metres over rugged and slippery ground; they were like mountain horsemen from Banjo Paterson's ballad 'The Man from Snowy River'. The 3rd Brigade's 9th Regiment rode on ahead, with their scouts killing or capturing any Turks defending the outskirts of Es Salt who did not flee. Fortunately, the Turks were mainly in isolated small pockets rather than one long line of trenches.

The 9th Regiment, led by their commander, Lieutenant-Colonel William Scott, had little trouble with their courageous and capable horses riding towards Es Salt over rocky and jumbled ground. Where possible, they galloped up towards the Turks shooting down at them from high on ridges, or leapt over their trenches in the ditches as the Light Horse had done at Beersheba. When they reached a major fortified stone barricade, they just jumped their horses over this obstacle and then turned on the German or Turkish defenders with their rifles and bayonets; or, in some cases, they dismounted and killed the enemy with bayonet or revolver in hand-to-hand combat — once again like the charge at Beersheba.

After that, Brigadier-General Wilson ordered the 3rd Brigade's 8th Regiment, led by Major Shannon, to gallop the last few kilometres into the town of Es Salt itself, which they reached even though the last of the Turkish defenders were firing at them from hill tops and trenches with machine guns and rifles. But the Australians galloped so fast, and returned enemy fire so quickly and accurately, that they forced the frightened defenders to flee. Just before nightfall, they got through into the main street of Es Salt itself, which ran between ridges, with houses built up layer on layer beneath a castle dating from the Crusades. Leading troopers shot or captured any remaining Turks defending the ancient town and stopped many of those fleeing. One of these men, Lieutenant Charles Foulkes-Taylor, 28, from Western Australia, riding ahead with a small group, killed or captured so many prisoners that he won the Military Cross. With typical Australian bravado, he even captured German and Turkish troops after his revolver ran out of ammunition, just by pointing the empty barrel at them and demanding they surrender!

So despite resistance by the Turkish defenders, the Light Horse captured Es Salt, and before nightfall. So far, so good; the elusive Es Salt was in British hands once again. James Rathie said, 'When we rode through Es

Salt we found boxes of ammunition and gun shells lying beside the road, over turned carts and wagons, lots of papers and even a typewriter. Then we found fresh bread — a regular windfall for our chaps'.

1 May

Although it looked like Allenby had now beaten Liman von Sanders, winning round two of the Es Salt battle, this sense of victory was short lived. The seemingly never-ending stream of Turkish reinforcements overwhelmed the raiders. The Turks defeated Grant's 4th Brigade, defending the Jordan crossing and driving the Australians away; and then those Turks rushed to Es Salt to dislodge Wilson's 3rd Brigade. Now Wilson would have to consider retreating from Es Salt. Suddenly, it was looking like another victory for Liman von Sanders.

When they did fight their way into Es Salt, the Light Horsemen rushed straight to the town's water supply so they could water their thirsty horses, in this case under the watchful eye of the local residents.

At the same time, Chauvel complained, 'The Arabs had just vanished into space'. There was no help to be had from Lawrence and his Arabs, even this second time around.

Hearing the news about the situation at Es Salt, Allenby and Chauvel realised they would have to consider retreat yet again or lose some of their best men, who were needed for the main target further north, Damascus. With aerial reconnaissance confirming thousands of Turkish troops arriving to defend Amman, Allenby understood that if he could not hang onto Es Salt, he certainly could not succeed with his planned follow up raid on Amman, which he had to abandon. Allenby ordered a fighting withdrawal.

James Rathie was relieved: 'Jaccos were everywhere in full force along the edge of the hills above us. Turkish snipers were taking pot shots at us, unseen machine gunners fired incessantly and bullets cracked overhead forcing us to keep our heads down and make for cover.'

2 May

The Australians fought on as hard as they could. Grant's 4th Brigade, having won so well at Beersheba, certainly did not want to retreat until they had to. As Colonel R.M. Preston wrote in his account, *The Desert Mounted Corps* (1921), soon after this battle: 'The Brigade headquarters and every man ... that could be spared from the service of the guns were also thrown into the fight. This little handful of men fought heroically, but hopelessly, against the ever advancing waves of the enemy, and at last was pushed back across our line of retreat to the south'.

The Australians even used captured enemy bombs against the Turks. Lieutenant-Colonel Arthur Olden of the 10th Light Horse Regiment later described this trick in his first-hand account, *Westralian Cavalry in the War* (1921): 'As a big body of Turks were advancing they commenced to shell our positions ... every available man was placed in the firing line, the horses were transferred to a deep ravine ... A large number of German bombs had been captured in Es Salt, collected in sacks and brought up on pack horses ... our gallant lads had loaded these strange and deadly missiles into the sacks just as if they were a collection of vegetables dumped them on the pack horses and brought them up the slippery stony tracks to their mates in the front line ... but as these bombs were different to anything we had seen a couple of them exploded prematurely to start with and the boys lost several fingers before they mastered the mechanism preparing the bombs for use against the Turks in the darkness'.

Preston added: 'Each time a Turkish attack broke and melted away before their fire, the enemy dead lay a little closer to our guns. And each time a short retirement was made ... the enemy pushed the guns further into the hills and each time there were fewer men and horses to move them. But at last there was no way out ... the teams were mown down by machine gun fire ... the remaining men and horses scrambled up the hills and the Australian troopers of the 4th Light Horse Regiment accompanied them fighting grimly and silently as an old dog fox run into by the hounds slashing right and left'.

3 May

The decision was made to withdraw from Es Salt, where Turkish reinforcements had swung the tide of battle against the British. The Turks embedded in the foothills surrounding the plateau also fought back strongly, so the British 60th Division and the mounted men all had to withdraw once again. Liman von Sanders had done it for the third time — first, having driven the British forces off the heights at Gallipoli, and then when they raided Es Salt the first and now the second time. The only justification for the Es Salt defeats was the same sort of rationalisation used at Gallipoli, as Allenby claimed he had diverted thousands of enemy troops away from his western coastal thrust, which for him was the main event. The British War Office had justified the lost lives at Gallipoli by claiming that the eight months they spent fighting there was useful because it diverted Germans and Turks from the main event, which was the Western Front.

But as Preston recorded, after receiving the order to withdraw all mounted troops from the assault on Es Salt, it was no easier to retreat this time than the last time. After his men mounted the horses and moved away, he wrote: 'Behind us we saw the Turks attacking ... in great style with bomb and bayonet ... and with a triumphant cry'. But at least the mounted men got away, with the New Zealand Mounted Rifles keeping the road open for the retreat.

James Rathie was relieved, having been so frightened of counterattack when up at the frontline one night that he said, 'I hoped our home folk were praying for us that night for only their prayers could help us out we felt'. But he was lucky: 'One shell came so close I could feel the wind of it on my hat and it burst about 20 feet away after going over us. My old horse thought he was hit and jumped off the path nearly on top of me'.

Many were killed, some injured. Trooper Stan Broome from the 12th Regiment would probably have had one of the lightest injuries, but was doubly lucky: 'We had a big stunt up the Jordan Valley, starting from 29 April and the next day my horse fell and I sprained my ankle. The shell fire was pretty warm but I hung it out till next morning. I was sent to the 4th Brigade Field Ambulance. While there, the Turks attacked us and I was lucky to get away. The ambulance was left and a doctor grabbed me and got me away'. Not only that, Broome added, but he also 'had a bout of malaria however a few doses of quinine cleared that up'. Nevertheless, within days Broome was back — on both feet and on duty.

4 May

By the end of 4 May, all forces had received their orders to withdraw and were on their way back down off the foothills of Es Salt and Amman, crossing the Jordan River and back onto the west side, into the comparative safety of the British-occupied Jordan Valley. 'Thus ended our second Amman stunt,' James Rathie wrote. 'We had been six days across the East side of the Jordan and never wanted to see that side again. We all had very thankful hearts that we got out safe and sound'.

Not that the Jordan Valley was all that safe, even for off-duty troopers, according to Signals Sergeant Hammond of the 11th Regiment, who claimed there were scorpions and hairy black spiders as big as a man's fist.

'The digger's instinct for gambling throve amidst these hazards', he wrote, 'and many a piaster was won and lost on the fierce conflicts staged by the soldiers between scorpions and spiders that fought to the death in a tin hat'. After the Jerusalem-based scientific department offered a reward for the asp that had reputedly bitten Queen Cleopatra in ancient Europe, and was rumoured to live in the Jordan Valley, Hammond said, 'Every digger who was not actually in the firing line could be seen tramping to and fro with a forked stick in his hands ... hardly a stone was left unturned'. But because such a wide variety of reptiles were soon delivered, 'It was not long before a frantic note came cancelling the order for live snakes'. In fact, an Australian assistant in the laboratory told one of the snake catchers to stop delivering, saying, 'You must think we are running a flaming sideshow here'.

Many of these Light Horsemen had performed well, including Signaller Ephraim McHugh, a storeman from Wedderburn, Victoria, who received a Distinguished Conduct Medal, serving with the 4th Light Horse, 'for conspicuous gallantry and devotion to duty during the operations at Jisr Ed Damieh and Black Hill from 30th April to 4th May 1918. Although operating under the most adverse conditions, and nearly always under a heavy machine-gun and rifle fire, perfect communication between regimental headquarters and all three squadrons, also brigade headquarters was established, and maintained throughout. This excellent result was mainly due to his untiring effort, his organisation and control of his men, and his record and gallantry on all occasions'.

McHugh's mate from Wedderburn, Trooper Robert Gregson, also of the 4th Light Horse Regiment, was among the lucky ones. A grocer in civilian life, Gregson survived battle after battle, and he returned to his hometown, where he later died and was buried. Nevertheless, he fought in Palestine for two years in some of the 'hottest scrapes', was repeatedly shot at, with mates dying all around him, suffered a broken arm, nearly died from malaria — which kept him in hospital for weeks in 1918 — but was among the first riders to liberate Damascus when the 4th Light Horse rode in as part of the Allied force on 1 October 1918. Later promoted to corporal, Gregson returned to Australia and took up residence in Wedderburn, as did McHugh, who later married Gregson's sister Lois.

A country boy, Trooper Victor Dignam from Menangle Park — who had earlier stolen an English officer's mare by secretly substituting his bucking gelding for the mare by swapping the identification numbers of the hooves, and whose spelling was not as good as his horsemanship — explained the retreat in a letter back home: 'There will be a Note in the Palestine papers about the 1 of May. Fighting East of the Jordan where we were in some verry hevvy Fighting on the Eastern Banks of the jarden and had to fall Back a bit but made the Tarks pay the price. They came over a flat from the River to fut hills where our Bradage was, they were as thick as flyes about three time is miny as up was. Our Sargent was Killed he was blone in too with a schell. We had on ather man Killed and 4 wounded.

'Well you say in your litter that Dad wanted to know if the priests and Chaplarns went into the farigng Line. Yes they go rite up into the Line with us. And at the battle of Telalsher I seen a Chaplaine of ours Killed. his name was Dunbar and he had 16 bullits. Where he had had a Machane gun turned on him. well I think that is all for this time. So with best lave and wishes for all fram Victor xxx.'

But good things sometimes came to those who waited, and just after the retreat in May 1918, the slow wheels of the military bureaucracy finally concluded their year-long processing of the Distinguished Service Order that had been considered for Major Thomas Bird, a farmer and grazier from Gresford, New South Wales, described in official correspondence as 'a thoroughly efficient and reliable officer quite capable of commanding a Regiment'. Bird had fought well at Gaza in March 1917, and helped to capture a Turkish divisional commander; he had also captured a troop of Turkish cavalry and then, when ordered to retreat from this failed assault on Gaza, he had led the orderly withdrawal from Gaza. In an official letter to his father, W.H. Bird, at Orinduina, Gresford, the Australian Imperial Force now advised:

'HIS MAJESTY THE KING had been graciously pleased to approve of the award for distinguished services in the field for Major Thomas Bird', confirming it had been promulgated in the Commonwealth of Australia *Gazette* of 18 April 1918. The plucky Bird — who was also 'Mentioned in Dispatches' — was lucky to live long enough to see his decoration confirmed, as some of his fellow Light Horsemen had died before the bureaucracy had confirmed the reward for their bravery.

Thick dust was a recurring problem for the Light Horsemen riding through the Jordan Valley — sometimes, the choking troopers complained, they could see no further than the ears of their horse.

Captain Jack Davies, who had won the Military Cross at Beersheba, was now ordered to find Lawrence of Arabia, who was camped near Jerusalem. Although he spoke very poor French (the main second language used by the Arabs), he eventually found an Arab who spoke perfect English and who told him to go to an Officers' Club where Lawrence would appear in half an hour's time. On arrival at the club, he was met by Lawrence, looking spick and span in his army uniform, and was able to brief the leader of the Arab Army in secret with Allenby's latest battle plans. Although Davies does not comment on Lawrence, a 7th Light Horse comrade wrote later: 'Lawrence was regarded as being super-human by all the Lighthorsemen [sic] and was always our own particular "little hero". Although few, if any, of us ever saw him he was always spoken about in a most friendly and familiar way, and I am sure many of us came to imagine that we personally knew him quite well. Any time that we managed to surprise the Turks we felt it was due directly or indirectly to Lawrence and we always had the feeling that he was "just out there somewhere" which made us feel safe and happy. He was never regarded by us as just a soldier — he was much more than that — he was a powerful and hidden ally. He was a far greater man than we ever imagined — he was a genius'.

As well as being a useful staging post for Allenby's forces on the advance towards Damascus, the biblical Lake Tiberias aka Sea of Galilee (where Christians believe Christ once walked across the water to calm wild waves) provided some respite for the weary troopers, who were given leave to swim in the lake.

Meanwhile, back in the Jordan Valley, surviving troopers got a chance to star in a newsreel film for cinemas back home — as Trooper Stan Broome of the 12th Light Horse wrote home: 'The Duke of Connaught and the King's uncle will inspect us next Monday and they are taking moving pictures of us. It is the first time the King's representative has inspected the A.L.H. General Chauvel, commander of the Desert Column and all the horsemen in Palestine, inspected us the other day and gave us a lot of soft soap over our war work, especially the Beersheba charge.' Broome confirmed he was polishing his boots and saddle for the film, saying: 'If you see the moving pictures of the Light Horse advertised soon after this arrives, it will be us! We are to do a charge against trenches I believe that will be screened also. Everyone here wishes they would stop their "tommy-rot" and let us have a spell'.

Allenby certainly thought men like Broome deserved a spell. Having failed to win the first and second battles for the towns of Es Salt and Amman up on the heights, Allenby was aware of the high price paid by his gallant troopers. Admittedly, he had captured Es Salt twice but only held onto the Turkish garrison town briefly before he was expelled by Liman von Sanders. It was ignominious and reminded his critics of the previous defeat of the British forces at Second Gaza, under the leadership of Murray. But there was no going back. With the hot dusty summer approaching, and so many men killed, wounded, or exhausted, he now had to fall back, regroup, and take stock.

The future did not look bright. Liman von Sanders had succeeded twice now in expelling British and Anzac forces from his high territory. It was a great day for the conquering German hero from the 1915 Gallipoli campaign. Now he had led the Turks to their second victory in the Middle East since Second Gaza in April 1917.

Not only that, but the head of the Ottoman Empire, the Sultan himself, now appointed as head of the Seventh Army in Jordan the Turkish officer from Gallipoli who had done more than any other to defeat the British with their Anzac allies — Mustafa Kemal. So the old conquering comrades — von Sanders and Kemal — were back together.

From now on it was going to be much harder for Allenby to win battles, especially as the British War Office was increasingly demanding he send more troops to the troubled Western Front — including 60,000 British infantry to France to stop the German Spring Offensive, which had started in March 1918 and threatened to sweep across France to the English Channel. With his back to the wall, Allenby now had to decide whether to retreat back down south away from these tenacious Turks or bravely push on to Damascus.

PART V
SYRIA 1918

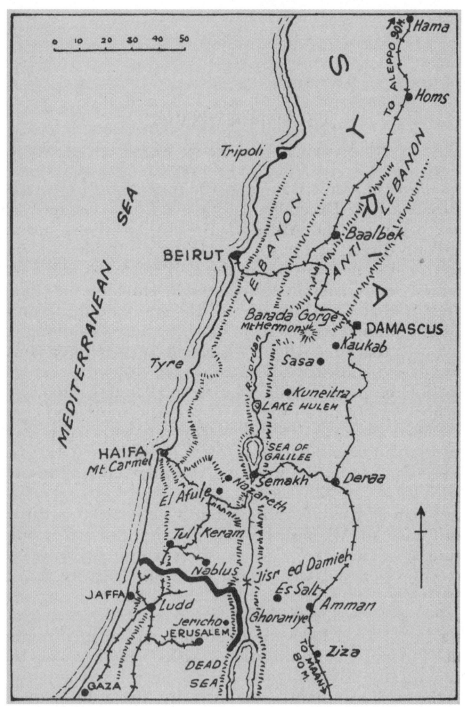

With his Egyptian Expeditionary Forces advancing north on both sides of the Jordan, supported by Lawrence of Arabia and his Arab Army on the eastern side of the river, Allenby was closing in on the last Turkish stronghold of Damascus by late September 1918.

10.
DAMASCUS, 16 SEPTEMBER– 11 NOVEMBER 1918

THE 'ROAD TO DAMASCUS' EXPERIENCE

As Damascus was surrounded by rugged hills, the Light Horse had to approach through valleys, risking ambush as they headed for this make-or-break battle where they feared the Turks would mount a last-ditch stand. 'Damascus Incident' painted by H. Septimus Power. (AWM ART03647)

My dear Chauvel, I do congratulate you on your ably conducted and historic ride to Damascus, and on all the rest of the performances of the Cavalry in this epoch-making victory. You have made history with a vengeance and your performance will be talked about and quoted long after many more bloody battles in France will have been almost forgotten ... and it was the Cavalry who put the lid on the Turks' aspirations forever!

SIR PHILIP W. CHETWODE, COMMANDER,
BRITISH 20TH INFANTRY CORPS, OCTOBER 1918

BACKGROUND TO THE BATTLE

Having been defeated at the battles of Es Salt and Amman, Allenby bided his time, falling back and regrouping during the long, hot, dusty summer before setting out on the road to Damascus.

It was just as well because, coincidentally, given the well-known biblical precedent of Saint Paul on the road to Damascus, where he was inspired to convert to Christianity, by the time Allenby's forces drove the Turks north, captured all the enemy towns along the way and approached their long-awaited destination, there would be plenty of unexpected and historic *experiences* for the competing players on the road to Damascus. In fact, it was such a race to this finishing post that some of the leading players experienced upsets almost as dramatic as those biblical precedents.

The contestants included Lawrence and his Arab Army, which had led the powerful Arab revolt and dreamed of reaching Damascus first, liberating the city from the Ottomans, installing Feisal as the king, and establishing the long-awaited Arab rule promised by the British. But Lawrence and the Arabs were upstaged by both Australian and British forces. Allenby and his dominant British forces were meant to arrive first in Damascus to claim control for Britain, with Allenby planning a symbolic entry like his conquering walk into Jerusalem; but a troop of carefree Australians beat their British masters to Damascus. The irreverent Australian Light Horse 10th Regiment — whose men had ridden so far and so fast ahead of all other forces — could not have cared less about the political protocol of symbolic arrivals. They rode in first because they just happened to get there first, and it suited them to take a short cut through the city — even if it did upset their superiors' best-laid plans.

But of course those who suffered the worst 'experience' were the Turks and their German leaders, who were defeated after their last-ditch stand at their final stronghold. They were driven out of town, still being led by Britain's old Gallipoli foe, Mustafa Kemal.

Another 'experience' was that of the Arabs and other citizens living in Damascus. They now had to switch from their centuries-old colonial ruler — the Ottoman Empire — to the occupying forces led by the British.

All these events followed that most famous experience on the road to Damascus for the opponent of Jesus Christ, Paul aka Saul, an event familiar to the Christians among the British and Australian forces, especially Allenby and Chauvel. For according to the biblical story in the Book of Acts, Chapter 9, verses 3 to 6 (King James version), this was where he had his conversion:

'And as he journeyed, he came near Damascus: and suddenly there shined round about him a light from heaven: And he fell to the earth, and heard a voice saying unto him, Saul, Saul, why persecutest thou me? And he said, Who art thou, Lord? And the Lord said, I am Jesus whom thou persecutest: it *is* hard for thee to kick against the pricks. And he trembling and astonished said, Lord, what wilt thou have me to do? And the Lord *said* unto him, Arise, and go into the city, and it shall be told thee what thou must do'.

Saul later explained that the voice of Jesus then commissioned him to become a 'messenger to the Gentiles', a complete change for Saul, who had always been a passionate Gentile-hating Pharisee, and believed the Jews alone had the place of honour in God's eyes. But he felt compelled, as Jesus ordered him, 'to turn [the Gentiles] from darkness to light and from the power of Satan unto God, that they may receive forgiveness of sins, and inheritance among them which are sanctified by faith that is in me'.

As seen previously, Allenby's 'Christian soldiers' had noted in their diaries or letters the religious significance of many of the towns and villages they captured en route to Damascus — especially Jerusalem, Bethlehem, and Jericho. Before Damascus, though, they had their sights on Nazareth, which was where the archangel Gabriel visited Mary, telling her she would become the mother of the saviour, and also where that saviour would grow up. As Idriess wrote earlier: 'At times we felt we were riding through the pages of the bible'. In fact, when the devout Allenby captured Megiddo, he announced the time had come to start the final battle. This may have been because Megiddo used to be known as

Armageddon, and that was where Saint John had predicted, in the Book of Revelation, that the final battle would be fought before the return of Christ. Allenby knew capturing Damascus would not shape the future of the world, but this lifelong Christian still believed it would be the end of the Ottoman Empire, which had shaped this part of the world for centuries.

By Megiddo, Allenby was certainly ready for the final push. After that four-month summer break, he had come up with a clever plan for the advance and tactics for tricking the Turks, which he was keen to put in place. By September 1918, Allenby had reorganised his troops and had the biggest force yet. He boasted

To Christian Light Horsemen, Damascus was best known for the biblical story of Paul's 'Road to Damascus experience' where this rebellious religious activist was converted to Christianity.

140,000 men in his three army corps, 57,000 rifles, 12,000 sabres, and 540 guns. He was determined to defeat the weakened Turks once and for all. Bean said Allenby knew from reliable intelligence that their total force was only 103,500, and that all three Turkish armies were 'in very bad shape' — the Fifth Army, Mustafa Kemal's Seventh, and also the Eighth Army. Yet Allenby estimated the enemy only had 26,000 rifles, 3,000 sabres, and 370 guns. To make matters worse, Turks were deserting in increasing numbers, averaging more than 50 a week.

Charles Bean reported that apart from reconstructing his British divisions, Allenby also restructured the Australian Mounted Division, turning it into a purely Australian force. Within this he created the 5th

Light Horse Brigade, commanded by Brigadier-General George Macarthur-Onslow, made up of two extra Light Horse Regiments, the 14th and 15th, created with Australians from the Imperial Camel Brigade, which Allenby had disbanded.

As he wanted these regiments to fight as cavalry, Allenby also issued swords to the troopers in this new brigade. On paper, the Turks did not stand a chance because the experienced and successful Chauvel now commanded four divisions — the largest cavalry force in history. In August, the 4th Light Horse Regiment (which had charged at Beersheba) had been issued with swords and trained in traditional cavalry tactics in preparation for the next offensive against the Turks.

Allenby and his men expected great things from this advance on Damascus.

Yet weather could undermine even this great force, so timing was critical. That is why Allenby had decided that he must mount this final offensive north in September, and capture Damascus in early October, before the rains came in November and December. This was an ambitious plan, as his forces were still nearly 100 kilometres south of Damascus, with their frontline stretching across the Holy Land south of the Sea of Galilee from Haifa on the coast across to the east just south of Deraa (the vital railway junction town used by the enemy to move troops by train from battle to battle).

16 September

As Allenby knew that Liman von Sanders, who had defeated the British at Gallipoli, also saw Damascus as a last stand, he tricked the Turks into thinking he would advance from the eastern side of the Jordan Valley inland rather than from the coast. The Turks were so convinced that when a devout Muslim Indian sergeant deserted the British ranks and told Liman von Sanders the truth, the German general disbelieved him, claiming he was a plant sent to trick them. Mustafa Kemal, by contrast, *did* believe the Indian but was overruled by Liman von Sanders. Kemal, who detested Liman von Sanders, had learnt his lesson from the tricky pretence the British and Australians organised so skilfully at Gallipoli to conceal their nocturnal retreat — once bitten, he was twice shy.

To aid his deception, Allenby ordered the creation of a make-believe camp headquarters to be maintained inland, with fake horses; he also set up his fake headquarters in Jerusalem at a fancy hotel. Chauvel created empty tent camps to pretend his HQ was based elsewhere, 80 kilometres away at Talat el Dumm, in another valley. Having succeeded in tricking the Turks for weeks before the evacuation at Gallipoli (where they had rigged up self-firing unattended rifles in trenches), Chauvel and his Australian troopers had good experience in deception, using fake horses, unattended campfires, electric lights, and gunshots in what was really a 'ghost camp'. Engineers also dragged big sleds around to stir up lots of dust that looked, from a distance, like troop movements. The Turks were certainly taken in, because they reported at this time 'some regrouping of cavalry units only on the coast' but otherwise 'nothing unusual to report', Bean wrote.

By the final advance towards Damascus, the Royal Flying Corps and the 1st Australian Squadron, with its ace pilots, were easily defeating any German bombers who dared to venture into their airspace.

Meanwhile, in the dead of the darkest night, the real moves were made for the start of the attack on Damascus. Allenby ordered Chauvel to move his real headquarters from the inland Jericho road to the coast in readiness for the last great offensive. The air force, which by then had gained superiority over the German air force, was mapping the Turkish positions around Damascus with little opposition. The 1st Australian Squadron was by then described as ' the finest that ever took to the air' by the British air force commander, Air Vice Marshall Sir John Salmond.

17 September

Allenby ordered the British and Anzac forces to advance north just inside the coast on the western side of the Holy Land. He paid a visit to Chauvel to wish him luck.

Chauvel certainly hoped fortune would favour his attempts this time to defeat Kemal, who had forced him off the beach at Gallipoli and who, as commander of the Turkish Seventh Army, now blocked Chauvel's path to Damascus. Luckily, Chauvel's other Gallipoli nemesis, Liman von Sanders, had refused Kemal's request to unify all three Turkish armies in order to create a larger force to stop Allenby's advancing men. This refusal by his German superior infuriated the Gallipoli hero and further undermined the solidarity between the Germans and Turks.

Always the diplomat, as Allenby's forces advanced further north, the Desert Column commander, Lieutenant-General Sir Harry Chauvel, negotiated peace agreements with local Arab chiefs.

Based over near the coast in the village of Sarona, just north of Jaffa, with his troopers at Jaffa and Ludd, Chauvel made his plans. He would first capture Nazareth and El Afule to the north-east, both communication centres and headquarters. Liman von Sanders was based in Nazareth.

Allenby also commissioned Lawrence to continue fighting further east, inland, doing the groundwork for the forthcoming advance by blowing up important railway lines and stations on the far eastern side of the Allied advance — hopefully putting the important rail junction town of Deraa out of action.

19 September

Allenby now ordered the great advance north using all his forces, both in the air and on the ground. It would be the last major offensive — its objective, Damascus.

The assault started with a massive bombardment from the air and the ground to help Allenby's infantry attack the Turkish line at its coastal end as the infantry advanced along the coast. His infantry immediately broke though Turkish defences on the coast, capturing Tul Keram and heading north.

Chauvel's Desert Mounted Corps rode north just inland of the coast from Jaffa towards Jenin. Meanwhile, two Indian cavalry divisions advanced north — minus that one devout Muslim sergeant who had deserted a few days earlier. Soon, the mounted forces penetrated deep into the Turkish rear areas, severing roads, railways, and communications links.

The Turkish resistance was collapsing, as the demoralised troops would rather surrender than fight for these last bastions of the old Ottoman Empire. Allenby's forces seemed to be everywhere. The British infantry led by Chetwode and Bulfin, along with Chauvel's mounted men, advanced on El Afule, conquering this village and taking 1,500 prisoners. Chauvel's men rode north, capturing Nazareth, but not before Liman von Sanders had managed to escape in a Mercedes wearing his pyjamas, much to the disappointment of Chauvel. They had also captured the little town of Jenin en route with 3,000 German and Turkish prisoners, as well as Megiddo. It was becoming a rout.

Meanwhile, further east inland Lawrence blew up a four-arched bridge at Mafraq, in a classic lightning strike that was very successful, apart from the fact that the Rolls Royce he was travelling in (instead of on his usual camel) broke down temporarily as he retreated from angry Turks, who threatened to shoot him until his driver got the vehicle going again. But at last this deadly Arab Army was really part of the team, as Lawrence said: 'The Arab movement had lived as a wild-man show, with its means as small as its duties and prospects. Now Allenby counted it as a sensible part of his scheme; and the responsibility upon us of doing better than we wished, knowing that forfeit for our failure would necessarily be part-paid in his soldiers' lives, removed it terrifyingly further from the sphere of joyous adventure'.

Next, Lawrence and his Arab Army raiding party bravely attacked the biggest railway terminus south of Damascus itself, Deraa, and with his increasingly skilled demolition experts successfully blew up the railway tracks, to the south then to the north. They also cut off the telephone lines, thereby isolating this important Turkish stronghold, so the Turks could not use Deraa for transporting either troops or supplies. They went on to disable all the rail and communications equipment at nearby Mezerib and then at Nasib. In most of these hit-and-run raids, Lawrence was lucky to escape, because the Turks defended railway lines and junctions from within strong fortifications, and their German comrades bombed Lawrence and his fearless raiders from the skies above.

20 September

Brigadier-General Wilson's 3rd Light Horse Brigade took Jenin, capturing 2,000 Turks and Germans — most happy to surrender. Later on the night of the 20th, the 10th Regiment of Wilson's 3rd Brigade also captured another 3,000 Turks retreating from Jenin. More Turks kept turning up overnight, and by first light on 21 September there were 8,000 prisoners.

The 4th Cavalry Division captured Beisan, then the 5th Cavalry Division captured Haifa on the coast; the 5th Light Horse destroyed the Samaria railway.

Finally, as Bean reported, after infantry action, the Australian Mounted Division also advanced in greater numbers than before from the Jordan Valley towards the previously elusive Es Salt and Amman, which were by then poorly defended. This time, victory would be easier, as rather than isolated battles, the move against Es Salt and Amman was part of a wider cavalry thrust towards Damascus itself by a well-coordinated and larger moving frontline.

Whenever the casual Australians rode confidently into ancient towns like Nablus, the locals stopped in their tracks and stared in amazement at these slouch-hatted bronzed bushmen, so scantily clad compared to them.

22 September

And so it was that once his forces had captured the old Ottoman town of Megiddo, aka Armageddon, Allenby had his first 'road to Damascus' experience. It suddenly dawned on him that the road ahead was clear and he could race on to Damascus. So he convened a conference with Chauvel, pulled out his maps, and announced he had decided to continue his advance right through to Damascus. It was a bold decision — with the remnants of three Turkish armies blocking his path — but he believed fortune favoured the bold.

After all, this juggernaut had already rolled over the plain of Esdraelon, had taken 13,000 prisoners, conquered the village of Jenin, won the hard-fought Battle of Semakh, and also secured the villages of Kuneitra and Sasa — so he was keen to maintain the momentum.

Allenby ordered Chauvel to advance further with the Australian Mounted Division, and with the 5th Cavalry Division following on, ordered them all to advance west of Lake Tiberias (the Sea of Galilee). He ordered the 4th Cavalry to advance to the east of the lake, where Lawrence was expected to follow, with his Arabs also riding up inland east of the lake, with a greater force than ever, thanks to Allenby's generosity. Said Lawrence, 'Allenby had now put three hundred thousand pounds into my independent credit account to cover personnel and equipment. With us now journeyed at least two thousand Sirhan camels, carrying our ammunition and food'.

When he finally led his conquering Light Horse Regiments into Damascus, Lieutenant-General Sir Harry Chauvel put on the biggest show of strength he could, to demonstrate who now controlled Damascus.

Most of the Light Horsemen were happy to push on, especially after the victory at Jenin, where they had discovered hundreds of bottles of sweet sparkling German wine. As 'the big brass' had made the mistake of assigning a couple of troopers to guard this treasure trove, it was not surprising that many of their fellow troopers soon had relaxed, happy grins on their faces and were ready and willing for anything.

23 September

So the grand advance continued. By now, even the Australian troopers among Chauvel's coastal forces hoped to defeat the Turkish Seventh Army, still blocking their progress north, because they wanted to get back at Mustafa Kemal, whose forces had slaughtered so many of their mates at The Nek and other battles at Gallipoli. British infantry soldiers felt the same — some of them had also been defeated by the Turks at the Dardanelles in the bloodbath at Cape Helles.

Allenby's wide moving frontline was now much more supported in the air by successful pilots like Captain Ross Smith in his magnificent — but one and only — Handley-Page bomber. He was one of many fearless and skilled Australian pilots flying for the Royal Australian Flying Squadron, including Captain Peters and his navigator-gunner James Traill (who had delivered the carrier pigeons to Lawrence that the Arab leader had eaten), and who by now had established great track records shooting German aircraft who opposed them.

Lawrence recounted how he, Smith, and another pilot were sitting down to a hot breakfast of eggs, sausages, and coffee at Lawrence's camp when suddenly two German aircraft appeared in the sky, heading for the Arab Army with bombs. Lawrence wrote: 'Our Australians scrambled wildly to the yet hot machines and started them in a moment. Ross Smith with his observer leapt into one and climbed like a cat up into the sky.' The planes headed straight for the oncoming enemy aircraft and engaged them with their machine guns. Lawrence continued: 'Ross Smith fastened on the big one and after five minutes of sharp machine gun rattles, the

German dived towards the railway line. As it flashed behind the low ridge there broke out a pennon of smoke and from its falling place a soft dark cloud. An "Ah" came from the Arabs about us'. Both enemy aircraft were destroyed. When the Australians landed, Lawrence wrote, Smith 'jumped gaily out of his machine swearing that the Arab front was the best place. Our sausages were still hot; we ate them and drank tea'.

Australia's Palestine war correspondent, Henry Gullett, confirmed that story, explaining why the Arabs were so appreciative: 'By now the Australians were dominating the air aided by the most unlikely allies as Australian airman [sic] have been engaged in a fascinating enterprise among the Arab allies. These pilots lived with the Arabs in their camps taking off for much effective bombing to far flung places that could only be reached from outlying Arab camps. One day they shot down two Hun planes among the Arabs who raced forward frantic with delight and excitement'. As Arabs loved looting the enemy, Gullett said, 'this adventure had a profound effect on our Arab Allies and spurred them on to increase their fine efforts'.

This spur was important, as Allenby was depending on Lawrence and his Arab Army to continue moving north on the eastern side of the advance, and to blow up more rail lines to stop any Turkish troop reinforcements. Lawrence said Allenby had nothing to worry about, because 'Allenby's smile had given us Staff, supply officers, an intelligence branch, and ordinance expert, a shipping expert and everything we needed'.

Pilots like Ross Smith provided so much valuable intelligence — including that many Turkish troops were now retreating — that these airmen were having more and more influence on the outcome of battle.

Just after Smith and other pilots flew Lawrence back to his camp south of Umm Tayeh, they were able to stop yet another German aircraft attacking that camp.

Later, Captain Peters flew up from Lawrence's camp to engage another German plane with his navigator, James Traill. Peters and Traill not only chased the enemy plane back to Deraa, but, when the German plane landed, set it alight with their deadly fire. Then the sharp-eyed marksman Traill shot the two airmen trying to escape.

But Lawrence was so angry that the German aircraft were bombing his Arab camps with raid after raid that he asked Captain Ross Smith and his fellow Australian pilots to get rid of them. Smith, who always relished a challenge, went off to the coast to collect a bigger plane — a Handley-Page bomber. In company with a couple of Bristols, Smith took off from Lawrence's camp and flew towards the German airfield at Deraa, ready to shoot any enemy planes out of the sky. On arrival, they shot to pieces or bombed every German plane on the ground at the Deraa aerodrome, dropping nearly a tonne of bombs and setting fire to both planes and hangars — thus removing an obstacle to the British advance towards Damascus.

24 September

Over in the east, Allenby's forces had also finally captured Es Salt and Amman, when they defeated the remnants of the defending Turks there as part of the relentless advance north.

This third-time-lucky victory was a combined effort, as Henry Gullett explained: 'Simultaneously while Chaytor's New Zealand Division were overrunning Es Salt on the east of the Jordan River where they captured 350 prisoners, the Australian Light Horse were also moving upon the Hedjaz railway after an all night march. The Light Horse then straddled the railway towards Damascus and they captured a complete train under steam and blocked the road ... the enemy fought resolutely and the struggle was the sharpest the cavalry experienced so far. Severe hand to hand fighting took place before the enemy, made up largely of Germans and strongly equipped with machine guns, was overcome'.

When Major-General Chaytor's forces, advancing from the Jordan Valley along with the Australian Mounted Division, had finally overrun the elusive Amman, they captured 2,500 prisoners from the retreating

Turkish Fourth Army. The Turks were now on the run — in fact, Bean reported that 5,000 of the enemy were now cut off south of Amman and trying to head north, dodging Allenby's forces.

By the end of the Palestine campaign, the commanding officers (but never the envious troopers) were using motor vehicles whenever they could because speed had become so critical, especially with events like the race to be first to Damascus.

Allenby had been very wise to bide his time, as Turkish resistance had moved north and weakened during that waiting time. It was something of an anti-climax; after securing Es Salt and the Hedjaz railway, Allenby's forces easily captured Amman against demoralised and retreating Turkish forces. As Gullett wrote: 'The Light Horsemen were never more eager to win'.

'The enemy casualties included 60 killed and thirty wounded, prisoners included 22 officers and 350 other ranks — nearly half of whom were Germans', Gullett continued. 'But by then the present position of the Turks' whole front line was desperate in the extreme.'

It had taken a long time, many months, to capture the stubborn and well-defended heights of Es Salt and Amman but it was worth it — Chaytor's forces captured 10,300 prisoners and 57 guns at a cost of just 139 casualties.

25 September

Allenby had ordered the advance against Lake Tiberias because he knew Liman von Sanders was using the lake, about 80 kilometres south of Damascus, as a natural buffer, with enemy defences entrenched at the southern and western ends. Now Allenby ordered Chauvel to send his experienced 4th Light Horse Brigade straight to the southern end of the lake to expel the enemy defending it.

At dawn on 25 September, Chauvel's 11th Light Horse Regiment successfully charged the southern end of the lake from the east. Although half their horses were hit by enemy fire, after a series of fierce battles the 11th Regiment overcame the defenders, killing 100 (mostly Germans) and capturing hundreds of Turkish prisoners. A little later, Chauvel's 12th Regiment, supported by the 4th Machine Gun Squadron, attacked the enemy's defences at the western end of the lake. After fierce fighting for a few hours, the 12th also succeeded in displacing the enemy defenders there. So Liman von Sanders' natural defence of the lake suddenly evaporated, removing another obstacle for the advance on Damascus.

28 September

Chauvel's Australian Mounted Division, heading north on the west of the lake, fought against a tough rearguard of German machine-gunners and Turks were forced further to the north.

The 5th Light Horse Brigade's commander, now Lieutenant-Colonel Donald C. Cameron, reported a big turning point to Allenby. The Turkish commander, who was cut off from his northern comrades and retreating from south of Amman, offered to surrender! The Turkish leader said they would throw down their arms on one condition: that the Australians would protect these routed and exhausted troops from marauding Arabs threatening to kill them. When 2nd Brigade Commander, Brigadier-General Ryrie, arrived with his 7th Regiment, he and Cameron agreed to the Turks' request because the Arabs — from the Beni Sakr tribe near Ziza Station — were not part of Lawrence's loyal followers, but were instead a rebellious tribe who were circling around, shouting threats and firing their rifles menacingly into the air.

Although they had established temporary headquarters in the field, the increasingly harassed Turks had to abandon these as Allenby's forces closed in on Damascus, often fleeing so quickly that they left their tents behind.

So the Australians recruited the newly surrendered Turks into their ranks before nightfall; along with Ryrie and Cameron's forces, the Turks then defended the position from the Arabs, who continued to threaten the now-united Turkish and Australian force. Shoulder to shoulder, the Turks and Australians fought together throughout the night. Next morning, when a New Zealand brigade arrived reinforcing the Allies and scaring off the hostile Arabs, the Turks then meekly handed over their weapons. They joined the swelling number of Turkish prisoners. But for one night they fought alongside each other, making a mockery of their years of mutual hostility. These friendly Turks then joined Chaytor's large groups of prisoners — then more than 10,000, all captured on this initial drive towards Damascus.

30 September

Allenby's forces, led by the Desert Mounted Corps, were closing in on Damascus. It was only a matter of days now, and different men were hoping to cross the finishing line first.

Not that the fight was over yet. Even as the German and Turkish forces retreated towards Damascus, tails between their legs, they suddenly turned around and took a stand at Kaukab, on a ridge with a higher vantage point, against William Grant's 4th Brigade chasing them. But using their increasing momentum under the command of Lieutenant-Colonel Murray Bourchier, the 4th and 12th Light Horse Regiments, which had fought together so well at Beersheba, charged the Turkish frontline and overcame their resistance.

At the same time, the 5th Brigade rode rapidly north to the west of Damascus to encircle and cut off the Turks fighting at Kaukab, who surrendered knowing they could neither escape nor defeat the Australians, who were by then reinforced by French cavalry. Kaukab, by the way, is said to be the exact spot on the road to Damascus where Saul aka Saint Paul converted to Christianity.

By now, with Damascus in sight, it was on for young and old. The 5th Brigade positioned itself on top of the steep Barada Gorge, and, from these rocky heights, shot at Turks fleeing north. When Wilson's 3rd Brigade joined them, the retreating Turks, by now evacuating Damascus in droves, did not stand a chance. With frightened Turks fleeing left, right, and centre, Damascus had all but fallen.

Everybody wanted to be first into Damascus — the finishing line. So the rivalry intensified between all attacking forces: the British, Lawrence, and the Anzacs. Even different Light Horse brigades and regiments were talking competitively about who would be first to ride into this almost mythical capital city of the desert. This was the end point of a long series of battles that had started with the Anzac Mounted Division's great breakthrough at Romani in August 1916.

It was very important at the highest level, because whoever entered first could claim victory and then assert control of Damascus and Syria. As the commander-in-chief of the Egyptian Expeditionary Force, Allenby had given strict orders that nobody was allowed to enter Damascus without his permission.

Everybody had different expectations, official and secret.

Lawrence wanted to be first with his Arab Army to install Feisal as king; in fact, he had already smuggled in flags to be hoisted on key buildings to proclaim Feisal's new possession. As Lawrence confirmed in his post-war book *Seven Pillars of Wisdom* (1926), the British 'promised to the Arabs, or rather to an unauthorized committee of seven Gothamites in Cairo, that the Arabs should keep, for their own, the territory they conquered from Turkey in the war. And that glad news had circulated throughout Syria'.

But the British and French had also created that secret and more powerful Sykes-Picot Agreement sabotaging that promise. Signed in May 1916, it proclaimed that all territory conquered would be divided between the British and French superpowers. Their agreement, with a map featuring different coloured regions (blue for France and red for Britain), awarded the coast of Syria (which became Lebanon) to France, and Iraq (both the central Baghdad region and the Basra region in the south) to Britain. The French would also control the north of Syria, Iraq, and Jordan, and the British the south, but with an Arab chief allowed to manage affairs under the colonial powers. Palestine was awarded to international control, but with the British becoming the dominant player. There was nothing left for the Arabs to control.

The British sought as much control as they could and planned to either govern the lands they conquered or to install puppet governments to do so for them; especially where explorers discovered oil, in places like Mosul.

Although the stakes were very high for the three main players — the British, French, and Lawrence — the Australians really just wanted the thrill, honour, and glory of being first.

But, in the end, it was a case of first come, first served. On 30 September, the eve of the planned event, the Australians were well out in front, ahead of both Lawrence and the British.

In fact, any Australian unit from the Desert Mounted Corps could have been first. The 5th Brigade, now commanded again by Brigadier-General Macarthur-Onslow, took the lead initially, racing along the road to Damascus, but was then ordered to go up into the hills on the road towards Beirut. Even though Macarthur-Onslow wrote that 'All ranks were greatly elated at the prospect of being the first troops to enter DAMASCUS!', the troops were ordered to bivouac high in the Barada (Abana) Gorge above the Beirut Road and railway line (full of fleeing refugees) to capture or shoot retreating Turks. Lieutenant-Colonel Bourchier's 4th regiment (with Cameron's 12th Regiment, which had charged at Beersheba) was also eager to be first, but was diverted with other duties. Finally, Wilson's 3rd Brigade hoped to be first, but at the last minute were ordered to wait in the hills closer to Damascus, then to send their 10th Regiment (which had fought at The Nek) ahead to the north of Damascus and cut off Turkish troops escaping on the road to Homs.

Britain's 5th Cavalry Division, commanded by General Henry MacAndrew, approached Damascus from Kuneitra as far as it could, competing with the Yeomanry Mounted forces commanded by General Barrow, but they were still 21 kilometres away.

Lawrence and his Arab Army were mustard-keen and rode though the night, hoping to be first and to liberate their treasured city, as a first step to establishing the free Arab nation state they had been promised. They were well behind the leading Australians, however, and although Lawrence arrived overnight and set up camp near Damascus, he made the mistake of getting up too late in the morning.

1 October: Enter the Australians — then Lawrence

The highly symbolic entry into Damascus became a fiasco. It was important, because traditionally the first conquerors to enter could take control in their own name. Although Britain's top brass, General Allenby (who had earned this honour), wanted the Australians to wait for the British to enter Damascus first, and Lawrence and his Arab Army (who had also earned this honour) wanted the British and the Australians to wait for the Arab Army to enter first, a bunch of Australians mucked the whole thing up by just cruising in unofficially, unannounced and by mistake.

4–5am

The Australians who had crawled out of their blanket rolls and saddled up at 4am were the troopers of the 10th Regiment, who had just been ordered to get up early and stop any Turks escaping along the Homs road to Aleppo, north of Damascus (including their old foe Mustafa Kemal, believed to be in Damascus). But as they could not work out how to find that road, they trotted into Damascus to ask directions! So the first into Damascus — and for purely practical reasons — were the battle-hardened troopers of the 10th Regiment. And according to Henry Gullett, these Australian troopers riding towards this holy grail could not have been less official or appropriate as conquering heroes: 'Unshaven and dusty, thin from the ordeal of the Jordan and with eyes bloodshot from lack of sleep they rode with the bursting excitement of a throng of schoolboys ... exuberant horsemen ... some with their swords flashing in the early sunrise'.

Having won so many battles in the Palestine campaign, the Australian Light Horsemen had become a bit of a legend by the time they captured Damascus — even if some of them seemed to know it, according to artist David Barker.

As Bean also reported, once the 3rd Brigade commander Wilson got the orders from above, during the night of 30 September, he sent his 10th Light Horse Regiment to find and block off that road to Aleppo. So, as

Bean continued, these unassuming Australians were the first to enter the long-desired city of Damascus at 5am on 1 October — only because they were looking for the way to the Homs road.

After being ordered to block escaping Turks, Wilson, who did not have a good map of Damascus or the area, reckoned the easier route to the road to Homs was not over rugged hills but straight through Damascus — so he sensibly got permission to 'pass through' the city. It would be the quickest way, though more dangerous, as thousands of German and Turkish troops could still be inside Damascus. Even so, Wilson thought his men would get through the narrow streets of the enemy stronghold if they galloped as fast as they always did.

'Believing that Damascus was still in Turkish hands', Bean wrote in his official history, 'the 10th Regiment headed by the brigade scouts and Major Arthur Olden (from Ballarat) — after making its way through the terrible debris in the Abana Gorge (littered with Turkish corpses) reached an open road running alongside the Abana River, which was empty. So they spurred on their horses from a walk to a trot as they saw before them shafts of sunlight bathing the minarets of Damascus with the early dawn light also shimmering on the exotic gardens of the city. Soon as the sun rose further they could see the bright city shining in all its glory like some mythical treasure — and so they broke from a canter into a gallop (leaving a cloud of dust behind them) and stormed into the great and ancient city of 250,000 souls'.

Nevertheless, even though they were just looking for locals to give them directions, the men of the triumphant 10th Regiment were now greeted as conquering heroes.

The locals certainly all stepped back for them — the noise of their horses' hooves on the cobbled streets would have been so dramatic, especially echoing from the ancient buildings either side as this rising, thunderous roar got closer and closer.

It would also have been a spectacular sight. The men were brandishing swords that gleamed in the sunlight. Bean wrote: 'They were greeted by a fusillade of shot but mainly from excited Arabs firing into the air in friendly demonstration.'

6am

Soon they reached the centre of Damascus and found a crowd at the Serai — the central civil administration building. Here, the bemused 10th Regiment reined in their horses, sleepy-headed troopers rested in their saddles, some with heads drooping from the early start and others looking around wide eyed at the odd assortment of locals gathering around them. Major Olden and Major Timperley dismounted, pulling their revolvers out of their holsters, and walked right into the building, which was full of robed Arabs.

This was a noisy and excited gathering of Arab notables, who had already taken control of the city from the Turkish administration. When the civil governor stepped forward, the 10th Regiment leader, Arthur Olden, warned him that Chauvel's Mounted Desert Column now surrounded Damascus with thousands of troops. Suitably impressed, the governor quickly wrote an assurance promising peace and safe conduct for Olden's troops on their mission to ride through the city en route to the road to Homs. The governor even provided a guide for the 'liberating' Australians.

6.30am

Olden accepted the surrender note and then sanctioned Emir Said as governor, taking the Arab's word for the fact that he was now the official ruler of Damascus.

6.45am

When Olden and Timperley emerged back into the sunlight, clutching this document guaranteeing safe passage, they were amazed to see hundreds of cheering Arabs surrounding the troopers sitting astride their horses. The grateful Arabs were even feeding grapes, peaches, and sweet cakes to the astonished horses and fastening colourful flowers to their bridles!

Bean says that 'It was only with great difficulty that the Australians disengaged themselves from the Arab welcome'. But they were there on another mission. In fact, according to the Regimental Diary, one increasingly impatient Light Horseman called out in a broad outback accent to the Arabs mobbing their horse, 'Could you just get out of the bloody way, mate, we're trying to find our way to that blooming Homs Road'.

7am

Eventually, having obtained their guide — an Armenian, Zeki Bey — to the Homs road, by 7am the 10th Regiment (having made history on the side) 'were soon clear of the cheering shooting crowd', the official correspondent Bean concluded.

Later, the 10th Regiment made more history: they fired the last shots in the Palestine campaign when they reached Khan Ayash, 30 kilometres out of Damascus. When ordered to attack the enemy, one of their officers, Colonel Daly, led a mounted charge that not only defeated the Turkish troops but also — for the first time in any Australian Light Horse mounted charge — snatched and captured an enemy flag. And this was also the last Light Horse engagement in Palestine.

Meanwhile, Lawrence woke up in his camp 25 kilometres south of Damascus, slowly shaved, had breakfast, and got dressed in his best flowing robes, determined to make a big impression for his grand entry into the city he had been dreaming about for years. He wore these robes, he said, because, 'The Arabs never had to ask who I was, for my clothes and appearance were peculiar in the desert. I always wore the pure whitest silk, with a gold and crimson Meccan headrope, and gold dagger. By so dressing I staked a claim, which Feisal's public consideration of me confirmed'. It was a big day for the leader of the Arab Army; he knew he had to be first to Damascus to claim victory for his Arabs and thus control of Syria, which he had promised them once he had installed Feisal as the king. Lawrence knew the future of the whole country would depend on who entered Damascus first.

He knew Allenby was at least a day or two behind him. He also believed Allenby's 'Gentlemen's Agreement' would hold: Allenby had by now agreed to allow Lawrence and his Arabs to enter first, because the Arabs could then assume control of Syria, which had been awarded to the French in the Sykes-Picot Agreement. (Allenby, who secretly resented his French Allies, preferred the Arabs, as they would limit French influence in this important oil-rich region). Lawrence also believed Allenby's order that 'no British or Australian troopers were allowed to enter Damascus unless absolutely forced to do so'.

It was a great moment for the Australian Light Horse when they conquered Damascus: it brought to a triumphant conclusion their campaign — which had started with the Battle of Romani in August 1916 — to rid Palestine of the Turks and dismantle the Ottoman Empire.

Setting off in his Rolls Royce, he had no idea that he was already well behind the Australian 10th Regiment (who argued later they had only entered Damascus because they were 'absolutely forced to do so' to find the Homs road to Aleppo). Then, to make matters worse, Lawrence was delayed for a while when a non-commissioned Indian officer guarding the approach to Damascus stopped him for questioning, thinking Lawrence and his party were Turkish, and trying to take them prisoner.

Eventually, the Rolls drove off again towards Damascus, led by Lawrence's advance guard of the 5th Cavalry Division and some of his own Arab leaders on horseback, Nasir and Nuri.

8.30am

Lawrence and his party drove through the ancient main streets, which were still crowded with spectators who had greeted the 10th Regiment and who now assumed this party was a follow up from the Australians; and so they were not so welcoming nor excited. Gullett described this entry: 'Lawrence rode into town with a few Arab horsemen on the heels of the advance guard of the 14th Cavalry Brigade. The Arabs believed that they shared with the Indians the honours of the first entry. Galloping with loud shouts down the streets, trailing their coloured silks and cottons and firing their rifles — they made a brave display. Their melodramatic demonstrations were in sharp contrast to the casual hard-fighting Australians who had risked all, nearly two hours earlier, thrilled the Christians but aroused the great Moslem crowds to a frenzy'.

Arriving at the city government building (the Serai), Lawrence leapt out of his Rolls, ran up the crowded stairs in his flowing robes, and entered the antechamber where his advance guards, horsemen Nasir and Nuri, were already meeting with 'the new governor', Emir Said, a pro-Turkish Algerian (anointed by the 10th Regiment just hours earlier). Emir Said announced he was now the governor, with his pro-Turkish Algerian brother Abdul Qadir (an old opponent of Lawrence) as his deputy! They were already governing Damascus with the support of Shakri el Ayubi, whom they pretended came from the house of Saladin. This carried weight, as the body of the last great conquering Muslim warrior, Saladin, who had captured Jerusalem from the Crusaders in 1187, was buried in the Umayyad mosque in Damascus, which Muslims revered. Emir Said and his brother had authority, they claimed, because they had personally greeted the conquering 10th Regiment and surrendered the city.

Lawrence was furious; as leader of Feisal's Arab Army, he had anointed Feisal as king and appointed Ali Riza al Rikabi as governor back in June 1917, when the Committee of the Seven had met and agreed on the post-war rule of Syria. Lawrence had even set up a committee for the transition of power to Feisal from the Turks. Shakria el Ayubi was only supposed to be the deputy to Lawrence's pick, Ali Riza al Rikabi. But Ali Riza al Rikabi had earlier deserted his post in search of Chauvel, whom he believed had more power than Lawrence and could install him as governor with greater authority. While his back was turned, the Algerian brothers had taken over the transitional committee, got the numbers, and seized power. It was a mess. Lawrence later wrote he was 'dumb with amazement'.

Meanwhile, when one of the disgruntled Arabs from one faction suddenly hit another from a rival faction on the cheek and threatened to kill him, they started punching and fighting each other until Lawrence and others pulled them apart. Lawrence may have ridden for two years with the Arabs, learnt their language, lived their lifestyle, and fought their cause, but he still could not understand them, let alone predict or control their behaviour.

And so the post-war political racial, religious, and tribal bickering had begun on day one.

9.30am

Chauvel left his base at Kaukab, a few kilometres south of the city, at 8.30am and drove into Damascus, arriving at 9.30am. He went in search of Lawrence, with whom he planned to establish the new government. The quick-thinking Lawrence, on meeting Chauvel, pretended that a 'majority of the citizens' had elected Shakri el Ayubi (who he wanted to govern now that his first choice Ali Riza al Rikabi had left town) as the head of a military government. Chauvel believed him and committed his Desert

Mounted Corps to support Shakri's new (but unofficial) government. Later, realising Lawrence's power, Qadir, one of the Algerian brothers, fled, and so Lawrence imprisoned the other one, Emir Said, to avoid any future challenges.

Chauvel then returned to his base to prepare an official parade of the conquerors for the following day.

2 October, noon

Ordered by Allenby — and representing him — as the conquering leader, Chauvel rode through the town on horseback, leading a victory parade that was the biggest and most impressive ever to enter Damascus and one that showed who was in charge now.

This military column represented, Chauvel wrote, 'every unit in the Corps including artillery and armoured cars, with the three divisional commanders and their staffs riding' also in the parade. This show of strength would have impressed the locals as it featured the British Yeoman and gunners, New Zealand Light Horse, Indian Lancers, and French Cavalry, while a squadron of the 2nd Light Horse Regiment rode alongside Chauvel as his bodyguard.

Lawrence had asked Chauvel to let Feisal's Arabs ride ahead of the British forces 'to clear the way', and Chauvel allowed 'a small detachment of the Sharif's gendarmerie to ride ahead waving large colourful Hejaz flags in the most unmilitary manner'. Although Chauvel thought this would placate Lawrence, he also believed this would show the locals which force had the most military might, as Chauvel's included armoured cars, heavy artillery guns, and machine guns. Sergeant Frank Organ, who led a squadron from the 4th Light Horse, wrote that the parade was so long that the last members did not arrive till 3pm.

Bean reported the success of this parade and its impression on the locals, saying, 'On the afternoon of the 2nd October Damascus a city of 300,000 — which till then was in ferment of looting and lawlessness, was quietened down by Chauvel with the age old method of an impressive parade of his battle-stained mounted troops riding through its streets and so the local people then re-opened their shops'.

These local people gawking at the parade included Arabs of every status, ethnic group, clan, religious faction, and background, but nearly all wearing long galabiehs of different colours. The majority of the onlookers were Syrians, of course, some in traditional flowing robes, some in European suits, jackets, and trousers. There was also a sprinkling of armed uniformed men representing the gendarmerie. Displaced Turks were there, too, in a wide range of dress including the classic fez, as well as Armenians, Greeks, and Jews in their distinctive dress. There were also Druze, with their colourfully painted cheeks and exotic hairstyles, from the Hauran region. It must have been an eye-opener for Chauvel and his Australian troopers, most of whom had never left home before. In fact, one of Australia's youngest soldiers, Alec Campbell, 16, an AIF infantryman from Tasmania, had written home back in 1915, when in Egypt bound for Gallipoli, telling his mother that 'all the fully grown men over here walk around the street in women's dresses in broad daylight'.

By the end of that big military demonstration, the people of Damascus were convinced that the British and not the Arabs would be ruling. They may have seen Feisal's Hejaz flags at the front, but the would-be king himself did not arrive until 3 October — three days after the 10th Regiment had entered the city and won the hearts and minds of the locals.

Lawrence was angry with Chauvel and his Australian forces, saying: 'The sporting Australians just saw the campaign as a point to point with Damascus as the finishing post. We saw it as a serious military operation in which any unordered priority would be a meaningless or discernable distinction. We were all under Allenby and Damascus was the fruit of his genius'. Not surprisingly, he never admitted in his reports, articles, or books that the Australians beat him to this Damascus finishing post.

After the parade, Chauvel moved into town to set up his HQ. First of all, he cabled Allenby, confirming the capture of Damascus and generously including Lawrence and his Arab Army, saying: 'The Australian Mounted Division entered the outskirts of Damascus from the north-west last night and at 6 A.M. today the town was occupied by the Desert Mounted Corps and the Arab Army'. Allenby then cabled the War Office confirming this: 'We took Damascus at 06.00 today. Details follow'. The War Office later issued a communiqué announcing that 'At 6 am on 1 October Damascus was occupied by a British force and a portion of the Arab army of King Hussein'; and that was how Lawrence and his Arabs, although they arrived later, were able to claim they were equal first into Damascus with the 10th Regiment.

But Chauvel, who knew his 10th Regiment was really first into Damascus, now got on with the administration of this conquered city, as the civil governor authorised by Allenby. Proudly, he wrote to his wife from the desk of the former Turkish governor of Damascus: 'I am now writing this on Jemal Pasha's desk in his own house in Damascus'.

He had lots of work to do before his troops departed for home. This practical work included such tasks as repairing the electricity for the city and cleaning up the collapsed hospitals.

The Australian Light Horsemen had dreamed of conquering Damascus since early 1916 — in fact, Ion Idriess was boasting about riding triumphantly into Damascus when his 5th Regiment was still in the Sinai! Sadly, by the time Chauvel's grand entrance into Damascus actually took place, the greatest scribe of this whole story was back in Australia, recovering from malaria and wounds. Later, Idriess would embark on an exercise program, teaching himself to walk without a crutch, and working out in a gym to get his shrapnel-wounded body back to normal, which by 1920 he had succeeded in doing, against the odds.

It was probably just as well for Idriess, as this city of their dreams turned out to be a nightmare. These brave and skilled conquering heroes had entered a deadly city of disease, where, soon after the last shots were fired, many gallant Light Horsemen died (as did their vanquished enemy, the Turks, in their thousands). For now, despite surviving battle after battle in the desert over the last three years, Light Horseman after Light Horseman contracted insidious diseases spread by the sick and dying in and around the disgusting hospitals of Damascus, which were rife with malaria and influenza. As Sergeant James Williamson of the 2nd Light Horse Brigade (2nd Signal Troop) wrote to his girlfriend, Maude: 'I was very pleased to leave Damascus miles behind me with all its filth and diseases — as it is such a filthy city. You could not imagine it Maude — it's the worst place I have ever seen'.

Once the war ended, the Egyptian Expeditionary Force no longer had to care for the hundreds of thousands of Turkish POWs they had been capturing since the Palestine campaign began in the Sinai in August 1916.

Bean wrote: 'A most dreadful legacy of war remained in the crowds of sick and dying and dead left behind by the retreating Turks in their appalling hospital, and in the onrush of malaria and pneumonic influenza that now mowed down the divisions of the Desert Mounted Corps. Their recent passage through areas swarming with infected mosquitoes and unequipped for prevention struck down a great part of the force. Yet these weakened Australians tried to help the even weaker Turks. Lieutenant Colonel T.J. Todd of the 10th Regiment' (which had entered Damascus first) 'was a sick man himself, but he took charge of 16,000 sick and dying Turkish prisoners organised in a camp at Kaukab and heroically fought for their lives against the apathy of the Arab authorities, before dying himself of the diseases he was treating them for'.

Even Idriess had contracted malaria earlier, well before Damascus. His account of the disease provides a vivid example of how infected Light Horsemen suffered. As he was also then wounded (which he saw as a blessing, as it got him out of the war), his story could apply to thousands, many of whom were not so lucky. As he wrote, 'It's a long time since I made an entry in the old diary. Here goes for the last entry.'

Even as the army was advancing north, 'I felt wretched through some form of malarial fever — Jaffa fever they call it. The last phase of activity I remember was watching New Zealanders charge through the Turkish shells and take a ridge ... I can remember the bayonets flashing, the hair-raising New Zealand war cries and the screaming "Allahs" of the Turks'. But 'From then on I was too sick to notice or care what was happening'. Then Idriess felt worse, complaining, 'if hell is any worse I don't want to go there'. Although feverish, sweating, hallucinating a lot of the time, and also being unconscious every now and then, he reported: 'The doctor with a lot of trouble managed to pull me through and one morning feeling much better, I went on sick parade to get my wretched septic sores dressed'.

But then, having never been seriously wounded since landing at Gallipoli in 1915, Idriess's luck turned even further. 'I was sitting down waiting my turn talking to the Red Cross sergeant on a gully-bank when — whee-ee-eezz crash! Instinctively we had thrown ourselves on our faces but the shell exploded too close. I spent awful seconds wondering if I was hit mortally. A whirlwind of bells was ringing within my head, and I knew that until the bells quietened I would not be able to think clearly at all. The first recognisable feeling was the numbness, with my mind trying to telephone to all parts of my body to find out which were still there and which were broken. Then quick as a flash I realized I had a good fighting chance although I still felt numb down my back. The bloody hole in my arm and also thigh did not matter. I should have been blown to pieces but there was not even a bone broken, just a dozen shell splinters'.

Idriess continued: 'They put me in a sand-cart ambulance ... after a painful bumpy journey hallucinating most of the way reached a dressing station ... where they probed out some of the shell splinters ... then a motor ambulance ... then on a stretcher to the Australian Casualty Clearing Station I think in Jaffa ... full of men suffering from malaria ... where I lay in a restful fever guessing the war was over for me'. Idriess guessed right: after more treatment at Ramleh, where he was treated by 'a captured Turkish doctor', he was taken 'by a captured Red Crescent train ... through the desert to Kantara on the Canal and on through the streets of Cairo to a final clearing station with my leg now starting a haemorrhage ... where the doctors confirmed the war was over for me'. He concluded: 'I am to be returned to Australia as unfit for further service. Thank heavens!'

Others were not so lucky. William James Japhet (Billy) Smith, cousin of George Smith from South Australia, made it to Damascus, but that was as far as he got. He had already been stricken with chronic rheumatism, was 'weak and wasted', and had to retire from active service and become an ambulance driver. But now he contracted malaria, and sadly died eight days before the Armistice, with the Turks confirming the victory of the EEF, which he had fought so hard to achieve.

But one of those conquering troops who survived long enough to liberate Damascus, James Williamson, who hated the place, envied Idriess, as all he wanted by then was to get back to Australia to see his girlfriend again — hoping he could recognise her. On 7 October 1918, he wrote to Maude: 'It is five years or more since I saw you last and a lot of changes can take place during that time ... although I received your letter containing your photo yesterday at first glance I did not seem to think it looked like you at all but I think I could just still recognise you if we met'.

Williamson, from New South Wales, had only met Maude once, as she lived in far-away South Australia.

Even though Damascus had turned out to be a hell-hole, on 2 October 1918, the newspapers broke the story as good news, with varying degrees of accuracy and political bias. The first Official Communiqué announced in different newspapers: 'Damascus surrendered at 6 a.m. yesterday. On the morning of the 1st October the town of Damascus was entered by our mounted troops and also the Arab army. Over 7,000 Turks surrendered. Half the remaining Turkish Army had been destroyed at Damascus. After guards had been posted the troops were withdrawn from the town'.

Reuters then expanded on the story, claiming 'the capture of Damascus represents a great Allied victory as it is one of the most important Turkish bases in Asia Minor and the principal supply centre for the captured Turkish armies. Its capture will create an enormous impression throughout Islam'.

Looking back on this historic moment, Australian correspondent Henry Gullett attributed the success of this great ride towards Damascus to efficient organisation. 'Despite the extraordinary distances covered the Australian horses are still fit. One of the finest features of Allenby's triumphant progress had been the remarkable efficiency of the Army Service Corps. On every advance the men and the horses have been well fed — there was no sign of the cavalry's splendid drive weakening'. The mounted men were also given time off for resting, swimming, and fishing in places like the Sea of Galilee, he said. The success of the mounted cavalry capturing Damascus was not only due to their years of experience, he said, but because some carried swords like cavalry of old, which they often used as a more lethal weapon.

Recalling one of these sword fights, Eric McGregor of the 12th Regiment wrote: 'When we marched on the town of Samat under the guidance of the 4th Cavalry Division who directed us to the point of assault and halted for final orders we came under terrific rifle and machine gun fire as the enemy had guns concealed in many buildings. But we attacked along with the 11th Regiment who charged mounted with drawn swords right up to striking distance'. After killing and wounding as many from horseback with their swords, the brave warriors of the 11th leapt off their horses alongside the 12th Regiment and 'engaged in a desperate hand to hand encounter with their swords while the 12th used the bayonet in and outside the buildings before many enemy dead and wounded lay marking this bloody scene'.

Having demanded swords, McGregor said 'the cavalry men of the 11th showed how well they could use these age old weapons'. The sword-wielding warriors 'suffered rather heavily losing many killed and wounded — as the enemy were princely Germans who put up a determined fight but they suffered much more heavily than we did and lost a whole Garrison of prisoners to us. Their superior officers later considered it "a magnificent performance" especially as there had been no artillery support'.

After his Desert Mounted Corps' epic 200-kilometre advance, Chauvel wrote triumphantly again to his wife: 'We have had a great and glorious time, and the Chief who motored from Tiberias today to see us, has just told me that our performance is "the greatest cavalry feat the world has ever known".'

Later military historians would agree with 'the Chief's' assessment.

3 October

Not to be outdone (although he was two days late), Feisal arrived with his Arab Army on a special train from Deraa. He then quickly switched to horseback, and, with his bodyguard of 40 to 50 horsemen, got ready to ride into Damascus. After Lawrence got Chauvel's permission, Feisal and his mounted men paraded through the already conquered city to stage a triumphal entry with all their Hejaz banners flying. Hopefully, there were still some spectators left who had not become bored with the series of triumphal conquerors riding into town.

Allenby also arrived that day by Rolls Royce, not for another parade, but for meetings with Chauvel and other leading lights, including Feisal, in the newly conquered city, aimed at sorting out who would be boss from then on in Damascus, Syria, and other parts of the Middle East.

Never had so many people had so many different experiences on the road to Damascus. These modern-day experiences certainly rivalled what happened to Saul aka Saint Paul all those years ago.

No matter *who* was first in Damascus, the fact was that the city was now captured and the Ottoman Empire was on its last legs. It had all been worthwhile, as it then appeared Allenby's forces had helped bring the war to a close! The *Daily News* London reported a communiqué received from Zurich on 3 October 'with the good news that Turkey has informed Germany of her determination to propose peace to the Allies'.

26 October

An Australian armoured-car detachment, which had travelled up the Homs road, finally captured Aleppo. They were supported by the Australian Mounted Division, who followed on from Damascus once they had recovered from sickness. Aleppo was an easy and final battle, as most remaining Turkish troops had all but withdrawn by then.

Bean wrote: 'These were the last actions of the Light Horse in the war'.

30–31 October

Finally, on 30 October, after a successful negotiating session, Turkey officially signed an armistice at Mudros. It came into effect the next day, putting an end to the fighting in this long Palestine campaign.

11 November

The Armistice with Germany signed on 11 November 1918 put an end to the world's worst war to date, which had started on 3 August 1914. Twenty million people had been killed and many more wounded and scarred for life.

Sadly, however, it did not stop the political fighting in all theatres of that war. Allenby's forces had won the war in Palestine and dismantled the oppressive Ottoman Empire, but they never won the political victory that would enable long-term peace. In fact, throughout the Middle East, armistice or not, the different sides continued to fight for control. It was superpower against superpower and Arab against Arab, beginning soon after Allenby's liberation of Damascus and Syria, which his forces had fought so long and hard to achieve. From that time onwards, the politics of the Middle East and especially Syria would become an unexpected and enduring nightmare that would stretch well into the future. More than 100 years later, as this book went to press, the war being fought for the control of Syria was the major conflict being fought on the planet.

POSTSCRIPT

POLITICAL BETRAYAL BREEDS FUTURE CONFLICT

In the history of the world, there never was a greater victory than
that which was achieved in Palestine, and in it, also, as in France,
the soldiers of Australia played a great part.

PRIME MINISTER WILLIAM HUGHES, SEPTEMBER 1919

The year after World War I ended, Australia's politically astute Prime
Minister, Billy Hughes, who had just returned home after signing
the Treaty of Versailles, praised both the Light Horse and the Australian
Imperial Force (AIF) during a speech to parliament. He was right, of
course. The Light Horse under Lieutenant-General Sir Harry Chauvel had
helped win the Palestine campaign, punching well above their weight. It
had been one of the greatest Allied victories of the war. He was also right
about the AIF's enormous role on the Western Front, where, under the
Melbourne-born commander-in-chief of the Australian Army, Lieutenant-
General Sir John Monash, they had helped win the war in Belgium and
France. (A little known fact is that a small contingent of Light Horse
troopers had also helped the AIF while serving on the Western Front in a
wide variety of roles.)

But unfortunately, the Allied leaders who negotiated the terms of peace
for that Palestine campaign were not as politically astute. In fact, the
way they sorted out the new post-war arrangements sowed the seeds for
today's modern conflicts in the Middle East. These Allied leaders ignored
pre-war and war-time promises to the Arabs and imposed self-serving and

unjust post-war governments that contained the kernel for future rebellion and war.

The Australian Prime Minister, Billy Hughes aka 'The Little Digger' was a strong supporter of the Australian Imperial Force, and won the hearts of the Light Horsemen when he told parliament, 'In the history of the world, there never was a greater victory than that which was achieved in Palestine'.

For a start, Britain and France — the superpowers of the day — betrayed Lawrence of Arabia and his Arab forces by not giving them the Arabian territories they had promised in return for helping to drive the Turks out of Palestine. Yet had it not been for Lawrence's Arab Revolt and the Arab Army that grew out of it, the British and Allied forces, including the Australian Light Horse, may not have been able to liberate this land. The Arab Army fought a parallel and complementary campaign beside the Egyptian Expeditionary Force, fighting as a guerrilla unit by destroying Turkish fortifications, railway and communication lines and forcing the Turks to retreat. These Arabs only helped the British because they believed they could inherit and govern their lands once the Turks were driven out.

Britain's military leader in the Middle East, General Sir Edmund Allenby, had actually promised Lawrence and the Arabs that if they helped the British drive out the Turks they could govern these lands.

Assigned by the British to help lead the Arab forces against the Turks, Lawrence united their warring tribes for this purpose. He told Prince Feisal, the leader of the Arab Army, that the Arabs would be given control of their own lands once they had liberated them. In turn, Lawrence said, 'Feisal had won over and set aflame all the different tribes bringing a sense of shared nationality to their minds inspiring them to sacrifice everything to achieve their long desired dream of self rule'. That is why Lawrence wanted the Arab Army to liberate the final town, Damascus, ahead of the British so they could claim their long-coveted prize. He and his Arabs believed it would be a case of 'first come first served'. Although Lawrence and his Arabs only arrived second, behind the Australians, Lawrence quickly helped Feisal establish the Arab National Council before Allenby and his British troops took over the town.

Unbeknown to Lawrence, Feisal, and the Arab forces, however, the British and French had signed that agreement in the early part of the war — the Sykes-Picot Agreement — in which the two superpowers divided Arabia between themselves, excluding the Arabs from government and ownership. This highly secretive and political 'gentlemen's agreement', signed in May 1916 with 12 clauses, was drafted by two upper-class, well-travelled Middle Eastern experts, Britain's Lieutenant-Colonel Sir Mark Sykes, 6th Baronet, and France's François Georges-Picot, 45. The agreement assumed victory over the Turks and the dismantling of the old Ottoman Empire, and divided the post-war Middle East into British- and French-governed territories. It included that map with the future British and French prizes coloured in red for and blue. Britain planned to seize most of Iraq — which had oil reserves — and control Palestine (where the British hoped to create a new nation for the Jews). France planned to take over most of Syria and Lebanon. Britain would also supervise puppet Arab governments in any other remaining land on the map to the south and France would do the same to the north. The ever shrewd commander-in-chief of the Egyptian Expeditionary Force, Sir Edmund Allenby, who led the liberating forces and urged Lawrence and his Arabs to fight harder to the end, knew this was the secretly planned outcome.

So no matter how hard the Arabs fought and no matter how fast they rode to try and get to Damascus first — they did not stand a chance. And this was the heartless betrayal eventually revealed at the post-war negotiating sessions that shocked Lawrence, Feisal, and the Arabs, and soured the victory of that uneasy coalition.

But with hindsight, if the superpowers *had* allowed the Arabs to govern all Arab lands instead of dividing the newly won territory between themselves, the Arabs might have established a peaceful *modus vivendi* as masters of their own destiny — instead of rebelling against their European masters and fermenting the bloody conflicts that have undermined peace in the Middle East to this day. Had the British not helped create the new state of Israel in Palestine in 1948 based on the Balfour Declaration hatched by Zionists during World War I, the Arabs in Palestine itself could perhaps have lived a more peaceful life.

In early October 1918, Allenby told Feisal to 'moderate his aims and await decisions from London' when they met in Damascus, saying at the outset that the French would control Lebanon. Allenby also explained he was in supreme command of all administration, but that both French and British governments 'agreed to recognize the belligerent status of the Arab forces fighting in Palestine and Syria, as Allies against the common enemy'.

But Prince Feisal told Allenby that Lawrence had promised him the Arabs would administer the whole of Syria, including access to the Mediterranean Sea through Lebanon, if his forces reached northern Syria by the end of the war — and they knew nothing about France's claim to Lebanon.

Australia's Lieutenant-General Sir Harry Chauvel, who had commanded the Desert Column, then carefully recorded the formal meeting between Allenby (the Chief) and Feisal at the Hotel Victoria, Damascus, 3 October

1918, revealing how Lawrence and Feisal saw this as a betrayal. Chauvel wrote:

'The Chief explained to Feisal:

'(a) That France was to be the Protecting or Mandatory Power over Syria.

'(b) That he, Feisal, as representing his Father, King Husein, was to have the Administration of Syria (less Palestine and the Lebanon Province) under French guidance and financial backing.

'(c) That the Arab sphere would include the hinterland of Syria only and that he, Feisal, would not have anything whatever to do with the Lebanon, which would be considered to stretch from the Northern boundary of Palestine (about Tyre) to the head of the Gulf of Alexandretta.

'(d) That he was to have a French Liaison Officer at once, who would work for the present with Lawrence, who would be expected to give him every assistance.

'Feisal objected very strongly. He said that he knew nothing of France in the matter; that he was prepared to have British assistance; that he understood from the adviser that Sir Edmund Allenby had told him that the Arabs were to have the whole of Syria including the Lebanon but excluding Palestine; that a Country without a Port was no good to him; and that he declined to have a French Liaison Officer or to recognise French guidance in any way.

'The Chief turned to Lawrence and said: "But did you not tell him that the French were to have the Protectorate over Syria?" Lawrence said: "No Sir, I know nothing about it." The Chief said: "But you knew definitely that he, Feisal, was to have nothing to do with the Lebanon". Lawrence said: "No Sir, I did not."

'After some further discussion the Chief, Allenby, told Feisal that he, Sir Edmund Allenby, was Commander in Chief and that he, Feisal, was at the moment a Lieut-General under his Command and that he would have to obey orders. That he must accept the situation as it was and that the whole matter would be settled at the conclusion of the War. Feisal accepted this decision and left with his entourage (less Lawrence) and went out of the City again to take on his triumphal entry which I am afraid fell rather flat as the greater bulk of the people had seen him come in and out already!

'After Feisal had gone, Lawrence told the Chief that he would not work with a French Liaison Officer and that he was due for leave and thought he had better take it now and go off to England. The Chief said: "Yes! I think you had!", and Lawrence left the room.

Chauvel concluded his recording of the meeting with the words, 'The Chief afterwards relented about Lawrence and told me (Chauvel) to tell him (Lawrence) that he would write to Clive Wigram about him and arrange for an audience with the King, also, that he would give him a letter to the Foreign Office in order that he might explain the Arab point of view.'

As leader of the Arab Army, Lawrence of Arabia had promised King Feisal and other Arab chiefs that they would be given Arabian territory to rule if they supported the campaign.

Although the British and French superpowers initially refused to install King Feisal as a monarch in return for mobilising the Arabs to serve in Lawrence of Arabia's Army, Lawrence finally got him installed as king of British-controlled Iraq.

Lawrence left Damascus next morning for England. This betrayal, so carefully recorded by Chauvel, affected the rest of Lawrence's life, as he resigned his military commission soon after, found it difficult to fit back into British society again, drifted from job to job in the British defence forces, changed his name, became a recluse hiding in the countryside, refused a knighthood personally offered by King George V, and published his version of events. He was killed in a motorbike accident on an English country road in 1935. In his books, especially *Seven Pillars of Wisdom*, he writes about his belief that the Arabs achieved more than enough in that desert war to have earned territories of their own.

Yet in 1921, Lawrence had made a temporary comeback. By then, he had become a famous figure celebrated in the British media, which published more and more stories about his achievements, and also in the theatres, which staged Lawrence of Arabia Lantern and Lecture Shows that attracted hundreds of thousands of patrons. He had also played a role as an Arab specialist at the subsequent Peace Conference in Paris, where the French used the Sykes-Picot Agreement to try and grab even more land in the Middle East. He had warned the conference that if French rule was imposed on the unwilling Arabs of Syria, 'There will be trouble and even war between the French people and the Arabs'.

Then the new Secretary of State for Colonies, Winston Churchill, listened to Lawrence (whom he appointed his official adviser on colonial affairs) and subsequently created a new nation state called Transjordan (later Jordan) and installed Abdullah Hussein as leader, with Amman as its capital. Fighting back even harder, Lawrence also persuaded Churchill to install Feisal as king of British-controlled Iraq, so that the Arab leader who had done so much to drive the Turks out at least got a face-saving position. Sadly, neither of these Arab leaders lasted long due to factional infighting, worsened by King Feisal's untimely death in 1933, and before long, both Jordan and Iraq were beset with problems that eventually undermined peace and stability, leading to today's conflicts.

The Australian Light Horse did not help Lawrence's political post-war cause either, as they gazumped him and his Arabs by stealing into Damascus first, angering Lawrence. After he got to Damascus, hours after the Australians, he asked them to retreat into the background, so he could ride into town officially and capture this strategic Turkish stronghold with his Arabs in a colourful show of flowing robes.

Light Horsemen like Norman Crosthwaite could now tell their sweethearts they were coming home.

After his long and distinguished service in Palestine, Lieutenant Reg Garnock won a rare award: the Sultan's Order of the Nile.

The Australians had never liked the Arabs during the war, though, so they did not care whether or not the Arabs were given control of these newly captured territories. The 5th Regiment trooper Ion Idriess said most of the troopers actually hated their Arab 'comrades' — especially the nomadic Bedouins — who were meant to be fighting alongside them against the Turks. Idriess reported many times that he had seen that the Bedouins mutilated the bodies of wounded Australians left to die on the battlefield and dug up bodies from the shallow desert graves to rob the dead of their possessions.

Then, on 10 December 1918, a raiding party of exhausted New Zealand Light Horse troopers ran out of patience with the Arabs and blotted their copybook. These troopers raided an Arab village in revenge after an Arab from that village crept into their camp in the dead of night to steal things — as they had through most of the desert war. But this time the Arab thief killed New Zealand trooper Leslie Lowry, who had tried to stop the thief when he was woken by the Arab pulling his kitbag out from under his pillow. The sleepy Light Horseman caught up to the fleeing Arab, grabbed him before the thief escaped, and tried to wrestle his kitbag from the robber's hands.

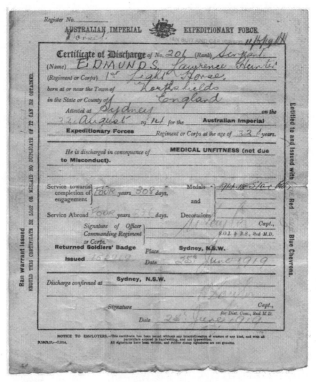

Like all Light Horsemen, (Lawrence) Hunter Edmunds was relieved to have survived the war after so many battles in which he could have been killed — and so he treasured his Discharge Certificate, which he then left to his descendants, who keep it in pride of place.

The thief pulled out a revolver and shot Lowry in the chest before bolting empty-handed. Lowry was found bleeding to death on the sand. His rescuer, trooper Ambrose Stephen Mulhall from the Australian 3rd Light Horse, reported that Lowry told him that, 'A Bedouin from the nearest Bedouin village had tried to steal his kitbag, shot him and then ran to the nearest Bedouin village'. Mulhall then reported, 'Lowry died in agony'. His abandoned kitbag and an Arab skullcap were found nearby.

Incensed by this crime, Lowry's mates — who like Lowry had just spent years liberating these Arab's lands from the Ottoman Empire — took revenge. By then, the New Zealand Light Horsemen had run out of patience, so they tracked the murderer's footprints to a hole in the fence near Surafend, an Arab village near a Jewish settlement, Richon le Zion, close to the Mediterranean coast not far from today's Tel Aviv. Then an angry posse of these New Zealand Light Horsemen raided the murderer's village to avenge Lowry's death and to teach the Arabs a lesson.

Official World War I historian for the Desert Campaign, Henry Gullett, later reported the incident: 'They were angry and bitter beyond sound reasoning. All day the New Zealanders quietly organised for their work in Surafend and early in the night marched out many hundreds strong and surrounded the village'. Gullett also claimed some Australian Light Horsemen got involved, saying, 'In close support and in full sympathy were large bodies of Australians. Entering the village the New Zealanders grimly passed out all the women and children and then, armed chiefly with heavy sticks fell upon the men and at the same time fired their houses. Many Arabs were killed, few escaped without injury; the village was demolished. The flames from the wretched houses lit up the countryside, and Allenby and his staff could not fail to see the conflagration and hear the shouts of the troops and cries of their victims. The Anzacs having finished with Surafend, raided and burned the neighbouring nomad camp, and then retreated quietly back to their lines'.

Although they were aware of Lowry's murder, the Light Horse commanding officers were angered by this undisciplined killing spree, and they conducted an internal inquiry into the massacre. This established little, however, because the Light Horsemen were all sworn to secrecy, so none of the hundreds who took part were punished. Their commander-in-chief, Allenby, however, called the Anzac Mounted Division to attention and denounced them from his horse.

Proud Australians maintained traditional Light Horse regiments right up until World War II, hoping to be called upon to repeat the feats of the Desert Column in World War I, but the mechanisation of warfare meant they were never called upon; so Australians kept the tradition alive through ceremonial parades and horse-riding events.

Allenby had said earlier: 'The Australian Lighthorseman combines with a splendid physique, a restless activity of mind. This mental quality renders him somewhat impatient of rigid and formal discipline, but it confers upon him the gift of adaptability, and this is the secret of much of his success mounted or on foot. In this dual role ... The Australian Lighthorseman has proved himself equal to the best. He has earned the gratitude of the Empire and the admiration of the world'.

But now Warrant Officer Nick Curtin, a Tasmanian, of the 3rd Regiment, reported Allenby saying: 'Since I have been with you you have done some wonderful things. You overran the Turks in Beersheba and you did this, and you also took so many thousand prisoners, and you did that. That was good but ah, you put the blotch on yourself when you killed some innocent Arabs. I thank you for what you have done ... but I hate you for what you did to the Arabs. I thought a lot of you once, but I think it of you no more'. And with that condemnation of some of the men (mainly New Zealanders) who had helped him drive the Turks out of Palestine, dismantle the Ottoman Empire, and liberate Palestine, Allenby turned his horse's head and galloped off.

As many of the wonderful Walers came from Tamworth, the local council, people of Tamworth, and local ABC radio broadcaster David Evans created this lifelike statue to honour the memory of those great Light Horsemen and their mounts.

But that condemnation was nothing compared to the final orders from commanding officers of the Egyptian Expeditionary Force. For the troopers were told they would have to leave their beloved horses behind when they sailed back to Australia.

The men had been looking forward to sailing back home with their mounts and putting them out to graze back on the properties from where they came. They had dreamt and talked often around the desert campfires of the good times they and their beloved Walers could enjoy back home. Now they had to deal with the gut-wrenching order to leave them behind.

The order was clear-cut — 'The horses stay behind'. The commanding officers claimed that it was impractical to take tens of thousands of army horses back to Australia; there were not enough transport ships and there was not enough room on the ships to create horse stalls, and anyway, the quarantine regulations would stop the horses being admitted to Australia.

By the end of the war, the Light Horsemen had formed such an intense bond with their horses — who had carried them for years, galloped into battle, stood patiently by if they were wounded, and provided unconditional companionship — that they had become mates.

The order from on high demanded all Walers were to be classified either A, B, C or D, according to their condition and age. All C and D horses were to be shot. They were first to have their shoes removed and their manes and tails cut off (iron and horse hair were saleable). Worse, the horses were to be skinned after being shot. Seven pounds of salt was allowed for the salting of each hide, to be sold as leather.

Horrible as these orders seemed, many men thought that it would be better to shoot their horse than leave it to be cruelly treated by the local Arabs. Some tried to have their Walers included in the C and D group for shooting. Others asked permission to take their horse for a last ride and returned carrying saddle and bridle, with the explanation: 'He put his foot in a hole and I had to shoot him'.

Hundreds of the Walers that had charged Beersheba or endured the Sinai or carried their 'Billjim' on the last great advance into Damascus were taken to olive groves outside Tripoli and tethered in picket lines. They were then given a last nosebag of fodder and shot. Many troopers found it touching that, to the very last, their horses trusted their uniformed figures and their rifles, and that gunfire held no fear for them.

Eventually, late in 1919, the last of the Light Horsemen arrived back in Australia. The regiments broke up and all men returned to homes, families, farms, and jobs to try and resume their lives. The Light Horse of the 1st AIF may have only existed for five years, but in time, it generated a reputation that a century later was romanticised more than any other Australian military force of World War I.

Yet back then it was a bittersweet return to Australia. Major Oliver Hogue of the 14th Regiment, who wrote under the name Trooper Bluegum, summed up the feelings of many Light Horsemen in his poem, 'The Horses Stay Behind':

In days to come we'll wander west and cross the range again;
We'll hear the bush birds singing in the green trees after rain
We'll canter through the Mitchell grass and breast the bracing wind
But we'll have other horses. Our chargers stay behind.

Around the fire at night we'll yarn about old Sinai;
We'll fight our battles o'er again as the days go by
There'll be old mates to greet us. The bush girls will be kind.
Still our thoughts will often wander to the horses left behind.

I don't think I could stand the thought of my old fancy hack
Just crawling around old Cairo with a Gyppo on his back.

Perhaps some English tourist out in Palestine may find
My broken-hearted Waler with a wooden plough behind.

I think I'd better shoot him and tell a little lie: –
'He floundered in a wombat hole and then lay down to die'
May be I'll get court-martialled; but I'm damned if I'm inclined
To go back to Australia and leave my horse behind.

APPENDIX 1

WWI & PALESTINE TIMELINE

1914

28 July: War declared in Europe

4 August: Britain and Australia join the war

1 November: First Australian troops sail for Europe

3 December: Australian troops arrive at Egyptian training camp at Giza

1915

25 April: First Anzacs land at Gallipoli

12 May: Light Horse start landing at Gallipoli

7 August: Light Horse fight in bloody Battle of The Nek

19 December: Anzacs including Light Horse evacuate Gallipoli and sail to Egypt

1916

Sir Archibald Murray is Commander-in-chief of Egyptian Expeditionary Force, which includes British and all Allied Forces

January: Light Horse train for desert warfare in Egypt

March: Harry Chauvel appointed Commander, Australian and New Zealand Mounted Division, which includes Australian Light Horse, serving within the Desert Column

11–14 April: Jifjafa Raid — first Australian Light Horse action

19–20 July: Western Front: Battle of Fromelles — the AIF's first battle on Western Front with nearly 2,000 Australians killed in one day's fighting

23 July–3 September: Western Front: Battle of Pozières — 23,000 Australian casualties in six weeks

4–5 August: First big Light Horse battle: Battle of Romani.

6 December: Lloyd George becomes prime minister of Britain, replacing Asquith

20 December: Battle of El Arish, Sinai

23 December: Light Horse Battle of Magdhaba, Sinai

1917

9 January: Light Horse Battle of Rafa, Sinai–Palestine border

26 March: Light Horse First Gaza Battle, Palestine

Lawrence of Arabia make plans for the Arab Revolt

17 April: Light Horse Second Gaza Battle, Palestine

29 June: General Sir Edmund Allenby appointed Commander-in-chief, Egyptian Expeditionary Force (replacing Murray)

6 July: Lawrence and his Arab Army capture Aqaba in the first major victory for the Arab forces

31 October: Light Horse win Battle of Beersheba with history's last successful cavalry charge

1 November: Light Horse fight battle at Tel el Khuweilfe; Light Horse sets out on the great drive up the Plain of the Philistines

1 November: Light Horse Third Battle of Gaza, Palestine

19 November: Heavy rain hits Palestine

17 November: EEF mounts the advance on Jerusalem, Palestine, capturing Holy City by 9 December.

11 December: General Allenby enters Jerusalem on foot

1918

May: Australian Army formed on Western Front with five Divisions under the Australian Commander in Chief, General John Monash

22 March: Light Horse starts battles of Es Salt and Amman, Jordan

25 April: Australian Army helps Allies recapture Villers-Bretonneux on Western Front from the Germans

4 July: General John Monash commands the Battle of Hamel defeating Germans in turning-point victory on Western Front

8 August: Australian Army helps Allies win conclusive Battle of Amiens on Western Front

12 August: King George V knights General Sir John Monash in the field

19 September: Light Horse begins advance on Damascus, Syria

1 October: Light Horse (10th Regiment) is first to enter Damascus helping to capture this last Turkish stronghold and dismantle the Ottoman Empire

30 October: Turkish leaders sign armistice at Mudros, ending war in Palestine

11 November: Germany signs armistice on Western Front, ending World War I

Appendix 2

WHO WAS WHO

Leaders and Units relevant for the Australian Light Horse — although these changed throughout the war

King of Britain
George V

British Prime Minister
Herbert Henry Asquith 1914–1916
David Lloyd George 1916–1922

Egyptian Expeditionary Force
Commander-in-chief:
General Sir Archibald Murray 1916 – June 1917
General Sir Edmund Allenby June 1917 – November 1918

Eastern Force
Lieutenant-General Charles Macpherson Dobell
Included Desert Column, Anzac Mounted Division, Imperial Mounted Division, 53rd (Welsh) Division, the Imperial Camel Corps Brigade, the 52nd (Lowland) Division, and the 54th (East Anglian) Division.

Imperial Mounted Division (January 1917)
Major-General Sir Henry Hodgson
A mounted infantry, Light Horse, and Yeomanry division
Included 3rd and 4th Light Horse Brigades and British Yeomanry 5th and 6th Mounted Brigades.

The Australian Mounted Division
This was actually the Imperial Mounted Division until the Australian government demanded the name be changed to the Australian Mounted Division.

It later included the newly formed 5th Light Horse Brigade as well when the Imperial Camel Corps was broken up, because Britain demanded its Yeomanry forces transfer to their main theatre Western Front.

Desert Column
Lieutenant-General Sir Philip Chetwode 1916–1917
Lieutenant-General Sir Harry Chauvel 1917
This included Australian Mounted Division and Anzac Mounted Division and the Imperial Camel Corps Brigade.

Anzac Mounted Division
Lieutenant-General Sir Harry Chauvel 1916–1917
Major-General Edward Chaytor 1917–1918
Brigadier-General Granville Ryrie 1918–1919
Included 1st and 2nd Light Horse Brigades, New Zealand Mounted Rifles Brigade, and British 22nd Mounted Brigade

Imperial Camel Corps Brigade
Brigadier-General Clement Leslie Smith
1st Battallion (Australian)
2nd Battallion (British)
3rd Battallion (Australian)
4th Battallion (Anzac) (from May 1917)

Yeomanry Mounted Division June 1917
This included 6th, 8th, and 22nd Yeomanry Brigades.

Desert Mounted Corps
Lieutenant-General Sir Harry Chauvel 1917–1919
Included two Indian cavalry divisions (recruited to take the place of the Yeomanry forces sent to France)

Light Horse Brigades and Regiments (Australian)
Brigade commanders changed during the war.

1st Light Horse Brigade
Lieutenant-General Sir Harry Chauvel/ Brigadier-General Charles Cox
1st Regiment: New South Wales
2nd Regiment: Queensland
3rd Regiment: South Australia and Tasmania

2nd Brigade
Brigadier-General Granville Ryrie
5th Regiment: Queensland
6th Regiment: New South Wales

7th Regiment: New South Wales

3rd Brigade
Major-General F.G. Hughes, then Brigadier-General Lachlan Wilson
8th Regiment: Victoria (Fought at The Nek, Gallipoli)
9th Regiment: South Australia, Victoria
10th Regiment: Western Australia (Fought at The Nek, Gallipoli, First to Damascus)

4th Brigade
Brigadier-General William Grant then Lieutenant-Colonel Murray Bourchier
4th Regiment: Victoria (Fought at Beersheba)
11th Regiment: Queensland, South Australia
12th Regiment: New South Wales (Fought at Beersheba)

5th Brigade
Brigadier-General George Macarthur-Onslow/Lieutenant-Colonel Donald C. Cameron
14th Regiment: Former Camel Corps
15th Regiment: Former Camel Corps
A French Regiment
New Zealand 2nd Machine Gun Squadron

Divisional and Corps Troops
13th Regiment: Victoria
Section of 4th Regiment: Victoria

New Zealand Mounted Rifles Brigade
Brigadier-General Andrew Russell 1914–1915
Major-General Edward Chaytor 1915–1917
Brigadier-General William Meldrum 1917–1919

APPENDIX 3

TRIBUTE: THE ANZAC ON THE WALL

I wandered thru a country town, 'cos I had some time to spare,
And went into an Antique Shop to see what was in there.
Old Bikes and Pumps and Kero lamps, but hidden by it all,
A photo of a soldier boy ... An Anzac on the Wall.

'The Anzac have a name?' I asked. The old man answered 'No',
The ones who could have told you mate, have passed on long ago.
The old man kept on talking and, according to his tale,
The photo was unwanted junk, bought from a clearance sale.

'I asked around,' the old man said, 'But no one knows his face,
He's been on that wall twenty years ... deserves a better place.
For someone must have loved him, so it seems a shame somehow.'
I nodded in agreement and then said ... 'I'll take him now.'
My nameless digger's photo, well it was a sorry sight
A cracked glass pane and a broken frame ... I had to make it right
To prise the photo from its frame I took care just in case,
Cause only sticky paper held the cardboard back in place.
I peeled away the faded screed, and much to my surprise,
two letters and a telegram, appeared before my eyes

The first reveals my Anzac's name, and regiment of course
John Mathew Francis Stuart ... of Australia's own Light Horse.
This letter written from the front ... my interest now was keen;
this note was dated August 7th, 1917

'Dear Mum, I'm at Khalasa Springs, not far from the Red Sea
They say it's in the Bible ... looks like a Billabong to me.
'My Kathy wrote, I'm in her prayers ... she's still my bride to be,
I just can't wait to see you both, you're all the world to me.
And Mum you'll soon meet Bluey, last month they shipped him out
I told him to call on you, when he's up and about.'
'That bluey is a larrikin, and we all thought it funny,
He lobbed a Turkish hand grenade into the Co's dunny.
I told you how he dragged me wounded; in from no man's land
He stopped the bleeding, closed the wound, with only his
bare hand.'
'Then he copped it at the front, from some stray shrapnel blast,
It was my turn to drag him in, and I thought he wouldn't last.
He woke up in hospital, and nearly lost his mind
Cause out there on the battlefield, he'd left one leg behind.'
'He's been in a bad way Mum, he knows he'll ride no more
Like me he loves a horse's back, he was a champ before.
So Please Mum can you take him in, he's been like my own brother
Raised in a Queensland orphanage he's never known a mother.'
But Struth, I miss Australia Mum, and in my mind each day
I am a mountain cattleman, on the high plains far away.
I'm mustering white-faced cattle, with no camel's hump in sight,
and I waltz my Matilda, by a campfire every night
I wonder who rides Billy ...!! I heard the pub burnt down!!
I'll always love you ... and please say Hooroo, to all in town'.

The second letter I could see, was in a lady's hand,
An answer to her soldier son, there in a foreign land.
Her copperplate was perfect, the pages neat and clean
it bore the date, November 3rd 1917.

'T'was hard enough to lose your Dad, without you at the war
I'd hoped you would be home by now ... each day I miss you more'

'Your Kathy calls around a lot, since you have been away,
To share with me her hopes and dreams, about your wedding day.
And Bluey has arrived ... and what a godsend he has been
We talked and laughed for days, about the things you've done and seen'

'He really is a comfort, and works hard around the farm,
I read the same hope in his eyes, that you won't come to harm.
Mc Connell's kids rode Billy, but suddenly that has changed.
We had a violent lightning storm, and it was really strange.'
'Last Wednesday, just on midnight, not a single cloud in sight,
It raged for several minutes, it gave us all a fright.
It really spooked your Billy ... and he screamed and bucked and reared,
And then he rushed the sliprail fence, which by a foot he cleared'

'They brought him back next afternoon, but something's changed I fear,
It's like the day you brought him home, for no one can get near.
Remember when you caught him, with his black and flowing mane?
Now Horse Breakers fear the beast, that only you can tame,'
'That's why we need you home son ... Then the flow of ink went dry ...
This letter was unfinished ... and I couldn't work out why.

Until I started reading, the letter, number three
A yellow telegram delivered news of a tragedy.

Her son killed in action ... Oh! What pain that must have been,
the same date as her letter ... 3rd November 1917
This letter which was never sent, became then one of three.
She sealed behind the photo's face ... the face she longed to see.

And John's home town's children, when he went to war,
Would say no greater cattleman, had left the town before.
They knew his widowed mother well, and with respect did tell,
How when she lost her only boy ... she lost her mind as well.
She could not face the awful truth, to strangers she would speak
'My Johnny's at the war you know ... he's coming home next week.'

They all remembered Bluey, he stayed on to the end.
A young man with wooden leg, became her closest friend.
And he would go and find her when she wandered, old and weak,
and always softly say ... 'Yes dear ... John will be coming home
next week.'

Then when she died, Bluey moved on ... to Queensland some did say.
I tried to find out where he went, but don't know to this day.
And Kathy never wed, a lonely spinster... some found odd.
She wouldn't set foot in a church ... she'd turned her back on God.
John's mother left no Will, I learned, on my detective trail.
This explains my photo's journey, of that clearance sale.
So I continued digging, cause, I wanted to know more.
I found John's name with thousands, in the records of the war.

His last ride proved his courage... a ride you will acclaim
The Light Horse Charge at Beersheba of everlasting fame.
That last day in October back in 1917,
at 4pm our brave boys fell ... that sad fact I did glean.

That's when John's life was sacrificed, the record's
crystal clear.
But 4pm in Beersheba is midnight over here ...
So as John's gallant sprit rose, to cross the great divide,
Were lightning bolts back home, a signal from the other side?
Is that why Billy bolted, and went racing as in pain ...?
Because he'd never feel his master, on his back again ...!
Was it coincidental ...? Same time ... Same day ... Same date ...!
Some proof of numerology ... or just a quirk of fate ...?

I think it's more than that you know, as I've heard wiser men,
Acknowledge there are many things, that go beyond our ken

Where craggy peaks guard secrets, neath dark skies torn asunder,
Where hoof beats are companions, to the rolling waves of thunder

Where lightning cracks like 303's, and ricochets again,
Where howling moaning gusts of wind, sound just like dying men
Some Mountain cattlemen have sworn, on lonely alpine track,
They've glimpsed a huge black stallion ... with Light Horseman
on his back.
Yes Sceptics say, it's swirling clouds, just forming apparitions.
Oh No, My friend you can't dismiss all this as, superstition.

The desert of Beersheba ... or a windswept Aussie range,
John Stuart rides on forever there ... I don't find that at all strange.
Now some gaze upon this photo, and they often question me,
and I tell them a small white lie, and say he's family.

'You must be proud of him.' they say ... I tell them, one and all,
That's why he takes ... the pride of place ... the Anzac on the wall.

ACKNOWLEDGEMENTS

I wish to thank those giants from World War I upon whose shoulders I have stood when using many quotes from official World War I Commonwealth Correspondents Charles Bean and Henry Gullet, and also from the unofficial Scribe of the Light Horse in Palestine, Trooper Ion L. Idriess — they all wrote so well, provided such useful eyewitness on-the-spot accounts, and helped bring the story back to life. I also thank Angus & Robertson — a former publisher of mine — for permission to reproduce quotes from Idriess's 1932 book, *The Desert Column,* and his kind descendants; also the late Elyne Mitchell of Towong Station (who introduced me to the work of her father, General Sir Harry Chauvel, while she was serving as Patron for the Man From Snowy River Centennial Celebrations I was organising in Corryong in 1995); also Roland Perry for permission to refer to his landmark book, *The Australian Light Horse* (Hachette, Sydney, 2009). All quotes attributed to Charles Bean come from *Anzac to Amiens* (Australian War Memorial, Canberra, 1946); quotes attributed to Henry Gullett come from *The Australian Imperial Force in Sinai and Palestine* (UQP & Australian War Memorial, 1984); and quotes attributed to T.E. Lawrence come from *Revolt in the Desert* (George H. Doran Company, New York, 1926).

I thank the team at Scribe, including visionary founder, owner, and managing director Henry Rosenbloom, Amanda Tokar — who so skilfully managed this book as well as three earlier books — Anna Thwaites, and Marika Webb-Pullman, the wonderful editor of this book; also Dr Brendan Nelson, Director of the Australian War Memorial, for finding time to write the inspirational foreword while he was busy commemorating the 100th anniversary of World War I; and also the dedicated Avalon Beach photographer and historical scholar John Stone, who scanned and then painstakingly photoshopped nearly all the pictures in this book, which he improved out of sight.

I also thank my wife and best friend, Jane, who helped research and write up extracts from the letters, diaries, and journals contributed by descendants of the Light Horse, and who so critically reviewed the edited manuscript and supported this book for years; John Mapps, my personal editor, who did the first edit of the manuscript and who also edited three of my earlier historical books; Glenda Lynch, 'Researching Australia', Canberra, who found many letters and diaries at AWM, as she did for my *Gallipoli Diaries* (Scribe, 2014).

Artist Leslie Sprague, who alerted me to the books of our shared mentor Idriess, with whom he shares a love and great knowledge of the outback and Aboriginal history, culture, and art. Michael Dillon, for helping film the 31st October 2017 documentary based on this book for Foxtel History Channel, *Palestine: last light horsemen tell all*, and for supportive research for many years; also David and Claire Paradice, who have so generously supported my Light Horse projects over the years.

I thank generous contributors from all around Australia who lent me their ancestor's original letters, diaries, photos, and albums, including Trish Murrell, who provided the first archival material — pictures from the World War I scrapbook of Major Thomas Bird, which scholar Gary Clift scanned and digitised before also supplying valuable information and contacts. These contributors also included Kath and Maurice Halloran, and Cec and Beau Traill of Tamworth; Tempe Onus near Moree and Elsie Ritchie of Sydney; Lyn Richardson of 'Eurella' horse stud; Peter Haydon of 'Bloomfield' station, Blandford, New South Wales; Meredith Bayfield; Marie Keys; Jamie Barka; Louise Davies; Jenny Hobson; Stuart Murray; Ross Harmer; Beryl Gregson; David Tate; Jock Munro; Tess Hoysted; Ruby Brooksby; John Chanter; George Falkner; Richard Caldwell; Ruth Rock; Brian Kelly; Lachlan McDonald; Tracey Colley; Mike Tucker; Barry Rodgers; Eric Edmunds; Stewart Johnston; James Williamson; Rebecca Broome; Peter Ingram; Betty Friend; Ray and Barbara Meers; Lorna

Roberts; Lea Taylor; Blanche Cooper; Jenny Merrell, and a special thanks to Judith Dewsnap, who provided heart-wrenching photos and letters of Colin Bull, who was killed at Beersheba and is featured in the endpapers.

I also thank media supporters Anne Newling, Rebecca Gracie at Tamworth's *Northern Daily Leader*, and Stephen Burns of *The Land* for publishing my appeals for the Light Horse letters, diaries, and photos; also radio stations who broadcast appeals for archival material from 2008 onwards, including Tom Menzies, producer, Breakfast Program, Fiveaa, Adelaide Radio; Wayne Taylor, presenter at RadioWest & HOT FM Networks WA; and Rosemary Greenham, producer ABC WA.

Finally, I thank Roger Scales — a modern day Light Horseman booked to ride in the centennial 'charge' at Beersheba — for providing inspiration after we organised the inaugural Man from Snowy River Festival in 1995 at Corryong, Victoria with General Sir Harry Chauvel's daughter, Elyne Mitchell; Peter Reid for scholastic encouragement and discovering the poem, 'The Anzac on the Wall'; Chris Bowen, a fellow World War I scholar in Stroud; Earl de Blonville, for little known information on Lawrence and his contacts with Mustafa Kemal; David Iggulden, author and World War I scholar; the late Stuart Dyson, who so generously gave me many World War I reference books; David Evans, former ABC Broadcaster in Tamworth, who inspired the magnificent Light Horse Waler Statue at Tamworth; Amanda Mooy, for secretarial and research assistance; Sarah Jacoby, nee Desborough, for information on those killed in action at Beersheba; Viscount Robin Bridgeman from the House of Lords, who gave me the useful 1918 book full of wonderful pictures given to his father, by Walter Stopford, in 1967, *The Times: History and Encyclopaedia of the War. Part 187 Vol.15 The Capture of Jerusalem*; Sibella Lee, for providing resources; and the patient and professional Brian Slavin, for keeping my ancient computer working.

PICTURE CREDITS

Most of the pictures in this book came from the many individual contributors — kind-hearted Australians named in the Acknowledgements — who provided photo albums, scrapbooks, and loose photos from their private collections — especially Trish Murrell, who lent the author the priceless photo album of her ancestor Major Thomas Bird.

The remainder came from original World War I first-edition publications produced during the war itself, and the author gives thanks to those publications for the use of these photos many of which are 100 years old. The author is also especially grateful to the late Stuart Dyson, who gave the author many first-edition World War I publications (published during the war itself or just after the war) full of pictures, for which the author gives thanks including: *The Kia-ora Cooee. The Official Magazine of the ANZAC Forces in Egypt, Palestine, Salonika & Mesopotamia* 1917–1918. *Australia in the Great War: the story told in pictures* (a magazine series in eight parts raising funds for the Australian soldiers Repatriation Fund (Commonwealth Government and Cassell & Co, 1915–1919); *Australia in Palestine* (Angus & Robertson, 1919); *The Times: History and Encyclopaedia of the War. Part 187 Vol.15 The Capture of Jerusalem* (March, 1918); also *Revolt in the Desert*, by T.E. Lawrence (George H. Doran, New York, 1926). The author also thanks Elyne Mitchell, the daughter of General Sir Harry Chauvel, for copies of photographs she kindly provided. The author has also used photographs from his extensive personal collection of archival photographs, which he has acquired over the last 40 years.

Most of these pictures were scanned and improved by the highly skilled and dedicated Avalon photographer and historical scholar John Stone.

The author also thanks the Australian War Memorial for the use of any of the above images published during World War I that may also now be in the AWM collection (where this was known, the author has published the accession number with the photograph).

Every effort has been made to trace copyright, and if advised of any omissions, the author will correct these in later editions.

INDEX